TRIUMPH OF
GOOD WILL

"I don't think the people of good will, as they thought about it, felt that we ought to hold down a whole segment of society. But at the same time, we always had."

—Terry Sanford, on his race for governor

How Terry Sanford

TRIUMPH OF

Beat a Champion of Segregation

GOOD WILL

and Reshaped the South

John Drescher

University Press of Mississippi
Jackson

www.upress.state.ms.us

08 07 06 05 04 03 02 01 00 4 3 2 1

∞

Library of Congress Cataloging-in-Publication Data

Drescher, John, 1960–
    Triumph of good will: how Terry Sanford beat a champion of
segregation and reshaped the South / John Drescher
        p.   cm.
    Includes bibliographical references and index.
        ISBN 1-57806-310-8 (alk. paper)
            1. North Carolina—Politics and government—1951–
2. Governors—North Carolina—Election—History—20th
century.   3. Sanford, Terry, 1917–   4. North Carolina—
Race relations.   5. Afro-Americans—Segregation—North
Carolina—History—20th century.   I. Title.

F260.D74   2000
975.6'043'092—dc21   00-035925

British Cataloging-in-Publication Data available

For the three sisters
—Dean, Anne Elizabeth, and Grace

It was well into the fourth hour of the fight now. The boat was still working out to sea and David, with Roger holding the back of his chair now, was raising the fish steadily. David looked stronger now than he had an hour before but Thomas Hudson could see where his heels showed the blood that had run down from the soles of his feet. . . .

"Am I doing anything wrong," David asked bitterly.

"No. You're doing perfectly."

"Then why should I quit on him?"

"He's giving you an awful beating, Davy," Roger said. "I don't want him to hurt you."

"He's the one has the hook in his goddam mouth," David's voice was unsteady. "He isn't giving me a beating. I'm giving him a beating. The son of a bitch."

. . . It was no good. The great fish hung there in the depth of water where he was like a huge dark purple bird and then settled slowly down. . . .

"Well," David said with his eyes tight shut. "In the worst parts, when I was the tiredest, I couldn't tell which was him and which was me."

—Ernest Hemingway, *Islands in the Stream*

CONTENTS

Acknowledgments   xi

Introduction   xv

Chapter 1.
Sanford   3

Chapter 2.
Lake   32

Chapter 3.
Kickoff   59

Chapter 4.
Wild-Card Lake   86

Chapter 5.
Shooting at Sanford   113

Chapter 6.
Lake, Apart and Afire   137

Chapter 7.
Attacks and Lies   164

Chapter 8.
Showdown   191

Chapter 9.
JFK and Mr. GOP   220

Chapter 10.
Epilogue   247

Notes   275
Bibliography   305
Index   311

ACKNOWLEDGMENTS

I could not have written this book without the support of the Wildacres Leadership Initiative and its Friday Fellows program, which is named for former University of North Carolina System president Bill Friday. I was lucky to be chosen in 1995 as part of the first class of Friday Fellows. Through the efforts of then executive director Clay Thorp, I got to know Terry Sanford, who graciously agreed to meet with me periodically and let me quiz him on life, leadership, and politics.

On the night of April 11, 1996, at a corner table at the Washington Duke Inn in Durham, North Carolina, I had dinner with Sanford and his former aide, Ed Wilson Jr., an attorney from Eden who also was in the first class of Friday Fellows. Sanford was a great storyteller and he enchanted us into the evening with political tales—among them, his memories of his 1960 campaign for governor against strong segregationist I. Beverly Lake. As we were leaving the restaurant, Sanford received a phone call from a reporter, who told him that Lake had died earlier that day. I didn't know much about Lake. The next day, back in Charlotte, I read Lake's obituary and immediately thought there was an important story to be told about his race against Sanford. I called Ed Wilson and told him I wanted to write a book on that campaign. "Go for it," he said. Those were the first of many encouraging words I received from my Friday Fellow colleagues. As I wrote the book, five fellows read my work: Wilson, Richard Fuqua of Charlotte, Katy Harriger of Winston-Salem, Leslie Takahashi Morris of Chapel Hill, and Deborah Ross of Raleigh. I am indebted to them for their comments, support, and friendship. The Wildacres Leadership Initiative also supported this book financially by providing a grant to cover travel and research costs. Also, the Blumenthal Foundation paid to have a copy of the book placed in a public library in every county of North Carolina. Many thanks to Herman and Anita Blumenthal of Charlotte and their son Philip. They are key supporters of the Wildacres Leadership Initiative and the Blumenthal Foundation.

I deeply appreciate the support I received from my colleagues at the *Charlotte Observer*. Editor Jennie Buckner, Managing Editor Frank Barrows, and Deputy Managing Editor Cheryl Carpenter allowed me to have time off in the fall of 1998 to write the book. When I took that leave from my job as front-page editor, my colleagues took turns filling in for me. Because that involved working nights, and they still had their other editing responsibilities, I owe them in a big way. My thanks to Mary C. Curtis, Steve Gunn, Brian Melton, Cynthia Montgomery, Trisha O'Connor, Jon Talton, Tom Tozer, and Jim Walser.

I am grateful I struck up a long-distance relationship (thank goodness for e-mail) with Craig W. Gill, senior editor at the University Press of Mississippi. Craig recognized that Terry Sanford's victory in 1960 was important not just to North Carolina but to the entire South. His comments made the book better. Also, I am grateful he speeded up the editing and production of this book so that it could be published in 2000, the fortieth anniversary of Sanford's victory.

My two most important sources for this book were on opposite sides of the fray. Terry Sanford, who died in 1998, was generous with his time. We talked three times about the 1960 race, not including that night at the Washington Duke Inn. Sanford was warm and friendly, with a sparkle in his eye that made you understand why even his political opponents often liked him. He was a great man and I feel fortunate to have spent some time with him. (I'm also thankful that his wife, Margaret

Rose Sanford, loaned me a scrapbook and gave me access to her husband's papers in the Duke University Archives.) My other most important source was Lake's son, I. Beverly Lake Jr., an associate justice on the North Carolina Supreme Court, as his father was before him. I first talked with Justice Lake for an article I wrote for the *Charlotte Observer* after Sanford's death. Lake knew I thought Sanford's election important to the state, yet he cooperated fully with my work on this book. He gave me exclusive access to hundreds of pages of his father's speeches, which are not available in a university library. I interviewed him five times and he invited me to his house to watch videotapes of his father's campaign speeches. This book is better—more precise, more authoritative, more complete—because of his cooperation. He disagrees with my premise—that Sanford's election was pivotal in turning North Carolina and the South in the right direction—and yet I hope he finds this book fair and balanced.

I could never find the words to properly thank my parents, Ann and Jack Drescher of Raleigh, for their support on this project and every other one I've undertaken in forty years. What an advantage it is to go through life knowing that two people are always behind you. They were, and are, great parents who believe in their three children. If I'm half as good a parent as they are, I'll consider myself a success.

Finally, I'd like to thank my wife, Deanna. This book was a crazy idea. When I came home from work that night in April 1996 and told her I wanted to write a book, we had two children in diapers and an almost-six-year-old who burned so hot with energy she could melt steel. Deanna is a former third-grade teacher who believes in opportunity for *all* children. She was busy with a variety of volunteer efforts, especially her passion—helping out at our children's public school. Life wasn't exactly slow at my office. I had a job—it seemed like two jobs—as city editor of the *Observer*. That was not the time to add another project to our lives. Yet she consented and was a good sport, as always. (It helped that she wore an "I'm serious about Sanford" button in 1972 when he was running for president and she was ten years old.) When I was on leave from my job and traveling to Washington and Atlanta and Chapel Hill and

Fayetteville to research, she kept our lives on track. When I was home, she tried to give me as much time as possible to write in the far corner of our old house, in what became known as "the Sanford room." Later, when we were on summer vacation and I broke away each afternoon to interview a source or to rewrite a chapter, she always understood. I am very lucky.

INTRODUCTION

In the spring of 1960, two talented, capable men—each with great passion and conviction—opposed each other in a pivotal governor's race that shook North Carolina and changed the South. Terry Sanford and I. Beverly Lake were, in the one-party South of that era, each Democrats. Yet they were different in almost every way. Lake, a middle-aged former law professor, believed deeply in segregation. Sanford, an ambitious young politician-lawyer, believed in expanding opportunities for all people. They were two compelling and complex figures, each with respect and disdain for the other. Their showdown provided North Carolina voters a stark choice at a crucial point in the state's history.

In choosing Sanford, those voters permanently changed the course of the state and, indirectly, the South. Sanford became a bold, aggressive governor of unusual energy and creativity. His schools program added twenty-eight hundred new teachers, raised average teacher pay by 22 percent, and doubled library money. He helped establish a statewide system of community colleges. He started the anti-poverty North Carolina Fund, which President Lyndon Johnson later used as a model for his War on Poverty. He named the first woman to the North Carolina Supreme Court—Susie Sharp, who later became the first woman in the United States to be elected chief justice of a state supreme court. He convinced legislators to create the North Carolina School of the Arts, the first residential state-supported college for the arts in the nation, and the Governor's School, a summer leadership program.

Word of Sanford's achievements spread across the nation. A study by political scientist Larry Sabato of the more than three hundred governors who served during 1950 to 1975 concluded that Sanford was one of the twelve best; of that dozen, ten served longer than the single four-year term Sanford was permitted by North Carolina law. A Harvard University study in 1981 gave Sanford even higher praise, ranking him as one of the ten best governors of the century, along with such national figures as Woodrow Wilson and Huey Long.

Shortly before he was elected governor of Maryland in 1994, Parris Glendening told voters he would model his administration after Sanford's. Glendening first noted Sanford when he was studying for his doctorate in political science and read Sanford's 1967 book, *Storm over the States*, which called for making state governments more modern and professional. Glendening admired Sanford for his emphasis on education, his innovation, and his eagerness, as he governed, to include all types of people with different backgrounds. "Progressive governors in the South are more common now but he was extraordinary for his time," Glendening said. "Sanford asked himself: What can I do now to position the state for the long term even if there's not a pay off for a long time? He focused on education. He understood that successful economic development was based on the quality of your education system." Sanford's success showed southerners that there could be a new approach to governing. "He showed people you could be progressive, fair and inclusive and be elected in the South," said Glendening, who was raised in Florida. "That sent a powerful message; 1960 was phenomenal. I believe he did open the way." Glendening taught at the University of Maryland for twenty-seven years, with an emphasis on state and local government. Sanford, he said, was one of the best dozen governors of the century: "There's no question about it, not only because of what he did but how he inspired others and his courage to stand up for change to get things done."

Sanford was admired nationally but his impact was greatest in the

South. He was the first New South governor, representing a style and philosophy that would later become popular with southern politicians and voters. Across the region, governors who came after him—including Jimmy Carter in Georgia, Bill Clinton in Arkansas, Jim Hunt in North Carolina, Dick Riley in South Carolina, and William Winter in Mississippi—emulated Sanford's model of governing, emphasizing good race relations, improved education, and robust economic development. Riley, who later became U.S. education secretary, said, "He opened doors in the South at a very difficult time and made it possible for subsequent leaders to be able to do tenfold what they would have without him." When Sanford died in 1998, President Clinton noted his impact on him and other southern political leaders. "I have admired Sen. Sanford since my earliest days in politics," Clinton said. "His work and his influence literally changed the face and the future of the South, making him one of the most influential Americans of the last 50 years."

William Winter watched Sanford's 1960 campaign from afar in Mississippi. He was encouraged by Sanford's election, which to him showed that a new type of politics could succeed in the South. "Terry Sanford represented in North Carolina the same sort of vision that I felt John F. Kennedy represented for the country," Winter said. "It was on the basis of that impression from a long distance away that I found myself very much attracted to Gov. Sanford." When Winter ran for governor in 1967, he read and reread Sanford's book on his education program, *But What about the People?* It became Winter's handbook. He didn't win then but was elected governor of Mississippi in 1979 and continued to be influenced by Sanford's book and his administration. Sanford's election and style of governing, Winter said, "helped establish not only for North Carolina but for the rest of the South a model of what a progressive southern governor needed to be about. . . . Anyone who had any understanding of the issues we had to confront in the South had to be influenced by Terry Sanford's vision and leadership."

In North Carolina, one of Sanford's disciples was Jim Hunt. In the late 1950s, Hunt served two terms as student-body president at North Carolina State College. The 1960 campaign drew him into real-world politics. "Terry was a breath of fresh air," said Hunt, who went on to serve four terms as North Carolina's governor. "He was a very strong and forceful personality who just resonated with the idea that we could do things. We could change things in North Carolina and make it much better. We didn't have to be a laggard in personal income, education attainments and opportunities for our people. We could change it. And he very boldly proposed those changes. Terry, to a young person like me, was at once a man who stood for and would work for a different kind of North Carolina. . . . There was a spirit about Sanford and his people and his time that has impacted me greatly. It's a spirit that says these issues that affect people are important and we can do something about it. There's this whole idea that, hey, this is fun. This is worth throwing yourself into totally. This is exciting. This is worth doing. That's a dimension of politics and government that often is missing and frequently is not spoken of. Terry had that about him. He threw himself heart, body and soul into his campaigns. He talked about the possibilities of our state and our people. It was that spirit of enthusiasm and zest for it that certainly infected me."

To an unusual degree, Sanford described his prospective governorship to North Carolina voters. From the beginning, he was confident—perhaps too confident—he would be elected. He used the campaign to build consensus for his activism and his ideas, which included a tax increase for better schools. The first year of his governorship began, in effect, as he campaigned in 1960. On a rainy morning in January, a full year before he would take office and ten months before he would win the election, Sanford was planning his administration when he met with a group of supporters in the small town of Louisburg, north of Raleigh. He had not officially announced for governor. A few Sanford organizers walked to the microphone and spoke awkwardly, their feeble, corny attempts at humor garnering only a few snickers. It was the kind of dull but worthwhile event other candidates dreaded and avoided. Indeed, for the most part Sanford's competitors weren't holding similar meetings, or not many of them, anyway.

Yet Sanford attended such meetings time after time after time, relentless as the tide, seeking support for a governorship he had not yet won. "I need your help. I need your interest," Sanford said in his deep, smooth voice. "I can't get along without you after we've won the election. If we're going to achieve for North Carolina any kind of program of progress which will have some meaning, then we'll need to work together and I'll need to have your continuing interest." It's impossible to understand Sanford's success as governor without first knowing the campaign from which his administration was born.

Perhaps the most important aspect of Sanford's legacy as governor was his belief in opportunity for all. In his inauguration speech, Sanford said, "No group of our citizens can be denied the right to participate in the opportunities of first-class citizenship"—which, as the writer Jonathan Yardley has pointed out, were fighting words in the North Carolina of 1961. Sanford was the first southern governor to call for employment without regard to race or creed. In 1963, on the one hundredth anniversary of the Emancipation Proclamation, he launched Good Neighbor Councils to encourage businesses to hire blacks and to further racial cooperation. "The most difficult thing I did was the most invisible thing," Sanford said shortly before he died. "That was to turn the attitude on the race issue. I realized that the lines of history were intersecting right there as I took the governorship."

Despite the gains North Carolina made on civil rights during the Sanford administration, that wasn't Sanford's campaign issue in 1960. Improving schools was. Indeed, Sanford tried to avoid the issue of race. Lake would not let him, however, and the campaign was racially raw. North Carolina's major politicians generally had avoided the race issue; race had not been the central issue in a gubernatorial campaign since 1900 (although it had been the main issue in the 1950 U.S. Senate race). But the 1954 Supreme Court decision banning segregation in schools changed politics across the South. Most blacks were impatient for change; most whites were afraid of it. Given that the Lake-Sanford race was the first contested governor's race after the 1954 decision, perhaps it was inevitable that race would be a major issue. Lake's passion for segregation guaranteed it.

Four decades after the campaign, Beverly Lake's candidacy has faded from memory and his views on race are largely discredited. Sanford became a role model for progressive southern politicians and a legendary figure to many North Carolina Democrats. Sanford's election as governor is taken for granted. Given today's racial mores, one cannot fathom a hardline segregationist winning the governor's mansion in North Carolina. But that was not true in 1960. Lake was smart and determined. A political novice when the campaign began, he quickly became a formidable candidate. He whipped two Democratic veterans in the first primary before locking up with Sanford in their one-on-one showdown.

For four weeks in June 1960, the state was gripped by the prospect of a hard-line segregationist becoming governor. Voter turnout in the first primary easily broke all records in North Carolina, including the one set a decade earlier during a fiercely fought U.S. Senate race. Almost 16 percent more votes were cast in the first primary than in any other gubernatorial primary in North Carolina history; turnout in the second primary was not quite as high but still more than the previous record and also a record for primary runoff. Years after the runoff, former U.S. Sen. Robert Morgan, who managed Lake's 1960 campaign, said that two political figures stood out for the strong loyalty they inspired in their supporters—Beverly Lake and Terry Sanford. "I'm durned if I believe I can transfer my support to anybody else like those two candidates can," Morgan said.

If not for Sanford's superior political skills and years of preparation, Lake might have won. Sanford's victory was an oddity. In the civil rights period from 1957 to 1973 in the South, only twice did racial moderates defeat strong segregationists in a governor's race. Sanford's win was one, and Carl Sanders' 1962 victory in Georgia was the other. And only once did a racial moderate beat a strong segregationist in a runoff primary—Sanford's victory over Lake.

On September 8, 1960, two months before Sanford was elected, seven-year-old William Campbell became the first black student to integrate a public school in Raleigh when he walked through a crowd of reporters, supporters, and opponents and into Murphey Elementary School. He attended the second-grade class taught by Mrs. Abbott, where he was welcomed by his teacher and accepted by his classmates.

Others, including some school parents, were not so happy about young William's presence. Some older students tried to intimidate him. His parents, who were civil rights leaders in Raleigh, received threatening phone calls and bomb threats. William's mother feared for her son's safety. His father, a battle-tested president of the local NAACP, later called his son's first day of school at Murphey "one of the worst days of my life." At PTA meetings, some white parents left when the Campbells arrived.

The following January, Terry Sanford, his wife, and their two young children moved into the governor's mansion, just a few blocks from Murphey School. The Sanfords sent their children to public schools, and Betsy, eleven, and Terry Jr., eight, attended Murphey. "It never occurred to us to not do that," said Sanford's wife, Margaret Rose. Sanford no doubt became one of the few governors in the South, if not the only one in that era, to send his children to an integrated public school. Newspapers across the country carried pictures of the Sanford children entering the school.

Four decades later, Bill Campbell, who became mayor of Atlanta, remembered Sanford's decision to send his children to Murphey as one of many that sent a message to the rest of the state and the South. "In my view, Terry Sanford's sensitivity and courage on the issue of race is what allowed North Carolina to escape the violence of the civil rights movement that so terribly wounded many other cities and states across the South," Campbell said. "Sanford deserves the lion's share of the credit for that. He set the tone. He set the moral tone, that the highest elected official in the state stood for equality for all people and would use the force of his office in order to ensure that people were treated fairly. . . . He took enormous political and personal risks and really emerged as one of the great figures of the South. In my view, Terry Sanford was one of the greatest governors in the history of the United States and clearly, given what he did, the finest Southern governor."

To become governor, Sanford had to beat Beverly Lake. Here's how he did it.

TRIUMPH OF
GOOD WILL

Chapter 1

SANFORD

In the early 1950s, in his bungalow on Hillside Avenue overlooking downtown Fayetteville, North Carolina, Terry Sanford kept a notebook in a bedroom dresser drawer. In the notebook, Sanford, then a young lawyer aspiring to be governor, jotted strategies for responding to race-baiting politics. While knotting his tie or emptying his pockets, an idea would come to him, and Sanford would pause to scribble:

> Never get on the defensive.
> Have a network of people to tell you about false rumors and materials.
> Be aggressive with a positive program in the beginning.

Sanford started writing in the notebook during the 1950 U.S. Senate race between conservative Raleigh attorney Willis Smith and liberal Sen. Frank Porter Graham, formerly president of the University of North Carolina. Graham was University of North Carolina president when Sanford was an undergraduate in the late 1930s and a law student in the 1940s. Sanford, like many Chapel Hill students, revered the kindly, warm man they called "Dr. Frank." Graham invited students over to the president's house on Sunday afternoons, and Sanford visited a dozen times. Graham opened another world for Sanford, a small-town boy from Laurinburg, southwest of Fayetteville, near the South Carolina border. Graham talked of the plight of textile workers and women and black people—the kind of talk, Sanford commented years later, that could get you thrown out of office in the South. Sanford and Graham became friends.

In early 1950, after Graham had been appointed to the U.S. Senate by maverick Gov. Kerr Scott to fill a vacancy, Sanford supported the campaign of his mentor. Sanford, then thirty-two, was not a newcomer to politics. The year before, he was elected state president of the Young Democrats, a stepping-stone for ambitious, young politicians. He plunged into the 1950 Senate race, a racially raw campaign that turned many North Carolinians against each other. Graham led Smith and two other candidates in the first Democratic primary with 48.9 percent —just short of the majority needed to win the nomination outright.

In the runoff a few weeks later, Graham was defeated with racist tactics, including widespread fliers, from the anonymous "Know the Truth Committee," that said, "WHITE PEOPLE WAKE UP." "Do you want," the ad asked, "Negroes working beside you, you wife and daughters in your mills and factories? Negroes eating beside you in all public eating places? Negroes riding beside you, your wife and your daughters in buses, cabs and trains? Negroes sleeping in the same hotels and rooming houses? Negroes teaching and disciplining your children in school? Negroes sitting with you and your family at all public meetings? Negroes going to white schools and white children going to Negro schools? Negroes to occupy the same hospital rooms with you and your wife and daughters? Negroes as your foremen and overseers in the mills? Negroes using your toilet facilities?" If you do, the ad said, vote for Frank Graham. If you don't, vote for Willis Smith: "He will uphold the traditions of the South."

Smith supporters used an array of tricks. Among them were ads that purported to be for Graham but actually were intended to sway white voters to Smith. For example, a black man walked into the offices of the *Daily News* in Washington, North Carolina, requested anonymity, and placed an ad. It was addressed "To the Colored Voters" and signed "Colored Committee for Dr. Frank Graham." The ads referred to recent U.S. Supreme Court rulings favoring integration and said, "These and other liberal rulings will mean nothing unless we have far-sighted, honest and fair administrators. We think Dr. Frank Graham has all the qualities. . . . Our vote counted in the last primary. We did it before—We can do it again."

In a different tactic, well-dressed blacks rode through eastern North Carolina in a car with "Graham for Senate" banners. The riders worked for Smith backers. Many of the tricks were believed to have been performed locally without the knowledge of the Smith campaign. Yet Smith was comfortable discussing certain issues of race; he carried handbills showing that in the first primary, Graham carried more than 95 percent of the vote in six black precincts in Raleigh, Durham, Greensboro, and Charlotte. Smith said those lopsided totals were a menace to democracy.

In the runoff, Sanford picked a precinct of mill workers in Fayetteville and learned how to organize. He went house to house. The precinct voted for Smith in the first primary, but swung to Graham in the runoff, one of the few precincts in the state that switched to Graham. Reacting to the racially oriented attacks, many whites in eastern North Carolina, where blacks made up a higher percentage of the population, abandoned Graham. There was a mob mood at the end of the primary, one observer later noted, and Frank Graham was lynched politically.

Sanford was bitter about the campaign, which he thought dirty and vicious. It scarred him forever. Shortly before Graham died in 1972, Sanford suggested to him that Smith's death three years after his election was God's retribution. The race left Sanford afraid of racial politics. But he knew if he were to run for governor, he might have to tackle the issue— or it would tackle him. Graham was just so nice and sweet, Sanford said, he let the Smith forces get off the defensive. Sanford was determined that when he was in charge, he wasn't going to get beat on the race issue. So he plotted and studied and waited for his day to come, when he would have to deal with the hottest, thorniest issue of that era for a liberal Southern politician. He continued to write in his notebook, until he had twenty-five or thirty pages of notes and strategies:

> Don't give them any quarter.
> Counter-attack on another issue.
> Don't let somebody drag you into something you don't want to do.

Sanford was born in Laurinburg in 1917, the second son of Cecil Sanford and Elizabeth Martin Sanford. Two younger daughters were to follow. Eventually, the family lived in one-and-a-half-story frame house on McLaurin Street, two blocks from downtown. His father operated a family hardware store, J. D. Sanford and Son, until it went out of business when the Great Depression struck in the late 1920s. Then he held a variety of jobs, including selling insurance to poor people, working for the WPA, and later keeping books for an oil company.

To his lifelong friends, it seemed Sanford was born politicking. As a young child, he sometimes received a spanking from his mother because he would go visiting, forget to tell her where he was going, and spend hours talking as she searched for him. He delivered newspapers and telegraphs and sold the *Saturday Evening Post* and *Ladies Home Journal*. He once said that he knew just about every house and person in Laurinburg, a dusty little farm and trading town surrounded by cotton and tobacco. He also sold vegetables in what was politely called New Town but more typically, by whites anyway, called Nigger Town. The Sanfords, like most people in the early 1930s, didn't have much, but still New Town was to young Sanford a shock. "I never have forgotten the plight that they found themselves in," Sanford said decades later. People were hungry. Outdoor toilets were in disrepair.

Terry Sanford reckoned his family was "on the downside of average" financially but was still well respected because of the roles his parents played in the community. Cecil Sanford was a quiet man who liked politics and the First United Methodist Church. "He was a very private person," said John Mitchell, who worked with Cecil Sanford at Service Oil Co., where Sanford was a bookkeeper. Cecil Sanford was the superintendent of Sunday school at First Methodist. The Sanfords used to walk to church. They attended Sunday mornings for Sunday school and the Sunday service. They went back on Sunday nights. They also attended church on Wednesday nights. "I'll tell you the truth," Terry Sanford said later. "I got about all the church that I wanted—maybe a little bit more."

Terry Sanford inherited his love of politics from his father. Cecil Sanford liked liberals and anti-establishment candidates. In 1936, for governor he vocally supported renegade Ralph McDonald, a college professor who called for "a New Deal for North Carolina." McDonald lost to the establishment candidate, Clyde Hoey, the brother-in-law of former Gov. O. Max Gardner, who had created a powerful organization—the Shelby Dynasty. Terry Sanford said of his father, "I always went with him on whoever he was for, so I sort of got in the habit of being for the challenger. . . . I had a pretty good example of a man that always thought he was right and seldom won." When he was older, Terry Sanford's favorite president was Franklin Roosevelt, because he remembered the little guy. His parents regarded FDR as a savior.

Terry Sanford inherited his outgoing personality from his mother, a longtime schoolteacher much loved by the townspeople of Laurinburg. "She was a wonderful person. Good personality," Mitchell said. "She was well-liked by everybody in town." Miss Betsy was highly respected as a teacher. She had a good sense of humor; she sometimes lost her glasses, only to find them on her head. She also told her children that the people who lived in New Town did not have the same opportunities as white people. While typically it was his father who led Sanford into politics, during the 1928 presidential campaign between Herbert Hoover and Al Smith, eleven-year-old Sanford marched in a torchlight parade through downtown Laurinburg carrying a sign that said, "Me and Ma are for Al!" At school, they had Al Smith buttons and pencils.

While his parents could be strict, they also gave Sanford enough freedom to roam. He was mischievous and played tricks on his family. "I suppose if I'd been caught and paid the penalty of everything wrong I did, I wouldn't be sitting her talking with you," Sanford once said to an interviewer. His parents let him smoke rabbit tobacco. When he was twelve, they let him buy an automobile—for one dollar. He tried to avoid work as much as possible, but with no allowance, he would cut grass, wash windows, or paint to have some money. One day he talked his mother into allowing him and a friend to spend the night in a swamp, so they could try to catch an insect that only comes out at night. Another time, on the way back from a family beach trip, he and his older brother rode in the trunk of the Sanford's old Ford. They were to knock if they had any trouble.

Terry knocked. The Sanfords stopped the car. Terry said he had a sore throat—and then fell unconscious. Carbon monoxide had seeped into the trunk. A physician told the Sanfords if they had traveled much further with the boys in the trunk, the boys would have died.

As a teenager, Sanford was liked, yet was different from the others. He didn't hang around Charlie Williamson's pharmacy with the small-town drugstore cowboys. He was good-natured, adventurous, handsome, and bright, but there was a different air about him. He was always doing something or working on something or off on a trip or to a meeting or to a movie. "He was like the prodigal son. You were home all the time, and he wasn't," his mother once said. At Pine Lake Camp, where he worked, Sanford would take long, solitary walks when the other were sleeping. At Boy Scout camp, he liked the group activities but he was often seen swimming by himself for long periods in the camp's big lake.

He was average at sports; he struggled with football but enjoyed tennis, fishing, and sailing. He liked the outdoors and was an Eagle Scout at fifteen. He played the saxophone in a band he formed with some friends. His own mother said that he was not outstanding in high school. The only thing his Latin teacher could remember about him was how he used to lean his chair back in the library; she thought he was going to fall back. Girls teased him about his dimples. Dickson Phillips, who knew Sanford as a boy in Laurinburg and later became his law partner, said that young Sanford stood apart. "He was not one of the boys," said Phillips, a retired federal appeals court judge. Phillips said that Betsy Sanford communicated to her son "that there were better things to do than hang around the drug store, play high school athletics, which were painfully inadequate in those days, and carouse around at night at road houses. That's what the peers were doing. That's what we all did. He was about other things."

The Sanfords stressed education. Betsy Sanford had gone to college and Cecil Sanford went briefly to a business school. They expected their children to go to college. Terry Sanford visited Chapel Hill and the new campus at Duke University. He ended up starting at Presbyterian Junior College, in nearby Maxton, which is now part of St. Andrews College in

Laurinburg. He hitchhiked to class every day. Eventually, he headed to Chapel Hill and the University of North Carolina to finish his college education.

In Chapel Hill, he continued to scrounge for money to pay the bills. He delivered the student newspaper, the *Daily Tar Heel,* to the west side of Chapel Hill during one of the snowiest winters in years. He washed dishes and waited tables at Swain Hall, the dining hall. He managed his dormitory. Before he left Laurinburg, he bought a suitcase he took to Chapel Hill, but he didn't pay for it for a year; every time he went back home and saw the merchants, Mr. Hammond and Mr. Monroe, they wanted to know when he was going to pay up. But there were benefits to hitchhiking back to Laurinburg. When he came home from college, his mother always baked a coconut cake.

Chapel Hill changed him. He was struck by the spirit of the place— the new thoughts, the different types of people from across the state and the country. "I probably would have followed a different path and probably been a different kind of person if I hadn't gone to Chapel Hill," he said. Frank Graham opened his eyes further to the lives of sharecroppers, women, textile workers, and blacks. He was introduced to student government; they didn't have class officers in high school in Laurinburg. He was elected speaker of the University of North Carolina Student Legislature. A classmate recalled that Sanford was "a nice fellow, easy to get along with. He was a fellow you knew would get somewhere. [Sanford] seemed mighty mature as a freshman. He knew enough to be attractive to people and he had a suave attitude about him then." He called his friends "buddyro" and played tackle on the Grimes dormitory touch football team that went undefeated one year. Among his new friends were northerners Louis Harris, the future pollster, and Richard Adler, who would compose the Broadway musical *Damn Yankees.*

He went to Chapel Hill thinking he might become a doctor, but after graduating in 1939, he enrolled in the law school. During his first year in law school, he met an outgoing undergraduate named Margaret Rose Knight of Hopkinsville, Kentucky. She was an English major, which he thought intellectual. She was dating a friend of his. Sanford thought she could do better, but it took a year before he had the nerve to ask her out. Although he had dated in high school, she became his first steady girlfriend.

Before he graduated from the law school, Sanford joined the FBI, with director J. Edgar Hoover offering him a job in December 1941. He was assigned as a special agent to Columbus, Ohio, and St. Louis, where he enjoyed the life of a bachelor. When he later applied to join the Society of Former FBI Agents, he received a letter from one of his former colleagues. "My first impression was to blackball you on account of all the calls I had at our room in the Forrest Park Hotel after you left from female callers," the former agent wrote. "How you ever got out of St. Louis single is more than I know."

Although as an FBI agent he was exempt from military duty, Sanford decided to enlist. He entered the army in 1942, four weeks after he stopped in Hopkinsville and married Margaret Rose Knight. At Fort Thomas, Kentucky, where he was sent for training, he was told that paratroopers ate steak every night and received fifty dollars a month in extra pay. He volunteered for parachute duty. His first meal with the paratroopers was bread, coffee without cream, and cold turnip greens. But he did get the extra pay. And he had another motivation: He wanted to be where the action was. He ran up and down a hill all winter and qualified as a jumper. He won a chance at officer training and was assigned to the 517th Parachute Infantry at Camp Mackall, a few miles from Laurinburg. He stayed with the outfit, which came to be known as the 517th Parachute Combat Team, throughout the war. He fought in five campaigns, in Italy, France, Belgium, and Germany, including the invasion of southern France and the Battle of the Bulge, where he was wounded by shell fragments.

He entered as a private and was discharged as a first lieutenant. To rally his troops, Sanford used to say, "Stick with Terry and you'll fart through silk"; he later exhorted his political troops with the same words. Sanford thought highly of the colonel who commanded the 517th. "He had a great sense of the military in terms of tactics and strategy but he also had a great compassion," Sanford said later. "He didn't want anybody killed and he didn't take any unnecessary risks." The 517th consistently met its objectives, giving the group great confidence. They thought: *You just turn us loose and we'll end this war.* The fighting gave Sanford confidence but it also left another mark on him. One day, on a hillside in Belgium, he watched friends dying all around him. The time he got after World War II was a gift, he thought.

After the war, he finished law school in 1946, having made a wealth of friends and contacts who later became a key part of his political foundation. He stayed in Chapel Hill for two years as assistant director of the University of North Carolina Institute of Government; he helped in directing the annual Boys' State programs held in Chapel Hill. He was active in politics; Sanford and his neighbor and friend, University of North Carolina law student Bill Friday, helped manage the election of O. Max Gardner Jr. as president of the Young Democrats Clubs. Sanford and Friday, who became president of the University of North Carolina system, remained friends and associates for the rest of Sanford's life. Sanford was busy in Chapel Hill, but it was time for a change. He was thirty years old. He had put himself through college, served as an FBI agent, and married. He had fought in the Battle of the Bulge, was awarded the Bronze Star and a Purple Heart, and helped save the world. There was one thing left to do. He was ready to start running for governor.

Sanford had known since he was an undergraduate he was going to run for governor, although he didn't tell anybody then. Now he thought it was time to leave Chapel Hill. He considered his options. First, where would he live? He didn't want to go to a small town. He had an offer from a law firm in Charlotte, the largest city in the state, but thought he would be middle-aged before he'd get enough recognition to enter politics. He didn't like Raleigh, the state capital, as a political base. Fayetteville wasn't far from his hometown, and it was big enough for a law practice to thrive. It was, he thought, the perfect size for him to quickly emerge as a leader. It was in the east, which he considered his home. His friend Paul Thompson loaned him five hundred dollars to pay off some debts and help him get started in Fayetteville. He and Margaret Rose moved there in 1948, and Sanford practiced law. First he worked with Charlie Rose Jr., whose son would later serve in Congress. Then Sanford joined L. Stacy Weaver in forming Sanford and Weaver; later, he brought in old Laurinburg friends Dickson Phillips and Donald McCoy.

Sanford threw himself zealously into Fayetteville's social and civic life. Within two years, he was a Rotarian, chairman of the Cumberland County chapter of the Red Cross, member of the advisory board of the Salvation Army, president of the Fayetteville Jaycees, a director of a hospital for black people, chairman of the Boy Scout troop committee, active in the American Legion, a captain in the National Guard, and a steward at Hay Street Methodist Church. A newspaper ad in 1949 included his picture and urged readers to tune in to WFLB radio that night to hear Terry Sanford, attorney and president of the Jaycees, talk about better schools and roads. When the *News and Observer* of Raleigh named him its Tar Heel of the Week in September 1950, reporter Jack Riley noted, "He hasn't found time for many hobbies." Sanford conceded that he enjoyed fishing for shad in the Cape Fear River, hunting deer at Lake Waccamaw, or "just fooling around the river in a boat."

He found time to politick. In 1948, he actively supported Harry S Truman for president, while much of the local Democratic leadership supported Strom Thurmond. Sanford brashly offered to debate the Dixiecrats' state treasurer, who lived in Fayetteville. A year later, the Young Democrats Club (YDC) from that district nominated him to be state president, a traditional stepping-stone to elected office. The Seventh District YDC printed a pamphlet introducing Sanford to YDC members, pointing out his accomplishments at the university, in World War II, and in Fayetteville. The YDC president was to be chosen at a three-day convention in New Bern in September. Candidates competed hard for the prestigious office. Max Gardner Jr. was helping Sanford. Gardner called his friend Clint Newton, who was in the textile business in Shelby. "He thought Sanford was in trouble," Newton said. He asked for help. Newton flew to New Bern and met Sanford for the first time. "We just became inseparable friends," Newton said.

Bill Staton, a young lawyer in Lee County, also received a phone call from a friend who knew Sanford. "I was told a young man named Terry Sanford wanted to run for president of the Young Democrats Clubs of North Carolina and eventually hoped to be governor," Staton said. Sanford's organizers were looking for a Wake Forest College graduate who could recruit other Wake Forest grads into Sanford's camp. A few weeks later, Sanford and their mutual friend visited Staton in his law office and talked at length. "I was impressed with Sanford and made a commitment to be of some help," Staton said. "I thought he was an alert, intelligent, bright man. I thought if you were going to be interested in politics at that particular time in the state, riding with him held a lot of hope for the future." Staton and Newton became two of Sanford's closest and longest-running political allies.

The Sanford forces rallied his friends from Chapel Hill, the American Legion, and the Jaycees, as well as newcomers like Staton. He turned back a candidate supported by Gov. Kerr Scott, and at the convention in New Bern, Sanford won the presidency. That fall, Sanford ran into Governor Scott at a football game in Chapel Hill. He introduced himself. Scott recognized the name and chuckled. "Well, I'm glad to meet you," Scott said. "You know, it does a man good to get beat every now and then." That was the beginning of a relationship that endured until Scott's death, one that grew close and eventually helped make Sanford into a bona fide statewide candidate.

As YDC president, Sanford campaigned for Frank Graham in 1950 and ran YDC meetings, presiding "with poise and efficiency," the *Fayetteville Observer* noted. During Graham's campaign, Sanford kept a notebook in which he pasted clippings from the "Under the Dome" political column in the *News and Observer*. When the Graham campaign announced a county campaign manager, the paper would publish the news. Sanford arranged the managers by county in the three-ring notebook; the counties were grouped by congressional district. A few business cards also were pasted in the appropriate county.

In 1952, Sanford ran for the state senate against a former two-term legislator. Sanford's campaign ad in the newspaper pictured him and said simply, "Terry Sanford, State Senate. I would greatly appreciate your support, and I will try always to represent you in a conscientious and straight-forward manner." Sanford easily won the Democratic primary, getting 75 percent of the vote, and was unopposed in November. He served one rather unremarkable term in Raleigh. He took care of the folks back home, working on several local measures. He got legislators to allow Cumberland County commissioners to use twenty thousand dollars in Alcoholic Beverage Control money to pay for the county tax revaluation. He worked to extend the jurisdiction of the Spring Lake police to three miles outside the corporate limits. He proposed that precinct lines in Fayetteville coincide with ward lines drawn for city elections.

Despite working on often mundane local legislation, he became a favorite of reporters looking for intelligent quotes on big, statewide issues. "If you were doing trend kind of stuff, he was the man to talk to," said Joe Doster, who covered politics and government for the *Charlotte Observer*. "You'd call Sanford or go by and see him and ask him about his views on something and how it affected the state. He had a reputation as a guy with some vision. He seemed to have a pretty clear idea about where he thought the state ought to go and what it ought to be doing." Woodrow Price of the *News and Observer* said, "Terry was a real whiz in those days. He was a brain. He had a lot of friends who were brains too. . . . He was an easy-going, easy-talking fellow. He could be pretty tough if he wanted to. But he was the kind of fellow you could get along with."

Sanford remembered his term fondly for making friends and emerging as an independent voice. He voted against the appropriations bills because he thought it wasn't debated enough. He opposed Governor Umstead's reorganization of the highway commission. But he believed he had fought those measures, and a few others, without making enemies. He was more convinced than ever that if you wanted to change the state, the place to do it from was the governor's office, not the legislature. Sanford served one term and did not seek reelection. He wanted to learn how Raleigh worked, but he didn't want to make a career out of the legislature. As usual, he had something bigger on his mind.

* * *

In early 1954, at the Carolina Hotel in Raleigh, former Gov. Kerr Scott named Terry Sanford the manager of his campaign for the U.S. Senate. Scott, although unpopular with many, was a living legend among the rural people in the state. Six years earlier, Scott had turned the state upside down. North Carolina's politics were dominated then by business interests and the political organization of the Shelby Dynasty. Scott was different. He was state agriculture commissioner when he ran for governor; the press liked to called him "the Squire of Haw River," a reference to his rural home in Alamance County. Scott called his supporters the Branch Head Boys, because they lived out at the branch of the river, isolated by unpaved roads.

In some ways, the Scott-Sanford alliance was an unusual one. Scott was rough, rural, and brash. Sanford was smooth, urbane, and friendly. But on the issues, they thought much the same, and Scott took a liking to Sanford. Also, Sanford could expand Scott's base with his ever-growing list of contacts. At the news conference at the hotel, Sanford said, "We're going to make this one of the cleanest campaigns ever conducted in North Carolina, I will assure you of that. We intend to be frank and candid all the way through this campaign."

Scott ran against Sen. Alton Lennon, who was appointed to the job when Willis Smith died in 1953. Scott inherited most of Graham's supporters, who viewed the Scott campaign against the conservative Lennon as a rematch of the second primary they'd lost four year earlier; they called the '54 match-up "the Third Primary." For Sanford, managing Scott's campaign was a pivotal experience. He wanted to redeem Frank Graham's loss. He also wanted to test his theories on how to respond to race politics; this would help him when he ran for governor.

Scott's term as governor—North Carolina then limited its governors to one term—was marked by road building, capital improvements to schools and ports, and what some saw as racial liberalism. Scott, a cigar-chewing dairy farmer, appointed a black man to the state Board of Education; this was believed to be the highest-ranking state post held at the time by a black person in the South. On May 17, 1954, when the U.S. Supreme Court issued the *Brown* decision outlawing segregation in public schools, the Lennon campaign leaped at the opening. The Democratic primary was twelve days away. Lennon said that Scott and his top associates supported integrating public schools. "Agitators are in North Carolina now," Lennon said, "trying to influence the election of Kerr Scott" with a "scheme to bloc-vote citizens of North Carolina."

In that era, when Jim Crow ruled and segregation was ingrained in daily life, no mainstream white politician in the South advocated integration; to do so would have been political suicide. "I have always opposed and I am still opposed to Negro and white children going to school together," Scott said. He also said that the Supreme Court's decision should not become an issue in the seven-candidate Senate primary. "I feel certain," Scott said, "that no candidates would favor the end of segregation, and I am sure they will join me in hope and prayer that we can avoid stirring up fear and bad feeling between races in North Carolina." Newspapers across the state criticized Lennon for raising the issue.

The following Wednesday, three days before the Saturday primary, an ad appeared in the *Winston-Salem Journal* eerily reminiscent of the dirty tricks from the Graham-Smith campaign. At first glance, the ad appeared to be designed to help Scott. It said that Scott, as governor, had increased the number of black state employees dramatically. The ad urged a vote for Scott for Senate, saying he was a "friend of the Negro." Scott, the ad said, increased appointments of blacks to state boards by more than 300 percent. The ad was signed by J. H. R. Gleaves, president of the Progressive Civic League, a black organization. The ad praised Scott so highly that Sanford was suspicious that it was a setup to turn off white voters. He was right. Later in the day, Gleaves disavowed the ad. Gleaves said that a white man had approached him about an ad. Gleaves, however, said he did not authorize the ad.

Sanford, taking a page from his dresser-drawer notebook, went on the offensive. He wired newspapers and radio stations, saying fake ads had been spotted. Also, he said the Federal Communications Commission had been notified of possible false radio ads. Sanford was not worried about the consequences of the ad in Winston-Salem. With that city's large percentage of organized black voters, he thought the ad might help as much as it hurt. But he wanted to stop the spread of unsigned ads like those that had devastated the Graham campaign four years earlier.

Then came a bolt of lightning from the east, where Frank Graham had been struck fatally on the race issue four year earlier. Sanford and Scott aide Ben Roney had built a network that was to alert them at the first hint of racial ads and flyers. "We were geared for dirty politics," Sanford said later. After the Supreme Court decision, they had expected racial issues to rise. On Thursday, two days before the primary, the Scott campaign received a phone call: A large stack of reprints of the Winston-Salem ad had been delivered to a service station in Columbia, in coastal Tyrrell County.

Sanford moved swiftly on several fronts. In Winston-Salem, Sanford turned loose his supporters and in a matter or hours determined who was behind the ad—Mayor Marshall Kurfees. The mayor, a Lennon supporter, said that he wrote the ad, persuaded Gleaves to sign it, and then paid for it to run in the *Winston-Salem Journal*. Gleaves, a Scott supporter, confirmed the story of his friend Kurfees.

Sanford wanted to stop the spread of the reprints in the east, so he wired Lennon's managers and threatened legal action if they distributed them. Sanford believed the reprints violated state and federal laws requiring political literature to be signed. He called the State Bureau of Investigation and the FBI and asked them to investigate. Sanford's threats worked. Several of Lennon's local leaders said that they would not distribute the flyers. In Pitt County, in the heart of eastern North Carolina, Lennon's manager stopped distribution, apparently after the Scott campaign started fighting them.

The reprints galvanized Scott's forces. In some counties, Scott supporters sought to confront people distributing the flyers; in two counties, Scott leaders offered one hundred dollar rewards for information leading to the arrest of those distributing the reprinted ads. The Scott campaign used an airplane to distribute its own flyers, which said that distributing the *Winston-Salem Journal* ad could result in prosecution.

The reprints were being carried down the coast. In tracking their distribution, Sanford received help from Woodrow Price, a reporter from the

News and Observer of Raleigh. Price had wandered into the Scott head-quarters in the Carolina Hotel. He was an avid fisherman who knew the coast well; he also had stumbled into the biggest story of the campaign. Working a phone in Scott's headquarters, with Sanford near him, he tracked the man distributing the flyers, who was dropping the flyers at county offices.

Sanford set out to get his hands on the leaflets. Working through a labor leader in Durham, Sanford arranged for a tobacco factory worker to approach the Lennon campaign and ask for a bundle of flyers. The undercover Scott man received one thousand flyers and instructions on where and how to distribute them. After the factory worker gave a written statement to the press, Sanford had him ushered into a hotel room, where a Scott loyalist shielded him from reporters for the next day or so. Confronted with a racially oriented appeal, Sanford hit back—and hard. "Some people might consider it a little bit shifty but I didn't," Sanford said of sending an undercover Scott supporter to the Lennon campaign. "I thought it was fair game, and I thought it was brilliantly executed, if I do say so."

Sanford fed the story to the *News and Observer*, the dominant paper in eastern North Carolina. It also was sympathetic to Scott. On Friday morning, coverage of the reprinted flyers dominated the paper's front page. A double-deck headline, spanning five columns, said, "Alton Lennon Forces Flood State with 'Phony' Race Issue Leaflets." Coverage included a large picture of a stack of leaflets obtained by the undercover Scott supporter. Three stories ran on the front page—Kurfees' admission that he was behind the ad; Sanford's request of federal and state investigations; and Woodrow Price's account of the distribution of the reprints.

Price's story included an account from the undercover Scott supporter. He said that he had received instruction from Lennon's publicity director, C. A. "Abie" Upchurch Jr., on how and where to distribute the reprints. Upchurch had advised him to work at night, putting the flyers in mailboxes in the rural areas and front porches and mailboxes in the mill districts. It was a reversal of roles for Upchurch, who had been publicity director for Frank Graham four years earlier. According to the undercover

Scott supporter, Upchurch said, "They beat me with this [in '50] and it ought to be good enough to try it again."

Sanford, his competitive juices pumping, was not done. He worked deep into the night Friday, keeping on top of the spread of the reprints. He told Woodrow Price that the FBI was investigating distribution of the flyers. Price was unable to get the FBI to comment. Nonetheless, the *News and Observer* published the story, basing it on Sanford's comments, and displayed it on the front page on election day as the dominant story of the day with the headline "Voters Give Decision Today; FBI Probes Race Circular." Sanford said years later that the FBI indeed did wire him that it was investigating. No prosecution resulted. But Sanford achieved his short-term goal: He put the Lennon campaign on the defensive and alerted voters that there was something suspicious about the flyers.

Sanford's counterattack was not without risk. His attacks elevated the issue and made more people aware of the original ad and reprints. The Lennon campaign purchased a full-page ad in the *News and Observer*, defending the ad as legitimate and reprinting parts of it. "Nothing Phony about This!" said the new Lennon ad. Still, despite all the attention, Sanford knew from the Graham campaign that it was more dangerous to let charges and dubious flyers go unanswered. A whispering campaign, especially about race, could be devastating in a close election. Sanford considered his handling of the matter one of his great victories in politics and he retold his moves and countermoves gleefully. Low on sleep but high on adrenaline, pushing buttons and making phone calls, Sanford fought the race issue head on—and won. "We put that prairie fire out," Sanford bragged years later. "We might have gotten our hands a little burned doing it but we damn well put it out in two days time."

On Saturday, Democrats narrowly chose Scott as their nominee, giving him about 51 percent of the vote. North Carolina was then a one-party state, and Scott won easily in November. Sanford's strategies from his notebook had been tested—and they worked. "If we hadn't caught it, Alton Lennon would still be the United States Senator," Sanford said about twenty years later. Besides, he said, "We had the greatest fun of any campaign I've ever been in."

For Sanford, then thirty-six, the Scott campaign was the political break of a lifetime. He ran a successful, high-pressure, statewide campaign, which prepared him for running his own campaign. In running Scott's campaign, Sanford displayed a golden touch with people, especially young people, a touch that would become a trademark. Sanford— sincere, a good listener, even tempered—convinced people he cared about them. "I always appreciated the attention he gave to those who worked in the campaign," said Jessie Rae Scott, Kerr Scott's daughter-in-law, who worked in the campaign headquarters. "I remember the worshipful and awestruck attitude that some of the younger people had toward Terry. It was very obvious."

As Scott's campaign manager, Sanford developed a close relationship with the state's dominant politician. Sanford now had a statewide network on which to build. Even before Scott officially announced Sanford as his manager, Sanford had traveled to thirty counties. By the end of the race, he had worked with Scott supporters in all one hundred counties. Sanford had been at the right place at the right time and had joined the right team. He had performed well, and now he was the heir apparent to lead the team. He had Kerr Scott's blessings. Shortly after Scott won the primary, Scott, Sanford, and Ben Roney went to the beach. "Senator, I sure would like to be governor," Sanford said. Scott said, "Well, why don't you run? I'll vote for you."

After the 1954 Senate race, Sanford devoted himself to building his own organization for a run for governor. He considered running against Gov. Luther Hodges in 1956. Hodges was lieutenant governor when Gov. William Umstead died in 1954. As lieutenant governor, Hodges had presided over the state senate during Sanford's term in '53. Sanford was not impressed with the former business executive and political newcomer. He didn't think Hodges worked well with people. "He was also a very aloof, arrogant person at that stage in his life, and he made a lot of people in the Senate extremely uncomfortable," Sanford said later. He didn't like Hodges much as governor, either. "Hodges," Sanford said, "didn't look like he knew what government was all about."

When no major candidate stepped up to challenge Hodges, Sanford considered the race right up until the filing deadline. He believed Hodges, who had no real political organization, could be defeated, and that he ought to be challenged. But Sanford, then thirty-eight, had a feeling he wasn't quite ready to be governor. Also, running against an incumbent was far more difficult than running for an open seat. And Sanford thought Hodges, a moderate on race, was taking the right course on the most explosive issue of the day, a direction that ought not to be risked by the emotions of a campaign. On the deadline day for filing, he wavered. He and law partner Dickson Phillips drove up from Fayetteville to Raleigh, and Sanford had the filing fee in his pocket. They walked toward the elections office. But instead of filing, they visited Hodges as the deadline passed. Hodges welcomed them in. An aide to Hodges told him, "Well, governor, you got by without opposition." Sanford didn't say a word about what almost happened.

Instead, Sanford worked on building his organization. He worked hard to win the people who supported Kerr Scott. Sanford noted they were different from his network of University of North Carolina grads, Methodists, Jaycees, and Young Democrats. The Branch Head Boys weren't professional people and they lived away from towns. "They were people, by and large, that I would not have been involved with," Sanford said of Scott's strongest supporters. "They were people that I might have had some difficulty reaching. They particularly were valuable to have on my side when racism became a big thing in the campaign because they were out in the rural areas where they, by being for me, would dispel a great many of those fears."

Sanford wanted to inherit Scott's supporters and Scott encouraged it. When Scott was in the Senate, Sanford visited him in Washington once or twice a month to talk politics. Scott contributed one dollar to a future Sanford campaign with a notation that said "to be held until Terry runs for governor." Scott died in office in April 1958. On the Sunday before he died, Kerr Scott walked to church in Hawfields with his younger brother Ralph. Kerr Scott told his brother that he wanted to live long enough to see Sanford elected governor. "He told me," Ralph Scott said, "that Terry has the character and the integrity, the background and the experience that North Carolina needs. And he said that Terry's as clean as a hound's tooth."

After Kerr Scott's funeral, Sanford, Ben Roney, and Ralph Scott went to the home of Scott aide Roy Wilder in Spring Hope in Nash County, east of Raleigh. They sat in a back room of Wilder's two-story log house and talked about who might be appointed to Senator Scott's seat. They hoped it would be his widow. They learned that night that Governor Hodges had appointed Everett Jordan to the seat. Jordan was a conservative textile manufacturer who was Scott's opposite, both in style and politics.

The Scott family did not like the appointment. Sanford lashed out bitterly at Hodges. "Sen. Scott's friends are deeply offended," Sanford told a reporter. "Jordan is the one man who fought Kerr Scott almost from the day Kerr Scott gave him an appointment in the Democratic Party organization. He fought the 'Go Forward' program. He fought Kerr Scott when he ran for the Senate." While Jordan claimed Scott was a friend, Sanford said acidly, "Jordan should stand on his own position and record, whatever they may be, without the benefit of the pious hypocrisy of claiming friendship with a man who is dead and unable to defend himself."

Sanford, even though he was courting support across the state, did not care about alienating Hodges. The two differed politically. They were from different generations and had little in common personally. Privately, Sanford called Hodges "liver lips." Instead of working for Jordan, four members of Scott's Senate staff quit. Each of the four—Roney, Wilder, Betty Carter, and Peggy Warren—later worked in Sanford's campaign for governor.

After Kerr Scott died, his relatives continued to support Sanford. Ralph Scott was a power in the state senate and a Sanford supporter. Kerr Scott's son, Bob, who ran the family farm, became a political ally of Sanford's and a regular correspondent. In the mid to late 1950s, Bob Scott sent Sanford county-by-county lists of agriculture extension agents and vocational agriculture teachers. Sometimes, Bob Scott sent political reconnaissance. In a letter to Sanford in 1959, Scott noted that former

Wake Forest law professor I. Beverly Lake, a strong segregationist, was traveling the state, gauging support for a run for governor.

Bob Scott himself had political ambitions, although they were not yet well developed. In a letter to Ben Roney, who had been a key aide to his father and was then working for Sanford, Scott asked if he could accompany Roney on a political swing across the state to get experience. Roney obliged. Scott, who had not been involved in his father's campaigns, got a political education from a master pol, traveling the two-lane highways of eastern North Carolina, stopping at every country store for a soft drink, a package of peanuts or crackers, and some political talk. How was Sanford doing there? Who's for him? Who's against him? Have the other candidates been through? Scott learned to just take a swig of soda and not drink the entire bottle; otherwise, he'd be bloated with soda by the end of the day. For Scott, who later would become governor, Sanford's campaign was his introduction to state politics.

Scott wrote letters to his father's friends, saying Sanford had absorbed much of his father's philosophy. Sanford also wrote to Scott supporters, pointing out his affiliation with Kerr Scott and asking for support. He maintained a close relationship with Scott's widow, Mary, who adored Sanford. In his frequent travels across the state, Sanford would stop and visit Mary Scott. Sanford called her "Miss Mary" and sent her drafts of political speeches to critique. She told him the latest scuttlebutt. "Did you hear Jesse Helms yesterday on TV?" she wrote Sanford in August 1959. Helms, who had supported conservative Willis Smith in the 1950 Senate race, was then executive director of the North Carolina Bankers Association. About a year later, he would start his career as an editorialist for WRAL-TV. Helms would later say that Mary Scott was mistaken and he did not make the television appearance that she described in her letter to Sanford. However, Mrs. Scott described Helms's talk in great detail and with great certainty. While Helms was not working then for WRAL-TV, it's possible he gave a speech that was filmed and later televised.

In the letter, Mary Scott wrote that Helms "was giving an impartial (?) talk on the candidates for gov. He was never a Scott supporter. He says you have a fair organization, that [John] Larkins has the sheriffs behind him, which in itself is a good organization. . . . He said each of you were for God, Mother, the Country, Education and against sin. Said the press was playing Lake as being a violent segregationist, which was not true. That at present he had no financial support but might overcome that. Also that he was the best informed of the three. That leaders in law and banking were about evenly divided in the support of you and Larkins, that you could be expected to get strong support from the Scott group. (This from him was not favorable I judge.)"

When a portrait of Scott was given to the state in 1959, at a special joint session of the legislature, Sanford was at Mrs. Scott's side and spoke glowingly of his mentor. "Well, he was rough—and tough; a rough, tough gentleman," Sanford said. "And history will say of him . . . long after the fleeting barbs of outraged gentility are lost in limbo, that he got things done." Mrs. Scott would soon return the favor. Sanford officially would announce for governor in early 1960 and Mrs. Scott would attend, weather permitting. "I don't know what size crowd you will have," Bob Scott wrote Sanford, "but it might be well to be certain that the news boys are aware of her presence for what it may be worth." When that day came, Sanford indeed would make sure that the news boys—and everyone else in the state—was aware of her presence.

If Sanford hid his ambition to be governor when he was a student in Chapel Hill, he did not in Fayetteville. "Not a day passed that I didn't make some move in that direction, maybe a minor one," he said later. "But I intended to be governor."

Indeed, some found him callow, too ambitious, too political. They thought he had not achieved enough professionally or politically to run for governor. But others, often closer to his own age, thought him a bold, vigorous, forward-thinking leader, with genuine ambition for the state. After Scott's campaign in 1954, Sanford maintained a core group of close supporters who periodically got together. "About eight of us got together and we were backing Terry all that time from '54 to '60. It was common knowledge he was running," said Woody Teague, a Raleigh lawyer who met Sanford during the Frank Graham campaign. Among the group were

24

Teague, Bill Staton, Paul Thompson of Fayetteville, and Henry Hall Wilson of Monroe, who would become part of President John F. Kennedy's congressional liaison staff.

Many of Sanford's allies served in World War II. "We came back with a lot of confidence. We had gotten the job done," said Clint Newton, a fighter pilot in the war. They also came back with a different perspective. "Here you have all these people coming back, having been so provincial and suddenly exposed to France, Italy, Sicily, North Africa, England—you name it," Newton said. "We found our respective towns were not the center of the universe. We wanted to make North Carolina better. So many of us went to UNC with its liberalism and seeing the racial factors and this sort of thing. Our state lacked a good educational system. There was a small group of idealists. Sanford was at the core of the idealism. . . . When Sanford said he wanted to run for governor, we got together and expanded the group and divided the state up."

Sanford sought to build what he called "a civic enterprise" base, something more than just a purely political base. He thought it important that people knew him, perhaps outside of politics, and trusted him. "It all comes back to knowing people who in a crunch are ready to go to work in a political campaign," he said. In the mid to late 1950s, he traveled the state, meeting with supporters. With his friendly, low-key style, he did not seem insincere or as if he were trying too hard to please. Yet he worked doggedly.

He was consumed by running for governor. Roy Parker, whose family owned a newspaper in Ahoskie in eastern North Carolina, remembers Sanford visiting the paper in the summer of 1958—nearly two full years before the 1960 primary. It was unheard of in those days for candidates to campaign so early. "He organized and got moving long before anyone else even thought about it," said Parker, who covered the governor's race for the *News and Observer*. "It wasn't even seemly in those days to campaign a year or so before. Generally, you didn't even think about that kind of politics until the year it began." Bert Bennett, a University of North Carolina friend who became Sanford's campaign manager, started working on the campaign in late 1959. By then, Sanford already had set up much of the organization. "He was a hell of a worker. He had all the ingredients to gear himself to go," Bennett said. "He was a great organizer. He prepared himself to be governor—mentally, physically, organizationally. . . . If you don't have that burning, gut desire, forget it. He had all of it."

A legend around Chapel Hill had Sanford pulling into a gas station in the early 1950s. The gas station owner filled Sanford's tank, chatted with him, and later that year received a Christmas card from Sanford. Christmas cards kept coming every year until 1960, when the station owner suddenly discovered why he had been receiving all those Christmas cards from gubernatorial candidate Terry Sanford. "I won't deny it. That could have happened," Sanford said later. "When we started building our organization we sent out our share of cards."

Typical of the relationships Sanford developed was his growing friendship with T. G. "Sonny Boy" Joyner, who grew cotton and peanuts in Northampton County, in the northeastern part of the state. In December 1957, Sanford visited the Joyners at their sprawling two-story manor house (built in 1801) and spent the night. In a "Dear Sonny" thank-you note, Sanford wrote: "I surely did enjoy seeing you and Ruth and I appreciate all of your good Northampton hospitality. I was mighty glad to have a chance to meet your pretty wife, and it was nice of her to get up extra early to fix our breakfast. I shall always be grateful to you for your interest and your help in shaping up things, and I hope you will keep me informed of anything you think I ought to know." In January 1959, Sanford sent Joyner a plug of Kerr Scott's favorite tobacco, embedded as a paperweight. Joyner became one of Sanford's most important supporters. When he campaigned in 1960, Sanford and his friend Lauch Faircloth spent the night at Joyner's house—in the same small bed. "People down in that part of the state don't think a thing about doubling up in a double bed," Sanford recalled. Faircloth, a businessman who would later defeat Sanford and serve in the U.S. Senate, also was a key Sanford supporter. "As I recall," Sanford said, "he didn't snore."

Sanford made friends, and kept them. They were loyal to him. His political ambition required help from many others, including his wife, who was taking care of their two young children, and his law partners, who picked up some of his workload. "A lot of people had to walk behind Terry," said law partner and childhood friend Dickson Phillips, adding, "I never picked up anything behind him that he wouldn't have picked up behind me. As far as I'm concerned, he never defaulted on anybody." His friend Woody Teague said, "His personality was always upbeat. He never did look on the dark side of things. He found ways to do things rather than ways to not do things." His friend Sonny Boy Joyner said that Sanford had an unusual sweetness about him: "He was a little different from the average man. He was so kind. He had a touch that people liked."

He befriended a wide range of people who seemingly had little in common. His political circle now included people like Raymond Goodman, sheriff and political kingpin of Richmond County. Sanford, who always loved the outdoors, attended the annual hunting gathering in Bertie County of Monk Harrington, a manufacturer of farm equipment. The gathering grew into a major social and political event, attracting hundreds of men, including many of the state's political leaders. Sanford fit in.

Yet he also was comfortable with younger, more cerebral college students or recent graduates. In the late 1950s, he met Jim Hunt, the student body president at North Carolina State, and Eli Evans, the student president at Chapel Hill, both of whom would become supporters. "I remember being excited that someone that young and dynamic could be governor," Evans remembered. "It was so revolutionary that someone was going to try to assemble the World War II veterans and this was going to be a new generation. With Luther Hodges as governor and Dwight D. Eisenhower as president, you didn't think of people like Sanford running for governor. You didn't envision that young of a person being elected to a high office like that. . . . Terry did enjoy meeting young people and saw young people as adding to this campaign." Evans was in the military in 1960 and didn't work in the campaign, but Hunt, who was known then as Jimmy Hunt, helped organize college campuses for Sanford. Sanford's first full-time campaign staffer was Tom Lambeth, a 1957 University of North Carolina graduate who had served with Sanford on a search committee during Lambeth's days in Chapel Hill.

Sanford courted younger people. One night, before the campaign began in earnest, Sanford and Margaret Rose invited four or five couples over to their spacious, two-story brick house in one of Fayetteville's nicest neighborhoods. The Sanfords had moved there from their Hillside Avenue bungalow a few years earlier. All of the invited couples, including Jessie Rae and Bob Scott, were in their late twenties or early thirties. On a grill in the backyard, a relaxed Sanford cooked his distinctive hamburgers—each burger had two patties, with a slice of tomato between. Sanford was a well-known, established figure: a former state senator and campaign manager who was known to be running for governor. Bob Scott, then thirty, was flattered by the invitation and the attention Sanford gave his guests that night. After dinner, in his living room, Sanford talked informally, not about himself but about the state's needs, and how young people needed to be involved in politics. "Young people had no one paying attention to them before that," Bob Scott said later. "He involved young people and made them feel important. He had a special knack for doing that. He did not want to surround himself with people who were hidebound by tradition. He did not want to hear too much of what you can't do because of past tradition. He didn't have much time for that kind of thinking."

Other than building his organization, Sanford tried to prepare himself in other ways. He recognized he was not an outstanding orator. His quick wit often did not come across when he delivered a speech. Years later, Alabama Gov. George Wallace would say of Sanford, "Terry Sanford? Hell, you ever heard him speak? He'll bore yo' ass off." Brandt Ayers, who covered Sanford's 1960 campaign for the *Raleigh Times*, said, "Terry's biggest problem is that he's got a mind of 24-carat gold and a tongue of lead." Sanford said that he never tried to copy anyone else's style. "Maybe I should have but I've always just tried to be myself," he once said. "I suppose at times that's come across rather dull. But in any event, I never did try to look like Kerr Scott or talk like Kerr Scott or speak in such general terms as Frank Graham or mimic John Kennedy or Franklin Roosevelt."

28

Refining and controlling the message were more important to Sanford than being entertaining. When he ran Kerr Scott's campaign, Sanford got Scott, who often said whatever was on his mind, to agree to stick to a written script. Scott obliged—except for the time, out of nowhere, he promised he'd give a bull calf to anyone who walked a certain route in eastern North Carolina that he had walked. Sanford turned it into a campaign event—the Great Bull Calf Walk. Other than that, Sanford said, the Scott campaign "got a little dull but that was all right. The object was to win, not to entertain the public."

Nonetheless, Sanford's supporters were interested in his improving his speech giving. In the late 1950s, Sanford invited Ben Roney and Roy Wilder, the two Scott men, to hear a speech he was going to give in Rocky Mount. Sanford shouted out the opening to his speech. Roney and Wilder were aghast. "When Terry started talking, it scared the shit out of us!" Wilder said. "The first words—he just boomed out. God almighty! We looked at each other and without saying anything, we thought, this is lousy." When they asked Sanford why he spoke so loudly at the beginning, he said that Albert Coates, director of the Institute of Government at Chapel Hill, had taught him to take charge at the beginning of a speech.

Wilder had worked as a newspaperman in New York and thought Sanford could get valuable coaching there. In a memo to Sanford in 1959, Wilder described a recent trip to New York and wrote, "About this business of making you a more presentable speaker: the man I'm touting you to is Ormand Drake, presently director of Town Hall. He comes high, about $50 a session, and is highly recommended." Sanford and Wilder went to New York together. Drake put Sanford at the front of an auditorium. Wilder sat in the balcony and Drake sat downstairs in the main section of seats. Drake directed Sanford to start giving his speech. As Sanford talked, Drake gave him pointers. Sanford absorbed the instruction but had one habit that Wilder could not get him to stop: When he spoke, Sanford often kept one hand in his pants pocket. Wilder thought it distracting. Sanford did it anyway. Three decades later, when Sanford ran for the U.S. Senate in 1986, Wilder wrote him a letter, again advising

Sanford to take his hand out of his pocket when he spoke. But Sanford never stopped.

Sanford traveled across North Carolina, speaking to groups and testing out different themes. In July 1959, he swung through the western part of the state. When he returned, he told the hometown *Fayetteville Observer* that it was too soon to announce his candidacy, but that he already knew what his main issue would be—improving public schools. In a speech in Durham in November, Sanford called for a "mid-twentieth century crusade" to improve public schools. He said, "The time has come for us to launch a long-range program to make our public schools second to none in the nation." Afterward, he told a reporter, "I am presenting this as the platform of the next administration. I would like, with the help of the people of North Carolina, to lead that administration. I hope it will begin with the campaign for the governorship." He said that North Carolina's public school graduates did not measure up to those of other states. He blamed "apathy, the lack of determination of our people, people like you and me." In a follow-up story in the *Fayetteville Observer*, Sanford said that he wasn't blaming teachers: "We are not providing them the means for them to do a better job." Sanford gathered endorsements and supporters. Bert Bennett, one of Sanford's old friends from Chapel Hill, resigned his post as Democratic chairman in Forsyth County so that he could run Sanford's campaign.

Sanford also studied issues, including the debate on segregation. He kept newspaper articles on the subject. In 1956, he wrote to his friend Roy Wilder, "I believe we ought to have copies of all accounts of the Pearsall-Lassiter debate." He referred to Tom Pearsall, who chaired a state committee that drafted a response to the U.S. Supreme Court's *Brown* decisions outlawing segregation, and to Thomas Lassiter, the editor of the *Smithfield Herald*, who opposed the Pearsall Plan. Sanford wrote to the school system in Little Rock, Arkansas, requesting information on the Little Rock school board's plan for integration as well as legal information that had been prepared for the superintendent there. Sanford collected literature on race relations, including a booklet called "Methodism's Challenge in Race Relations" and a fund-raising letter from the NAACP Legal Defense and Educational Fund.

As the new year began in 1960, Sanford was on the verge of officially starting a race that he, in reality, had been running for at least six years. He had served in the legislature. He had managed the successful statewide campaign of a North Carolina legend. He had traveled to every county in the state. He had lined up support, written hundreds of letters, hired staff, and given speeches across the state. He was prepared politically, probably more prepared than any candidate for governor of North Carolina had ever been.

Yet he knew there was one issue—what the writer Marshall Frady later called "the immemorial dark obsession of Southern politics"—that was largely beyond his control. Race would arise. How, when, by whom—there was no way to know. But Sanford suspected it would come up. Would his candidacy be consumed by fear and hysteria, as Frank Graham's was in 1950? Or would he control the fire and run the race on his terms, as Kerr Scott did in '54? The tone of the campaign, and the daily dialogue that emerged, depended largely on who else ran. Sanford knew that John Larkins, a former legislator and former state Democratic Party chairman, would run. Sanford thought Larkins, a pro-business, mainstream conservative, was unlikely to raise the race issue. Some other state government veterans were considering running, but none particularly worried Sanford. One other, more unpredictable, candidate lurked. Up the road in the old college town of Wake Forest, I. Beverly Lake, the state's most articulate voice for segregation, was considering entering the race.

Chapter 2

LAKE

On a hot afternoon in late June 1950, I. Beverly Lake sat next to his sixteen-year-old son, Beverly Jr., on their side porch at 403 North Main Street in Wake Forest, North Carolina. From the swing facing Main Street, the Lakes had a fine view of the comings and goings in the small college town north of Raleigh. Their house, built about 1850, was a block from Wake Forest College, a small Baptist school where Dr. Lake taught law. So many faculty members lived on leafy Main Street, in the houses surrounding the Lakes, that it had taken the nickname "Faculty Row."

As the Lakes enjoyed the day from the shade of their porch, a rumble emerged from the south, near the campus. A caravan of cars moved toward them, with drivers honking their horns and hollering out the windows. In the crowd was Willis Smith, candidate for the U.S. Senate. Smith and his supporters were driving from town to town, seeking votes in his campaign to unseat Sen. Frank Porter Graham. The sun was strong; by the end of the day, Smith's face was sunburned. Smith and Lake once practiced law together in Raleigh but had fallen out. Lake believed that Smith, who had been president of the American Bar Association, had tried to blackball him from that organization. Lake was supporting Graham, and the Smith caravan knew it. After boisterously passing the Lakes, who were in plain view from the street, not even fifty feet away, the cars turned around on Main Street—and drove past the Lake house again, honking and yelling. "Son," Lake said when the din diminished, "don't ever get into politics."

If Lake did not like politics, he, like many North Carolinians, found the racially raw Graham-Smith campaign even more distasteful than usual. During the campaign, Lake addressed a radio audience and urged listeners to return Graham to the Senate. He deplored the Smith supporters' emphasis on race. "For the first time in the memory of most North Carolinians an effort is being made to gain votes for a candidate for high political office in this state by stirring from its 50-year sleep the dreadful monster of race hatred," Lake said in his address. "Shocking as this callous indifference to the welfare of our state is, it is perhaps well enough that this attempt has been made to revive this evil thing most of us had thought dead. If, indeed, race hatred in North Carolina be not dead, but only sleeping, then let us welcome the opportunity to give it its death blow in the senatorial campaign."

Two weeks after Smith defeated Graham in the June primary runoff, Lake wrote to Graham, offering his support and decrying the racially oriented tactics of some Smith supporters:

> To have had a part in that fight for decency and good government is an honor. I shall always recall with satisfaction that in it I was associated with you. . . .
>
> The two weeks that have passed have not blunted the edge of our keen disappointment but we are beginning to learn to live with it and carry on a fight which must eventually be successful because it is one for the Christian way of life. It is clear that those who were with us in the primary have no intention of quitting and are glad they followed your leadership and are ready to do so again.
>
> It is hard to realize that thousands of North Carolinians are gullible enough to be defrauded by a campaign such as the opposition conducted. It must have hurt you deeply to see those for whom you have worked so faithfully and so effectively turn to another because of a blind, unreasoning racial fear deliberately dragged in and played upon by the other side. Though discouraging, their prejudice and gullibility can be understood. What is beyond understanding is that informed people could stoop so low as to conduct so dishonorable a campaign.

> I take great encouragement from the fact, and I know it means
> much to you personally, that there are a quarter of a million North
> Carolinians whose confidence in you and the principles for which you
> stand is so strong that neither fraud, threats, bribery nor even their
> own prejudices could turn them aside.

The typed letter, on Wake Forest College stationery, was signed "I. Beverly Lake, Professor of Law." Ten years later, Lake would become the state's leading voice for segregation, and many of Graham's strongest supporters would work passionately to keep him from becoming governor.

Lake loved the town of Wake Forest and lived almost all of his life there, within a few blocks of the college. "I'm still a small-town North Carolinian," Lake said when he was an old man, living on Main Street, just a few blocks from the house in which he was born. His father had come to Wake Forest in 1899 to teach physics at the college. Beverly Lake, born in 1906, was the youngest of five children. His mother died six weeks after he was born. Four years later, his father married his mother's sister. All his life, Lake cherished a picture of his mother and stepmother taken at his parents' wedding. He once said proudly, "I'm about the only person who has a beautiful picture of his mother and stepmother taken together." His late mother he referred to as "Mother." His stepmother he called "Mama."

It was his stepmother, Virginia Prudence Caldwell Lake, who raised Lake and instilled in him a strong sense of the family's history and southern heritage. Her father, John W. Caldwell, was the colonel of a Kentucky regiment in the Civil War. According to Lake family history, at the end of the war, when defeated Confederate troops were supposed to turn their flags in to Union troops, Caldwell's men declined to do so. Instead, they gave the flag to Colonel Caldwell. The flag was a family heirloom passed down to Beverly Lake, who treasured it. He believed it was the only unsurrendered Confederate battle flag in existence. In the Old South spirit of honor and valor, he once said, "It would take a whole lot more than an order from the commander in chief of the Federal Army to get that flag away from me." When he was a member of the North Carolina Supreme

Court, Lake hung the flag in his chambers. He kept his grandfather's Confederate uniform displayed in his house. For much of his life, before and after his 1960 campaign for governor, he traveled the state, speaking to Sons of Confederate Veterans and other groups interested in the Civil War. He showed them the flag and Colonel Caldwell's uniform.

Lake was a sickly, delicate child. He was taught at home by his stepmother until he was nine years old, when he entered the fifth grade at the small schoolhouse around the corner from Main Street. He remembered finally arriving at the schoolhouse, looking up through the ceiling and seeing blue sky. Angus Jackson, a childhood friend of Lake, remembered him as small but energetic. "In football, he was the last one chosen because he was smallest," Jackson said. "He was a scholar, not an athlete. . . . When we were interested in football and baseball and cracking the whip, I think he was interested in history and mathematics. He was very serious." Lake did enjoy baseball; he pitched and played shortstop. His father had been captain of the baseball team at the University of Richmond. As young teenagers, Lake and boys from Wake Forest would organize a town team and play boys from the nearby hamlets of Youngsville, Rolesville, and Franklinton.

Wake Forest, which is now a fast-growing suburb of Raleigh and the Research Triangle Park, was in Lake's youth a country village without paved streets. "We had a very close relationship, not only in school, but among the people of the town, both white and colored," Lake said. His stepmother used to put food on the back porch for people not so well off. College students came to classes in the fall and rarely visited home until Christmas. The passing of an automobile was enough to bring children rushing out of their homes. Among the favorite pastimes of the children—and college students—was to walk to the town's rail station and see who was on the noon and afternoon trains that stopped on their way through Wake Forest. College students would flirt with the girls on the train.

The college was the center of life, giving the town's children some diversions that most small-town children did not enjoy. Troupes of traveling actors would perform. Children from a nearby orphanage visited the college every year to sing. And, most enticing of all to many of the boys, athletes from other colleges would visit to play teams from Wake Forest College. Starting at age five, Lake would sneak away from home to watch practices and games. He marveled at Wake's Harry Rabenhorst, the best football player he had ever seen, who once punted a ball nearly the length of the field against State College. When a State player fumbled the long punt, Wake Forest recovered in the end zone for a touchdown, a play Lake could recall with great detail and zest nearly seventy years after it happened.

The public school in Wake Forest had only eleven grades. In the tenth grade, Lake was the only student in that grade, which, he once joked, would have given him a fine opportunity to be valedictorian of his class the following year. Instead, he entered Wake Forest College at age fifteen, majored in physics and math, and graduated at the age of eighteen in the spring of 1925. While Lake had always used his middle name of Beverly, in college some of his friends affectionately called him "Ike" or "Ikey," a nickname derived from his first name—Isaac. As a middle-aged man, when he was called "Ikey" it almost surely was by an old college chum. In college, he was a member of the Euzelian Society, a literary society and debating club. Participation in such clubs was mandatory at Wake Forest when Lake entered, and Lake thought they helped Wake Forest men become superior public speakers. In his final undergraduate year, he was senior critic, analyzing debates and offering students comments on how they could improve.

Lake grew increasingly interested in law. Because he was the child of a faculty member, tuition to the law school was free. He decided to attend Wake Law School for a year. That small law school was not then accredited, and Lake wanted to attend an accredited school. He applied to Harvard Law School, where future U.S. Supreme Court Justice Felix Frankfurter was on the faculty. He was accepted, although not without an early glitch. When he was registering, a woman from Harvard asked him from which high school had he graduated. Lake, then only twenty, told her he had never graduated from high school. "What are you doing up here if you haven't graduated from high school?" she asked, incredulously.

Lake

Lake explained: He left high school early to attend college. If he had thrown a firecracker under her desk, Lake once said, it wouldn't have surprised her more.

He graduated from Harvard in 1929 and started shortly after with the Raleigh law firm of Smith and Joyner at twenty-five dollars a week. The partners were Willis Smith, the future U.S. senator who was about to become speaker of the North Carolina House, and William Joyner, a Harvard graduate. Three years later, Lake left the firm to become the fourth law professor at Wake Forest—a career move that changed his life. He spent most of the next twenty years teaching law at Wake Forest. The faculty was small, so he taught each of the different classes over the years: constitutional law, corporations, negotiable instruments, partnerships, torts, and real property.

He was an extraordinary professor. A half century after taking his classes, his former students praised his intellect, teaching ability, civility, and warmth. In his gentle way, he demanded maximum effort. It was not uncommon for Dr. Lake to question one student for the entire class period. "He was my mentor in law school," said Robert Morgan, who would later become North Carolina's attorney general and then a U.S. senator. "I have never known of a former student who didn't have the highest regard for Dr. Lake." He was "very genteel, civil, a warm person," Morgan said. "He was so smart—brilliant."

Allen Bailey, a prominent Charlotte attorney and former Lake student, said: "He was a fantastic teacher. He made that which was complicated very, very simple and easy to understand. He was just a tremendous human being and teacher. His students appreciated the qualities they saw in him. He was such a gentleman. I never saw a greater gentleman in my life. He was courteous and so polite to everyone, including his students. He would go out of his way to help you do anything in the world. That didn't mean he was easy on you when it came to trying to teach you something. He just demonstrated his willingness to help you do what you wanted to do. You just couldn't say no to him. You wanted to excel in his classes for him, if for no other reason." Bailey and Morgan were in the Wake Forest law class of 1950; Lake ranked it as one of his two most out-

37

standing classes. Among others in the class of '50 were Norman Wiggins, who became president of Campbell University; Hiram Ward, later a federal judge; and Charles Whitley, who went on to serve in the U.S. House.

Lake's influence reached beyond the classroom and deep into the total life of the law school community. On Saturday evenings, Lake sometimes joined students in playing softball at Caddell Field. "He demanded much of his students," Wiggins said, but he loved them. "He called them 'my boys.' He visited with them when he met us on campus. . . . He and Mrs. Lake went far beyond the call of duty to make the students and other guests feel at home when they came calling on a visit." Lake, who lost most of his hair during his years as a law professor, once joked to them, "You see, I pulled all of my hair out grading your papers." It was obvious, though, that Lake was fond of his students, and he kept up with many of his former students for decades. They were all white males, reflecting the social and legal mores of the times. Decades later, when it became far more common for women to practice law, Lake did not like seeing women in court. "I just don't like to see a sow's ear made out of a silk purse," he once said. Another time he said, "In my opinion, the ideal lady is one who is or considers becoming a home-maker, which I think is the finest career for a woman of all."

Lake married Gertrude "Trudy" Bell of Raleigh at about the time he began teaching at Wake Forest. Their two-story frame house on North Main Street had five bedrooms. The Lakes almost always had students boarding, sometimes as many as five. Students were in and out of the house endlessly. In feeding them, Trudy Lake favored buffets; among her favorites were a shrimp creole made with okra for lunch and an oyster stew for dinner. When unexpected guests arrived, as they often did, she could always add another quart of milk to the stew. She recalled how a student, about to drop out of school, came by the house to talk with Dr. Lake. They talked and talked. Mrs. Lake went to the kitchen and fixed cinnamon toast and hot chocolate. The boy decided to stay in school. Trudy Lake thought it unclear whether the student's decision was based on Dr. Lake's advice or her cooking.

Lake took three brief breaks during his tenure as a law professor. During World War II, he was the federal director of rationing for fifty-two counties in eastern North Carolina. Two years later, he received a doctorate in the science of law from Columbia University in New York. And in '51, with conflict in Korea emerging, he was asked to go to Washington to help draft possible rationing regulations for the National Production Authority. Each time, he returned to his love—teaching law at Wake Forest. But in the early '50s, it became clear that Wake Forest College was going to move about one hundred miles west to Winston-Salem. Lake despaired that the college, the focal point of his life nearly since the day he was born, was going to move. He decided he could not move with it. In 1952, Lake joined the staff of North Carolina attorney general Harry McMullen.

In his new job, Lake became a public figure increasingly known across the state. He was the attorney general's expert on utility regulation. His job was to represent the public before the state Utilities Commission, which decided how large a rate increase to grant utilities. Lake had not planned on working on utility issues when he joined McMullen's staff. But in a staff conference one Friday, McMullen assigned Lake to fill in for another attorney and represent the state on a rate hearing—on the following Tuesday. The attorney general's staff had assembled a three-foot-high stack of documents for the hearing. Lake knew nothing about the case. He had never seen the Utility Commission operate. He did not know its procedure. Now he had the weekend and two work days to prepare. He went to the hearing full of anxiety, fearful he would say something that would cause everyone to laugh at him.

Lake survived the hearing, became the attorney general's main lawyer on utility issues, and gained a reputation as a strong consumer advocate. He thought the Utilities Commission, which was appointed by the governor, to be heavily slanted toward the utilities. He believed commission members were appointed by the governor based on recommendations from the utility companies. The utilities, Lake said, were "a little inclined at times to be selfish in their views and exorbitant in the rates they wanted to charge." When the state disagreed with the decision of the Utilities Commission, the state could appeal to the North Carolina

Supreme Court. Lake appealed aggressively, winning the praise of editorial writers at the *News and Observer* of Raleigh.

It was not, however, the arcane world of utility regulation that was to gain Assistant Attorney General Lake the greatest attention. That would come on a more visceral issue. On May 17, 1954, Lake walked down a Raleigh street, a clear garment bag from a dry cleaner over his shoulder. Inside the bag was his grandfather's dress gray coat from the Civil War. That day, the U.S. Supreme Court issued its *Brown v. Board of Education* decision that outlawed segregated public schools. A man stopped Lake on the street. "Mr. Lake," the man said, looking at Colonel Caldwell's uniform, "I didn't know we were going to war so soon."

Lake joined the battle. The Supreme Court ordered a second round of arguments on the school integration issue, this time on how and when its decision should be put in place. North Carolina wasn't a party to the case, but McMullen, the attorney general, asked Lake to write North Carolina's friend of the court brief and present it to the Court.

Lake, like most white southerners and some scholars, had no trouble disagreeing with the Court's *Brown* decision. To many southern leaders, the day of the Court's decision was known as Black Monday. Immediately, some constitutional lawyers criticized the decision for relying on sociological reasoning to brush aside seventy years of precedent on the meaning of the Fourteenth Amendment, which guaranteed every American equal protection. They questioned the constitutional basis for the decision. So did Lake. He thought the Court had reached too far. A court's job is to interpret and enforce the law; it was state legislatures' or Congress's job to write the law, he thought. While the Fourteenth Amendment forbade discrimination and required equal opportunity, he said that it did not require blacks and whites to attend the same schools.

With trademark self-confidence, Lake flatly disagreed with the notion that separate was inherently unequal. The Constitution did not require integration, he said. "It required the state to give all children an opportunity, each child the opportunity to become the best educated man or woman he or she could be," he said years later. "But it didn't require the state to put them all in the same classroom. . . . Separate is not inherently unequal. That's just all I can say about that. . . . The man who says that separateness is necessarily inequality is just wrong."

Lake believed that schools for blacks and whites in North Carolina were equal in quality and curriculum—an idea strongly contested by blacks who wanted to send their children to white schools. In 1900, the amount the state spent per black student was less than half that spent per white student. In the 1930s and '40s, federal courts began to push harder and harder for proof of equal treatment, and North Carolina responded. In 1940, the state spent 65 cents per black child for every dollar it spent on white children. By 1950, North Carolina spent 85 cents per black child against every dollar spent on white children. Blacks' school buildings also had received less money. When the value of school buildings was estimated in 1952, white schools held 82 percent of the total value and black schools 18 percent. Yet blacks made up 29 percent of all public school students.

In his brief, which was filed in October 1954, Lake quickly made it clear that the state of North Carolina disagreed with the Court's decision. Lake acknowledged that he had no solution "to the extremely delicate and dangerous problem which has arisen in North Carolina by reason of this Court's decision." But he presented a series of reasons why subsequent decrees and timetables to carry out the Court's order should be made locally and not by the Supreme Court. While the Court had the power to order a school board to stop violating the Fourteenth Amendment, the Court did not have the power to dictate a solution to the school board, the brief said. If courts were to decree a solution, those decrees should come from federal district courts, not the Supreme Court.

Lake said that attempting to quickly integrate public schools in North Carolina could lead to a second civil war. "An attempt to compel the intermixture of the races in the public schools of North Carolina forthwith would result in such violent opposition as to endanger the continued existence of the schools," the brief said. "No other problem has so deeply moved and disturbed the people of the State since the dark days of the early [18]60s." The Court should not allow its decision to be guided by public opinion, the brief said, but neither should it ignore reality, especially when children could pay the consequences.

He referred to surveys prepared by the attorney general's staff, asking North Carolina's superintendents what would happen if schools were desegregated immediately. Of the 165 responding, 7 believed desegregation would occur peacefully; 148 said there would be serious problems of discipline; 141 thought large numbers of parents would withdraw their children from public schools. Lake also reported the results of another survey, this one of sheriffs and police chiefs across the state. Of the 198 responding, 191 believed there would be violence that would interfere with school.

In arguing for as much local control as possible, Lake said that North Carolina's larger population of blacks made its challenges more difficult than those of many other states. Even if every other condition were the same, Lake said, integrating one Negro child with ninety-nine white children in North Dakota is a far different problem for a school administrator than bringing together seventy-one Negro children with twenty-nine white children in Northampton County, North Carolina.

Lake argued that North Carolina had shown good will in building a public school system which, he said, treated blacks equally and provided equal opportunities. The state educates more blacks than any other, the brief said. It employs more Negro teachers than any other state. And, on average, black teachers made more money than white teachers. That was because black and white teachers were on the same pay scale. Black teachers had fewer job options and tended to stay in their teaching jobs longer. That seniority gave them slightly higher average salaries.

Lake, influenced by the prevalent cold war attitudes, also tied North Carolina's system of separate but equal schools to fighting communism. In doing so, he got in a dig at the Court and inferred that its ruling in the *Brown* case was less than the American way. "There is peace and friendship between white and Negro North Carolinians today which all North Carolinians desire to preserve," he wrote. He said that the State Department should use North Carolina's separate but equal school system as a model at home and abroad.

Lake believed blacks could not keep up with whites in the classroom. He referred to state statistics showing the percentages of white and black children who were older than normal for their grade. From these figures, with no analysis of why children started school late or why they were held back a grade, Lake concluded that one white child out of six was "retarded" and one black child of three was retarded. About half the black children who were older than normal for their grade were one year older than their classmates. Nonetheless, Lake considered such children retarded; he did the same for whites. The brief said it would create great difficulties in heavily black areas to put thousands of Negro children, one-third of whom are retarded, in classrooms with white children.

Lake's brief was well received, even by the big-city editorial writers who were considered far more liberal than most North Carolinians. In an editorial titled "Model for the South," the *News and Observer* said that the brief might have overstated fears of integration. But it concluded, "All in all, the brief presents the Southern problem as well as the State problem with force, with dignity and with persuasiveness. A good job has been done for the State and a good pattern set for the South." The *Asheville Citizen* said, "The brief, in sum, speaks well for a State that is neither passive nor restive, neither docile nor rebellious, in the face of constitutional inevitabilities. North Carolina can be proud of it."

The brief, which Lake would argue before the Court in the spring, wasn't North Carolina's only response to the Court's desegregation decision. In August 1954, Gov. William Umstead appointed a committee, chaired by former North Carolina House Speaker Thomas Pearsall of Rocky Mount, to develop a response to the *Brown* decision. As the committee was beginning its work, Governor Umstead died; his successor, Luther Hodges, asked the committee to continue. Lake and Attorney General McMullen communicated often with committee members.

The nineteen-member committee, which included three black members, agreed that the state should have two main objectives: To preserve public schools and to preserve the peace. The committee said that desegregation could not occur immediately. Many committee members feared that large numbers of whites would take their children out of public schools, crippling public education. The committee's key recommendation was that the legislature transfer all responsibility for pupil assignment to local school boards, which could tailor solutions to their communities.

At Governor Hodges' request, Pearsall, the chairman, worked out a final draft of the bill with a small group, including legislators and lawyers from the attorney general's office. Pearsall found that McMullen constantly deferred to Lake, who drafted a version of the bill. The bill gave local school boards great discretion in pupil assignment. Parents could ask the board to review pupil assignments and could request assignment to another school.

By giving authority to local school boards, and not the state Board of Education, the state hoped to eliminate the possibility that a single lawsuit could force desegregation of the entire state. Black parents would have to litigate one school board at a time. Some blacks said that the legislation appeared to be avoiding the Court's desegregation ruling. At the end of March 1955, the all-white legislature passed the Pupil Assignment Act. North Carolina's leaders had not defied the Supreme Court ruling; neither had they embraced it. They were trying to buy time.

In April, Lake traveled to Washington to argue his brief before the Supreme Court. Dr. Lake, the former law professor, was in his element. Justice John Marshall Harlan listened with his chin on his hand as the justices paid close attention to Lake. "Race consciousness is not race prejudice," Lake told them. "It is not race arrogance. It is not intolerance and it is not to be confused with racial injustice. It is a deeply ingrained awareness of a birthright held in trust for posterity."

Lake responded adroitly to questions from the justices. The most pointed came from Justice Frankfurter, who had taught Lake at Harvard Law School; while at Harvard, Frankfurter had been an adviser to the NAACP, which, in the *Brown* case, argued for integration. It wasn't unusual for Frankfurter to fire a rapid series of questions at an attorney. During the first *Brown* arguments, Frankfurter shot so many questions at NAACP attorney Thurgood Marshall that Marshall struggled to keep his cool. "Frankfurter was a smart aleck, you know," Marshall said later with a glare.

Lake argued that federal courts could find certain practices in North Carolina schools unconstitutional and could direct the state to stop those practices. But he said that courts could not direct the states to take certain specific measures to achieve a goal. Not even Congress, Lake said, had the "authority to assign children to this or that building owned and operated by the state." That prompted a long debate between Lake and Frankfurter, during which, at one point, Lake pointed his finger at Frankfurter, emphatically making his point. Frankfurter, for his part, interrupted Lake several times in mid-sentence, as in this exchange:

> FRANKFURTER: The direction of the court, the affirmative direction, to admit a certain student in a certain institution, surely that isn't beyond the powers of a court, because of any doctrine of inherent limitation or separation of powers or what not.
>
> LAKE: Well, sir, it is our—
>
> FRANKFURTER : I don't get the force of your argument that there is some suggestion that there is a limitation of the powers of the court to direct an institution or anybody else to do something if there is a legal duty to do so.

Later in his argument, Lake said that the states were under no federal mandate to operate public schools and a desegregation order would not apply to a state which shut down its public schools. Frankfurter replied acidly, saying the state "could bring up its children in ignorance if it wanted to." Lake tweaked: "It could do that also. The state *could* abolish the public school system."

After Lake finished and the 2 P.M. recess was called, he was detained by several attorneys who congratulated him. Attorney General McMullen stood by, obviously pleased. Fred Helms, a Charlotte attorney and member of the Pearsall committee, watched Lake before the court and considered Lake's arguments superb. Helms reported to Governor Hodges that Lake was "clear-cut, frank, unequivocal and unapologetic."

In May 1955, the Court released its opinion on how desegregation would proceed. It granted states an indefinite time period to desegregate their schools but required them to move "with all deliberate speed." Thurgood

Marshall hated that phrase and blamed Justice Frankfurter for developing it. To Marshall, it meant states would move slowly. The Court essentially had agreed with Lake's key points. U.S. district court judges would hear disputes. A memo written mostly by Chief Justice Earl Warren said that North Carolina and four other states "impressively presented" their views to the Court. The memo served as the starting point for the Court's written opinion. "These briefs and arguments were both informative and helpful to the Court," the memo said.

A month later, in a speech to the Raleigh Kiwanis Club, Lake reacted to the Court's decision. In doing so, he clearly identified the enemy—the NAACP. His comments appear to be his first public criticism of the NAACP, which would become his sworn adversary for the next ten years and beyond. Across the country, the NAACP was suing to get black children admitted to white schools. The NAACP was Lake's opponent during the *Brown* re-arguments; on the first day of testimony, when Lake was barely able to begin before Court adjourned for the day, Lake was preceded by Thurgood Marshall, who argued for desegregation to occur later that year. The NAACP, Lake told the Kiwanis Club, was the "implacable enemy of our Southern social structure. It has able leadership, a well-filled treasury and a singleness of purpose." Those were probably the kindest words he ever spoke about the NAACP.

Lake told the Kiwanis Club he would not offer a proposed solution to the Court's desegregation decision. But he offered a number of principles to guide a solution. The first was that "pride of race is not wrong. I make no apology for my pride of race for it is not based upon and does not involve hatred of or injustice to another race." He said the English, Scotch, and Germans who settled the South brought a philosophy of government and a belief in God that allowed them to build a way of life "which has never yet been equaled by any colored or mongrel race anywhere on earth."

While Lake didn't offer a plan of action to the Kiwanis Club, it wasn't long before he did. In giving a speech to the Asheboro Lions Club in mid-July, Lake touched off several days of newspaper stories and drew a surprised Governor Hodges into the debate. Lake urged each community in the state to charter a nonprofit charitable corporation to operate one or more private schools. These schools could admit white children only. If public schools stayed open and segregated, there would be no need to open the private schools. But if the public schools were integrated and then closed, the private schools would be ready to go. For parents who could not afford private school, the state could subsidize their education by giving them scholarships—a sort of GI Bill for children. "The NAACP is our enemy, not the Negro people," Lake said in Asheboro. "We shall fight the NAACP county by county, city by city, and if need be, school by school and classroom by classroom to preserve our public schools as long as possible while organizing and establishing other methods of educating our children."

The speech marked a turning point in Lake's public career and launched him as the undisputed public leader of the staunch segregationists. He said that he was speaking as an individual and not as a state official, but that didn't matter to the press nor the NAACP. A high-ranking state official had raised the possibility of closing public schools—an approach that had been advocated seriously in other southern states but not in more moderate North Carolina. After an emergency meeting in Raleigh, the NAACP asked Governor Hodges to fire Lake from his job as assistant attorney general. The group said that Lake had openly advocated defiance of the U.S. Supreme Court.

Hodges was knee-deep in a mountain stream, fishing for trout, when a state highway patrolman tracked him down. Hodges learned of the NAACP's resolution from the patrol car's radio. He considered Lake's position extreme and said that it was premature to talk of abandoning public schools. He emphasized that Lake was speaking for himself and not the state. But Hodges said that he wasn't going to ask the attorney general to fire Lake. And he hit back at the NAACP. "I am amazed that this private organization, whose policies are determined in its national office in New York and are obviously designed to split North Carolina citizens into racial camps . . . should have the effrontery to make such a request," Hodges said. He would do all he could to retain Lake, whom he called a "distinguished lawyer." Lake's new boss, Attorney General William Rodman, who was named to the post when Harry McMullen died suddenly in June, also backed Lake. "The Negroes, if they will evaluate carefully what has been done for the schools, will be appreciative and will strive to keep the schools going," Rodman said.

Hodges, however, soon viewed Lake as a threat to the moderate course the governor wanted. But Hodges also thought Lake could be a formidable campaign opponent in 1956, when Hodges would seek a full term as governor. As early as August 1955, the *News and Observer* reported in its "Under the Dome" political column that Lake was considering a run for governor. So Hodges tried to keep Lake in his camp—an increasingly difficult task, given Lake's independence, strong positions, and growing stature. Lake was in demand across the state as a public speaker, and, increasingly, supporters urged him to run against Hodges. Lake, who had never considered himself a politician, declined to run. But he recognized that almost mysteriously, without his intending so, he had become a major statewide public figure. After the fallout from the Asheboro speech, he told his family, "Life won't be the same."

Lake didn't back down from his Asheboro remarks. Soon he expanded on them. While he had grabbed the attention of strong segregationists across the state, he also had gained the attention of the national NAACP. When Roy Wilkins, NAACP executive secretary, visited North Carolina in early August, he attacked Lake bitterly. "Every Negro voter, every Negro office-holder, every precinct worker ought to be on Gov. Hodges' doorstep demanding the resignation of Beverly Lake," Wilkins said. "For Beverly Lake has shown himself to be assistant attorney general of the white people of North Carolina. He is using his high office to tell white people how to deny black people their rights before the law. We dare the Lakes and the Hodges and the state Board of Education and the Negro stooges over the state to let the people decide. The people are far ahead of the politicians on this matter, and the children and young people are far ahead of even their elders." North Carolina, Wilkins said, was not the progressive southern state he had thought it to be. When Wilkins was done, the battle lines had been drawn clearly and permanently. The NAACP was on one side. Beverly Lake was on the other.

* * *

Shortly after his friend Harry McMullen died, Lake decided to leave the attorney general's office. He might have been unhappy that Governor Hodges did not appoint him attorney general. Hodges and Lake had not gotten along well for several years, even before Lake's Asheboro speech. Lake, who had represented the attorney general's staff in several meetings chaired by Hodges, sometimes challenged Hodges' positions—and Hodges did not like to be challenged. Because of that, Lake probably did not expect that Hodges would appoint him attorney general. Lake was ready to depart, and had even rented office space, when the NAACP called for his resignation. He decided to stay longer so it wouldn't look like the NAACP had forced him to leave office. In October 1955, he left the attorney general's office and went into practice with his friend A. J. Fletcher.

The return to private practice did not diminish Lake's public profile or his eagerness to join the desegregation fray. After the Supreme Court's second desegregation ruling in May, Governor Hodges formed a second Pearsall committee. This committee had two full-time lawyers: W. W. Taylor Jr., a legislator and former student of Lake's, and Tom Ellis, a Willis Smith supporter in the 1950 Senate race who led the motorcade past Lake's house in Wake Forest. Taylor and Ellis took a hard-line position. They urged Hodges to, among other things, seek repeal of the sections of the state constitution requiring the state to operate public schools. "The eventual goal of this [integration] movement is racial intermarriage and the disappearance of the Negro race by fusing into white," they wrote.

The committee's report took a more moderate tone. The committee, which was all white, tried to strike a balanced position that was difficult, if not impossible, to achieve. The state's leaders wanted to obey the Supreme Court. They also wanted to maintain segregation. The state needed to create a "safety valve" that would assure parents that their children would not be forced to attend school with children of another race. The committee's recommendations came to be known as the Pearsall Plan. That plan called for a public vote to achieve two goals. First, local school systems could close their schools if a majority of voters in the system agreed to it. Second, the state would pay tuition grants for the private-school education of children who didn't have a public school to attend or whose parents objected to their attending an integrated school.

A lawyer who worked on the Pearsall Plan put it this way: "We have to publicly have a goal of opposing integration and doing everything in our power to prevent it from happening, while at the same time planning to let it happen. We know we're going from A to Z but we don't know yet how we're going to get to Z, and when we find out, we can't admit we're getting to Z."

The legislature approved the Pearsall Plan in a special session in July 1956—but not without a fight from the allies of Beverly Lake, who thought it did not go far enough. A group of legislators, including Lake's former student Robert Morgan, developed an alternative that was known as the Lake Plan. Under the Lake Plan, the state would no longer be required to operate public schools. Also, the legislature—not voters in the state's approximately 170 school districts—could close schools. So the Lake Plan made it far easier to shut down large numbers of public schools. The North Carolina House and Senate could close down every school in the state.

The Lake Plan was drafted by Lake and introduced by Morgan in the senate and Rep. Byrd Satterfield in the house. Satterfield described Lake as "perhaps the greatest constitutional lawyer in the South" and "a man with no prejudice towards any race." The legislature held three days of public hearings, which attracted an unusual amount of interest. People across the state followed the debate on a statewide network of radio and television stations. Lake told legislators that while the Pearsall Plan was basically good, it did "not go far enough in controlling situations that might arise." He said that the legislature needed the flexibility to tackle problems as they occurred.

Hodges called a press conference to refute the Lake Plan and support the Pearsall Plan. For two days, legislators debated a variety of amendments to the Pearsall Plan, all of which failed. Hodges, Pearsall, and allies won easily in the legislature. The break between Lake and Hodges was complete and permanent, with Lake becoming an ardent, frequent critic of Hodges.

The public would vote on the issue on September 8. The Hodges forces organized speakers to travel the state in support of the Pearsall Plan. Among the speakers were Terry Sanford of Fayetteville and future U.S. Sen. Jesse Helms of Raleigh—marking one of the few times in their careers they agreed. There had been speculation that the Kerr Scott wing of the Democratic Party would oppose approval of the Pearsall Plan. That speculation was based on the theory that Senator Scott viewed Governor Hodges as a possible reelection opponent in 1960 and would not want to do anything to help him. Scott's brother Ralph, a leading legislator, criticized the plan but voted for it.

Sanford ended the speculation by announcing in early August that he supported its approval. He pointed out that many of Kerr Scott's legislative allies voted for the Pearsall Plan. Sanford said that he was for the Pearsall Plan all along. "It is essential to have this legislation," he said. "I think that it is imperative also that we should realize that after this legislation is approved, the governor still will have a terrific job to do. Passing the Pearsall Plan is not the final answer."

Sanford traveled the state, speaking in behalf of the Pearsall Plan and offering a preview of how he would handle issues of race when he ran for governor. In a speech to the Junior Woman's Club of Ahoskie, in eastern North Carolina, Sanford preached reason and restraint. He called for expanding public school opportunities for all children. He did not criticize the Supreme Court's original *Brown* decision, as Lake did. "I cannot and will not approach this question of the Supreme Court's decision by screaming, crying or in sullen despair," Sanford said. "The Supreme Court may be just as wrong as Corrigan, but response must be calm, quiet and deliberate reason. You do not curse away the darkness of the night; you illuminate your area by holding up a light. The people of North Carolina have reasoned their way out of many difficult situations, and we will reason our way out of this one."

Sanford said that the state needed some type of plan; otherwise, in a crisis emotional legislators could move unwisely to fill a vacuum. He said that the Pearsall Plan provided a safety valve, to be used only if needed; he hoped it wouldn't be used. And he pointed out that it gave local voters the power and flexibility to do what they thought was best for their schools. Years later, Sanford called the Pearsall Plan "a brilliant piece of strategy" that calmed the state, and he credited Pearsall and Hodges for "superb diplomacy." "It seemed to be more than it was," Sanford said. "It satisfied people: 'We've got the Pearsall Plan.' I'm talking about people on both sides of the issue."

Voters approved the plan by a margin of more than four to one. The Pearsall Plan was more show than substance. The plan was an effort by the state's leaders to reassure whites that their state was taking action on the issue of school desegregation. No school system ever tried to use the provisions of the Pearsall Plan to close its schools. It was declared unconstitutional by federal courts in 1966.

By the fall of 1957, Lake was seriously considering running for governor in 1960. The school boards in Charlotte, Greensboro, and Winston-Salem had allowed token integration; a total of about ten black students were attending previously all-white schools. Lake denounced the actions of the three school boards and said that North Carolina's moderate approach was wrong. Drifting into integration would lead to disaster. In an interview distributed statewide by the United Press, he bluntly predicted segregationists would win big in the 1960 elections. He stopped short of announcing he would run for governor.

At about the same time, Lake gave a televised address—his first television appearance—at the request of WRAL-TV. In the speech, Lake went further in urging defiance of the U.S. Supreme Court decisions. The governor, Lake said, should decline to enforce the Court's rulings, which were invalid. "Therefore, the state of North Carolina will take no action, directly or through its counties or cities, to put that decision in effect," Lake said. He said that the state should not use its National Guard or police to enforce a decree from any federal court requiring integration.

Several times, Lake addressed the great fear of many white people of that era—that blacks and whites would marry and have children. White public figures of the 1950s often cited "the mixing of the races" as the ultimate goal of those favoring integration. The NAACP, Lake told his television audience, "[is] trying to condition your children, even before they are old enough to be conscious of sex, to accept integration not only in the classroom, but in the living room and the bedroom as well." He urged viewers to not cast their votes in 1958 and 1960 for any candidate who did not plainly state his opposition to integration and pledge to do whatever he could to stop the NAACP.

Lake also attacked Governor Hodges repeatedly and stridently: What had Hodges done to show Negroes why separate schools were best for them? Nothing. What had Hodges done to preserve the state's constitutional rights? Nothing. What had Hodges done to reveal the NAACP in its true light? Nothing. He said that Hodges should have directed the State Bureau of Investigation to investigate the NAACP's membership, contributors, leadership, and goals, and then make that information known to the public. He compared allowing token integration in the three North Carolina school systems to Neville Chamberlain's conceding part of Europe to Hitler and Mussolini. A gradual retreat would lead to a total retreat. "So it always is when a man, a state or a nation deviates from fundamental principles in the hopes of appeasing an arrogant aggressor who despises those principles," Lake said. "We cannot afford to buy 'peace in our time' from the NAACP by admitting a few Negroes to white schools this year and a few more to other white schools next year."

Hodges, known as the "Businessman Governor," did not favor integration. He had appointed two committees to study how to respond to Supreme Court decisions; each committee was dominated by segregationists. When the school boards in Greensboro, Charlotte, and Winston-Salem integrated some of their schools, Hodges declined to offer his endorsement. He criticized blacks who did not agree with his belief in voluntary segregation. "Where are the Negro leaders of wisdom and courage to tell their people these things?" he asked. Many blacks were highly skeptical of him. At a Founder's Day Program at North Carolina Agricultural and Technical College, a black college, Hodges' speech was interrupted by rustling, hissing, and loud talking. Blacks said that Hodges had improperly pronounced "Negro" as "nigra"; Hodges said if he did, he did not mean to. The black press didn't like him; one black newspaper called him a "dupe of brazen white supremacy advocates." Yet Lake believed Hodges was "blinded by the glitter of moderation" and was a participant in a policy of appeasement and "retreat, retreat, retreat." Hodges had frittered away four years in the battle against segregation, Lake believed. He strongly hinted he would run for governor.

Among those pushing Lake in the late 1950s to run for governor were several members of the Patriots of North Carolina, a white supremacist group with an impressive board of directors. The Patriots, with twenty thousand members, were the state's largest and most influential segregationist organization. Their founder and president was Dr. Wesley Critz George of Chapel Hill, former chairman of the Department of Anatomy at the University of North Carolina School of Medicine and one-time president of the North Carolina Academy of Science. George believed blacks were biologically inferior to whites and could never equal whites' intelligence and creativity. To preserve the white race, George said that black and whites must never have children together. "The protoplasmic mixing of the races" would result in the nation becoming "progressively Negroid," diminishing the white race, George said. At least partly because of his background in science, George received national attention for his views.

George and Lake began corresponding in 1957, exchanging speeches on preserving segregation. A year later, George introduced Lake to a group in Mecklenburg County, home of the state's largest city, Charlotte. "We have gathered here to protest the attitudes and actions of those politicians who, in their gamble for Negro votes, look upon our children and grandchildren as expendable white poker chips," George told the group. He said Lake was "a brilliant, scholarly young man" who was "devoted to the interests of our people."

In early 1958, George began a campaign to get Lake to run for governor. He sent typed letters to former Patriots (the group appears to have been replaced by another similar group in 1958) asking potential supporters to make a financial pledge to Lake. "I have reason to believe that

Beverly Lake would consider entering the primary for Governor if he had some assurance of a grassroots desire for him to run," George wrote in March 1958. "No one else has appeared on the scene, so far as I know, who is so well qualified by ability, courage and will power to tackle the situation in which we North Carolinians find ourselves today. We can't afford to let the NAACP and pro-integration-minded politicians take over North Carolina. The way we can prevent this is by our votes."

George wrote to Lake regularly, giving him updates on his fundraising. Lake responded, asking for more help. In the summer of 1959, Lake asked George to assess his strength in George's home county and a neighboring county. It would take at least fifty thousand dollars, Lake wrote, to operate a state headquarters and buy some television air time. "I do not want to run unless this can be assured in advance," Lake wrote to George. If he could raise fifty thousand dollars to get a campaign started, Lake said he could raise another hundred thousand dollars during the campaign. George continued to work for Lake and in early 1960 he chaired a committee that approached Lake about running for governor.

Other former members of the Patriots also actively supported Lake. State Rep. John Kerr Jr. of Warrenton, a former Speaker of the North Carolina House, told leaders in his area not to commit to a candidate for governor until Lake announced his plans. If Lake ran for governor and had a segregationist message, Kerr said he would support Lake. "I realize, of course, that he will have to have a few other planks as well to decorate the platform as much as possible," Kerr wrote to George in 1959. Spencer Bass, a Tarboro physician and former Patriots director, proposed another role for Lake. Bass feared segregationists were "losing the battle of propaganda in this state." In a letter to George, he proposed a new, pro-segregationist newspaper that would comment on editorials from the *News and Observer* and reprint editorials from conservative newspapers. He recommended that Lake serve as legal advisor to the paper and that Wesley Critz George and Jesse Helms of Raleigh, then with the North Carolina Bankers Association, serve as associate editors.

By early 1960, Lake and Robert Morgan were talking about how to put together a Lake campaign for governor. Bill Staton, a former law student of Lake's, received a visit from his old professor. Lake phoned Staton in Lee County, where he practiced law, and said he would like to visit. Lake was traveling the state, gauging the level of support. Staton, who had lived at Lake's house when he was a student, admired his former professor. But he had been a friend and supporter of Terry Sanford's since he helped Sanford win the presidency of the Young Democrats in 1949. Staton was on board for Sanford's campaign for governor. Lake, always gracious, said he understood. Lake asked Staton about some others in the area who might support him. Staton, still loyal to his old professor, gave him some names of some potential supporters.

At Wake Forest College, Lake had gained a reputation among some as being a liberal, a reputation that followed him to the attorney general's staff as he challenged the utility monopolies. His former student and good friend Robert Morgan said in 1973, "Beverly Lake was generally thought of as a liberal. . . . Dr. Lake was very much of a populist, and still is." In the 1950 Senate campaign, when Sen. Frank Graham visited Wake Forest, Morgan and Lake worked at Lake's kitchen table, writing Lake's introduction of Graham.

Morgan thought there were two reasons, each stemming from the 1950s, why Lake became so firm in his segregationist views. Lake's work on the *Brown* case was one reason. "You know, when you do that, when you prepare and work on cases, you become more firmly convinced in your views," Morgan said. Morgan also thought Lake's Asheboro speech, and the resulting flap it caused, staked him out as a strong segregationist. "That pushed Lake into taking stronger positions than he normally would have taken," Morgan said. Woody Teague, another of Lake's students who was friendly with him at Wake Forest, said, "Lake was a nice fella. Lake taught me and he was a liberal. Just as soon as the *Brown* decision came about, he went from being highly liberal to being conservative." Others also said they believed Lake had changed in the '50s. "I have known Beverly Lake for years, but some time during the last ten years something has happened to him," William C. Archie, dean of the college of arts and sciences at Emory University and a North Carolinian, wrote to Terry Sanford in 1960.

The man who in 1950 had given a radio address in support of Frank Graham, the South's leading liberal, was now on the other side. Lake saw no inconsistencies in his support for Graham and his strong segregationist views that emerged. "I did support Dr. Graham in 1950 and later a man in one of the western counties wrote and told me I had changed since making my speech for Graham," Lake said. "There was no difference between what I said then and what I was saying in 1960. The terminology was different but the idea was the same. The reason I supported Dr. Graham was that I thought he would do more good at the time, because he would get more attention in Washington. . . . But if I had known then what I know now I would never have supported Dr. Graham."

Lake's characterization of his 1950 address for Graham generally was accurate. In that address, he said that both candidates supported continued segregation. "North Carolina believes in the practical wisdom of recognizing the differences between our two great races," Lake said then. "We believe a great state cannot be built either on a stupid ignoring of race differences or a diabolical magnifying of race differences into race hatred." Integrating public schools would be "the greatest calamity to North Carolina since the Civil War, because it would mean the death of public education," he said, with private schools opening for the children whose parents could afford them. Lake said that the best way to beat national efforts toward integration was to send Senator Graham back to Washington "where his sane, practical thinking and his understanding of our North Carolina method of racial cooperation, race separation and race pride" would convince his Senate colleagues.

Lake's radio address, however, also contained several statements that were racially moderate, if not liberal, for that era. He publicly criticized the tactics of many Smith supporters, and this in itself aligned him with liberals; in criticizing the tactics, he was preaching racial moderation. He proudly told the story of a black student, the son of the principal of Wake Forest's black public school. The student competed against white and black students across the southeast and won a scholarship to Columbia University, where he made the honor roll. "Wake Forest is proud of Robert Best—proud of him as a product of our Wake Forest public school system," Lake said. A black student attending a mostly white university was a controversial idea then to many Southerners. Indeed, Willis Smith supporters during the 1950 campaign circulated handbills saying that Graham had appointed a black student to West Point. It wasn't true, but the question of whether Graham appointed the student haunted Graham throughout the campaign. Few white public figures would have praised a black student as Lake did in his radio address, especially during that racially charged Senate campaign.

Lake insisted that he had not changed during the 1950s and that he had always been a conservative. "People started calling me a liberal because of the utilities bill," he said. "You ask any of my boys that I taught during the period if I was a liberal or a conservative. . . . I am definitely a conservative." Some of his former students, including Sanford supporter Bill Staton, did remember him as a conservative. Regardless, by 1960 I. Beverly Lake's stance on segregation was strong and clear. As the new year began, he watched to see whether a suitable candidate would enter the governor's race and try to preserve segregation—or whether he himself would have to carry the flag for the Old South, as his grandfather had almost exactly one hundred years earlier.

Chapter 3

KICKOFF

In January 1960, four months before the Democratic primary, Sanford received polling information and campaign advice from Louis Harris, a friend from his Chapel Hill days who had become a nationally recognized pollster. Harris's firm interviewed twelve hundred voters. Harris himself traveled the state and talked with one hundred voters. In a shrewd and prophetic analysis, Harris noted that the governor's race was wide open. Many of the men who had dominated North Carolina politics in the 1940s and '50s would be of little or no influence. Mel Broughton, Clyde Hoey, and Kerr Scott, all former governors and senators, had died. Frank Graham had moved out of state. Governor Hodges, who never had a strong political organization, had decided not to run for the U.S. Senate. New forces were building. A new generation was about to come to power in an election that could shape the state for years. While various candidates had ties to previous leaders, in 1960 each candidate was going to have to make it on his own, on the issues of the day.

There was much good news for Sanford. Harris looked at scenarios with various candidates—Sanford; former state Democratic Party chairman John Larkins; Speaker of the North Carolina House Addison Hewlett; state treasurer Edwin Gill; state senator Arthur Kirkman; and former Wake Forest law professor I. Beverly Lake. Sanford led the pack, although by a small margin. If no candidate received more than 50 percent of the vote in the Democratic primary—and no candidate was likely to get a majority—there would be a runoff. Sanford polled strongly against each of the candidates in a one-on-one face-off. His support was broad, and strong even among business and professional people who typically supported a more conservative candidate.

Sanford, however, had soft spots. Surprisingly, he was not doing well with farmers and rural residents—the people who had been Kerr Scott's most loyal followers and were expected to be a key part of Sanford's base. In a two-person race, tobacco farmers supported John Larkins over Sanford by 55 percent to 45 percent. This lack of support among rural voters, Harris said, was "the one really glaring source of weakness" to emerge from his research.

Sanford also needed to improve his standing with women, especially young women. Sanford struck voters as deeply sincere, with a firm, mature manner. While voters saw him as responsible, it also could make him forbidding, especially to younger women. "Terry Sanford himself simply must smile more and demonstrate a touch of levity when coming into contact with women, especially those under 35," said the Harris report. "Smile more, be more gracious and bending in manner, although neither be unnatural about it, nor to lose the quality of firmness that is so appealing." The report noted that President Eisenhower was viewed by most voters as firm, yet he also communicated warmth.

Harris also urged Sanford to make improving education his dominant issue—his "political trademark." While education was a top issue in many states, North Carolina was rare in its passion for the issue. Those polled had an intense, fierce desire for improvement. Yet they associated improving schools with Larkins, not Sanford. Harris laid out a platform for improving schools. Teachers needed public support. They needed substantial pay raises. Standards also needed to be raised. The governor must make improving schools his top priority and he should urge the people to get behind him. If Sanford could wrest the schools issue away from Larkins, he could cruise to victory.

Harris's report included excerpts of interviews with voters. A woman, identified only as a thirty-eight-year-old wife of a lawyer in Wilmington, said of the governor's race, "Now the biggest problem is the school situation. We need more schools, more teachers, the classroom number is too large. I'm not concerned with integration. I think if we keep moderate, things will work out. The big thing is to improve the schools. . . . I, for one, would be willing to pay higher taxes. . . . I'd be for Terry Sanford. . . . He is in sympathy with the views of Frank Graham and Kerr Scott. . . . He is a moderate on integration, not like Lake. . . . Sanford is not the best speaker but he is better than Hewlett."

She was among the more liberal voters surveyed. A retired textile executive from Gaston County held a different view of Sanford: "As far as candidates for governor go, I am not sure who I would favor, but I can say I would be definitely against Sanford. He is not the type of man I would vote for because of his philosophy, which affects his thinking. He was in too deep with Graham and Scott for me to trust him in there as governor. . . . If we get sound business people like Hodges in there, we will make out just fine. But keep those spenders like Sanford out."

A forty-four-year-old black man, a storekeeper from Apex, said, "I would vote for Sanford over Hewlett or Larkins. I like Sanford because he is a young man. I don't know much about him. I don't have much choice in voting for one who has my philosophy. All are politicians but Sanford is a little more progressive. I can't say there is much I don't like about him, least nothin' I can justify. Of course, I can justify it against Beverly Lake. But I can't accuse Sanford of that. I don't like none of Lake's opinions on nothin', most of all on civil rights. . . . I believe in mixed [integrated] schools. It would waste less money and save tax money. We need a better program for the schools."

Some white voters associated Sanford with holding the line on segregation. A fifty-two-year-old widow who followed politics said this from her front porch in Salisbury: "The big problem is that poor folks need more. They get nothin' right now. Course they should cut that welfare money for the colored. . . . Put the colored in their place and get on with it all. Now for governor, I'm for this fella Sanford. He's right good. He's a right smart fella. He says what he means when he says it. . . . I do believe in givin' the colored their education but separate.

61

Yes, I'm sure Sanford would help education and keep the colored where they are."

With black voters, Harris found Sanford running strong. When asked about all six potential candidates for governor, Sanford ran first with support from 30 percent of black voters; the next highest candidate had 21 percent. Sanford was well known among blacks, and his previous association with Frank Graham helped. Harris urged Sanford not to openly court black voters, which could alienate whites: "This issue should be handled with the utmost care, for it is possible for Sanford to maximize the Negro vote without driving away the bulk of his white support."

Sanford was advised not to give an all-out endorsement of civil rights. But he could assure blacks in other ways that he would work to better their lot. Don't put anything in writing or out in the press. Instead, work through word of mouth and through channels of communication with blacks. "At this moment the white electorate is not deeply stirring over racial issues," Harris wrote, "though some rather ugly overtones can be brought out if one scratches only a bit below the surface."

In the hypothetical six-man race, Sanford was first with 25 percent. Gill, the longtime state treasurer, was second with 23 percent, and former party chairman Larkins was third with 21 percent. Lake, the former Wake Forest law professor, was last with 5 percent. Gill's support was thought to reflect mostly that voters were happy with the job he had done as treasurer; Harris predicted that Gill, if he ran, would fade once Sanford and Larkins campaigned vigorously. "In the end," Harris said, "the choice for governor will undoubtedly rest" between Sanford and Larkins.

Several of the six were likely not to run for governor. The more likely candidates were Sanford, Larkins, and Lake. In that three-man match-up, Sanford led with 45 percent. Larkins had 42 percent, and Lake, 13 percent. Of the 13 percent who supported Lake, most would choose Sanford over Larkins, by more than a two-to-one margin. Harris "strongly urged" Sanford to do what he could to keep Lake out of the race. If he could keep Lake out, Sanford could win more than 50 percent in the primary and avoid a runoff. Also, Harris noted that Lake could awake issues of race, and this could cast the entire primary and runoff in a different, more controversial light. "Therefore," he concluded, "the stakes are high in getting Beverly Lake out of the running."

Larkins was the first to formally announce his candidacy. On January 20, 1960, Larkins, a fifty-year-old lawyer from Trenton in eastern North Carolina, began a campaign that would be built largely around his experience as a legislator and Democratic Party leader. He called for a major road-building program and expansion of the state's community college system. A high school education was within reach of every child, he said. "It is time now," Larkins said, "to expand our goal and work toward providing every capable student with the opportunity to get a college education." To reduce escapes from prison, he called for better pay and shorter hours for prison guards and stiffer punishment for inmates who tried to escape. He said the state should work to improve farmers' markets. And he advocated the state set up a staff of experts to advise cities on how to clear slums. He offered no plan for paying for his proposals.

Larkins sold himself more than his ideas. His campaign literature said that Larkins had more experience in state government than all other candidates for governor combined. He had more experience in state government than any gubernatorial candidate in the history of North Carolina, his backers said. Larkins had served nine sessions in the state senate, been chairman of the state Democratic Party, served as North Carolina's representative to the Democratic National Committee, and twice chaired the powerful Advisory Budget Commission that helped develop the state budget. He had raised more than $1 million for the party.

Now Larkins hoped to cash in on his twenty-five years of loyal service. An aide estimated that half of the county party chairmen and three-fourths of the top law enforcement officers were supporting Larkins (he had served as the lawyer for the state sheriffs' association for twenty-five years). He was particularly strong in the west, where he had often helped Democrats fight Republicans in the area of North Carolina where the GOP was strongest. In mountainous Madison County, the entire Democratic executive committee agreed to manage Larkins campaign, an unprecedented show of respect and loyalty. Larkins had lived in different corners of the states, giving him contacts throughout. He went to elementary school in Fayetteville, high school in Greensboro, and got his law degree from Wake Forest. Because he was not yet twenty-one years old when he passed the bar exam, and could not get a law license until his twenty-first birthday, he briefly worked for a law firm in Charlotte, where he met his future wife. Shortly after, he started practicing law in Trenton, where his first office was in the former harness room of a livery stable.

Larkins had considered running for statewide office before but had never done so. He was more interested in a run for the U.S. House. But he declined to run against his congressman, Graham "Hap" Barden, and Larkins consistently supported Barden. Confident that Barden would continue in that seat, he opted to run for governor instead. On the day after Larkins announced his candidacy, Barden made his own announcement—he would not seek reelection. If he had known Barden wasn't going to run for reelection, Larkins said years later, he would have run for Congress. But having made his announcement to run for governor, Larkins decided to stick with it.

Larkins considered himself a conservative—and he did not want Terry Sanford, whom he thought of as a liberal, to ease into the governor's mansion without opposition from a conservative. He knew Sanford from when they both had served in the state senate. In late 1959, when Sanford was the only candidate sure to run, Larkins decided to oppose him. Among Larkins' closest advisers was former U.S. senator Alton Lennon, whom Sanford had helped defeat in 1954.

With his fiscal conservatism and loyal service to the party, Larkins expected to have the support of Gov. Luther Hodges. When Hodges became governor in 1954 after Governor Umstead's death, Hodges kept much of Umstead's team. That included Larkins, who was then Umstead's liaison to the legislature. Larkins resigned that role in 1956, but Hodges and Larkins, the state party chairman, continued to work together. In the next year their relationship frayed. Hodges appointed Republicans to some posts that Democratic activists thought should have gone to the loyal Democrats who helped put Hodges in office. In a meeting attended by Larkins and Hodges, several local Democratic chairmen told Hodges they were unhappy they were not being consulted about appointments. Larkins listened as Hodges was criticized. At a press conference the following week, Hodges said that Larkins let him down by not defending him at the meeting. Larkins responded that Hodges called the meeting to hear suggestions and complaints from the local party leaders. "I didn't know I was expected to debate each point," Larkins said.

Despite their disagreement, Larkins still hoped for Hodges' support. In 1959, Larkins lined up Woodrow Jones of Rutherfordton to be his campaign manager. On Christmas Eve, Larkins received a phone call from Jones. Hodges wanted to run for vice president at the 1960 Democratic national convention, and Hodges had asked Jones to manage his campaign. I've already committed to run John Larkins' campaign for governor, Jones told Governor Hodges. Could you, Hodges asked, get out of your obligation to Larkins? Larkins released Jones from his commitment. That left Larkins without a campaign manager only weeks before he was to announce his candidacy. Larkins, now more than ever, expected Hodges' support. He had done Hodges a big favor. Yet as he kicked off his campaign, he still did not have the backing of the governor.

In mid-January, Terry Sanford said that he would formally announce for governor on February 4, prompting a front-page article in his hometown paper, the *Fayetteville Observer*. The paper already had run a series of articles speculating on when Sanford would announce his candidacy, even though it had been widely known for a year that Sanford would run. Local leaders joined in. The mayor and chairman of the county commissioners issued a proclamation: "Whereas this candidate is one of our best known and most highly respected citizens, and whereas the people of Fayetteville and Cumberland County have great confidence he will serve the state of North Carolina with ability, integrity and great dedication. . . . Now, therefore, we do hereby proclaim that Feb. 4 is set aside as TERRY SANFORD DAY in Fayetteville and Cumberland County."

In the mountainous western part of the state, the pomp was too much for editorial writers at the *Asheville Citizen*, who didn't mind adding to North Carolina's east-west rivalry that dated back to the Civil War (many in the mountains remained loyal to the Union) and probably before. The designation of Terry Sanford Day, the paper said, was "an indication of how seriously the people of Eastern North Carolina take their politics." People in the east *do* take politics more seriously, Sanford thought. When he traveled in 1958 and '59, it seemed every counter man and filling station operator in eastern North Carolina knew there was a governor's race coming up. But in banking and business circles in Charlotte, they were only vaguely aware.

On February 4, a Thursday, Sanford left his law office on Hay Street around noon and walked to the old Market House to give the speech he'd been planning all his adult life. The Market House, in the center of a European-style traffic circle in the middle of downtown Fayetteville, was one of the most significant buildings in the state. It started out as the state capitol and later was a town hall and then a market house. It was there that North Carolina ratified the U.S. Constitution and chartered the University of North Carolina. General Lafayette was welcomed there during his 1825 visit to the city. Sanford sought to make the day worthy of the building's history.

Even the *Asheville Citizen* must have been impressed: In the cold, five thousand supporters came to cheer Sanford. They came from Parkton and Clinton, from Charlotte and Raleigh, from Lumberton and Southern Pines, from Aberdeen and Elizabethton, from Raeford and, of course, Laurinburg. They stood before a raised platform, crowded against each other. To fight the cold, most wore hats, although some also wore dark glasses to block the bright sun. Some people held signs, each supported by a stick, that said, "Terry for Governor" or "Terry is Tops." Sanford, wearing a dark suit with the top button of his jacket secured, held a folder as he took his seat on the platform next to Margaret Rose.

Motorcades from other cities received a police escort into Fayetteville. "It was," wrote Marjorie Hunter of the *Winston-Salem Journal*, "like the Fourth of July, the State Fair and a gubernatorial inauguration day all rolled into one noisy and colorful package on a cold but sunny day." Bands played. Red, white, and blue bunting was draped on the Market House behind Sanford. A huge sign, showing a picture of Sanford against a blue state of North Carolina, was unfurled from the balcony at the moment of his official announcement. As Bob Scott promised, his mother attended. She sat on the large platform with Sanford, his wife, and his parents, and received an ovation when she was introduced. Later Mrs. Scott posed with Sanford and his wife for photographers.

A new decade had just begun, full of energy and promise. An old president and an old governor were stepping down. Many of the young men who had fought World War II were in their late thirties or early forties and were ready to take over. In his speech, Sanford hailed a "New Day" in North Carolina and challenged its people to do better. "The time has come," he said forcefully, holding the lectern with both hands, "to quit holding back. I call on you to join with me to build a better North Carolina. Let's quit holding the line. The object of the game is not to defend the goal but to score a touchdown. The touchdown for North Carolina is expanding, growing, developing and building."

While the state has accomplished much, Sanford said, "Let us also be honest. We simply have not put to the best use our full potential. I have been impressed, in traveling across the state, that our people are becoming more and more aware of our shortcomings and are determined that now is the time when something must be done." He noted a "quickening of interest" in public schools, and said that improving schools would be the dominant issue of his campaign. "This is a New Day in North Carolina," Sanford said, "when we are facing opportunities unsurpassed, unprecedented, unequaled in all of the sweep of the state's history."

After his speech, Sanford talked with reporters. He confirmed that he had the support of textile tycoon Charles Cannon of Concord—a major coup for Sanford. Many thought Cannon, one of the state's most prominent industrialists, and other businessmen would more likely support John Larkins, who was considered more conservative and business oriented than Sanford. Cannon's support of Sanford showed that business support was likely to be divided among the candidates—and that Sanford would get his share. Sanford himself was somewhat surprised at Cannon's support. In late 1959, Cannon sent word he would like to see Sanford. Sanford, who didn't think he'd even met Cannon before, went to visit him in Kannapolis, north of Charlotte in the heart of the state's textile industry. Cannon was concerned about the level of health care in the state; taking care of the state Highway Patrol, which he admired; and making sure the worker's compensation reserve was financially sound. That was it. Cannon made no request regarding the textile industry or any other business matter. And Cannon gave Sanford his support. He explained to Sanford and his aide Tom Lambeth why he didn't support Kerr Scott when he ran. "Unlike you, he didn't come down here and seek support," Cannon said. Off in a corner later, Sanford said to Lambeth, "It's never a mistake to ask."

After his announcement, Sanford talked with reporters and elaborated on his ideas for improving public schools. The state needed to attract more qualified young people into teaching and keep them teaching. To do that, he said, the state needed to pay teachers more. A reporter asked if taxes would need to be raised to pay for his program. "Obviously, you can't get something for nothing," Sanford said. If a financial analysis showed "that it takes more money, I'll have the courage to recommend proper revenue sources." That meant, of course, raising taxes.

Sanford's comment about possibly raising taxes was lost in the day's events. Many newspapers didn't even publish the remark. But it was extraordinary. On the day he announced his candidacy, when candidates typically offer Mom-and-apple-pie platitudes, Sanford started laying the groundwork for a tax increase in the first year of his administration. Unlike most candidates, who view a campaign merely in terms of getting elected, Sanford viewed the campaign as the first part of his governorship. He was a first-time candidate for statewide office. Yet he was confident he would be elected governor, and he campaigned that way. And so it was that Terry Sanford's administration began not when he was inaugurated in January 1961, but almost a year before, when on the first official day of his candidacy he called for a new effort to improve schools and said he was willing to raise taxes to do so.

For a politician, the sublime moment comes when good politics and good policy are aligned and become one and the same. Sanford believed that was the case with a tax increase to improve public schools. Tom

Lambeth remembered Sanford speaking to a group in Greensboro in late 1959 about taxes. Lambeth thought it the first time Sanford said if it meant raising taxes to improve education, he would ask for the tax hike. "He got a lot of applause," Lambeth said. "He was sort of testing that out. I remember him saying after you could get people to applaud a tax increase if you frame it right."

In his book *But What about the People?* Sanford recalled a different speech as the first time he mentioned raising taxes to improve public schools. He was traveling the state, trying out his message. It was before his official announcement and Bert Bennett was with him, although Sanford had not yet named Bennett his campaign manager. It was probably late 1959. When he talked about roads and farm income and industrial development, the audiences were interested. When he talked about improving public schools, they applauded. At an event in a remote county, Sanford remembered a woman standing up to ask a question. She probably wasn't a heckler, Sanford noted, but she sounded like one. "Where are you going to get the money for all this stuff?" she demanded. Sanford looked around the room and didn't see any newspaper reporters. He decided to be blunt. "Where do you think we will get the money?" he said. "From taxes!" The audience applauded. After he left, Sanford turned to Bennett and said, "Do you realize what we experienced tonight? Voters applauded when I said we would get new school money from taxes. That's remarkable." Bennett laughed. "Yes, but I wouldn't be too sure," he said. "They thought you said you'd get the money from *Texas*."

Bennett's punch line might have been added to make a good story. Sanford later called it "the funny line . . . that we probably made up." But more importantly, Sanford had decided he would talk about his willingness to seek more taxes from the legislature if needed. Sanford framed the issue this way: In order to improve public schools, he would have the *courage* to seek more taxes. Sanford was telling voters that improving education was his issue; he believed in it so strongly that he would raise taxes if needed. He also was telling them that his character and political will were strong enough to do something unpopular, if it was the right thing to do. Most political consultants would advise against a candidate talking about raising taxes, Sanford would say later, and he probably was right. His position on taxes would become a major issue in the campaign.

After the press conference, Sanford attended a scheduled one-hour reception in his honor; it turned into a two-hour reception. Five hours after he had taken to the podium to give his speech, he was buoyant—talking, smiling and shaking hands. "Tired, heck no, I'm not tired," he said as the final group of guests filed out of the civic center. "I feel just as good now as I did when I stepped on the platform at the Market House. . . . I don't think things could have gone off any better."

His successful kickoff carried into the weekend, when Democrats from across the state came to the Hotel Sir Walter in Raleigh for the party's annual Jefferson-Jackson Dinner. Sanford supporters were everywhere. Many had committed to him months, even years, ago. One reporter estimated that two-thirds of the seven hundred Democrats attending were backing him. Sanford had put together an impressive coalition—a good number of businessmen and bankers, as well as the supporters of Frank Graham and Kerr Scott. "He's united the cats and the dogs," one politician said.

Working the crowd was I. Beverly Lake, who was still deciding whether to run for governor. Lake sparred with reporters and moved quietly among Democrats in the hotel lobbies. Some Democratic regulars worried about Lake entering the contest because they expected race would become a dominant issue. "It would set the state back ten years," said one Democratic county chairman. The general consensus was that Lake, running on a segregationist platform, could not win but that he could get enough votes to force a primary runoff between Sanford and Larkins.

Editorialists also fretted about race becoming a dominant issue. The *Charlotte News* noted that neither Sanford nor Larkins had a reputation as a demagogue or zealot. "Consequently, it is to be fervently hoped that North Carolina can be spared the kind of unseemly spectacle that has marred the political landscapes of several other southern states in recent years," the *News* editorialized. "We have in mind, particularly, a campaign during which candidates ring the changes rather outrageously on the race issue."

The *Charlotte News* considered Larkins and Sanford men of substance, although it couldn't help getting in a dig at Sanford: "It's not true that Mr. Sanford has been 'running since he was 12 years old,' as some cynics insist. But we are fairly certain that he broke into a kind of dog-trot in 1954 and has been picking up speed ever since." He was picking up the pace and the others were in danger of being left behind. He had waited a long time for that week, and it had gone well. But something else happened that same week, something he could not plan for, something that was part of a tide bigger than him and bigger than politics, something that eventually would rise up and carry the country along with it.

Three days before Sanford announced his candidacy, four students at North Carolina A&T walked into the Woolworth's on South Elm Street in Greensboro, purchased school supplies and sundry items, and climbed onto stools at the lunch counter. Because they were black, local custom did not allow them to sit at the lunch counter and eat. They asked for service. The lunch counter manager said no. The store manager said no. The students refused to leave. "I beg your pardon but you just served us at [that] counter," said one of the students, Ezell Blair Jr. "Why can't we be served at the [food] counter here?" The employees did not relent. Neither did the students. They quietly stayed in their seats. They said they would return the next day and remain until they were treated as white customers were.

The students' quietly defiant act prompted sit-ins and boycotts throughout the state and the South. In all, students in fifty-four cities in nine states joined. Students had boycotted before in other cities but never with this impact. Never had sit-ins caught hold and spread. This time, like some kind of spontaneous combustion in which the elements mixed in perfect measure, they did. In Greensboro, hundreds of students participated. Each day, they showed up at Woolworth's and the Kress five and dime nearby. Thousands more of their counterparts at predominantly black colleges across the state in Raleigh, Durham, Charlotte, and Winston-Salem did the same.

Some believed the college protestors might have been influenced by writer Harry Golden of Charlotte. In his book *Only in America,* Golden noted the strange, illogical custom in the South of serving blacks while they stood at lunch counters—but not while they sat. "The white and Negro stand at the same grocery and supermarket counters; deposit money at the same bank teller's window; pay phone and light bills to the same clerk; walk through the same dime and department stores; and stand at the same drugstore counters," Golden wrote. "It is only when the Negro 'sets' that the fur begins to fly." One of the Greensboro protestors, Franklin McCain, revealed his motivation when he said years later, "I grew up in a world that was really two worlds, that were separate and totally unequal. There was very little chance of your climbing out of the world to a better world that you knew existed, that you saw and tasted a little bit of every day. You could taste the pie, but you couldn't eat it."

Shortly after the Greensboro sit-ins began, black students arrived at the Woolworth's lunch counter in Durham accompanied by four white students from Duke University. The store closed at midday after police received a report that a bomb was planted in the building. The forty demonstrators moved to the S. H. Kress and Company Store, which closed minutes later. The students then crossed the street to a Walgreen Drug Store but the manager roped off the dining area moments before they arrived. "If we can stand up and be served," said a black, female student from North Carolina College, "why can't we sit down and be served?"

Then in Charlotte, 150 demonstrators filed quietly into eight downtown stores and filled the lunch counter seats. The well-groomed students did not protest outwardly when waitresses ignored their requests. They sat impassively while the stores closed their lunch counters and departed orderly when one store closed its doors. "I have no malice, no jealousy, no hatred, no envy," said Charles Jones, a graduate student at Johnson C. Smith University who led the Charlotte sit-ins. "All I want is to come in and place my order and be served and leave a tip if I feel like it. . . . Of course, this movement here and those in Greensboro, Winston-Salem and Durham are interrelated in that they are parts of my race's efforts to secure God-given rights. But they are not part of a plan and were undertaken independently. We did not consult with groups or individuals at the other schools. There is no organization behind us."

Not all the protests were peaceful. At the Woolworth's in downtown Raleigh, counter-protestors threw eggs that hit the lunch counter and splattered on some blacks nearby. The blacks, apparently college students, showed no emotion. The store closed twenty-five minutes early and the crowd dispersed without further incident. Next door, McClellan's variety store closed down early when a crowd gathered. Young whites taunted the black protestors but they did not respond.

The same week, forty-three black college students in Raleigh were arrested for trespassing when they tried to stage sit-ins at the McClellan's downtown and the Woolworth's at a shopping center. In High Point, young blacks and whites battled with bricks, bottles, and rocks; they met downtown and were separated by police, then continued their encounter away from downtown. In Durham, the Rev. Martin Luther King Jr., the civil rights leader who four years earlier had led the successful boycott of segregated buses in Montgomery, Alabama, visited and supported the students. When King toured the Durham Woolworth, scuffles between news photographers, police, and employees broke out. Employees and the police sought to seize cameras. The employees said the store was private property and no one had permission to take pictures.

That night, King spoke at a rally in Durham in support of the sit-ins. "The underlying philosophies of segregation are diametrically opposed to Democracy and Christianity, and all the dialectics of all the logicians in the world cannot make them lie down together," King said. He respectfully praised the students for their courage and for making a difference in the adult world. "What is fresh, what is new in your fight is that fact that it was initiated, led and sustained by students," he said. "What is new is that American students have come of age. You now take your honored places in the world-wide struggle for freedom." King told the students they must not be intimidated by fear of arrest: "If the officials threaten to arrest us for standing up for our rights, we must answer by saying that we are willing and prepared to fill up the jails of the South."

North Carolina's political leadership condemned the sit-ins. State attorney general Malcolm Seawell suggested city and college officials act against the "serious threat to the peace and good order" raised by the sit-ins. Owners of private retail establishments have a legal right to sell or not to sell to anyone they want, Seawell said, adding that the law did not require segregated eating places. He said that his office would help city officials draft ordinances to deal with any threat to peace and order. Seawell said that college officials had the right and probably the duty to block any action by students that threatened the peace of the community.

The executive director of the American Civil Liberties Union objected to Seawell's comments. In a wire to Seawell, he said that Seawell's statements contradicted rights guaranteed under the Fourteenth Amendment and that he was pressuring students to stop their boycotts. Seawell responded with his own telegram: "My statements with respect to the law in this state are none of your business. I stand by what I have said—if you like it, well and good—if you do not like it, you may lump it." Gov. Luther Hodges asked the heads of the state-supported colleges to do whatever they could to end the wave of sit-ins. "I want to make it clear," Hodges said, "that I have no sympathy whatsoever for any group of people who deliberately engage in activities which any reasonable person can see will result in a breakdown of law and order, as well as interference with the normal and proper operation of a private business."

For gubernatorial candidate Terry Sanford, the timing of the sit-ins could not have been worse. He wanted race to fade into the background of the campaign and disappear into the glow of his courageous pronouncements about improving public schools. Instead, newspapers carried an almost daily drumbeat of stories about sit-ins and confrontations. The sit-ins were not often front-page news; the idea that college students could lead a protest with serious, national consequences was, at the time, unthinkable.

Still, it was impossible to live in North Carolina and not know about the protests. The college students created a subtle undercurrent that would ripple throughout the course of the campaign. Sanford wanted the whole issue to go away—at least until his campaign was over. Campaigning in Wilmington, he said he hoped the lunch counter sit-ins would not become an issue in the governor's race. "There are a great many people working for a solution of the problem," Sanford said. "I don't see how it can be injected into the campaign." In Wake Forest, I. Beverly Lake saw it differently. He was offended by the sit-ins. As they continued for a second week in mid-February, Lake followed the protests and continued mulling a run for governor. Soon, he would speak out on both.

Since he had emerged as a major public figure in the mid-1950s, Lake had been urged by friends and fans to run for governor. Lake had never been active in politics. He didn't like politics and he didn't really want to run for governor. He really wanted to be named to the state supreme court. Lake worried that getting involved in politics would hurt his chances to be named to the bench. Also, he and Sanford had mutual friends. He encountered a friend of Sanford's the year before the primary. "Well now," said Lake, "I want you to understand that when you're talking about Terry Sanford, you're talking about one of my friends." Sanford supporters, perhaps remembering Lake's support of Frank Graham in 1950, hoped Lake would back Sanford. Nonetheless, for two years Lake had traveled the state, gauging support for a run for governor. In early 1960, he told supporters that he didn't think he had enough financial support to run. But then on February 5 he said, "I have gotten considerably more financial support than I had." He would make an announcement next week, he said, at a Young Democrats rally in the central part of the state, in the Lee County town of Sanford.

The rally was attended by most of the Council of State, the North Carolina officials elected statewide, including Attorney General Seawell. Terry Sanford also attended, as did Arthur Kirkman of High Point, a state senator who was considering a run for governor. Lake opened his speech to the six hundred in attendance by saying many friends had urged him to run for governor and he had given much thought to the issues confronting the state. He gave his eclectic views on a range of issues, sometimes sounding like an economic conservative, sometimes like an economic populist, always like a social conservative.

First he shellacked Governor Hodges, his former ally. Lake now had a well-developed contempt for the Hodges administration. In 1955, Lake said, the state had a surplus of $53 million. That surplus was gone, as well as a windfall that the state received from collecting two years of income tax in one year. "The next administration will have no surplus and no windfall," Lake said. Just to maintain state services at the same level, the next administration would have to identify $20 million in new revenue. The Hodges administration had engaged in "deficit financing," Lake said. Hodges was widely known as the "Businessman Governor." Maybe so, Lake said. His administration "may or may not be properly called a 'businessman's administration,'" he said. "It is not a business-like administration. It will be the duty of our party's candidate for governor to give this state a business-like administration of the public's business. As a state, we must live within our income."

Finished with Hodges, Lake moved on to public schools and tweaked those, like Sanford, who advocated spending more on schools. Of course more money was needed for building, equipment, and salaries. "But money alone will not give North Carolina the education our children must have," Lake said. He called for "a revival of learning" in public schools—but admittedly offered little direction on how to create that revival.

Lake seemingly held a mix of political philosophies, making it difficult for even his supporters to label him. Those views were apparent in his speech. The state's tax burden, he said, should be spread fairly between individuals and businesses. When the state agreed in 1959 to collect two years of income tax from individuals in the same year, it treated individuals unfairly, he said. Corporations for the most part were not subjected to that burden, he said. And in discussing the need for changes in utility regulation, Lake said that the Utilities Commission, which regulated the utility monopolies, needed more money and staff.

If some of his views were hard to put in a category, his views on racial issues were not. There were whites who were sympathetic to the cause, or at least the peaceful tactics, of the black students who began their sit-ins a week earlier. Franklin McCain, one of the Greensboro Four who started the sit-ins, remembered on the first day an elderly white woman who told the four how proud she was of their actions. Lake was not one of those sympathetic whites. He suggested heads should roll at the state's black colleges. "A merchant is free under our law to select the customers he wishes to serve at his lunch counter or any other counter, and should be protected in that right," Lake told the crowd. "If the administrative officers of any institution operated by this state are either unable or unwilling to exercise over its students sufficient control to prevent organized, group invasions of private property by the students, the state should supply the institution with an administration which can and will do so."

If anyone held any doubts, Lake made clear his support for segregation. "For almost a hundred years North Carolina has followed the policy of educating her white, Negro and Indian children in equal, separate schools," he said. "The results have demonstrated the wisdom of Governor Aycock and others who built our public school system on that policy. That system of public schools ought to be continued and it can be continued by the voluntary action of our people. They should be encouraged in that purpose. That policy should remain the policy of our state." It is the legislature—not the governor, not judges—which has the authority and duty to declare North Carolina's policy, he said. And, in another dig at Governor Hodges, Lake said that the legislature should be free from pressure from the governor.

With that closing on his trademark issue, it appeared Lake would enter the governor's race with a rush. His speech had been interrupted twelve times by a group of at least one hundred supporters, many of whom wore homemade campaign badges and held placards saying, "I. Beverly Lake for Governor." The crowd believed Lake had been building up to an announcement of his candidacy.

Shockingly, instead Lake withdrew. At the end of his speech, he thanked his supporters but said he did not have enough money to run. "I am not willing to prejudice these principles in the minds of our people by an inadequate presentation," Lake said, "so I shall not be a candidate in the primary this spring." With six brief sentences, he was out of the race.

"Run anyhow! We're for you," a supporter yelled at him. Another supporter blurted, "Damn!"

In an exchange with reporters, Lake left open the possibility of a candidacy if supporters said they had enough money for a campaign. "I am not going to try to raise any more money," Lake said. "If the money is brought to me, I'll have to consider again in light of those facts." State senator Robert Morgan, a Lake supporter, told reporters that efforts were being made to get Lake to change his mind.

Sanford knew earlier that day that Lake was not getting in. He followed Lake to the podium and praised him heartily. He said that Lake's announcement removed a heavy load from his mind and that Lake would have been an able and formidable contender. He agreed with Lake that the increasing centralization of government was a bad trend. "I believe in keeping our government close to the people in every way," Sanford said. Lake's friends admire him, Sanford said: "We have been friends for many years and I have noted something which I think is the finest recommendation a man can have. I did not have the privilege of studying under him, but over the years, in meeting hundreds of former students, I have noted that they all literally idolize him. This is a reflection of enduring qualities of character, and no man, teacher or otherwise, can desire greater acclaim." Sanford wished Dr. and Mrs. Lake happiness. "I know that he will continue to serve North Carolina with distinction," he said.

Sanford did not, of course, mention that he disagreed strongly with Lake on race. They had been on opposite sides of the Pearsall Plan in 1956 and generally viewed the race issue from a different perspective. While Sanford did not think the student sit-ins should be a campaign issue, Lake thought they should. While Lake rejected the *Brown* decision, Sanford thought the state should accept it and adapt. Still, Sanford said years later that he didn't have any problem flattering Lake that night in Lee County. "There was an admirable part of Dr. Lake," Sanford said. "He was a beloved professor, and that in my mind spoke very well of him. He had this blind spot on the race issue; he had this blind spot on the Confederacy. He thought the great tragedy of America was that the South lost the war. Other than that, Dr. Lake had a lot of good qualities. These

young men around us who were for me [such as former Lake student Bill
Staton], wanted us to avoid a confrontation. It wasn't hard for me to say
what I said because it was true. My speech was about what a great professor he was and how students loved him."

What was important to Sanford was that Beverly Lake was out of the
race, and, likely, so was any feverish discussion on the pace of integration.
Sanford was relieved. He could concentrate on talking about schools and
how to bring North Carolina into the New Day.

Malcolm Seawell was hot. Maybe Terry Sanford was unburdened by the
Lee County event, but Seawell sure wasn't. Sanford might have thought
he was making things better when he praised Beverly Lake—but it infuri-
ated the direct, blunt Seawell. He was appointed attorney general by
Governor Hodges in 1958, and he was loyal to the governor. Seawell had
expected Lake to hack away at Hodges; he had heard Lake speak before
and it was well known that Lake was a Hodges critic. Anyway, Seawell
just plain didn't like Lake. As attorney general, part of Seawell's job was
to defend the state's plan for handling school integration, including the
Pearsall Plan adopted by voters in 1956, a plan that Lake opposed. Seawell believed extreme statements on segregation had hurt the state's legal
position in defending its response to the *Brown* decision. And Seawell believed Lake was making extreme statements.

But what really irked Seawell was Sanford's praise of Lake; Seawell
took it as an endorsement of Lake's criticism of Hodges. The day after the
Lee County rally, Seawell told reporters he was considering a run for governor. Sanford left the impression that he "was embracing the slap at the
present administration," Seawell said. "I don't say that he intended it that
way. I just say that is the impression some got. . . . It disturbed me that no
mention was made [by speakers at the rally] of the chief executive of our
state and the very fine accomplishments of his administration." Seawell
said he would make a decision in about ten days.

Seawell and Sanford had been friends and allies for years. They had an
understanding, or so Sanford thought, that Sanford wanted to be governor and Seawell wanted to be on the state supreme court, as his father had

been. Sanford kept in close touch with him in late 1959 and early 1960, and Seawell told Sanford he would not run for governor. But within a week of telling Sanford he would not run, Seawell was approached by a group of business and political leaders aligned with Governor Hodges. The group asked Seawell to consider running. They didn't like Sanford or Lake and didn't think Larkins could win. In Fayetteville, Sanford arranged a meeting with Seawell and Dickson Phillips, his law partner who also was friendly with Seawell. Sanford knew Seawell was considering running; Sanford was surprised, upset, and fearful. If Seawell ran, he would attract many people who otherwise would vote for Sanford.

The three men met at the Green Lantern restaurant south of Fayetteville. Sanford told Seawell they thought alike on a lot of issues and had many mutual friends. He urged Seawell not to join the race. "It's not a question of my being a better man than you," Sanford said. "But you don't have a chance. I've got commitments you need to have. It's not that I'm better than you but I've been at it longer." Seawell said he had the support of sheriffs across the state. And he told Sanford he was disappointed that Sanford had not confronted Lake on the race issue. "Somebody needs to do it," Seawell said, "and you haven't been doing it." Sanford blanched. He and Phillips went back to their office knowing Seawell would join the race.

Seawell might have been unhappy with Sanford's praise of Lake. But Sanford and Larkins believed there were other factors at play. They believed Governor Hodges had recruited Seawell to run for governor. Sanford never expected Hodges' support. "I never was a big Hodges supporter," Sanford said later. Neither was Hodges a fan of Sanford. Hodges' son, Luther Hodges Jr., would later say his father considered Sanford too political, too likely to engage in the kind of spoils system Hodges tried to avoid. "Seawell was more his kind of person . . . less political," Luther Hodges Jr. said. He said his father tended to like people who had not been involved in politics. For some of the same reasons, Governor Hodges did not want Larkins, the longtime Democratic party man, to be governor. "There was such a difference in Larkins and my father; they just approached the world differently," Hodges Jr. said. Hodges was from a humble background; he viewed Larkins as part of the aristocratic elite that ran eastern North Carolina and kept out new industry unless it suited their needs.

Roy Parker, who covered politics for the *News and Observer*, said that as the field developed, Hodges looked for a candidate to run. He didn't want Larkins or Sanford. Lake was too extreme on race. "So what [Hodges] needed was a good, untainted, middle-of-the roader," Parker said. "He had to get somebody to be in the middle between Terry and Lake. But then John Larkins wouldn't back off. Luther thought, being governor and all that, he could dictate who to pick."

A week after the Lee County rally, Seawell, fifty, entered the governor's race. His cousin, H. F. "Chub" Seawell, had been the Republican candidate for governor in 1952 and won more votes than any Republican candidate in state history up to that time. Chub Seawell was a well-known raconteur and humorist who later would refer to President Lyndon Johnson as "Cousin Lendem Billions Nimrod Fountain Pen Beulah Land Father Divine Johnson." Malcolm Seawell, however, lacked his cousin's lighter touch. He was forceful and plain-spoken. "I am called a controversial person," said Malcolm Seawell. He agreed, in this sense: "When I have . . . been required to rule and make statements with respect to the law, I have done so without regard to race, color or creed, because the law applies with equal force and dignity to all of us."

That was a courageous statement. Not many southern white politicians of that era would have said it. While he didn't mention the *Brown* decision, implicit was that it was the law and North Carolina must follow it. Seawell was a staunch supporter of the state's schools policy, which had resulted in token integration in several of the state's larger cities. In announcing for governor, Seawell explained why he had been a vocal backer of the state's schools policy. For one, he saw the strife, turmoil, and bitterness in other southern states, and it threatened to close down their schools. Secondly, as attorney general, when he defended the state in federal court he thought he needed to appear "with clean hands."

That made Seawell almost a race liberal, by North Carolina standards. He once received an unsigned letter that said, in part, "When the peoples of North Carolina want your advice on education, they will ask you for it. When did you join the NAACP, you nigger lover?" But Seawell could be baffling. While many liberals thought he had an impressive record, especially in fighting racial violence, he could be unpredictable. In announcing his candidacy, he also spoke strongly against the black college students who were conducting sit-ins at lunch counters. He pointed out that trespass laws could be used against such demonstrators. "Here again we are confronted with the question of law," Seawell said. "Property rights still exist in this state and I hope that they will continue to exist with a people who believe in free enterprise."

Seawell first gained statewide prominence in the early 1950s when he was the solicitor, or prosecutor, in Robeson County, in the southeastern part of the state. The Ku Klux Klan was active in neighboring Columbus County and threatened to move into Robeson. Seawell had Klansmen put into jail for violating an ancient, little-known law. Then Seawell visited the jail. He told them they could resign from the Klan immediately or he would do his best to send them to prison. They got the message. Seawell immersed himself in the Klan's culture. He memorized the "Kloran," or rule book. He knew the Klan's handshake: A horizontal grip in which one person shook hands with his palm upward, and then the upturned palm was turned over. He learned the Klan pledge, part of which was, "I pledge my sacred honor, my life, my property and my vote" to the Ku Klux Klan. Seawell was credited with driving the Klan out of Robeson County.

Seawell went to the University of North Carolina Law School, then worked for the Institute of Government in Chapel Hill and was on the staff of the state Parole Commission. He briefly practiced law in Lumberton in Robeson County and then in 1942 joined the staff of the secretary of war in Washington. After the war, he returned to Lumberton and was elected mayor. He was appointed solicitor in 1950. Governor Hodges appointed him a superior court judge in 1955 and attorney general in 1958. Seawell's father also had been attorney general and a member of the North Carolina Supreme Court.

After he was appointed attorney general, Seawell quickly let it be known that he considered the *Brown* decisions the law of the land. While he disagreed with the decisions, Seawell said he would enforce the law. He said that defiance or massive resistance, such as that in Arkansas and Virginia, would backfire. "It is unthinkable to me that any people possessed of their senses would say, in effect, 'We will close our schools and let our children grow up in ignorance,'" he said. He knew he would defend North Carolina's position in court, and thought he would be more effective if he took a moderate, respectful tone regarding federal decisions on integration. In a speech to a group of attorneys in Chapel Hill, he said that a lawyer would look silly if he appeared in court with a client after denigrating the law and saying he would not abide by decisions of the court.

Seawell liked a good fight. In a July 4 address in 1959, Seawell issued a stern warning to the Klan, saying North Carolina would not tolerate violence. A few months later, in a Veteran's Day address, Seawell tweaked the strong segregationists, including those who had been members of the Patriots group. In his address, Seawell said that a person could not be a patriot unless he was determined to live by the laws of the state and nation. "The true patriot," Seawell said, "gives his allegiance to the law of the nation and of his state, rather than to the land itself where one resides."

As attorney general, Seawell received a human relations award from the North Carolina B'nai B'rith Anti-Defamation League, a Jewish organization, for his work against the Ku Klux Klan and his insistence that public schools remain open amidst the debate about integration. That prompted the Mecklenburg Patriots of North Carolina to call for his resignation. If he received an award from B'nai B'rith, Seawell had failed to serve the best interests of the state, the Patriots said. They added that B'nai B'rith "ranks with and is a companion organization" of the NAACP. Seawell responded in typical caustic fashion: He did not intend to resign. If he ever did consider resigning, it would not be because of a request from the Patriots. "And," Seawell said of the Patriots' spokesman, "I wish him a Happy New Year."

Seawell was Hodges' boy. Hodges had appointed him—twice. He

liked the way Seawell did his job. He liked the way he aggressively defended the state's schools policy. After a crowd had gathered one day in the capitol to watch a new state employee take an oath, Hodges asked Seawell to step forward. Smiling broadly, Hodges unwrapped a package and presented it to Seawell. It was an editorial cartoon from the *Greensboro Daily News*. The cartoon depicted Seawell and Hodges, wearing medieval armor, under school banners that said "moderation." Behind "Sir Malcolm of Seawell," Hodges was mopping his brow and saying "moderation, of course." Hodges told the crowd he was glad to have "attestation to show we are both moderates." He placed a hand on Seawell's shoulder and said, "Everybody knows there is no real difference between me and this wonderful fellow here."

Now, in early 1960, Seawell was a formidable candidate for governor. He was physically impressive: tall, gray-haired, and direct in manner. He held one of the most prominent offices in the state. He was widely believed to have Governor Hodges' support; Larkins called him "the Crown Prince of the Hodges Administration." When he announced, Seawell said he did not consider himself Hodges' candidate because he had not even discussed his candidacy with Hodges. He said that he admired much about the Hodges administration but that he would be his own man.

Sanford and Larkins believed Hodges picked Seawell to run, even though Hodges and Seawell denied it. "He [Hodges] brought Seawell in," Sanford said later. Larkins, shortly after he announced his candidacy, said he was shocked to learn that Hodges was not going to support him. Raleigh attorney Armistead Maupin told Larkins that Hodges had called him and asked him to manage Seawell's campaign. Larkins didn't think Hodges was vindictive in bringing Malcolm Seawell into the campaign. "I think he just made up his mind that neither Lake nor I should be governor, and so he got somebody to run that he thought could be elected over either of us," Larkins said years later. "After the primary, Governor Hodges told me he wanted me to know that although he had been accused of helping Malcolm Seawell, he did not lift a finger to help him. I told him I had several reports, including one from Armistead Maupin himself, that he had personally asked Maupin to become Seawell's cam-

paign manager. The governor said he had no recollection of that conference. So we dropped the subject, shook hands and remained friends."

Sanford was chagrined. "I had it under control. I thought the campaign was going to be John Larkins and me," he said later. Now, with
three strong candidates, a second primary was almost certain. Sanford
liked Seawell and considered him a friend. "It was a great disappointment
to me that he let [Hodges] talk him into that," Sanford said. "It really
caused us all kinds of trouble." If Seawell had not run, Sanford said he
would have named Seawell to the North Carolina Supreme Court when
Sanford became governor. But Seawell was running. At least Beverly
Lake wasn't running. Or was he?

Chapter 4

WILD-CARD LAKE

When Beverly Lake announced he would not run for governor, John Larkins immediately visited his old college friend in Raleigh. Larkins and Lake were fraternity brothers at Wake Forest College in the 1920s. Larkins, who knew Lake well enough to call him "Ike," considered himself and Lake to be conservatives. He asked Ike Lake if he would co-manage his campaign. Lake said he might support Larkins—if he did not become a candidate himself. Lake was leaving open the slight possibility that his supporters would raise enough money for him to get into the race. He told Larkins he wanted to wait a few days to see how much money his backers would raise.

Lake was swamped with letters and phone calls from supporters, asking him to reconsider and run for governor. The day after Lake's announcement in Lee County, Paul Hastings of Reidsville, a former director of the segregationist Patriots of North Carolina, wrote Lake a two-page letter saying how Lake could win the governorship. "To say that I was disappointed at your announcement . . . last night is putting it mildly," wrote Hastings. Lake was better known and better qualified than Sanford or Larkins, Hastings wrote; he did not mention Seawell, apparently not considering him a major threat. Hastings said that Lake had a duty to run. If he did not run, Sanford and Larkins would not be forced to take a position on the important issues. Lake, he said, would be denying many citizens the opportunity to vote for someone who shared their principles.

Hastings said that the timing was right for Lake to win. The sit-ins were creating a white backlash, he said, making Lake's segregationist beliefs more timely. "The present Negro demonstrations would mean more to you in votes than $50,000 to $100,000 in additional funds could get, and they would all go to you as you are the only one who has taken a public stand on the issue," Hastings wrote. "These demonstrations are really being talked about in this section and the people seem to resent them very much, especially when it is clear that the whole thing is promoted by an out-of-state group of scallywags. All of this has made the people more conscious than ever that the ultimate goal of these radical groups is complete integration is every area of life."

The Patriots disbanded in the late 1950s, but Hastings said that they could still elect Lake governor. A list of at least twenty thousand former Patriots sat in a Raleigh office. Hastings proposed mailing a letter to each, signed by former Patriots leaders, explaining Lake's beliefs and soliciting support. The letter would ask for at least $10 from each Patriot. Hastings believed at least ten thousand Patriots would respond—and Lake would have more than $100,000 in contributions. "We know how these people feel on segregation and that most of them feel strongly about it, enough so to give and to work for anyone who represents their views," Hastings wrote. "I do not know of any other candidate who knows that he has 20 odd thousand individuals strongly for him to begin a campaign as I am positive you have."

Among the more prominent supporters who wanted Lake to run was Dr. Clarence W. Bailey, a physician from Rocky Mount and another old friend of Lake's from their Wake Forest College days. Earlier in the year, Lake had called Bailey and told him he was considering running for governor. When Bailey read about Lake's Lee County speech and his money woes, he wanted to do what he could to get Lake to run. He telephoned Lake and told him he didn't like what he'd read in the paper. He invited him to come to Rocky Mount to talk things over.

Lake accepted. A small group met at Bailey's office at 147 North Main

Street in Rocky Mount, including Lake, Bailey, his son Jack, Bailey's son-in-law John Lewis, and Robert Morgan, then a state senator from Harnett County. According to Jack Bailey and John Lewis, the discussion went like this: Lake explained to Bailey why he had decided not to run. Bailey probed. "Beverly, what would it take for you to get in the governor's race?" he said. "How much money would you have to have to change your mind and get in the race?" Lake hesitated and did not give a direct answer. Bailey persisted. Lake finally answered: "I'd have to have $10,000 in the bank to start." Bailey reached into his bottom desk drawer, pulled out a checkbook, wrote a check for $10,000, and handed it to Lake. "Now," Bailey said, "does that get you into the race?" Lake was stunned. "I don't know," he said. He said he needed a campaign manager. Morgan quickly interjected that he would put his law practice on hold and run Lake's campaign. With that, Lake agreed to run. Beverly Lake Jr. said his father confirmed the general discussion described by Jack Bailey and John Lewis.

Morgan's involvement in that meeting and in the Lake campaign has been discussed by Lake partisans for years. In 1974, when he was running for the U.S. Senate, Morgan told the NAACP at a meeting in Charlotte that he served as Lake's campaign manager out of loyalty to his old law professor, not because he agreed with Lake's philosophy.

That outraged Lake and many of his supporters. Lake, who was then a member of the North Carolina Supreme Court, wrote letters to supporters, withdrawing the support he previously had given to Morgan. Lake wrote that Morgan urged him to run for governor and even wrote letters trying to raise money for a campaign. Also, Lake said that Morgan fully supported his segregationist approach. Lake said that Morgan gave the impression he yielded reluctantly to the request of an old friend to manage the campaign. "Nothing could be further from the truth," Lake said. For writing the letter as a sitting judge who was supposed to stay out of political campaigns, Lake was called before the state Judicial Standards Commission on a charge of unethical conduct. He was cleared. Lake also wrote Morgan a letter. Morgan decided to let the issue go. Caught somewhere between his present as a Democratic candidate for the Senate and his past as a key ally of a strong segregationist, Morgan could not win. He could either further alienate his beloved mentor or offend the black people of North Carolina. Morgan never opened Lake's letter and never talked to him about it.

In a 1998 interview, Morgan said that Lake had asked him several times to run his campaign. "I did not want to manage the campaign because I did not know how," Morgan said. Also, Morgan was busy serving as a legislator and practicing law. His law partner, Archie Taylor, went to Lake and said that Morgan was not physically up to managing a campaign for governor. Lake said he could understand that, and, in that case, he just would not run for governor. "I didn't want that responsibility" of having kept Lake out of the race, Morgan said. "I didn't know anything about [running a statewide campaign]. I'd never run anywhere except here. I reluctantly did it, not because of lack of respect for him but because I didn't know how to run a state campaign."

Did Morgan agree with Lake on the segregation issue in 1960, as Lake said? Morgan certainly sounded like Lake back then. When Lake was reconsidering entering the campaign in February, Morgan said that Lake's campaign would not be a campaign of racial hatred. But that did not mean that racial issues would not be discussed, Morgan said. It is illogical to deprive the people the chance to discuss and vote on one of the major issues, Morgan said, just as it would be illogical to refuse to discuss the subject of taxes. In a speech in Harnett County during the campaign, Morgan said, "If Dr. Beverly Lake is elected governor he won't sit idly by as [Governor] Hodges has done and let the NAACP and other evil outside influences make a mockery of North Carolina taxpayers [and] our way of life."

Was Morgan a reluctant participant in the Lake campaign, as Morgan said? Sanford and his allies had long considered Morgan a key Lake supporter. An unsigned note to Sanford aide Ben Roney in June 1959 said, "Archie Taylor, Bob Morgan of Harnett are on a Beverly Lake kick." In October 1959, Sanford supporter Henry Hall Wilson wrote to Sanford and enclosed a newspaper clipping about Lake. He also briefed Sanford on a recent political event in Asheville. "I'm sure you are aware of what appears to be a Lake hot bed of sentiment in Hoke and Harnett," Wilson wrote. "Little Robert Morgan was at Asheville but didn't appear to be cutting much mustard." Morgan and Sanford had been friends for years. They practiced law in neighboring counties. Although Morgan had a general practice and Sanford's was geared more toward corporate clients, they occasionally opposed each other as friendly rivals. Each was politically active, with populist instincts. Each had worked for Kerr Scott in 1954. Morgan attended an organizational meeting for Sanford in the late 1950s and told Sanford he would support him—unless his old mentor Beverly Lake ran. "He told me way ahead of time: 'If Dr. Lake runs, I'd have to support him,'" Sanford said years later. Morgan remembered it the same way: "I told him then if Lake ran, I'd have to support Lake." So Sanford knew from the beginning that Morgan would support Lake.

Morgan's actions indicated that he was fully committed to getting Lake to run for governor and that he would do all he could to get Lake to run. Morgan actively and publicly raised money for his candidate. Newspapers often quoted Morgan on the status of the fund-raising effort. Two days after Lake's Lee County speech, Morgan told the *News and Observer* he had accepted the chairmanship of the Lake for Governor Committee. Morgan said he would travel the state to raise money for Lake's campaign. The committee formed without Lake's knowledge "to raise the necessary funds to permit him to wage a vigorous campaign and to adequately present the issues to the public," Morgan said. Lake's decision not to enter the race triggered a wave of telephone calls and telegrams urging Lake to reconsider. If the trend continued, Morgan said, "I am confident . . . that we will be able to persuade Lake to change his decision and offer himself as a candidate for governor of North Carolina." A few days later, when a statewide fund-raising campaign was started in Winston-Salem, Morgan predicted Lake would have enough money to run. A Lake for Governor fund-raising letter urged supporters to mail their contribution to Robert Morgan.

On February 24, two weeks after Lake's withdrawal, Morgan told a reporter that sufficient funds were on hand to begin the Lake campaign. "I think it will influence him to get back in the race," Morgan said. "We don't have the half million dollars supposedly raised for one candidate or the $300,000 announced for another. But there's enough on which to begin." These were hardly the words of a man reluctant to join the fray. Contrary to his 1974 campaign speech to the NAACP, Morgan was a key player—perhaps *the* key player—in getting Lake to run for governor. And once Lake started running, Morgan ran Lake's campaign aggressively, with skill and tenacity.

While the money from Bailey was important, there might have been other factors that made Lake run. Lake said he was approached by "a man high up" in the Sanford campaign, whom he did not identify. The man told Lake he could have a seat on the state supreme court if he would stay out of the race, Lake said in 1978: "I told him if I had a choice of the two jobs, I'd take the court seat, but since he had said that to me I would run against Sanford." Sanford supporters are skeptical that this was a bona fide offer. Sanford, for all his New Day rhetoric and fresh-faced looks, was highly capable of playing the role of backroom pol. Years later, he told several interviewers he would have named Malcolm Seawell to the state supreme court if Seawell had not run against him. But in more than a half dozen interviews with the author and others, Sanford never discussed appointing Lake to the court. Several of Sanford's closest associates, including Dickson Phillips and Bert Bennett, were skeptical that Sanford authorized a deal that would have put Lake on the supreme court.

Other factors probably influenced Lake more. He apparently did not believe his old friend Larkins conservative enough on race. "He wasn't unhappy with Larkins as a person but he didn't think he could carry the battle," said Beverly Lake Jr. Larkins and Lake were different kinds of conservatives—Larkins was a pro-business conservative who was more moderate on race, similar to Governor Hodges. Lake was a hard-edged social conservative who was less conservative on business issues. Lake eventually told Larkins he would not support him.

Larkins had his own theory about why Lake entered: He believed that once Seawell entered, preaching the state's plan of racial moderation, it was inevitable that Lake, his antagonist, would run. They had become political opponents when they'd feuded over the value of the Pearsall Plan.

"Lake was determined that Malcolm Seawell would not be governor because they were at opposite ends of the political pole," Larkins said. Sanford agreed. "Coming in the way [Seawell] came in forced Lake to get in," he said.

Others believe Lake simply was swayed by the enthusiastic support of whites who wanted to preserve segregation and who believed in Lake and his message. "He had a lot of grassroots encouragement to run, out over the entire state," said Bill Staton, Lake's former student who supported Sanford. "He had people who were concerned the direction the state might be drifting towards with respect to race relations in the state. Dr. Lake responded to an undercurrent of feeling out over the entire state that there needed to be somebody in the race who would push that agenda."

On March 1, 1960, while lunch-counter pickets paraded on sidewalks below his Raleigh law office, Lake officially entered the race for governor. He spoke like a man arguing a case to a jury. His hands were clasped behind his back as he read his announcement to journalists and friends in his tenth floor suite of offices. In answering questions from journalists, Lake, fifty-three years old, sometimes sounded like a professor answering questions of his students.

He believed the candidates ought to discuss "the most far-reaching problem North Carolina has faced this century." Lake used the proper, well-spoken, well-constructed language of the professor, not the hard-edged, heavily dialectic language of the southern demagogue: "I consider any condition and any policy of our government which causes the people of North Carolina grave concern for their Constitutional liberties, the peace and good order of our state and the future of their children a legitimate subject for public discussion in this campaign." In plainer language, people were worried about race, it was a legitimate issue, and he was going to talk about it. "The Democrats of North Carolina," he said, "are entitled to have from each candidate a clear, public sentiment of his position on these questions before the primary."

He spoke warmly of the black people of the state. The friendship between blacks and whites was treasured. "It is based upon mutual respect and confidence developed through generations which have lived and built our social structure," Lake said. "If I become governor, I shall use every power I have, officially and unofficially, to preserve and promote that friendship and to resist all groups, from within or from without our state, whose programs will endanger it. . . . If I become governor, I shall use every power conferred upon me to continue that social order in North Carolina."

Responding to questions, Lake said he supported the Pupil Assignment Act, which allowed local school boards to assign students to schools, regardless of race. A few had allowed token integration. Lake said he drafted the bill as an assistant attorney general. But he said that the law was never intended to serve as "an impenetrable wall behind which we could rest in safety from the invasion of our school system by the NAACP."

Lake offered a dozen other planks in his platform, including improved schools; a fair distribution of the tax burden between individuals and corporations; the right of any owner of any store, restaurant, or cafe to decide which customers he or she will serve; improving facilities for and methods of farm marketing; and an independent legislature free from pressure by the governor's office. The last promise tweaked the Hodges administration for what Lake thought was meddling, although the statement was curious, if not disingenuous. Lake had just promised to "use every power" he had to preserve segregation. Would that not include using the powers of the governor's office to sway legislation? Lake had criticized Hodges for four years, saying he had not done enough on the race issue. For years he had, in effect, criticized Hodges for not leading. Now he was saying Hodges, in the legislature, led too much.

The day before his announcement, Lake appeared in New York on the nationally televised *Today* show, hosted by David Garroway, and gave his views supporting segregation. He joined a panel of three white adults and two black students to talk about sit-in protests. If the U.S. Supreme Court should hold that segregation in restaurants is illegal, "You would have chaos and confusion in the eating establishments all over North Carolina," Lake said. "Many of the very well-established restaurants, cafes, will go out of business." Among the panelists was a black female student from Virginia Union College. At one point, Lake said he wanted her "to say just what rights she thinks she has to go into a private store." Garroway reminded Lake that the participants had agreed not to question one another. When *Today* show planners learned that Lake was about to become a candidate, they limited his role. "Sorry I didn't have more time to say some of the things I wanted to say," Lake said at the press conference announcing his candidacy. "Frankly, it was the first time I'd ever seen the Dave Garroway show."

The NAACP responded quickly and forcefully to Lake's candidacy, saying it would vigorously oppose its old rival. Lake couldn't have asked for more. The NAACP was the enemy he loved to hate, and the strong public reaction given by the NAACP to his candidacy suited his needs perfectly. Now every segregationist in the state knew Lake was the NAACP's public enemy number one. Kelly Alexander of Charlotte, state president of the NAACP, said that the group would increase its voter registration drives in an effort to defeat Lake. "Dr. Lake's announcement on Tuesday as a candidate for governor presents a far greater threat to equality for the Negro than all other candidates from both parties combined," Alexander said. "The Negro citizens are interested in a candidate who will not review the race question from a deep-rooted segregationist viewpoint but with wisdom and understanding." Alexander said that a segregationist platform was "a grievous violation of Christian justice" and not justified "in this modern age of enlightenment and loudly proclaimed democracy." The Lake-Alexander exchange in the first week of March was just the beginning. Lake would criticize the NAACP in nearly every speech he gave in the campaign.

Lake's entrance also provoked a spasm of activity among the state's editorial writers. Some were pleased. The *Robesonian* in Lumberton was relieved at the temperate tone of Lake's announcement. It praised him for renouncing the support of any person or organization that would seek to create discord between whites and blacks. His candidacy meant resistance to integration would develop as a campaign issue. "But the moderate tone of his announcement offers hope that he will not wage a Faubus-type campaign to stir up and capitalize on racial disagreement," the *Robesonian* wrote. "Taking Lake's statement at face value, it seems possible now that North Carolina may have the most interesting governor's race in many years, without setting the state back that far."

Other newspapers were more alarmed. They praised Lake's concilia-tory tone but feared that his campaign would tear the state apart. The *Winston-Salem Journal* feared that the issue of race now would dominate. "That would be unfortunate, for it would open the door to the kind of smear campaign that Dr. Lake abhors," the *Journal* wrote. Other impor-tant issues might be lost in the fury. The paper urged North Carolinians to use restraint and discuss race without bitterness. The *Charlotte Ob-server* took a similar tone. The paper called Lake "an honorable man." But it feared his campaign would be taken in a dangerous direction by his sup-porters. Lake could deliver a statement on constitutional law that would do credit to former Supreme Court chief justice John Marshall. But, the paper wrote, that would be translated by many and put in terms of lunch counters and the NAACP and "would you like your daughter . . ." That's what happened in the 1950 Senate campaign, the *Observer* said, when one of the state's greatest men was smeared and vilified.

Some editorial writers, without hesitating, thought Lake's candidacy bad for the state. The *Smithfield Herald* said that the Supreme Court had declared school segregation illegal and debating the issue was moot. "These are times for level-headedness," the *Herald* wrote. "Level-headed-ness tells us that the next governor of North Carolina, even if his name is Beverly Lake, will not be able to turn back the clock and strike down the decisions of the U.S. Supreme Court against segregation." Other segrega-tion laws were on the way out. Campaigning against segregation might win votes—but it also could lead to the unproductive, unsuccessful kind of resistance seen in Virginia and Arkansas, the *Herald* wrote. It con-cluded: "Does North Carolina wish to travel that way?"

The conventional wisdom throughout the campaign was that while Lake might change the tone of the campaign, he would not be a threat to win. In July 1959, the *Goldsboro News-Argus* asked the state's newspaper editors, "As of now who do you think is the front-runner for governor?" Nearly one hundred editors replied. Most of them—62 percent—said Terry Sanford. John Larkins was next highest with 15 percent. Malcolm Seawell had 3 percent. Four other candidates were named. Beverly Lake was not mentioned. In a November column, H. W. Kendall, editor of the *Greensboro Daily News*, said that the governor's race was as muddled as North Carolina had seen in years. Sanford, Larkins, and House Speaker Addison Hewlett would run and two others might; he did not mention Lake. In a front-page story in December in the *Daily News*, five possible candidates for governor were mentioned—but not Lake.

Even in early 1960, when Lake was openly considering running, he was not given much of a chance to win or even make the runoff. At the annual Jefferson-Jackson Democratic dinner in February, "[t]here was general agreement that the race issue cannot elect a governor of North Carolina in 1960," the *Charlotte Observer* reported. Lake would not get far with such a campaign in the Piedmont, the central part of the state. He would do better in the east, the paper reported—perhaps enough to deny Sanford and Larkins a majority of votes and force a runoff between those two.

Three days after Lake announced he was running, the *Asheville Citizen-Times* editorialized that Sanford would finish first, with Seawell or Larkins finishing second and Lake probably fourth. As the campaign continued, journalists still did not believe Lake was winning many voters. On May 3, less than a month before the May 28 primary, managing editor Gibson Prather of the *Fayetteville Observer* told a Rotary Club that Lake was drawing some support from some rural areas in the east "but his campaign issue apparently has not drawn the support the Raleigh lawyer expected." Prather reported a recent poll of newspaper editors, showing Sanford and Larkins leading. Also in early May, the *Greensboro Daily News*, in its political notebook column, said that Sanford and Seawell would meet in a second primary, with Sanford the winner. "Smoky room experts" told the paper that despite possible gains in the east, Lake's emphasis on preserving segregation would not work statewide. The column repeated its prediction twice more that month.

Gene Roberts, who covered the campaign for the *News and Observer*, was more cautious. Lake's appeal was unpredictable, reported Roberts, who would become managing editor of the *New York Times*. He wrote, "There is talk that the candidate might get a strong 'silent vote.' And there is talk to the contrary that 50,000 or so vocal supporters are making Lake appear stronger than he actually is." The *Post-Dispatch*, in the small town of Rockingham, was one of the few newspapers that looked at other events in the state and thought Lake could be strong. "If the lunch-down invasions continue, we might predict a second race between Sanford and Lake," the paper wrote in an editorial. "Many a voter will give lip-service to one of the three candidates but come May 28th they'll stick in a ballot for Beverly Lake! This could be a protest against these lunch-counter raids whether they think Lake could do anything about integration, or not."

Black newspapers also thought Lake might run strong. The Raleigh *Carolinian*, which called Lake "the Tar Heel symbol of massive resistance," had heard the talk that Lake could not win. It disagreed. "There is a strong possibility that Lake, riding on the crest of a massive resistance wave, will become a Cinderella fighter capable of wearing his opponents down," it said in an editorial. The *Carolina Times*, the black newspaper in Durham, feared a repeat of the 1950 Graham-Smith contest. It worried that blacks and liberal whites would be complacent, never believing that Lake could win—and that Lake would pull off the upset.

The most authoritative research was conducted by Sanford pollster Louis Harris, and it showed that Lake was not a serious threat. After his first poll in January, Harris conducted a second poll of twelve hundred residents in early April. It showed Sanford with 32 percent, Seawell with 14 percent, Larkins with 13 percent, and Lake with 9 percent. The rest were undecided. The poll showed that most North Carolinians favored segregation or very slow integration. Only 14 percent, however, took a militant stand of all-out opposition to any integration. "While most southerners are still against segregation, they do have some hesitation to place the matter in the hands of an extremist," Harris wrote. "As Beverly Lake becomes better known in North Carolina it does not seem likely at this time that he will make any real inroads on the present position of the other three candidates in the race for governor."

The other candidates thought Lake was formidable. John Larkins knew his campaign was badly wounded. On paper, with his party experience and contacts, Larkins should have been a front-runner. But if, as it's been said, the three most important factors in politics are timing, timing, and timing, Larkins was in trouble, trouble, trouble. He lost his campaign manager just before he announced his candidacy. He planned on getting Governor Hodges' support, and then Malcolm Seawell decided to run. He asked Beverly Lake to be his co-campaign manager—but instead Lake entered the race, dividing the conservative voters that Larkins hoped would be his. Lake also would get the backing of some Wake Forest alumni who would have supported Larkins. "Many of them told me personally that the only reason they supported Dr. Lake was because he had been good to them in school and helped them get through law school, and it was just purely personal loyalty on their part," Larkins said, adding that many did not agree with Lake's hard-line stance on race. Larkins believed Robert Morgan's decision to run Lake's campaign "was purely a matter of personal devotion."

Sanford believed Lake to be a genuine threat. While Sanford said he did not talk privately with Lake in an effort to keep him from running, he said his supporters did. That gives some credence to Lake's claim that "a man high up" in the Sanford campaign offered him a supreme court appointment. The offer could have been made without Sanford's knowledge. Sanford did not believe Lake would run. "I had already pretty well finessed [Lake] out of the race," Sanford said years later. "I thought we were sailing along." Then came Seawell into the race and then Lake. "I knew very well that [Lake's candidacy] was bad, bad news, that we were going to have a racist campaign before it was over," Sanford said.

Racially oriented campaigns were breaking out all over the South, as southerners finally realized the Supreme Court decisions meant changes were coming. Sanford mentioned George Wallace's campaigns for governor of Alabama in 1958 and 1962. In '58, Wallace ran for governor as the more racially moderate Democrat and lost to John Patterson, who accepted the endorsement of the Ku Klux Klan. Wallace promised never to be "out-nigguhed" again. He wasn't. He won in '62 with a hard segregationist campaign. Hard-line segregationists won all over the South. In 1958, Ernest Hollings won in South Carolina, Orval Faubus in Arkansas, and Ernest Vandiver in Georgia. In '59, Ross Barnett won in Mississippi and Jimmie Davis in Louisiana. In '60 Farris Bryant would win in Florida.

With the civil rights movement growing, and with lunch-counter sit-ins spreading across North Carolina nearly every day, perhaps it was inevitable that a candidate would respond to the white backlash. With a campaign focused on the race issue, Sanford thought Lake could be strong. If the other three candidates divided the racially moderate vote and Lake won the hard-line segregationists, Lake would win a high percentage of the vote. Seawell's entry gave Lake an opening. "With four [candidates], Lake thought he could win," Sanford said. He disregarded Louis Harris's low estimate of Lake's strength: "He didn't know about the effects of a racist campaign. It's like a prairie fire." Bert Bennett, his campaign manager, shared Sanford's fear of the race issue. "You never knew from that silent voter that might look at you and you'd think were for you," Bennett said. While polls looked good, Bennett said, "They might lie to the polls." And if a voter lied to a pollster, he probably was voting for Beverly Lake.

Lake was different than the other candidates. Sanford, Larkins, and Seawell were established political figures. Lake had served briefly on the Wake Forest town board, but that was a far less partisan political experience than serving as chairman of the state Democratic Party or running a U.S. Senate campaign. When it came to campaigning, Lake was a novice. And now he was running for the highest office in the state. He was a middle-aged, Old South gentleman with a formal manner. Though loved by his former students, he could be stiff, especially in public. Once his son Beverly was talking with a friend who knew Dr. Lake. "You won't believe what I saw," the friend said. "I saw your dad cutting the grass." "He does that all the time," said Lake Jr. "But," the friend said, "he was in a three-piece suit."

Early in the campaign, Lake went to visit one of his supporters, a former student named John Burney, who was then the local prosecutor in the coastal city of Wilmington. Lake arrived wearing a Homburg hat, a felt hat with a soft crown and shallow, slightly rolled brim. Burney, an experienced campaigner and strong extrovert, took Lake behind a nearby ice factory and gave Lake a lesson in retail politics. Few of Lake's students, who held him in awe, would have dared advise him on anything. But Burney, who later served in the legislature, was an unusual and colorful man. Lake accepted his advice without reservation. They were getting ready to go to Brunswick County and some other rural areas. "He was very stiff," Burney said. He told Lake to get rid of the hat. Burney taught Lake how to meet people on the campaign trail, how to greet them when shaking hands. Burney coached Lake to say, "I'm Beverly Lake. I'm running for governor. What do you need for this area? More promises?" Burney explained: "You got to make them laugh. . . . He was very smart. After about the third stop you'd have thought he had been doing it all his life." Burney gave himself the title "Chairman, Tidewater Committee for Lake" and became one of Lake's key workers.

Lake was a serious person, said Tom Ellis, a Raleigh lawyer who was one of the most active workers in the Lake campaign. "My impression always of Lake was that he was a very intense individual and that he had very little lightness about him," Ellis remembered. "He was very intense on the issues and wrapped up in them." Reporters often wrote that Lake did not look like a politician. They said he was stiff and awkward. Lake was balding and dressed conservatively. He was on the small side—about five feet, eight inches tall and 160 pounds. He didn't smile much. He was often described as aloof, although quick to shake hands. He often seemed ill at ease. "I thought being out on the campaign trail was something he had to do but was something he didn't really enjoy much," said Joe Doster, who covered the campaign for the *Charlotte Observer*. "He was polite. He didn't kid around any. He never made any little jokes that I could recall. Very serious. . . . There was a little courtliness about him."

Gene Roberts of the *News and Observer* reported that Lake grew far more relaxed and comfortable as he campaigned more. In a swing through

Wake County in late May, Roberts wrote that Lake campaigned like an old pro. Earlier in the campaign, Lake was reserved when campaigning. On this jaunt through the towns of Garner, Rolesville, and Knightdale, Lake moved smoothly through stores in a counter-by-counter appeal for votes. He was relaxed and spoke easily with voters. "Mighty glad to see you. Pleasure to meet you," Lake said to shoppers and merchants. Sometimes he added, "I'll appreciate any support you can give me in Saturday's election."

In Rolesville, near his hometown of Wake Forest, Lake provoked laughter when he lifted his foot and pointed to a hole in his shoe. "I've just about wore out my car in the campaign and now my shoes are going," he said. A supporter flapped his arms against his side and crowed: "It's like Adlai Stevenson." While meeting voters and shaking hands, Lake did not mention his opposition to integration. Still, in Wake Forest, a carpenter said loudly, "When he's talking against the NAACP, he's saying what I feel." A plumber in Rolesville said, "Dr. Lake says he's against this here integration, so I'm for him." Beverly Lake Jr. said that his father grew to like one-on-one campaigning. "It became natural to him once he realized he wasn't in the classroom or the courtroom," Lake Jr. said.

Lake knew little about running a statewide campaign and Morgan, his campaign manager, had never run one. Unlike Sanford's campaign, which had been planned for years, Lake's campaign was built as it unfolded. "I was the rankest amateur in politics who ever ran for public office in North Carolina," Lake said later. "We ran that campaign on a shoestring, from my [law] offices. . . . We had a lot of volunteer workers. I think we had three ladies who were paid. We never did get a newspaperman [a publicity director] because we didn't have the money. We had no county organization. We started completely from scratch." Morgan had run his campaigns for the legislature, but those were local efforts. "I didn't know anything about running [statewide] campaigns—raising money, advertising," Morgan said. "We ran it like I had been running my state Senate races." Tom Ellis said that it was a campaign of political rookies. "There was no expertise. I had zip," said Ellis, who later would become a top strategist for U.S. senator Jesse Helms. Beverly Lake Jr. said, "The whole campaign was an amateur campaign. We didn't have any professionals at all."

Jack Bailey and John Lewis of Rocky Mount, who attended the meeting in which Bailey's father wrote a ten thousand dollar check for Lake, became key workers in northeastern North Carolina, along with their friend Bruce Peacock. Bailey described their network of supporters as a "loosely formed organization of amateurs that had not been involved in political circles before." Lewis said, "The bulk of the people supporting Lake were doing so on principle. Most of them had no experience in politics. . . . We were learning as we were going. That was my first political experience. I think the strength of Lake's campaign was while he didn't have the big money [and] the big names, the people that were for him were for him on principle and because they believed in him were willing to work."

Among Lake's supporters was Jesse Helms, then executive director of the North Carolina Bankers Association. Helms did not work actively in the campaign but he supported Lake. Helms, who attended Wake Forest College, met Lake there and admired him, first as a professor, then as a candidate. "Like countless others, I admired Dr. Lake's intellect and his courage in speaking out," Helms said in 1998. "There may have been times when I didn't agree with him but I don't remember one. . . . Of course, Dr. Lake quite properly doubted the wisdom of such things as forced busing, forced integration and other such federal actions that created animosity on both sides. They have, in my judgment, proved to have been unwise."

Helms and Lake became friends. In 1972, Helms asked Lake to support his first bid for the U.S. Senate; Lake agreed to do so. Helms, who was then working as an editorialist for WRAL-TV, asked Lake if he would speak to the station's owner about releasing him from his contract so he could run. The station was owned by Lake's former law partner, A. J. Fletcher. Lake agreed to talk to Fletcher, who allowed Helms to run. Helms then won the first of five terms in the U.S. Senate. "I have known Dr. Lake for a long time," Helms wrote to a supporter in 1988. "I have observed and admired his illustrious career when he constantly, often almost alone, defended the highest principles of this nation. He is a man of incredible courage; he is brilliant; he is dedicated. And he has served his state and nation well. Dr. Lake is a totally moral man."

Helms had a friend in the Lake campaign in Tom Ellis. They worked together on the Willis Smith campaign in 1950. Jack Bailey, who would later serve as Helms's campaign treasurer, said he met Helms through the Lake campaign. Bailey was in the business of supplying promotional materials. He had Lake signs attached to his car. When he and Helms parked near each other at a business convention in Pinehurst, Helms introduced himself to Bailey. "You and I got something in common. I like the bumper signs on your car," Helms said, according to Bailey. "You and I will probably be the only two people here who will admit they are for him."

Decades after the 1960 campaign, Helms said he had no role in it. "I don't even recall attending any rally involving Dr. Lake," Helms said. Several Lake supporters remembered Helms on the fringes of the Lake campaign, lending his support in small ways. "Jesse Helms came out of the Lake campaign. Helms was involved to a certain extent in Dad's campaign," said Beverly Lake Jr. Roy Parker, who covered the campaign for the News and Observer, said he attended a rally at which Helms introduced Lake. "Jesse was pouring it on, giving them the old pulpit speech," said Parker, who became a longtime adversary of Helms. Helms said he never introduced Lake. Helms did attend at least one Lake event. On the night of the May primary, Helms was photographed standing near Lake as Lake addressed hundreds of supporters.

The campaign was run out of the Fletcher and Lake law offices in Raleigh. It was built around Lake's former Wake Forest students, people like Robert Morgan and John Burney. While those were capable people, they didn't give the Lake campaign a large base of supporters. The campaign, perpetually short of cash, relied on guerrilla campaigning and innovative tactics to get as much punch as it could for its limited dollars. For several weeks, the campaign bought fifteen minutes of daily air time in the morning on WRAL radio in Raleigh. John Burney and Tom Ellis broadcast what they called "Radio Free North Carolina" and told listeners why they should support Lake. The show opened with the sound of a bell ringing—the Liberty Bell, according to the announcer. "It came on early in the morning," Ellis remembered. "We'd go to bed late, working on the campaign, and get up about half asleep and go over and talk to one another about the campaign and tell as many stories as we could about what was going on in the campaign." Each day, the show would have an unnamed mystery guest. One day the mystery guest was Burney, and he was interviewed by Ellis. The next day the mystery guest was Ellis, and he was interviewed by Burney. And then they would switch again.

Lake supporters organized bus trips throughout eastern North Carolina. They would rent a bus and travel to a town in advance of a Lake rally, trying to build interest and support. Sometimes there weren't many people on the bus. When they got to the town, they would run from window to window in the bus, ringing cowbells, trying to make it look as if the bus were full. "The paper would report a busload of people came through Elizabeth City and there wouldn't be four to five people on the bus," Jack Bailey said. "That's how naive we were. But it worked." They would drive through the hamlets of Murfreesboro and Scotland Neck and Rich Square with a loudspeaker on top of their car, making the case for Lake, sometimes talking to farmers in the fields. They developed a slogan: For Your Children's Sake Vote for Lake. They put it on stickers and yard signs. They kept the trunks of their cars filled with Lake signs and stopped to nail them on trees.

Beverly Lake Jr., who was a law student in Winston-Salem, organized a bus trip through the western and central parts of the state. Lake Jr., ten law school buddies, and their wives or dates traveled in the bus and hit twenty-eight counties in three days. They notified local newspapers before their arrival. Supporters gave them an escort into town. When the group arrived, a three-piece Dixieland band, which traveled with them on the bus for the three days, played "When the Saints Come Marching In." Lake Jr. and his friends would empty off the bus and shake hands. An emcee spoke to the assembled crowd. "Ladies and gentleman," he said, "we bring you greetings from the next governor of North Carolina, I. Beverly Lake." A cheer would rise. "The next governor is not here but we have the next best thing—his son." In Gastonia, the Lake event was interrupted by Sanford supporters, who had a wagon pulled by a donkey, presumably a Democratic donkey. The Lake emcee asked the crowd to note that the Sanford campaign was being pulled by a jackass, the Lake campaign by a Greyhound.

The most effective tactic for the Lake campaign was its televised rallies. John Burney came up with the idea. "I was sitting in my office one day thinking, 'What could I do for Dr. Lake?'" Burney said. "I knew TV was getting to be a red hot thing. I said, 'Why can't it be used in politics like anything else?' I said if you can sell soap, you've got to sell yourself. I went out to Channel 6 here and asked if they'd put on a live television show." The answer was yes. The Lake campaign bought thirty minutes of air time and held a live, televised rally in Wilmington featuring a speech by Lake—which the Lake campaign believed was the first live political rally ever televised in the United States. "When we went on the air that night, we'd never practiced one iota. We just went on," Burney said. It was such a success that Lake held similar televised rallied in other cities. The rallies successfully juxtaposed different eras of politics. The use of television was visionary and a precursor of what was to come in North Carolina, which became a national leader in the 1980s (for better or for worse) for high-dollar, television-saturated campaigns. But the rallies themselves were more reminiscent of the early part of the century, when candidates entertained audiences with arm-waving, high-pitched rhetoric.

The rallies, not all of which were televised, became the trademark of the Lake campaign. Terry Sanford called them "foot-stomping rallies"; he could have called them "Sanford-stomping rallies." Burney, Lake's set-up man, fired up the crowd and worked over Sanford. Then Lake took over. "I gave [Sanford] hell, good political hell," Burney remembered. All of the candidates had criticized Sanford for making too many promises. At one of the televised rallies, Burney bellowed, "They say politics makes strange bedfellows. I do hope Terry Sanford doesn't make any promises in his sleep." The crowd howled.

Burney was a large, hulking orator, an old-fashioned fire-breather. He would lean into the microphone when he spoke. When he delivered his punch line, he would step back, put his hands on his hips, tilt his head back—and listen to the roar of the crowd. He reminded audiences that the "I" in I. Beverly Lake did not stand for integration. "Lake gave us hell," said Sanford aide Roy Wilder. "People like John Burney were so damned good at their work. We'd get calls from our folks—'You've got to do something to stop this, to beat this.' John was a firebrand speaker. He can hold an audience and get them riled up." Bert Bennett, Sanford's campaign manager, also respected Burney's skills. "He could really get the heat on," Bennett said. "He could get the damn crowd stirred up. He could get the shoutin' and the hollerin' and the passing of the hat. He was good at it." Sanford was well aware of Burney. Before Sanford gave a speech in Kinston, the newly crowned Miss Kinston sang for the audience. "We've got the jump on the other crowd," Sanford said. "They haven't got anyone to start their program but John Burney."

The Lake rallies were good theater and stood out in the era of staid Gov. Luther Hodges. They provided a level of political showmanship that the state had not seen for years. Days before the rally, Lake supporters mailed letters and bought newspaper ads intended to draw a large crowd. The site of the rally—sometimes a large barbecue hall, sometimes a courthouse, sometimes an auditorium—was dressed up with pennants, placards, and Dixieland bands. Staunch Lake supporters regularly attended the rallies like avid football fans went to games. Carloads sometimes drove a hundred miles or more to attend. Children attended; they were given balloons that carried the slogan developed by Jack Bailey and John Lewis: "For Your Children's Sake Vote for Lake." At some rallies, Lake supporters marched up and down the aisles, shouting in preparation for the television lights. When the cue came from the cameraman, supporters jumped from their seats and shouted in unison.

An hour before a rally at a tobacco warehouse in Smithfield, southeast of Raleigh, workers found a spot outside the doors. They readied themselves to pass out buttons and Lake for Governor pennants, similar to college football pennants that fans took to games then. Inside the warehouse, campaign posters hung from beams. An eight-piece band began playing thirty minutes before the rally started. Early arrivers drank soft drinks. Suddenly, Lake's procession arrived, escorted by a police car with sirens wailing. Lake stepped from a sleek yellow Cadillac and was quickly surrounded by a cheering group of a hundred supporters. He posed briefly for pictures, then walked into the warehouse as the band played "Dixie." His supporters stood and cheered. They clapped their hands, stomped their feet, and chanted, "We want Lake! We want Lake!"

Before and after the rallies, cars and buses decorated with Lake paraphernalia drove through the streets while supporters yelled to pedestrians. Sometimes buses piped out "Dixie" from loudspeakers. Some of those attending rallies were showmen in their own right. Men sometimes would wear a sandwich sign proclaiming support for Lake. Some loaded their shirts with Lake buttons. A delegation from Craven County converted bumper stickers into headbands at one rally. One man wore campaign buttons in his ears like earrings. A sign painter from Fuquay wasn't to be outdone. He drove to one rally with a blazing red neon sign in the rear window of his car. The sign, which was visible for hundreds of yards, said, "Lake for Governor."

A televised rally in Rocky Mount was particularly successful. Democrats held their state convention in Raleigh on a Thursday in May. That night, the Lake campaign held a rally organized by Jack Bailey and friends. After the convention, hundreds of Democrats on their return to eastern North Carolina stopped at the rally at Josh Bullock's barbecue restaurant, which had the biggest dining room in town and could seat eight hundred to nine hundred people when all its rooms were connected. The dining hall was jammed. People stood in the parking lot and listened on speakers. It was a stroke of genius to hold the rally shortly after the Democratic convention finished. It also was pure luck. "We didn't even know what the Democratic convention was," Bailey said later. He and his cohorts scheduled the rally with no thought of the state convention. Once they learned what the convention was, they went to it and promoted their rally for that night. "It was absolute luck," Bailey said. "Bus load after bus load of folks who had come from all these little towns for the Democratic rally stopped in Rocky Mount for supper on the way home and went to the Lake rally."

Wild-Card Lake

Lake was introduced by John Burney. The TV audience missed most of Burney's warm-up act and instead heard a brief introduction. "And now ladies and gentlemen, after being in Raleigh, North Carolina, today at the state Democratic meeting, and seeing the great enthusiasm and the great demonstration that was witnessed there by the people of North Carolina today for Beverly Lake—we have a great turnout tonight of over a thousand," Burney said. And then he almost shouted: "I now present to you the next governor of North Carolina, the honorable Beverly Lake!" The crowd exploded. For thirty seconds, they clapped and cheered and hollered and stomped. Lake, wearing a white shirt and a dark suit, with a "Lake" ribbon in his left lapel, took the podium, smiling broadly. Behind him was a cinder block wall; over his left shoulder was a sign that said, "I. Beverly Lake for Governor: Take Lake."

Lake seemed genuinely touched by the support. "I want to tell you that this is an experience which Mrs. Lake and I shall treasure for the re- mainder of our lives," he said. "This is a thrilling climax to a wonderful day. . . . I want to tell you tonight some of the things I want to do when I become your next governor, as I am persuaded I shall become your next governor."

Lake did not smile during his thirty-minute address. His head pivoted, turning from side to side to address the wide audience in front of him. He often held the top of the podium with both hands. At most rallies he read from a typed speech, which he wrote himself, but this night he spoke without notes. He never stumbled. He spoke in a flat, determined voice. He was no John Burney but he had a strong command of the language, a forceful delivery, and an earnest style. He used words precisely—perhaps too precisely for a politician, Robert Morgan believed. "Dr. Lake had one fault," Morgan said later. "He used crisp [language]. His language, some- times even in his judicial opinions, was very emphatic. If he was against integration of the schools, he said so and he said so in no mealy mouthed terms. And that caused him a lot of problems. He had that knack of say- ing it in a few words, which causes you a lot of problems sometimes in pol- itics." Allen Bailey, who supported Lake in 1960 and managed his campaign in '64, agreed. "I tried many times to change a paragraph in his speech to present the very same thing he was saying but to present it in a less direct manner," Bailey said. Lake would reject the changes, saying, "That's exactly how I feel. I can't say anything except how I feel."

Lake opened his speech in the heart of tobacco country by talking about helping the small farmer. "The backbone of American independence has always been the independence of the small farmer," Lake said. "And we must preserve, we must cherish and we must encourage that independence in North Carolina." But he presented few specific ideas for helping farmers. He said he would cooperate with the state commissioner of agriculture in working to improve marketing facilities and procedures. He also said he would seek the advice of and cooperate with the leaders of the farm organizations of North Carolina. Although he had just begun his speech, and had broken no new ground, he already had been interrupted by applause five times by the raucous crowd.

The real cheering, however, was just ahead. After his brief comments about farming, Lake leapt into the heart and soul of his message: "I shall take as the major objective of my administration and I shall work on that objective every day throughout my term in my office, the preservation of the present public school system in North Carolina of separate, equal schools for the white and Negro children of this state." Men in white shirts and ties and women in dresses rose to their feet, roaring their applause. Many of them waved Lake signs.

Lake said he would work for more educational opportunities for every boy and girl in North Carolina. Lake said that not long ago he was asked, Mr. Lake, what is your program for the advancement of the colored people of North Carolina? "And I said to that audience as I say to you, I have no special program for the advancement of the colored people of North Carolina, just as I have no special program for the advancement of the white people of North Carolina," Lake said. "My program is for the advancement of all the people of North Carolina." The crowd again applauded loudly. In all, the crowd interrupted Lake with applause twenty-two times.

Lake took a shot at Terry Sanford, although he did not name him. Sanford campaigned on a platform of improving schools. "We have been doing a good job in public education in North Carolina," Lake said, "and I reject the suggestion by one of my opponents in this campaign that the children of this state are now getting a third-class education. The children of North Carolina are going to good schools. We have no apology to make to anyone for our record in public education of white children and of colored children." But he said he was not satisfied and would work to improve schools. He made six proposals, including cutting class sizes to twenty-five students per teacher; giving teachers the same sick leave given to other state employees; providing clerical help to relieve teachers from paperwork; and putting into high schools a more diversified curriculum, including separate curricula in agriculture, the building trades, and business office skills.

Lake did not say how he would pay for those improvements. He said those improvements, and all others in state government, had to be made with a sound fiscal policy. Without naming Luther Hodges. Lake criticized him. Hodges remained one of Lake's favorite targets. "I do not promise to give you a businessman's administration," Lake said, "but I do promise to give you a business-like administration." North Carolina had not been operating in a business-like way in the last four years, he said. A surplus of $53 million was gone. The state collected two years of income taxes in one year. "It has been said that the tax rate in North Carolina has not been increased," Lake said. "Please notice that word rate. No, your income tax rate has not been increased. It's just been applied to you twice."

Lake then circled back and talked about race. The NAACP's opposition to his candidacy was irresistible. Lake reminded the audience that the NAACP's chief spokesman in North Carolina had said that Lake, more than all the other candidates of both parties combined, was opposed to the program of the NAACP. Without a trace of a smile, Lake said, "To the best of my knowledge and belief, that is the only statement that man had ever made with which I am in complete agreement." The crowd roared. Lake remained poker-faced. The NAACP had good reason to oppose him, Lake said. "I have appeared and participated in three separate cases in the United States Supreme Court against that organization at its national level and at its local level," Lake said, "and I have not lost any of them."

He agreed the public schools must be kept open. He would use all the powers of the governor's office to keep them open. But it was not enough to keep schools open, he said. Schools must be effective. Children must be educated. The NAACP program of integration would destroy schools, Lake said. He was the candidate who could best fight the NAACP and, therefore, best preserve the schools.

While he wanted to fight the NAACP, Lake said he did not want to fight the Negro people. "Now I want you, every one of you, tonight and always and I want every person in our television audience to remember always, to distinguish between the NAACP and the Negro people of North Carolina," Lake said. The NAACP was not, he said, a Negro organization; it was an integrated organization. He opposed the NAACP; he didn't oppose progress for the Negro people. "For I favor the advancement of the colored people of North Carolina, just as you do," he said. There was no applause, only a short gap of silence. "The National Association for the Advancement of Colored People is not the North Carolina organization," Lake continued. "It is a New York organization. Its guidance is New York guidance. Its planning for North Carolina is New York planning for North Carolina. And we need no New York planning for North Carolina." The crowd applauded.

But Lake wasn't done with the NAACP. Whites and Negroes had lived in North Carolina for generations as friends and neighbors. "We have worked with our Negro neighbors. We have played as children with our Negro neighbors," Lake said. "We have had mutual helpfulness, mutual respect and neighborliness between the white people and the Negro people of North Carolina. We must not allow this vicious New York organization to drive a splitting wedge between the white people and the Negro people of North Carolina. And if I become your next governor, as I expect to do, I shall use every influence and power of my office to preserve the friendship between the white North Carolinians and the Negro North Carolinians. I shall defend that friendship by seeking to help you drive from North Carolina the NAACP!"

Lake said he believed in the power of public opinion, peacefully expressed but clearly expressed. He would do all that he could to encourage white and Negro public opinion in favor of preserving segregation. That was the foundation of "our whole social order in which both races have advanced together in every way that the advancement of a people can be made." Democracy could survive, he said, but only if the people made it survive. "That's why," he said in closing, "I'm asking you to help me become the next governor of North Carolina."

Lake really was different. North Carolina had not had a major candidate for governor focus on race issues since 1900. What other politicians wouldn't say, Lake addressed up front. All of the major, mainstream white politicians in North Carolina said that they were personally for segregation. But few of them actively fought integration. They might have explored how they could delay as much as possible or integrate as little as possible. But few would tackle the issue head on.

For at least six years, since the Supreme Court's *Brown* decision, southerners had been defensive about preserving segregation. Lake made supporting segregation respectable again. His rallies were celebrations of segregation. His supporters cheered him and cheered his message because he was the best of them. He was smart, successful, religious, generous, and courteous. He was a person of character. He didn't hate black people; he said he wanted to help them. He wasn't like the southern demagogues who spewed a message of hate. He showed that reasonable people could be ardently opposed to integration, his supporters believed. At the rallies, people were proud of Lake and proud that so many others felt as they did. Many, many more would not attend a rally. "There were an awful lot of people who were supportive of Dr. Lake but did not want to have their name identified with the segregation part of the campaign," Jack Bailey said. As Lake headed into the thick of the primary, that was the unresolved question that would determine the governor's race: How many silent Lake supporters were out there?

Chapter 5

SHOOTING AT SANFORD

Compared to Lake's rallies, which were colorful and boisterous, Sanford's were sedate. He was not entertaining in front of large audiences and it could be difficult to get a crowd fired up when your central message was about improving schools—a far less visceral message than Lake's. But Sanford was determined to own the issue of making schools better and the January poll from Louis Harris showed he had work to do. Just as he had methodically planned his campaign for years, he now set out to capture the voters' attention on education. In his persistent, determined style, Sanford spoke on the issue at every chance.

About three weeks after he announced his candidacy, he addressed a Women for Sanford group in Greensboro in late February and laid out his proposal for improving education. The speech was painfully vague in some areas. "I haven't any final answers," he said. He would continue to seek advice from parents, school administrators, teachers, and interested citizens. While Sanford didn't always have a clear vision of how to improve public schools, he knew improving them was his first priority. He didn't think the state had concentrated on making schools better in the 1950s and he wanted to change that.

That made him different. All candidates were in favor of better schools. But Sanford was rare, at least in the South, in the emphasis he placed on improving schools and his bluntness in saying the state was not spending enough on education. Cynics contended that the state's industrialists, who had dominated the state's politics for most of the century, did not want the masses too educated—only enough to operate their plants, factories, and mills, and to be content with that. Sanford had a different view of public school education—that it was more than preparing the elite for college. It was about allowing each student, of all races and economic classes, to develop to his or her full potential.

In his Greensboro speech, Sanford started with three principles. Two of them were so shallow, so undeveloped, it was difficult to tell what Sanford meant. He called for "a long-range program" involving planning ten years ahead. He didn't elaborate. Few could argue that the people who run public schools should plan. But what were they planning? For growth in enrollment? For updating textbooks and curricula? Sanford didn't say. He also called for "quality education." He defined quality as meaning "our children are educated, not just trained. Quality, which means our boys and girls can compete with the product of any school system. Quality, which means that the mind has the fullest growth." This was more platitude than policy. Who would argue against quality education?

His third principle was more substantive: "The responsibility of public education is primarily a state responsibility. I am opposed to shoving it off on the counties or cities. I am opposed to sitting around doing nothing and inviting the federal government to take over." That principle was significant and reflected Sanford's let's-get-after-it personality. Was the state going to sit around while its schools foundered and its wages lagged and the Russians shot Sputnik into space? Or was it going to get moving and do something? When he announced his candidacy in Fayetteville, he said it was a New Day with "a quickening of interest in public schools, with parents and other citizens not content with mediocrity." He was staking his campaign on the belief that voters, when it came to education, were willing to be bold.

He told the Greensboro audience that North Carolina needed more and better teachers; more rewards for teachers, possibly through private endowments; smaller classes; and more respect from the public. And, unlike most candidates, he backed it up by saying he would be willing to raise taxes to pay for it. North Carolina simply wasn't spending enough on its schools, he said. On average, states and their local governments spent $340 per student. North Carolina and its local governments spent $220 per student. "We are not doing the job because we are not spending enough," Sanford said. "All the talk about improved schools is hollow indeed if your candidate fails to mention the generally unpleasant subject of money. In this case, it is probably not so unpleasant because I believe people are eager to pay for quality education."

He continued to build his case for spending more: Good men and women were leaving teaching every month because the pay was too low. Young teachers, educated in North Carolina often at taxpayer expense, were leaving the state to teach where the salaries were higher. Salaries for career teachers were "extremely inadequate." It all built to this: "I would not be honest if I did not promise that, if revenues are inadequate, I will have the courage to recommend to the General Assembly and the people proper sources. This is fundamental."

Sanford traveled the state, delivering the same message, never wavering from his willingness to raise taxes to improve schools. He told Young Democrats at the University of North Carolina, "It includes the realistic admission that more money will be needed, and it includes the promise that I have the courage to ask for it." At a candidates' forum in Albemarle, Sanford said he would "have the courage to ask for new and additional sources of revenue . . . to make education the first consideration of state government and not the second or third or fourth. We cannot wait generation after generation for per capita income to be lifted. . . . We cannot wait until some time in the vague future when we have enough money." At a press conference in Raleigh, he said, "If we have got to have money to get out of the basement, let's have the courage to recommend sources to the legislature." At Davidson College, Sanford told students, "Education is going to cost a lot of money. It will come from taxes. I want a long-range program. We cannot hold the reins any longer. Everybody is for it but the question is who is going to fight for it."

When Sanford talked openly about his willingness to raise taxes, he was disregarding the advice of his pollster. Louis Harris found North Carolina voters willing, reluctantly, to raise taxes to make public schools better. Even so, Harris urged Sanford to steer clear of the finances and talk instead of the need to make schools better. He strongly advised Sanford not to talk about raising taxes: "People don't like to be reminded of the unpleasant part of the task but rather of the rich rewards. . . . Above all, do *not* talk in terms of higher taxes for schools."

But from the first time Sanford mentioned the possibility of raising taxes—when Bert Bennett joked that the audience thought he said *Texas*—he believed he was winning votes with the issue. "I always got applause," Sanford remembered. "I felt very confident that the people understood that if we wanted to do what we had to do, we also had to have the honesty to pay for it. . . . We were talking about opportunities of education for everybody, not just for the people that were college-bound to the liberal arts universities. This rang a true bell. People understood it. Their children were involved and they'd seen children not have an opportunity to develop their talents. It was a great issue. It was *the* issue. It was a genuine issue."

The gamble on taxes showed a side of Sanford that would emerge periodically throughout the campaign and his term as governor: He would take risks. Not wild risks, but calculated gambles. "Terry was a risk taker," Robert Morgan, Lake's campaign manager, said years later. "When you advocate [raising] the food tax, even if it was for the purpose of education, it took a lot of courage." Sanford thought many politicians and leaders were too cautious, too conservative. "While you don't stir up as many enemies, you don't develop as many enthusiastic friends by taking that cautious, middle-of-the-road thing, and it just never suited my nature," he said a decade after the campaign. "I've always been a 51 percent man, and thought that if we could move as far as we could and still carry 51 percent, that was the responsibility of leadership."

Sanford did more than advocate his proposals. He attacked the status quo, criticizing those who would do nothing. He called them "hold the liners," an expression Kerr Scott used, and he seemed to be including Governor Hodges. The state's political establishment talked a good game about improving education, Sanford said, but it did not deliver. "These people have the attitude that if you put your first emphasis on building up the state economically, then you will be in the position of doing something for education," Sanford said while campaigning. "But in the meantime, they want our education program to hold the line at minimum requirements. . . . Education must come first. A boy or girl from North Carolina cannot grow up with a bare minimum of learning and lead this state in the economic competition, which is so stiff in this scientific, technical, atomic age."

In another speech, Sanford bluntly criticized hold-the-liners who had "wrecked legislation in the General Assembly which was designed to improve our education. . . . Their program is to provide a place for our children to spend some time and, if they can get a good education by some chance, then all the better. They haven't the slightest intention of doing any more for education than hold the line. They didn't do anything in the past. Their friends haven't done anything. Their supporters haven't done anything. There has never been a better example of wolves in sheep's clothing." In case there was any doubt that he considered Hodges a hold-the-liner, Sanford clarified. The Hodges administration, Sanford said, "has not moved with the same kind of vision in the field of education for our children that it has used in bringing in new industry." Sanford expanded his criticism to Hodges' Highway Commission, which he said was "stubborn, cold, unfeeling, impersonal, mechanical and foolish."

In attacking Hodges, Sanford hoped one of the by-products would be to rally Kerr Scott's old followers. The Branch Head Boys had never had much in common with the "Businessman Governor," and when he named Everett Jordan to fill Senator Scott's seat, Hodges alienated more of them. Louis Harris had warned in January that the Scott people were not for Sanford as much as expected. In February, when he traveled the state and met with supporters, campaign manager Bert Bennett also found that Sanford was not doing well with Scott's supporters. Bennett took notes during his meetings. "Need to get branchhead boys organized; several say we do not have the grassroots support in this area that we thought we had," Bennett wrote during one meeting in eastern North Carolina. "Whitfield says not enough of the branchhead boys know who

Terry Sanford is and that he had any connection with Scott." Bob Scott said that his father's rural followers never felt completely comfortable with the more urbane Sanford. He didn't chew tobacco. He had a sense of humor, but it was based on his sophisticated, quick wit and wasn't like Kerr Scott's more blunt, salt-of-the-earth guffaws. In personality and style, Sanford was just different than the Squire from Haw River.

If Sanford wanted to provoke Hodges, he succeeded. Hodges said he would remain neutral unless his administration was attacked, although Sanford, Larkins, and Lake never thought he was neutral to begin with. At his weekly press conference in mid-April, six weeks before the Democratic primary, Hodges praised Seawell and criticized Sanford. "I like the way that candidate Seawell has the courage to speak out favorably on some of the things we are trying to do for the people of North Carolina. I wish others would do likewise," Hodges said. Asked to comment about Sanford's criticism of his Highway Commission, Hodges said, "I think in this case Mr. Sanford has gone a little too far. He is becoming impatient either with himself or with his campaign." Sanford had said the state should pave all unpaved school bus routes; Hodges said he was promising too much. Sanford backtracked from his criticism, saying Hodges was not a hold-the-liner.

Sanford asked women to play the major role in pushing for school improvements. He thought women generally were more idealistic and would have the passion to make better schools the state's top priority. They were more concerned about children and more likely to be frustrated about weak education, Sanford believed. The Sanford campaign aggressively assembled Women for Sanford groups across the state. In the 1950s, women generally played supportive roles in campaigns. Sanford was unusual in his eagerness to listen to what women had to say. He ran an inclusive campaign, a practice that would become more typical in the 1970s, '80s, and '90s, but one that was rare in 1960. Women, blacks, young people—Sanford included all in his campaign, ignored the stereotypes, and talked to them with respect. That was smart politics but it also reflected his personal values. The respect he gave people from all walks of life was perhaps Sanford's most endearing quality and the one that most set him apart

118

from the politicians of his era. Martha McKay of Chapel Hill organized women for the Sanford campaign and was included among Sanford's inner circle of advisers. "There was nothing going on then [in politics] about including women," McKay remembered. "But Terry never used people. If I was going to help, I was going to help. I was going to be part of it. So I was." She was one of about twenty women who helped develop Sanford's education platform and produced Sanford's pamphlet on improving schools.

McKay and her volunteers did much of the grunt work of the campaign, organizing committees, licking stamps and envelopes, and writing letters. They used every mailing list they could find, including their own Christmas card lists. "We flooded the state with letters to our friends," McKay said. Kays Gary of the *Charlotte Observer*, in an assessment of the candidates' strength in Mecklenburg County, said Sanford had what appeared to be "the most energetic and massive volunteer organization in local primary history." In almost every residential area, ranging from lower middle class to the wealthiest, Gary said that it was difficult not to find "a housewife who ha[d] just been or [was] going to a neighborhood coffee for Sanford. They're in his 'Education Crusade.'" McKay said, "As far as we were concerned, it really was a crusade. We were just wrought up, to say the least, about the situation in public schools." Sanford spoke to Women for Sanford groups in Elizabeth City, Goldsboro, Greensboro, Charlotte, and Asheville. He said that they would determine whether the state improved its schools. "You women," he said, "are the only people who can save the situation."

Sanford's three opponents attacked him for his willingness to tax and spend. John Larkins was astounded that Sanford would campaign on a platform of raising taxes. While Sanford's speaking style was boring, Larkins thought his message revolutionary. In previous years, some successful candidates for governor championed exempting certain products from the sales tax. Sanford was campaigning on a pledge that he would consider *adding* taxes. "It is amazing that the people of North Carolina would turn around in 1960 and support a man" advocating taxes, Larkins said later. "Things have a way of turning around." At an event in Elizabeth City, Larkins called Sanford "Terrible Tax Terry," a nickname that stuck. He also called him "High Tax Terry" and "Tall Talking Terry."

Larkins and Seawell routinely criticized Sanford for promising more than he could deliver. Larkins said that higher taxes could hurt efforts to bring new businesses to the state. Sanford endorsed the program of the United Forces for Education, a coalition of seven groups, including those representing parents, teachers, and school boards. In return, the United Forces endorsed Sanford. The United Forces plan would increase annual state spending by $45 per student at a cost of about $50 million a year. While Sanford said he would be willing to raise taxes if needed to pay for school improvements, he was vague about which taxes and how much they would need to be raised. When pressed by reporters, Sanford dodged: "I don't see how anybody can intelligently discuss that until we have a better idea of what revenue we are going to have."

Seawell repeatedly attacked his old friend Sanford. At a televised forum in April, Seawell said that it wasn't time for Sanford's New Day in education but instead for continuation of progress. "It seems that every four years someone invents public education," he said, adding that the public schools were doing a good job. On another occasion, Seawell said Sanford seemed to be suggesting that North Carolina had a second- or third-rate educational system. "His insinuation discredits the fine efforts of thousands of dedicated persons. . . . [It] simply reveals how little he knows about the problem or that he is committed to a campaign of trying to hoodwink the people with ridiculous promises." He said that Sanford's refusal to say where the money would come from was irresponsible. Seawell said that he was sympathetic to the United Forces program but that it could not be enacted without new taxes, and that money alone would not solve the schools' problems. Sanford took the high road: "I have always heard that if you didn't have a program of your own you had better attack the other fellow." He would stick to his program.

Lake didn't criticize Sanford as strongly as the others did, but he disagreed with Sanford's premise that the state first needed to spend more on schools. Lake said too many school problems were blamed on a lack of money. "The primary need is not an outpouring of funds but a revival of learning," Lake said at a candidates' forum. First the state needed to make sure it was spending its money wisely. Another time, Lake said that budget problems would make it difficult for the next governor to do more than hold the line on public school spending.

In early May, less than a month before the primary, Sanford caught a lucky break that shielded him from some of the criticism. Governor Hodges said that new projections showed the state would have about a $30 million surplus at the end of the 1960–61 budget year. Sanford had been saying that the state might be able to pay for school improvements without a tax increase. Hodges' announcement bolstered his claim. The surplus would, Sanford said, "go a long way in financing our school program. There is every reason to believe that future years will continue to give us increasing amounts of revenue. . . . The greatest significance of this report is to indicate how wrong those people are who keep saying that we cannot afford to give our children the education they need."

Hodges' projections were based on new figures for the 1959–60 budget year, which would end on June 30. Through ten months of that year, revenue collections were up 18 percent from the previous year. When that budget year was complete, Sanford predicted revenue would have grown 20 percent from the year before. Other candidates welcomed the news but were more cautious than Sanford. Lake believed the state would have difficulty just maintaining state services at their current levels. Seawell was pleased with the new revenue estimates but said that the surplus still was not enough to pay for the United Forces for Education program, which would cost about $50 million a year. Larkins concurred. There would be enough new money to pay for 15 percent pay raises for teachers, which he advocated. But, he said, there was not enough money to pay for the proposal supported by "High Tax Terry."

At one event attended by three of the Democratic candidates, Sanford drew the first speaking position. Hands outstretched, with palms down in an almost soothing manner, Sanford spoke in tempered tones of a New Day in North Carolina, including the need for his ambitious school program. When the other two candidates rose to speak, they spent much of their time shooting at Sanford's program.

During the primary, and especially in the final month of May, Larkins and Seawell attacked Sanford on a variety of fronts. Their consistent criticism showed they believed Sanford to be the front-runner. Larkins could be jaunty, even silly; one time, he strolled into Durham's city hall, approached a dark-haired secretary and identified himself. "I am looking for the support of black-haired, brown-eyed girls who are pretty," he said. "You qualify." She giggled. He moved on, changing his message as he met blondes and redheads. But he also could be harsh, although colorful, in his criticism. He had served nine terms in the legislature and worked diligently for the Democratic Party for years, attending four national conventions as a delegate. Now he was getting beat by a boyish forty-two-year-old who'd served one term in the legislature. It irked him.

Wild promises had been made, Larkins said. Of Sanford, he said, "One candidate for governor in particular has spent years crisscrossing the state, flinging campaign promises right and left on any and all programs which in his opinion will get a few votes. He knows as well as anybody that most of his promises, particularly those that run into the millions and even up to a half-billion dollars, are pure tommy-rot." In another speech, Larkins said, "Although his moon shots are fizzling on the launching pad, he still is the most promising young candidate you've ever seen." Larkins asked voters if they wanted his experience or a candidate "who, in place of experience, offers us only a big batch of cure-all programs, many of which have dubious merit and all of which are expensive." A poster reflected what Larkins believed was the most important difference between the two candidates. It said, "Why send a boy out to do a man's job—vote for John Larkins."

When a committee of the AFL-CIO labor union recommended Sanford, Larkins went after Sanford again. Union leaders had put a first mortgage on Sanford and if he were elected, they'd collect, he said. Sanford said he was not obligated to labor or anybody else. He blamed that attack on his old nemesis Abie Upchurch, who was an aide to Larkins. Upchurch was Sen. Alton Lennon's publicity director in the 1954 Senate campaign and was involved in distributing copies of the disputed, racially oriented material that ran in the *Winston-Salem Journal*. After Larkins' labor boss attack, Sanford said, "[Upchurch is] the well-known master of the political smear. We can expect sneaky attacks, unsigned leaflets, smears and misleading statements as long as Abe is calling the shots."

Upchurch then hit Sanford where it hurt—questioning his credentials as a Kerr Scott man. Upchurch said he worked for Scott for governor in 1948 and didn't see Sanford anywhere in the campaign. Seawell also picked up on the Sanford-is-no-Kerr-Scott theme. Terry Sanford was no Kerr Scott, a man who really knew the problems of the farmer, Seawell said. Sanford had never picked cotton, primed tobacco, nor sold tobacco on the warehouse floor, as Seawell said he had. Sanford had spent the last twelve years as a lawyer serving big business, Seawell said, while he had spent the last twelve years serving the people as district solicitor, superior court judge, and attorney general.

Lake's Harnett County chairman, lawyer D. K. Stewart, claimed that Sanford did not support Kerr Scott in either the first primary or the runoff primary for governor in 1948. "Oh, if the Squire of Haw River could see Terry Sanford now," Stewart said. "Fair-haired Terry of the triple tongue—all things to all people as long as the people vote and pay—has now turned his back on all the things Kerr Scott stood for. . . . The Squire was a conservative man; Terry Sanford is acting like a wild man in his desperate search for votes. . . . No indeed friends, as a loyal supporter of Kerr Scott—I voted for him and worked for him—I can tell you that Terry Sanford today is no true disciple of Kerr Scott."

The question of whether Sanford supported Kerr Scott when he ran for governor in 1948 was a sore spot for Sanford. He never said during the campaign whom he supported that year. Sanford owed his political career to Scott for choosing him to manage his Senate campaign. "Terry always said if it hadn't been for Kerr Scott, he'd still be a lawyer in Fayetteville," said reporter Roy Parker. In a 1976 interview, Sanford said he had worked for gubernatorial candidate Mayne Albright, a fellow World War II veteran, in the first primary in 1948. But he did not say if he was involved in the runoff between Charlie Johnson and Kerr Scott. His silence almost surely meant he did not support Scott. But it would have been embarrassing for Sanford, who for years had hitched himself so tightly to Scott, to admit that he did not support Scott in 1948.

Seawell also said that Sanford was making pie-in-the-sky promises. Sanford's proposals, he said, would almost double state taxes. "Sanford and I have a complete departure in our way of thinking," Seawell said. Indeed they had. They had been friends before the primary, but Seawell attacked relentlessly, in a biting, personal manner, all the way until the May 28 primary. They would never be allies again, as Sanford once thought they would. On the eve of the primary, Seawell said, "Never in the history of North Carolina have so many asked to do so much for one who has done so little for North Carolina." Seawell said that Sanford served one term in the state senate and did nothing then for education or farmers.

Sanford was witty and clever. He enjoyed taking his opponents' criticism and turning it back at them. To respond to the pie-in-the-sky charge, Sanford's campaign rolled out a huge apple pie, sliced it and served it to Young Democrats on the lawn of the Wake County courthouse. If it's pie in the sky, Sanford said, North Carolina should start cooking. "The thing that is worse than pie in the sky is talent hidden in the ground," Sanford said. "The children of this state can't wait." If Sanford was scathed by the attacks from Larkins and Seawell, he didn't act like it. He stayed calm and stuck to his message about improving schools. He pointed out that he had been accused of being a corporate lawyer and a tool for union bosses. "If you average out those statements, you'll find me safely in the middle," he said. He had been accused of being a Kerr Scott man and of not being a Kerr Scott man. "It looks to me," Sanford said, "like they're all mixed up."

Sanford believed voters wanted a candidate who looked, talked, and acted like a governor. He was confident in himself and confident he would win. He had worked on becoming governor for so long that he believed all the other candidates merely pretenders. That they tried to tear him down showed they were not fit for the office. "I've been running for governor, not against my opponents," he said in one TV commercial. He had not talked about personalities, not talked of smears and half truths.

"That's in keeping with the high office I'm seeking," he said. "I pledge to carry on that kind of campaign until the time of election."

As he sat at a table at a campaign event, listening to speakers, campaign manager Bert Bennett had a question for Sanford, who was sitting nearby. Margaret Rose Sanford had called and left word that Sanford needed to come home to Fayetteville and spend time with her and their two young children—Betsy, eleven, and Terry Jr., who turned eight during the primary campaign. Bennett scribbled on a napkin, "Terry, what makes you stay in this business?" Sanford wrote quickly and pushed the napkin back to Bennett: "To keep the sons of bitches out."

Sanford campaigned with zeal, almost maniacally. He hit nearly every county (he missed one or two) before he even announced his candidacy in early February, and then he traveled to all one hundred counties in the primary. During the primary campaign, from January through June, he would visit his law office once and his home about a dozen times. His campaign staff estimated he shook forty thousand hands. He shook so many hands in January, when he was traveling the state before his announcement, that a large blister bloomed between his right thumb and forefinger. It was purple at first, then black, then brown. It went away in February but returned in March. In the month before the May 28 primary, he had a long, red callus that began midway up his forefinger and extended to his thumb.

One Saturday in early May, Sanford shook an estimated two thousand hands in a long day of campaigning. In that frenzied tour of Wake County, Sanford covered 157 miles—147 riding and 10 walking—to visit thirteen towns and communities. He started before 7 A.M. In Zebulon, a sound truck blaring music led a caravan of Sanford cars into town. Campaign workers jumped from cars to hand out literature. Sanford reached for the hand of Rella Privette. She was holding groceries but worked a hand free to greet Sanford. Robert Perry, a farmer, got to Sanford next. "I'm pulling for you," he said.

In Rolesville, supporters waited for Sanford under the shade of a filling station shed. A man wanted to be the first to greet Sanford. He walked, with his cane, into the sun. "I've been reading after you," he said. "You just take off where Mr. Scott left off. I thought a whole heap of him." All during the day, a Sanford worker muttered, "We gotta keep on schedule." In Holly Springs, E. M. Paxton, eighty-four, said that Sanford sent him a letter in November but forgot to put a stamp on it. "They made me pay the four cents postage," he said. Sanford roared. He reached into the his pocket for some money but came up empty. A supporter loaned him a nickel, which he gave to Paxton. "That's a penny extra for interest," Sanford said. At the end of the twelve-hour day, only his reddened right hand showed the wear and tear of a full day on the trail. "I would keep on going," he said, "if I thought the press could keep up with me." Sanford smiled and laughed. His tie was straight.

Sanford aide Tom Lambeth often drove him. Once Sanford thought Lambeth, a cautious driver, was traveling too slowly in his secondhand, mid-1950s Ford Fairlane. "Pull over," Sanford said. He took the wheel and drove furiously. Lambeth did not think his car would last the trip, much less the campaign. Sanford wore out one car during the primary, Lambeth said. Woody Teague of Raleigh, who organized about ten counties for Sanford, said that throughout the campaign Sanford would get up at 6 A.M. and work until midnight. "He had fire in his belly," Teague said.

Sanford believed politicians needed to be tough and part of that toughness meant having great stamina. "Politics is a tough game," he said later. "People are throwing arrows and daggers and javelins at you all the time. You've got to certainly stand up to that. And I think not only tough in the sense of having a tough skin and not being thrown off course by that kind of an attack, I think toughness means willingness to go day and night. I think it means if I've got to see that person . . . that I have to go all night and see him and be back here in the morning for an 8 o'clock meeting, I'll do it. That kind of toughness."

Sanford paid attention to detail. He prepared. "He was an indefatigable worker," said supporter Martha McKay. Sanford was an early riser. Once McKay, who had three children, complained she did not have enough time to do something. He advised her to get up at four o'clock and work on it. "He was telling me to do what he did," McKay said. "He carefully looked at every element of a campaign or a trip or anything else he should look at. He planned and strategized."

Once, on his way to campaign at a tobacco market, Sanford stopped in Rock Ridge in Wilson County to pick up a young supporter, North Carolina State College graduate student Jim Hunt. After campaigning indoors, Sanford, Hunt, and some other supporters got back in Sanford's car. After driving a block, Sanford said that they needed to stop. "I called that fella the wrong name," he said, according to Hunt. "I know his name. I'm going to go back and call him by the right name." Sanford went back and spoke with the man. Then he and his entourage drove off. "That was the kind of attention to detail" that Sanford paid in building a campaign, said Hunt. "Most people would never pay attention to that detail. He planned his county organizations carefully. He knew the people, he went to them, he worked hard. Frankly, it's the kind of model I've used in my own efforts as I built an organization in every county in North Carolina. Having those friends—they know you, they'll stand up for you."

Through Sanford's religious, civic, and political connections—the Methodist church, the Jaycees, his legislative friends, Young Democrats, the Kerr Scott people, University of North Carolina friends, World War II veterans—he knew an amazing number of people across the state. Robert Morgan later said, "Terry Sanford has more people that he can get on the telephone tonight and say, 'How about getting out yonder tomorrow and helping Bob Morgan' than any other man." He studied people and knew their connections. Reporter Roy Parker said, "Terry knew the providence of every politician you ever saw—who he'd been for, who'd been for him, who could push him."

Yet as hard as Sanford worked, he never seemed to show it. He was stocky—five feet, eleven inches tall and about 190 pounds—with sandy hair, an easy smile, and a boyish, round face with dimples. He looked people in the eye. "I can see by the look and the facial expression whether I have their votes," he said during the campaign. He was friendly but a bit detached. "He was cool. He was the kind of person that was cool under fire," said Doris Cromartie of Charlotte, an active volunteer who often campaigned with Sanford. "You didn't stump him. Most of the time he took long enough to think about what he said. He seemed to value the opinions of the people around him, particularly Bert [Bennett]. You never needed to be intimidated to tell him what you thought. . . . He was quite a wit and great to work with." Sonny Boy Joyner drove Sanford from town to town in the northeast, stopping at filling stations and drugstores. "Sanford was not the type of fella who would throw his hand up [when talking]. He wasn't one of those fast-talking politicians," Joyner said. "There was something in that handshake that people liked. He was easy going. He was smooth."

Sanford rarely stumbled or found himself in a situation he didn't handle well. His friend Clint Newton remembered one of those rare occasions. Sanford was at a political event in the east when a man walked up, escorting a woman on his arm. "Mother," the man said, "I want you to meet Terry Sanford." Sanford thought he would flatter her. "You don't look old enough to be his mother," he said. "I'm not," she said. "I'm his wife." Sanford was embarrassed. Later he said to Newton, "Damn a man who calls his wife 'Mother.'"

That was a rare slipup. Raymond Goodman, the sheriff in Richmond County, organized his county for Sanford. One night, in the heat of the primary, Sanford visited his house. "There was such a fight going on, I wondered how he could be so cool," Goodman said. "He was cool and polished. He did everything right, in my book. He'd come across as a friendly, good person. People had a lot of confidence in Terry Sanford." Bill Staton of Lee County had known Sanford for more than ten years. "Terry had an unusual ability," Staton said. "He could get under great pressure and unless you knew him real well, you did not know he was under pressure. He had the ability to take it and make it calm and easy. He was excellent with people one on one. He was an extremely good campaigner one on one." Hoover Adams, editor of the Dunn *Daily Record*, supported Lake. But he liked Sanford's style. "He was never a vindictive sort," Adams said. "He was always calm, collected and unruffled. He had a great personality and he was just a great guy."

Aide Tom Lambeth never saw Sanford lose his temper. At one event, Sanford stood before a blackboard in a building in a rural community and described his program. "If I had a piece of chalk," Sanford said, "I could show you on the blackboard." Unsolicited, Lambeth spotted some chalk and piped up, "Here's some chalk." Sanford then was obligated to write on the blackboard, which he did. Later, Sanford said to Lambeth, "If I want some chalk, I'll ask for chalk." Said Lambeth, "That's as close to being sharp as I can ever remember him being."

Sanford had a knack for sleeping in the car for thirty minutes or so and appearing refreshed at the next stop. "He was always fresh," said Bert Bennett. "In the campaign, they don't give a damn if you've got a cold or you're catching hell at home or if the children are doing this or that. He was always there. He was a tough campaigner and always in good shape." Sanford said he tried to stay relaxed and never had any trouble sleeping. "During the campaign, when we'd just move out of a tense situation, I'd drive to relax," he said. "Mostly I was driven, though, because I spent a lot of time in the car sleeping or going over correspondence." Sanford enjoyed politicking. Ever since he was a young boy in Laurinburg he liked to get out and meet people. He liked making a first impression. While some candidates found campaigning distasteful and did it out of obligation, Sanford reveled in it. "He loves it," Bennett said. "And he works at it. And he had that knack. . . . a good nose for it." He brought into the campaign many people who had never been involved in politics before, Bennett said.

Sanford was an unusual political amalgamation—part old school pol, part cutting-edge visionary. He could drink bourbon with the boys after a day of hunting and he could talk with college-educated women about preparing school children for a new era of technology and change. Those different sides of Sanford were reflected in two of his leading campaign men—Ben Roney and Bert Bennett.

Roney, from Rocky Mount, was Kerr Scott's administrative assistant in Washington. He was a hard-living, backroom deal maker who lived for politics and knew eastern North Carolina better than any man alive— "[A] political genius," said Bob Scott. Roney was uncouth, often intentionally, and had a habit of calling his friends at 2 A.M. "He was a tough, hard-nosed, profane drinking guy whose every moment asleep or awake was politics," said his friend Roy Wilder. "He was unpopular with his enemies and a man popular with the folks on his side. Ben—he knew a hell of a lot of people. He knew where the bodies were." Bert Bennett, a successful Winston-Salem businessman, was Roney's opposite. He had been chairman of the Democratic Party in Forsyth County but had not had a leading role in a statewide campaign. "Bert Bennett, like Terry, was very inclusive," said Martha McKay. "He was not given to any kind of histrionics or show-off. He was calm, quiet, but very businesslike, very smart, a very good strategist."

Bennett and Roney came at the campaign from different perspectives. Roney was from the old school, where you wheeled and dealed with labor leaders and sheriffs and black leaders to win blocks of votes. A wad of cash could get out the right voters. Roney knew who to deal with in every county. Bennett thought a campaign should be run like a business. He carried a briefcase and had charts and graphs and maps of the state, broken into regions with a coordinator for each. He stayed in touch with the key Sanford people across the state, pushing them to build their organization. Typical of Bennett was this three-sentence memo he wrote to a Sanford supporter in Sampson County in March 1960. "Of your four counties, I have only Pender under a manager," Bennett wrote. "I have nothing yet from you on Onslow. I would appreciate your latest thinking along these lines." Neither Roney nor Bennett wanted much to do with the other. Sanford saw the value of each and made sure they coexisted.

On the campaign trail, Sanford loved to talk about education—and hated to talk about race. When he announced his candidacy, Sanford promised to "state clearly and in detail" his position on all matters of concern to voters. But when it came to race, he broke his promise. Beginning early in the campaign, when he said that the lunch-counter sit-ins should not be a campaign issue, he avoided talking about how and whether to integrate. "Everybody got burned in the Frank Graham campaign, that's for sure," said Martha McKay. "That was just a major blow to all the progressive forces. I think he probably was gun-shy on that topic and planned with care what he was going to do and why." Sanford later acknowledged that he tried to avoid commenting on the sit-ins. In doing so, he was following the advice of pollster Louis Harris. His polling in April showed that 54 percent of North Carolinians believed blacks seeking service at lunch counters should not be served; 22 percent thought they should be served. Most didn't see any specific action that the governor should take on the issue. Harris advised Sanford to avoid the issue.

Even before the sit-ins, Sanford believed race was going to be an issue in the campaign. Lake's entrance guaranteed that. But that didn't mean Sanford was going to be swept along by Lake or the news of the day. As he learned from the campaigns of 1950 and 1954, he was trying to control the issue and frame it in his terms. "I didn't basically disagree with the motivations of the students," Sanford later said. "I would have preferred they leave it to me to work these problems out. I said privately, 'If I were black, I'd be sitting there too.' It'd be my nature to be one of them. You had to admire those students. But I certainly didn't make any statement urging them to continue." There was no way for Sanford to be truthful and survive politically. So he kept quiet as best he could.

That wasn't easy to do. Nor should it have been. How and whether the state should integrate was the major issue of the day and a legitimate area of public debate. Lake was talking about race every day. Seawell was striking at Lake on the issue—and sometimes at Sanford. Seawell entered the race partly because he did not believe Sanford was standing up to Lake. Seawell knew Sanford was dodging the issue and he publicly urged him to take a stand.

Sanford responded. In a three-page statement released at the end of February, he ripped Seawell and stated his position. "I regret that the integration question has been brought to the front in this campaign by the heedless remarks of the ex-attorney general," Sanford said. "His demand that I answer and 'take a stand' on this issue is regrettable. . . . I'll admit, coming in the middle of a political campaign, that it puts me on the spot. I am sure that is what he intended to do, and while it is not for me to judge his motives, I suspect his motives were purely for his own selfish political advantage." Sanford said that he already had taken a firm position. If Seawell didn't know it, Sanford said, it was because he was too busy making hot-headed charges and careless "like it or lump it" statements. Sanford pointed out that he was one of the first people outside the Hodges administration, if not the first, to "put [his] neck on the line" and openly support the Pearsall Plan.

Sanford chose his words carefully. "The people of North Carolina are almost unanimously opposed to integration in the schools," he said. He said he was offended by the federal government ordering a solution. "I intend to represent the feeling of the people of our state, firmly but diplomatically, in resisting such pressure, by every decent and legal means. I will not falter," he said. Sanford gave himself plenty of room to wiggle. All he said was that North Carolina should be able to decide for itself how, when, and whether to integrate. But he didn't address how, when, and whether North Carolina should integrate. Also, he didn't say he opposed integration; he said most people in North Carolina did.

Sanford also said he would seek to promote better understanding between the races and more "economic opportunities for all people and especially those who have been denied wide opportunities for gainful employment." He did not elaborate. But in calling for more opportunities for all, including those who had been denied opportunity, he was treading where few southern politicians would go. He was sending a signal to blacks that he knew they had been denied opportunities and he thought that was unjust.

He also said flatly, "The schools of North Carolina will not be closed." Sanford then said again why he thought the issue should go away. Each of the candidates stood with the majority of North Carolinians, he said. Each thought the Supreme Court decisions were bad law. "It is my position, because of this, that there is no legitimate issue here," he said. "I am willing to take them at their word, Larkins, Lake, and Seawell, and to trust them all. I hope they will have their say and that we can avoid charges and counter-charges on racial matters, which cannot do the state any good and which will not serve any purpose except to make worse a situation already bad. I do not intend to make such racial charges."

Despite his attempts to diffuse it, the issue would not go away. In mid-March, he spoke to a near capacity crowd of University of North Carolina

Young Democrats at Chapel Hill. Sanford gave his thirty-two-point Positive Program for Progress. Point number seven was school segregation. A United Press International reporter called it the first time Sanford discussed school segregation in a campaign speech. "I think and I prayerfully hope that we in North Carolina will use our brains instead of our mouths, and that we can handle this matter with intelligence and calmness," Sanford said. "I stand with 90 percent of the people of our state who approve the present North Carolina approach, which is being copied by other southern states. I haven't seen any other workable plan proposed. We must not for purely political reasons allow our state to be consumed in racial bitterness."

Students weren't satisfied with that. With their peers across the state and the South embracing the lunch-counter sit-ins, they wanted to know what he thought of the protests. They asked him in a question-and-answer session after his speech. But Sanford would not give a position. "Racial issues have no place in a gubernatorial race because they can play on the emotions of people instead of reason," he said. If the candidates took stands, he said, uncontrollable emotions could erupt, with charges and countercharges. In the heat of the discussion, a student asked, "Do you know that the governorship is a stepping-stone to the Senate?" Sanford quipped, "Yeah, and it's a stepping-stone to political ruin, too."

Sanford knew that a candidate could not win by supporting integration. But he also believed that most white North Carolinians did not like the hard-nosed resistance they saw in other southern states. In one of his television commercials, Sanford addressed the issue and sought to define it on his terms. In the lengthy commercial, a friendly interviewer lobbed easy questions at Sanford. After a series of questions about his family, his military experience, and his education platform, the interviewer asked Sanford about school integration. Sanford said he did not think the 1954 Supreme Court decision was "good law." But he said he opposed any kind of massive resistance, which he said would only prompt federal courts to step in. "I think we can handle it if we use our brains instead of our mouths," he said, repeating a favorite line. He said that North Carolina's approach was a good one and other southern states were copying it.

Sanford was in a quandary. He wanted and needed the support of black voters. "It was ticklish. We never, never could lose the black vote or we were gone," Bert Bennett remembered. But if Sanford openly courted black voters, he would alienate whites. This was the dilemma identified by Louis Harris. "It is undoubtedly best, in view of past primary history, not to make overt gestures for the Negro vote in this state," Harris wrote. If Sanford openly courted blacks, he could lose his front-running status in Mecklenburg and other populous Piedmont areas. On the other hand, Harris said that there was no need for him to alienate black voters.

Bennett reflected the same dilemma in a letter to a supporter who had asked for advice in working with black voters. "It is difficult for us to give advice on local situations as you have to sort of feel your way," Bennett wrote in April. "As you well know, we certainly do not want any Negro or labor tag put on us as they have tried to do but by the same token, we want their vote." Bennett concluded: "On reading this over, this certainly doesn't answer your question."

Perhaps Sanford, his staff, and supporters were unsure of how to campaign on the race question and what their message should be. But when it came to responding to dirty tricks, Sanford believed he knew exactly what to do: Hit back. So when the Sanford campaign discovered unsigned, racially oriented leaflets in four counties, Sanford drew on his experiences from the 1950 and 1954 Senate campaigns and responded quickly.

On May 20, eight days before the primary, Sanford held a press conference in Raleigh and denounced "unsigned, derogatory, false and inflammatory" leaflets attacking his candidacy. They were found across the state—in Craven County in the east, Harnett and Robeson Counties in the south-central part of the state, and in Cleveland County in the west. Sanford angrily said that he was "pretty certain" of the people spreading the literature and called for the State Bureau of Investigation (SBI) to take action. He said that the leaflets dealt with the race issue and attacked him by name, although the Cleveland County leaflets were directed at one of his supporters. The leaflets favored two of the gubernatorial candidates, but Sanford would not name them. He declined to provide any de-

tails—or to show the leaflets to reporters. He considered not saying anything about the leaflets until after the election but decided to speak because "it's time that North Carolina put a stop to this kind of
campaigning."

The next day, the SBI said that it would investigate the leaflets. John
Larkins, however, zestfully pointed out the holes in Sanford's case. Sanford had not said what the leaflets said, who distributed them, or whom
they favored. "As a lawyer, Terry should know this is a mighty flimsy
case," Larkins said. He and Seawell demanded Sanford make the leaflets
public. Sanford refused. Robert Morgan also suspected Sanford was bluff-
ing. In a letter to Lake supporters, he said that the Lake campaign had not
produced a leaflet with derogatory remarks and that Sanford had not publicly released the leaflets. "If a client of mine begins a conference by
telling me how honest he is, I immediately doubt him," wrote Morgan, a
lawyer. "In the same manner, Sanford cannot stop telling how ethical his
campaign is—so watch him."

A few days later, the SBI identified the leaflets and said that they did
not violate state law. The leaflets were reprints of a March 26, 1959, editorial from the *Lenoir County News* in eastern North Carolina. The editorial, titled "We're Still for Larkins," said that Sanford was a
"moderationist" on the race issue and that Lake and Larkins were "segregationists." The editorial said, "Our spies in Cumberland County report
Sanford as saying, 'I'll win if they do not hang the Negro around my
neck.' The most logical inference one might draw from this is that Sanford fears his record or his stand on the burning issue of public school segregation."

It was against state law to distribute unsigned literature designed to be
derogatory. The SBI director said that the reprint carried the name of the
newspaper which printed it and said that it did not seem to be derogatory.
Another leaflet, which implied wrongdoing by a Sanford supporter in
Shelby, was more questionable, the SBI director said. But Sanford had indicated less concern about it. The issue quickly faded.

Sanford had swung hard—and barely connected. Unlike 1954, when
he turned the unsigned flyers to his advantage, his most recent attempt

mostly fizzled. It looked to many that Sanford had overreacted. The *Raleigh Times*, in an article on Sanford's smooth-running campaign, mentioned the flyer incident as the only stumble. "Many observers feel he dropped the ball" and it might backfire on him, the article said. Sanford did get some favorable press; the *Greensboro Daily News* editorialized that Sanford had rendered a public service by exposing the issue and urged other candidates to repudiate the tactics and warn their supporters. Sanford continued to milk the issue. "We have not attacked our opponents and have not resorted to smear techniques," Sanford said. He gave insight into his true motivation: "The public has been alerted—and that's primarily what we wanted done. By airing it out, I think we've helped dry up their distribution." He was trying not to get on the defensive, trying to control and beat back the race issue. Beverly Lake, however, had a different plan.

Chapter 6

LAKE, APART AND AFIRE

While Sanford wanted the race issue to go away, Lake wanted it out in the open. From Lake's entrance into the race in early March until the primary at the end of May, the two wrestled for control of the debate. Was the central issue making schools better, as Sanford said? Or was it fighting integration, as Lake said? When he announced he would run, Lake said that integration needed to be openly debated, and he did not waver from that belief. In a speech in early April, he confidently characterized the positions of his three opponents on school integration. One opponent believed the Supreme Court decision was the law of the land, Lake said, referring to Seawell. Another candidate "has declared himself to be a moderate. He hasn't said yet how he stands," Lake said of Sanford. The third candidate, Lake said of his old friend Larkins, "is like Brer Rabbit's Tar Baby: He ain't said nothing."

Lake proudly stated his position: "I have always been opposed and now am opposed to integration of our public schools." When pressed, the other three candidates often said something similar. But then Lake cut to the heart of what distinguished him from the others: He did not recognize the Supreme Court's decision as legitimate. The Court's *Brown* ruling, he said, "was in violation of the Constitution of the United States." He did not support it. He would not support it. "I promise you," he said, "if I become governor, I will use the powers of the office to preserve the school

137

system we now have." Another time, Lake said he would not call on the National Guard to enforce a judgment of a federal court to integrate: "I do not think that a governor who takes the oath to support the Constitution should call out the National Guard to do what he believes to be a violation of the Constitution, and I wouldn't do it."

Lake continued to point out the differences among the candidates on race. In mid-April, while the candidates moved about the state but before the race grew frantic, Lake traveled to the coast for two days of campaigning there. A few hours before a rally at the New Hanover County courthouse in Wilmington, Lake met with reporters. The chief difference between himself and the other three Democrats, he said, was in their attitudes toward the integration issue. Lake said that the other three candidates seemed to believe that the state already had dealt with the problem in 1955 by adopting the Pupil Assignment Act, giving local school boards great discretion in pupil assignment. Lake drafted that law as a member of the attorney general's staff. But, he said, "The Pupil Assignment Act is not a Gibralter behind which we can hide indefinitely." Lake knew that while the law allowed local school boards to block integration, it also allowed them to integrate—and a few systems had allowed a handful of black students into white schools. The state needed to do more to fight integration, Lake told reporters. School integration would be tragic for both whites and blacks. "If elected I will do all I can to avoid that situation," Lake said. "I would also take my election to mean that's what the people want."

A few hours later, Lake was the star of his first televised rally. John Burney came up with the idea of the TV rally and organized the first one in his hometown. The Lake campaign purchased thirty minutes of air time. The courtroom was filled with several hundred people. Spectators crowded into the balcony and stood in the aisles. They came from the neighboring southeastern counties of Pender, Columbus, and Brunswick, partly to see Lake, partly because they had never seen a live, televised political rally. Burney recruited his father's law partner, retired Col. Royce McClelland, to introduce Lake. They never practiced the introduction— or anything else. When the TV lights flashed on, McClelland froze for several seconds, finally recovering to introduce Lake. The rally energized the Lake forces and drew contributions even from South Carolina. The Lake campaign was so pleased it duplicated the televised rallies in other cities. They became Lake's trademark.

In his speech, Lake stuck with his message of fighting integration. After briefly greeting and thanking the crowd, Lake moved to his favorite target: the NAACP. In a jab at race moderates, such as Sanford, he said he would not be moderately committed to defeating the NAACP but "wholeheartedly" committed. "To its defeat I ask you to commit yourselves, for defeat it we can and defeat it we must," he said. Lake talked about some other matters, including the local issue of where a bridge should rise over the Cape Fear River. He, like Sanford, criticized Luther Hodges' Highway Commission and pledged to reorganize it.

Lake outlined his plan for improving schools, including reducing class sizes, hiring clerical workers to relieve teachers from paper work, raising teacher salaries to keep up with inflation and other states, and making the high school curriculum more diverse. In this speech and in others, Lake said that the state's finances were tight and that not all of his proposals could be fully in place within four years. For example, he said that the smaller class sizes could be phased in with each year's new crop of first graders. He said his was not a moderate program. It was, he said, a "far-reaching" program. But even a moderate program would have cost millions of dollars and Lake did not identify any way to pay for his ambitious proposals. He opposed a tax increase; he did not name other programs to cut or even say he would cut other programs. For a man who prided himself in shooting straight, and who was chiding his opponents for not openly discussing the race issue, when it came to making schools better Lake sounded like most politicians. He was making big promises without saying how he was going to pay for them.

Perhaps Lake simply thought he could get away with being vague. (He did; there were few, if any, newspaper articles during the campaign pressing Lake on how he would pay for his school proposals.) Or perhaps his real passion was preserving segregation and that was what he spent his time and energy thinking about. After discussing his school proposals,

Lake returned to warning his courthouse and television audiences about the dangers of integration. The NAACP didn't like him because he had fought the group three times before the Supreme Court—and won each time, he said. The first was when the Supreme Court decided how to put its *Brown* decision in place. The second involved the right of the hospital in Wilmington, which was privately endowed, to determine which doctors should have staff privileges. The third was when the Court affirmed the right of a local elections board to require a literacy test for voters.

The NAACP was sponsoring "an all-out attack to compel the complete intermingling of our two great races in all aspects of our daily life," Lake said. He offered the lunch-counter sit-ins as proof. The law allowed business owners to serve whomever they pleased. Those who didn't like it, he said, could start their own business and serve whomever they pleased. As governor, he said he would protect them in that right—just as he would protect the right of operators of restaurants, cafes, lunch counters, barbershops, and beauty parlors and other business owners to serve whomever they wanted at whatever price they wanted. It did not matter why a business owner refused to serve a customer. "'I don't want to' is a sufficient answer to some demands in North Carolina," Lake said, "and if I become your next governor I shall use every power of the office to see that it is still a sufficient answer to those demands when my term is over."

Lake believed most black people favored segregation. The NAACP did not speak for black people in North Carolina, he said; it was an integrated group run out of New York. He pitched for the support of black and white voters. Once the NAACP's program was exposed, he said, "Public opinion—white and Negro public opinion—will drive it out of the state and remove from North Carolina the political power of its friends. When that is done, the Negro people and the white people of North Carolina, living side by side, in peace and mutual respect and mutual helpfulness, just as we have always done, will continue to go forward to a richer, happier, fuller life and to a better North Carolina." Lake never offered evidence, in this speech or any other, for why he believed blacks favored segregation. Which black people were telling Lake they wanted segregation? He never said.

Lake's critics said that he talked more about race in eastern North Carolina and more about economic issues in the Piedmont and west. The east—a rural, agrarian area with a higher percentage of blacks—traditionally had been viewed by liberals as the most racist part of the state, more like the Deep South than any other section of North Carolina. Of the state's 4.5 million residents, about 1.6 million lived in forty-three eastern counties. In those counties, about 38 percent of the people were black; in the fifty-seven Piedmont and western counties, about 18 percent of the residents were black. The eastern counties had been crucial to Willis Smith's upset of Frank Graham in 1950. In the first primary, Smith won sixteen of the eastern counties; in the runoff, he held onto those counties and won fifteen others that Graham had won in the first primary.

In 1960 in North Carolina, blacks were nowhere near the potent voting force they would become. About 25 percent of the state's population was black. But largely because of Jim Crow barriers to registration, only about 10 percent of registered voters were black. About 90 percent of white adults were registered to vote; only about 30 percent of black adults were registered.

Lake occasionally gave less emphasis to his positions on race. For example, in a speech to Charlotte's Queen City Optimist Club in May, Lake mostly discussed attracting new industry, including the state's transportation and fiscal policies. He did not mention the NAACP or fighting integration. But that was highly unusual, and that same day Lake also gave a hard-edged talk on a Charlotte radio station about opposing the NAACP. A review of the full text of thirty-three of his campaign speeches and TV addresses shows that Lake spent most of his time talking about fighting integration.

Lake was an effective communicator. He spoke in a formal, old-fashioned, elegant manner, with precise language and diction. His backers sometimes praised him with the same language they later used to support his friend and supporter Jesse Helms: You knew where he stood. "He was a very sincere man," said Hoover Adams of the Dunn *Daily Record*, a Lake (and Helms) supporter. "He believed what he said. He didn't pull any punches. He was effective. He was very succinct. He could say more in a few words than anybody I had ever heard." Lake's friend, supporter, and former student Allen Bailey said, "He simply called it as he saw it. He was that honest with himself and everybody else." Whether you agreed or not, his message was compelling. Through his rhetorical skills and the force of his calm but determined personality, Lake drew the state's attention to him. Large crowds traveled to hear him. Journalists thought he was good copy and the state's editors spread his comments about integration on their front pages. In the months leading up to the May primary, Beverly Lake set the tone for the debate.

The NAACP had no defenders in the governor's race. Because the white reporters from the mainstream newspapers generally did not get a response from NAACP representatives, most of Lake's charges went unchallenged. Certainly Sanford, Seawell, and Larkins, seeking white votes in a highly competitive primary, were not going to defend the group. In a televised forum in April—the first time in North Carolina history that all Democratic and Republican candidates for governor appeared at the same event—Larkins and Sanford joined Lake in criticizing the NAACP. "The NAACP seeks either to run the show or suffer what it can advertise as persecution," Larkins said. Having achieved neither in North Carolina, Larkins said that the group was frustrated and frantic. He claimed that the NAACP sought to provoke white people and said that the sit-ins were timed with the May primary in mind. Sanford was more reserved but agreed the purpose of the NAACP was to "stir up strife." He continued to urge restraint in discussing the issue. "We should stand steady and work with our brains instead of our mouths," he said. "The more we stir it up, the more trouble we will have." The state could only realize its potential if it could "prevent the hopes and aspirations of our people from being consumed in racial bitterness."

A week later, in another attempt to diffuse the issue, Sanford said he did not think any of the four Democrats would receive the endorsement of the NAACP and "that pretty well wrap[ped] it up." Or so he hoped. The *Greensboro Daily News* noted that each of the Democrats was critical of the NAACP—and wondered why. The paper pointed out that the group pursued its goals of integration and equal opportunity peacefully and through the courts. Wasn't that the way the American system was supposed to work? Why did that so rile the candidates? While the editorial didn't say, the answer was obvious: Beating up the NAACP was a good way to win votes with many white North Carolinians. Black voters did not like Lake but did not see another candidate to rally around. They had hoped to support Sanford, one unnamed black source told the *Charlotte Observer*. But each of the candidates made "a whipping boy out of the NAACP, which may not represent all Negroes—but it represents more than anybody else." Turnout among black voters was expected to be low.

The NAACP was Lake's favorite target, but when it came to integration, he had others. One was Gov. Luther Hodges. In early May, in a fifteen-minute show on a Greenville television station in eastern North Carolina, Lake tore into Hodges, saying he had created the wrong tone for the state. He had adjusted "the halo of moderation to the angle [he] believes most likely to win the applause of the integrationist press," Lake said. Meanwhile, the lunch-counter demonstrations were launched in North Carolina. Why North Carolina? Because, Lake said, the NAACP was "led by the present administration's professed love for moderation to believe that North Carolina is the softest spot in the South." He said that all three of his Democratic opponents seemed to approve of Hodges' policies.

Without naming them, Lake had more criticism for his opponents. Lake said he had been criticized by one for fabricating a "synthetic issue designed to build hope where none exists." Larkins had made that comment. Lake said, "Do you think the matter of preserving our present system of public schools is a synthetic issue or do you consider it, as I do, the most important problem confronting North Carolina today?" If the issue was settled, Lake asked, did that mean Larkins would integrate schools during his administration? If the issue was not settled, then how would Larkins fight integration? Lake said that another of his opponents, in discussing the lunch-counter sit-ins, had called for sitting down with the NAACP and picketers to try to reach a settlement. "There are some things about which I am not willing to compromise," Lake said, referring to Sanford.

Lake said that a third opponent believed the Supreme Court's decision was the law of the land and the state must accept and obey it whether it liked it or not. Seawell often made that point. Lake asked, Would Seawell use his powers as governor to persuade your local school board to integrate with all deliberate speed? If he did not intend to encourage local school boards to put the ruling in place, what did he intend? Seawell had been silent on the key questions, Lake said. "I do not think this decision is the law of the land," Lake said. "I consider it a miscarriage of justice and a judicial violation of the Constitution." Therefore, Lake said he would do everything in his power to urge local school boards to delay and prevent integration. He said that North Carolina should clearly say that school segregation was the official policy of the state; this would openly defy the Supreme Court's ruling.

He also said he disagreed with his opponents on the Pearsall Plan, which gave local voters the power to close their schools if a majority of voters in the system agreed to it. Lake opposed the Pearsall Plan in the legislature in 1956, although he voted for it in the referendum that fall "because no other option was available." He said that it was too cumbersome to defend against integration and had never been used. In what was perhaps Lake's hardest-edged speech of the campaign, he also took his criticism of the NAACP a step further. He said that the group wanted to integrate churches, recreational activities, social functions, and marriage, "so as to reduce both races to a mixed-breed common denominator."

Lake hit on most of his key themes in the Greenville address, but others emerged during the primary. In a radio address in Charlotte, he referred to recent appearances at the University of North Carolina by civil rights leader Martin Luther King Jr. and black poet Langston Hughes. He criticized Governor Hodges for not speaking out against the appearances. Lake said he would "protect the state against use of its public institutions to honor and encourage spokesmen of the NAACP" who came to the state to attack "North Carolina's social system." He often criticized the lunch-counter sit-ins and boycotts. In several speeches, he called for a state law to ban organized boycotting of private businesses. That appeared to be the only state legislation related to race that Lake advocated during the campaign. Lake did not propose changing the law he drafted—the one giving local school boards the power to handle student assignment. Instead, he said he would use the governor's bully pulpit to urge local school boards to segregate white and black students.

Lake talked often of using the governor's office to create a climate of public opinion against integration. "I am opposed to the mixing of white and Negro children in the public schools of North Carolina," he said shortly after entering the governor's race. "In this I am not and shall not be a moderate, but I shall endeavor to be practical and to exercise self control. I am completely, whole-heartedly opposed to it and if I am elected governor of this state, I shall use the full influence of that office in every practical, lawful way to protect the educational opportunity of our children, white and Negro, against such intermixture." If federal courts destroyed the state's public schools, Lake said, the state could consider another educational system. The state could give grants and tax credits to parents who put their children in private schools, he said. On a radio call-in show in Charlotte, he said that if a federal court ordered a black student admitted to a white school, he would advise the local school board to comply. He would not recommend an armed guard to keep the child out. "We have to have some practical common sense," he said. But he would make it clear he opposed the admission of the child and he would encourage the child's parents to take him back to a school for blacks. "I would not advise the school board to welcome the child with open arms," Lake said. "I would regard that child as an invader."

Lake believed integration would hurt public schools by driving wealthier white children into private schools, draining the public schools of needed brain power and resources. It wasn't enough to keep schools open, he said; they needed to be effective. He used the example of the integrated schools of Washington, D.C., to illustrate his point. The schools there were open and well-paid teachers awaited. But white children were fleeing. Fewer than one in four students was white.

Lake said that North Carolinians who advocated gradually integrating the schools could afford to send their own children to private schools "if our public schools are allowed to degenerate into the blackboard jungles, which the program of the NAACP will make them." But he said that poor children, Negro and white, would not have that option. Lake had said "blackboard jungle" at least once before, in a speech two weeks earlier. While salaries were important to teachers, so were other considerations, he had said then: "How much salary would it take to attract your daughter to the blackboard jungle which integration has made of the public schools of the city of Washington?" Lake's use of "blackboard jungle" was unusual for him. These appear to be the only occasions in the campaign when he used a racial slur. It was out of character for a man who in both his public and private lives advocated good relationships between whites and blacks.

Lake warned against following the racial moderates, like Sanford. The only difference between the NAACP and the moderates, he said, is that the NAACP would integrate faster. He warned that if the NAACP succeeded, whites would be surrounded by blacks in their everyday living. Their schools would no longer operate effectively. Their communities would be filled with suspicion, tension, and fear. Their great-grandchildren would be of mixed racial background. "We cannot idly stand by and appease, placate and surrender a way of life," he said. If they thought the lunch-counter protests were isolated to chain stores, think again, he said. Next blacks would be seeking to integrate cafes, restaurants, barbershops, beauty parlors, dentists' offices, and doctors' offices.

As the campaign wore on, and Lake continued to prick his opponents, they tired of his hammering on the race issue. None of them thought integration was the central issue of the campaign. Of North Carolina's 173 school districts, 7 were integrated—barely. When school opened in the fall of 1960, 3 more districts integrated. North Carolina had about 1.1 million public school students. Of the more than 300,000 black students in school that fall, 82 attended an integrated school—far less than one-tenth of 1 percent. In Raleigh, 1 black student went to an integrated school. In Greensboro, 5 blacks attended school with whites. In Charlotte-Mecklenburg, 2 black children went to an integrated school. The integration in North Carolina was mostly symbolic. Four southern states—Alabama, Georgia, Mississippi, and South Carolina—had no black students attending school with whites.

Larkins and Seawell struck back at Lake, sometimes with venom. Seawell fought Lake the hardest. When Lake said he would treat a black child at a white school as an "invader," Seawell thought it unfair. Lake was talking about a young child who would have been placed in a school by action of a school board, not by the child's own decision, Seawell said. When Lake said that North Carolina was "soft" on integration, Seawell objected. North Carolina had respected the law of the land and moved forward, Seawell said: "We are not soft at all but intend to be strong under our system of law."

Seawell thought it outrageous that Lake claimed the Supreme Court's *Brown* decision was not legitimate and he therefore could disregard it. Seawell said he was personally opposed to integration. He did not like the Supreme Court decision either. But that didn't mean the state could ignore it. If each citizen decided what laws he or she would follow, anarchy would rule, he said. The state could not survive. "No one man may, with impunity, set himself up as being a super Supreme Court," Seawell said, "and no one man may seek to create a monster of defiance and lawlessness which would lead to the destruction of public education in North Carolina." Another time, Seawell said, "No one who takes his oath on the Holy Bible with his fingers crossed ought to be elected governor of North Carolina." Seawell also questioned exactly what Lake was advocating. Lake talked about creating an atmosphere of public opposition to integration. What did that mean? They created an atmosphere of opposition in Virginia and in Little Rock, Arkansas, Seawell noted, and that led to the closing of schools. Did he intend to close the schools? "I don't want paratroopers in North Carolina," Seawell said, "and that is what [this] atmosphere leads to, especially when led by a governor."

Hodges also defended himself from Lake's criticism. While "a few people" were tearing down North Carolina's "well-conceived and intelligent" approach, Hodges said that other southern states were copying it. He warned that a misstep could bring mass closings of schools or mass integration, either of which he said would be bad for the state. Most North Carolinians did not like the Supreme Court decision, he said. "But certainly, up until the present time, we have managed in North Carolina to meet the problem directly and intelligently," Hodges said, "and not simply indulge in an emotional binge of criticism against courts and against Negro organizations."

The other candidates sometimes attacked each other on the integration issue. Seawell said he was the only one of the candidates who stood up to be counted when some North Carolinians wanted to defy the Supreme Court's *Brown* ruling. "That was the time when men could be separated from the boys," he said. Seawell successfully defended the state's school policy before the Supreme Court when he was attorney general. He said that other candidates, worried of their political futures, had steered clear of the issue. Larkins said that Seawell was taking too much credit. Yes, Seawell defended the state's school integration plan in court, but he was just doing his job in defending a good law, Larkins said. Many leaders worked on the plan and they deserve the credit, Larkins said, pointing out that he had supported the plan when it was proposed.

In the daily campaign dialogue, Sanford was mostly silent on race, letting the other candidates trade insults as he continued to say improving schools was the number one issue. His silence did not mean he was not getting plenty of advice. He was, from all sides. A supporter wrote him a five-page memo advising him on how to handle legal issues associated with the lunch-counter sit-ins. The handwritten letter was labeled "Personal memo to Terry" and was signed "X." Seawell had said that trespassing laws could be used to prosecute the sit-in protestors. That advice, said the anonymous letter writer, "was hasty, ill-advised, poor legal advice in the final analysis—typical of his personal fever outrunning the state's good." The letter writer, clearly an attorney, cited case law that said the issue wasn't as simple as Seawell thought. There was a right to buy and sell goods in public commerce, he said. If police arrested the protestors, they could argue that their rights guaranteed by the equal protection clause of the Fourteenth Amendment were violated. X recommended finding a friendly reporter and dropping a hint that Seawell "may have

148

been ill-advised as [with] other hasty actions springing from personal impetuousness." There might be other ways to approach the sit-in problem—such as the use of private security guards—that might be easier to defend legally, X said.

Sanford stayed away from that issue and others related to race. When editors and reporters at the *Winston-Salem Journal* asked him if he had any ideas to improve race relations, Sanford did not mention the Supreme Court decision, North Carolina's Pearsall Plan, or even public schools. Instead, he said that the governor could get white people and black people to talk to each other in groups in their communities. "We certainly can't isolate ourselves and isolate the Negro," Sanford said. "The matter of communicating, knowing each other's problems and attitudes, will probably help solve a great many problems. I'd like to use the governor's office to encourage that kind of communication." That was a nice thought—in essence, that was the concept behind the Good Neighbor Council that Sanford would create as governor. But Sanford's comment dodged the issue of the day—whether and how quickly schools should integrate. That, no doubt, was the way Sanford wanted it.

Lake's strong, vocal stance favoring segregation raised this question: Was he a racist? The question was debated during the campaign and has been debated since by his supporters and opponents. His supporters argue passionately that he was not. They say that although he was a segregationist, he believed in fairness for all and was not a racist. Lake, they say, had only good will toward black people. "I never perceived in the slightest during those years I knew him so personally prior to 1960 that he was a racist," said supporter and former student Allen Bailey. "That was not part of my perception of him. I knew he was in fact a segregationist but there's a lot of difference in the two terms, at least in my mind. I think he was totally convinced that it was not in the best interest for the races to intermarry. He was convinced that was what was out in the future. And I think that's where he took his stand. . . . If he ever held any hostility toward black people, it never occurred to me. I never saw it. I never saw any difference in his treatment among the races."

Robert Morgan, who also knew Lake initially from his days at Wake Forest, said, "He believed in the segregation of the schools but he was not a racist. You have to remember who did believe in the segregation of the schools back then. Almost everybody. . . . He was the old southern gentleman . . . very caring about everybody, including blacks, but I guess people would call it paternalistic."

Lake supporter John Lewis traveled with him often in eastern North Carolina. "I knew the man well," Lewis said. "I knew what he thought. He said in the future, it might come to the point where integrating the schools might be good but at this point in history, I don't think it would be. He was for everybody having an equal opportunity for a good education." Roy Green, who took a leave from his job as a bus driver to drive Lake during his 1964 campaign for governor, said, "He was not a racist. He just didn't believe in integrated schools. There wasn't a racist bone in his body. He didn't ever say anything bad" about blacks.

Even some Sanford supporters and other observers were ambivalent on the question. Bill Staton, the Sanford supporter who was one of Lake's former law students, believed Lake's use of race during the 1960 campaign was racist because "he wanted to draw a distinction between the races, black and white." Staton said, "I don't think there's any doubt that he used race as the principle issue in his campaign. In an effort to win the nomination, he moved further and further in that direction." But prior to the campaign, Staton, who graduated from Wake Law School in 1942, said he saw no evidence that Lake felt animosity toward black people. "If you had asked me before the campaign if Lake were a racist, I would have said no," said Staton. "What he said, and what he did, did not raise the flag of caution in my mind." Dickson Phillips, Sanford's law partner and good friend, got to know Lake after the campaign. "He was absolutely persuaded we could and should live in a segregated society," Phillips said. "My perception was he was not mean spirited about it, that he didn't think a black person was a sub-human. But he thought there was enough of a difference that we ought to maintain a segregated society. . . . I'll bet he never would have treated black people poorly in a one-on-one situation."

Joe Doster, who covered the campaign for the *Charlotte Observer*, noted that Lake was steadfast in not campaigning against blacks. "He did not beat up on blacks," Doster said. "All he talked about was separate but equal was the true way. The idea that you could do violence to blacks was against his whole law and order background. In many ways, Lake was sort of a paradox. I was intrigued with the guy. You sensed this intellectual capacity there. You saw this position he was taking. And you're constantly trying to reconcile those. He had to know the policies he [was] espousing, while maybe not violent, were in the long run harmful to black people. He had to know that. While he was personally benign, the policies were not benign."

Lake's personal and public generosity was part of his appeal as a candidate and set him apart from other leading southern segregationists of the 1950s and '60s. He was not a hater. His supporters believed him to be a good man. He was a religious person; Lake was a faithful churchgoer and Sunday school teacher at the Baptist church in Wake Forest for most of his life. Roy Green, the driver who traveled often with Lake, recalled that each night in their hotel room Lake dropped to his knees to pray. One night in early May, Lake and other candidates took questions from a Charlotte-area radio audience. One caller asked Lake if he considered himself a Christian and, if so, how he justified his stand on segregation. "Yes, I consider myself a Christian, I have no doubt in my mind about that," Lake replied. For one hundred years, the state had educated its children in separate, equal schools, and each race had made great progress, Lake said. Integrated schools could not be run successfully, he said.

In a speech in 1959, Lake explained how his religious beliefs meshed with his views on race. In addressing the men's club of Grove Presbyterian Church in Harnett County, Lake referred to the New Testament and Paul's letter to the Galatians: "Ye are all children of God by faith in Jesus Christ. . . . There is neither Jew nor Greek, there is neither bond nor free, neither male nor female; for ye are all one in Christ Jesus." That did not mean that Christians did not recognize the differences between people, Lake said. It was important, he said, to look at the context of Paul's words. He wrote to people who were inquiring about who could become a Christian. Only one thing was necessary to be a Christian, Paul said—faith in Jesus Christ.

There is a oneness in man, Lake said. All humans feel pain and pleasure, companionship and loneliness, hunger, thirst, cold, heat, sorrow, joy. All humans die. But there are important differences, he said. He compared those differences to those among animals. "The Percheron and the Kentucky racer are both horses, the collie and the Pekinese are both dogs, just as the Chinese, the Negro and the Anglo-Saxon are all men," Lake said. "It may well be debated whether the Percheron or the racehorse has made greater contributions to the world, whether the collie or the Pekinese is the better pet for children, but it is absurd to say there are no differences between them except the pigmentation of their hair. The breeder of horses or dogs who makes that silly assumption and exercises no supervision over the associates of his animals will find that the world puts a low appraisal on his colts and puppies. The parent who, on the similar assumption, pays not attention to the associates of his children will find a similarly low appraisal has been placed upon some of his grandchildren."

God loved all his children, Lake said. "But God has not obliterated the differences between the sexes, nor has he abolished childhood." Have we sinned, Lake asked, because we separate our Sunday school classes by age and gender? Have Baptists and Presbyterians sinned by operating separate colleges for women? "If not," Lake said, "have we sinned by operating them as colleges for white women only? Wherein does one more than the other violate the truth that 'In Christ there is neither Jew nor Greek, neither male nor female'"?

The Negro and the Anglo-Saxon are both parts of the body of Christ, Lake said, and of the body of North Carolina. Both must live together in harmony. That requires justice. But that does not mean everyone should be treated exactly alike; this, he said, would be a grave injustice. "Justice requires that differences between people be recognized and that our treatments of individuals vary in accordance with those differences," Lake said. "It is not justice to require a 12-year-old boy to do the work expected of a young man. It is not justice for a teacher to give a well written and a

152

poorly written examination paper the same grade. It is not justice for a court to require a commingling of pupils in a classroom which will hold those with superior intellect to the faltering pace of the dull and less capable." Whites generally had the superior intellect, Lake believed. But, he added, black children should not be denied the educational opportunities given to white children. Nor, he said, should either race be forced to choose between integrated schools and no schools.

To Lake, it was vitally important that whites and blacks not have children together. Both races should be proud of their heritage, he said, and it was God's will to keep blacks and whites from having children together. "You and I are trustees of a birthright for children of Harnett County now asleep in their cribs," Lake said in concluding his speech. "They know nothing of racial heritages but we do. If, mistaking the doctrine of the Supreme Court, the NAACP and its allies for the command of God, we permit their heritage to be destroyed, we shall surely be accounted faithless stewards of the treasure God has committed to our keeping, and we shall deserve to be exiled to the outer darkness as unprofitable servants." To Lake, preserving segregation wasn't just a desirable public policy. It was what God wanted.

On the campaign trail, Lake often reached out to blacks and asked for their support. He said he would not forget the state's one million Negro citizens: "I shall be their governor as well as for the white people." In a speech in Wake County, Lake said that the Democrats' primary mission was good government for all—Democrats and Republicans, rich and poor, industrialist and laborer, white and black. Also, he said, "Every child in North Carolina, rich or poor, in city or in country, white or Negro, must be given the opportunity to get the best education he can and will take." While Lake did not discuss it in his speeches, his campaign literature called for a new medical school in Durham for blacks, affiliated with what was then called North Carolina College, a black institution. The state badly needed a medical school for blacks, he said, because black physicians on average carried a much heavier patient load than white physicians.

Lake talked often of the need for whites and blacks to live together in harmony. He repeatedly said that while the NAACP was his enemy, black people were not. He urged blacks to join his effort to drive the NAACP out of the state. "If you keep faith with your white neighbors and join with us in the defeat of this interracial, New York organization, we will keep faith with you and your children," Lake said in one speech. "Then the Negro people and the white people of North Carolina can go on living side by side as friends and neighbors in mutual respect and mutual helpfulness, just as we have been doing for generations. Then our colored people can really advance along with our white people in prosperity, in education, in freedom and in friendship."

In another speech, Lake said he was wholeheartedly committed to preserving the friendship between whites and blacks. While Lake's appeals to blacks might have been politically shrewd, allowing him to sound more moderate and reasonable, Lake rarely spoke solely for political effect. He meant what he said. He did have affection for many black people. He never grandstanded and threatened dramatic gestures, such as standing in schoolhouse doors to block federal marshals. "I have a lot of regard for George Wallace," Lake once said, "but it was ridiculous for him to try to block integration by standing in the schoolhouse door. That's not the way to do it. You have to be practical."

Lake said that it bothered him during the campaign when people said that he was a racist. "It made me mad because it wasn't true," he said in 1986. "I had then and I have now many, many friends who are colored." In another interview, just two years after the campaign, Lake said he never spoke harshly of blacks. "There are some people who thought I was speaking against the Negroes, because of my beliefs on the separation of the races," Lake said. "But I never said anything against the Negroes. I never have made a speech I wouldn't make to a Negro audience. They might not agree, and they might not like what I said, but I wouldn't hesitate to say it." In another interview, Lake said he never made a statement in private that he would not have made in public to a black audience. He said that black people were misled during the campaign by inaccurate reporters. Still, he said, "I also got some Negro votes and I feel I got more of them than were reported."

If a racist is a person who harbors ill will toward people of another race, then Lake almost surely was not a racist. But if a racist is a person who believes another race is inherently inferior, then one must come to a different conclusion about Lake. For Lake, like many white people of his era, believed that black people were intellectually inferior to whites. The subject arose occasionally during the campaign. "At the present time, there is a tremendous difference in the ability of the average white and Negro child to do school work," Lake said at one campaign stop. He said that it would take "10 generations"—more than three hundred years—to raise the achievement level of black students to the achievement level of white students. Lake seemed to be saying that blacks ultimately could achieve at the same level as whites. In other speeches and interviews given before and after the campaign, Lake did not raise that hope. In his 1959 talk to the Grove Presbyterian Church in Harnett County, Lake criticized the court for requiring "commingling of pupils in a classroom which will hold those with superior intellect to the faltering pace of the dull and less capable." He was talking of the Supreme Court's *Brown* decision.

Lake also revealed his thoughts on race in his correspondence with Wesley Critz George, the Chapel Hill medical school professor and founding president of the Patriots of North Carolina. George appears to have greatly influenced Lake, who adopted George's measured, academic tone. On issues of race, Lake's standard campaign speech in 1960 was similar to speeches George gave a few years earlier. While George believed that blacks were intellectually inferior, he, like Lake, did not call blacks names and did not speak in anger or hate. "We have worked out a system of social customs and laws, and personal and group understandings, that have enabled two greatly different peoples to live together in peace, mutual tolerance and helpfulness," George said in a mid-1950s speech that sounded much like Beverly Lake in 1960. "Under this system we have developed increasingly good, friendly and cordial race relations." George compared well-meaning integrationists to Neville Chamberlain and those who sought to appease Hitler in the 1930s. Lake used the same comparison when criticizing Governor Hodges in his 1957 speech on WRAL-TV.

In a speech George delivered at Dartmouth College, he explained why he believed blacks were intellectually inferior. The white race, he said, had creative talents and abilities that blacks had not demonstrated. The world's greatest civilizations were produced by whites, while blacks in Africa had not developed their continent. Whites invented the wheelbarrow, the wagon, the automobile, the locomotive, the steamship, and the airplane. Architecture, science, math, music—all were dominated by whites. And George said that blacks consistently scored less on tests measuring intelligence. George also confronted ministers who believed integration was the Christian action. God's will is sometimes misinterpreted, George said. He pointed to Abraham, who nearly sacrificed his son until an angel stopped him.

Lake believed what George believed. After reading George's Dartmouth speech, Lake wrote to George in May 1957: "I congratulate you upon it. It is, indeed, a scholarly and a common sense presentation of our side of this question." He liked George's speech so much that he referred to part of it while teaching his Sunday school class. God expects us to use our judgment, Lake wrote: "We have no right to shut our eyes to the accumulated experience of mankind and then trust Him to save us from our blunders in social relations. I am grateful to you for this contribution to my own thinking on the subject." A few years later, Lake would ask George to be his campaign co-chairman in Orange County.

In several interviews years after the 1960 election, Lake elaborated on his belief that blacks were intellectually inferior. "There are many tests which show the average black doesn't have the intelligence level of the average white," Lake said in 1978. "Tests also show that blacks are superior in athletics and strength but they wear out quicker because they have more disease and worse diets." In a 1992 interview, Lake said he had many black friends. "But I wouldn't want, I wouldn't want one of my great-grandchildren to marry one of their great-grandchildren," he said. "That's just a matter of pride and I believe that the white people are superior in development to the colored people." He added that there were many blacks he respected more than whites.

Lake said that it was not inconsistent to have race pride but to still treat people of different races with respect. "I'm delighted that I'm a white man and I'm delighted that all my descendants are white," Lake said. "I want that to be true. I think the white race is, in many respects, the white race is superior to the other races of the world in development. And we want to bring the other races up to our standard, rather than pull ours down to theirs. Racial pride is not inconsistent with decency and respect for other races. I have a great deal of respect for the Chinese, for example. They're remarkable people. In many respects, they probably surpass us in intellectual achievement. But I wouldn't want my granddaughter to marry a Chinese. There are just a lot of differences between our heritage. And heritage and environment and training as you're growing up has a great deal to do with your ideas of integrity and justice and right and wrong. And I would want my great-grandchildren, as so far as they do, I would want them to have the advantages that I had as a white man." Asked if he would object if his granddaughter married a third-generation Chinese immigrant born and raised in Wake Forest, Lake said, "Yes, I would. That may be unjustified prejudice, I don't know, but I wouldn't want my great-granddaughter to marry a man of Chinese heritage. Because I think you said three or four generations, I think heritage goes back far beyond two and three generations."

In the 1992 interview, Lake said he still believed segregated schools were best. He said he attended segregated schools and never felt that impaired his education. "I have respect for the Negro race," he said, "and I want to see every child—white, black, red or yellow—have an opportunity to become the finest person he or she can be." But, he said, "I think that there are differences between our races that ought to be recognized as legitimate differences and not necessarily making one inferior to the other. In some respects there should be equality." While grade schools should be segregated, there could be some integration in higher education to offer blacks opportunities that otherwise would not be available to them, he said.

Lake also said, "In my opinion, it may be or may not be wrong, the great mass of Negro people do not have as high standards of legal propriety as the great mass of white people. That may or may not be right but that is the way I feel. . . . Much of it is probably the way that they [blacks] have been trained and much of it is due to financial conditions in their homes. And other things, I don't know. But I think a good deal of it is due to, maybe I am in error in saying it is due to racial heritage, but I think that is probably a factor in it."

As far as public policy was concerned—and that is, after all, what campaigns are about—the issue in 1960 was whether black people could receive equal opportunities in a segregated society. Lake believed they could. He believed black people in North Carolina had been treated fairly. "Nowhere in the world are there better, more friendly relations between two different racial groups living side by side in great numbers than the relations between the white and Negro people of this state," Lake said in a campaign speech. "The white people of North Carolina have dealt justly with their Negro neighbors. We have no apology to make to anyone for our record in the education and development of the Negro people of this state and we make no such apology." Lake often referred to North Carolina's "equal, separate schools." He believed they were equal. "That policy [of separate but equal] has worked," Lake said in one speech. "In schools based on that policy, both white and Negro children of North Carolina have advanced toward education."

In his belief that black people had ample opportunity, Lake, like many white people of his generation, was blinded by an institution that was as natural to him as the sun rising in the east. Everywhere, in every facet of life, inequities abounded. Yet he was imprisoned by his idea of how society should be ordered and therefore unable to acknowledge those inequities. The man who believed deeply in justice and opportunity was willing to deny both to a whole class of United States citizens. The tragedy of segregation for black people was that it limited their opportunities and made them less than full partners in the American Dream. The tragedy for Beverly Lake was that it robbed him of friends and colleagues who could never, given the obstacles, rise to his academic, professional, and social standing. Lake lived life fully, often using his keen intellect to embrace new people and new challenges. Over the years, many of his professional adversaries spoke warmly of him. Yet Lake never embraced the black people who would have been his professional and social peers if given the chance. His rich life, which extended into his late eighties, was lesser for it. Still, in the spring of 1960 Lake's message about preserving segregation struck such a true chord with white North Carolinians that many were prepared to make him their governor.

Nine days before the May 28 primary, several thousand Democrats gathered in Raleigh for their state convention. Supporters of the four candidates for governor swamped Memorial Auditorium and turned the convention into a carnival. They paraded around the auditorium as drums, bugles, and a four-piece brass band played. The delegates waved pennants, giant photographs, and posters and released helium-filled balloons bearing the name of their candidate. The largest group of supporters appeared to belong to Terry Sanford. They wore blue-and-white buttons and carried blue-and-white placards. The loudest supporters, however, were those backing Beverly Lake. Outside, on the front lawn, the campaigns wooed delegates. The Lake campaign used a house trailer as its convention headquarters. Next to the trailer were several wooden kegs on which signs had been painted that said, "Have a drink of LAKE water." A sleepy donkey supported Terry Sanford by eyeing those who passed by.

The convention approved delegates to the National Democratic Convention in Los Angeles and adopted a platform, which included a plank advocating segregation. "We believe in the principle of separation of the races in our schools and all institutions involving personal and social relations," the Democrats said. That no doubt pleased Lake. But the keynote speaker, W. T. Joyner of Raleigh, also had a warning for the Democrats—although it seemed to be aimed specifically at Lake. Joyner praised the way North Carolina and Governor Hodges had handled the race issue. "The magnificent result of our Democratic leadership up to this date is that our schools are open, our children are being educated, there has been no school-connected violence," Joyner said. He urged the Democrats, "[K]eep your heads, keep your tempers, keep the state strongly Democratic and keep our schools open."

Joyner's speech reflected the fear among some Democrats that Lake was surging. Seawell and Larkins had spent most of the primary attacking Lake and Sanford. Lake's call to preserve segregation and Sanford's call to improve schools had dominated the debate. Larkins and Seawell increasingly were left on the outside. Larkins had known for a long time, since Seawell and Lake entered the race, that he was in trouble. His message—elect me because I'm the most experienced—never caught on.

Seawell also was having trouble being heard. His message seemed to be to elect him and continue the policies of Governor Hodges, including taking the moderate path on race. Seawell had challenged Lake head to head on race. He had portrayed Lake as an extremist whose election as governor would lead to federal troops and closed schools. But Lake seemed to be getting stronger, not weaker. H. W. Kendall, the editor of the *Greensboro Daily News*, surveyed delegates at the convention and reported that Sanford was in the lead. Seawell would be in a runoff. Larkins would get a good vote but his support was spotty. Lake was the unknown factor. Supporters of the other three candidates were worried about Lake, Kendall said. They believed Lake would get a lot of votes, but they did not know how to evaluate his strength. Many of his supporters were silent.

When Kays Gary of the *Charlotte Observer* spent several days talking with voters in Mecklenburg County, he had difficulty finding Lake supporters. Lake's local manager was not worried. Lake supporters often were silent about their candidate, the manager said. And his phone rang day and night with people asking how they could help. Gary kept looking. One day, he interviewed thirty-six people at a shopping center before he found a Lake supporter. "[Lake] is the most capable man and the smartest man of all the candidates," said the man, an assistant store manager. His wife supported Sanford. A laborer was "for Lake because he [was] the only one with any kind of stand" on segregation. At a small grill featuring beer, one customer was for Lake, saying, "It's about time somebody bucked the NAACP."

The *Observer*'s Jay Jenkins found more Lake support in the Piedmont counties between Charlotte and Durham, where textile mills and tobacco factories abounded. Lake had gained strength even in the liberal bastion of Orange County, home to the University of North Carolina. Lake visited nearby in the small town of Hillsborough and collected seven hundred dollars in three hours. Anyone who could raise that much money quickly in Hillsborough was "a genuine threat," according to the *Chapel Hill Weekly*. In Alamance County, which was home to a contingent of Patriots, Lake's name kept coming up, especially in rural areas and near textile mills. In Guilford County, Lake also was strong in textile villages, especially near High Point where there had been fights related to lunch-counter protests.

As the primary neared, Lake's campaign was confident. Typical of the Lake campaign's aggressive attitude was a newspaper ad that ran the day before the primary promoting a Lake television commercial. "We Dare You!!" said the headline. It continued, "To watch and listen to Dr. I. Beverly Lake's platform tonight . . . And not cast your vote for him for governor of North Carolina tomorrow." The newspaper ad said that Lake believed in a balanced budget; returning to basics in the schools; the right of the state to operate without interference from the federal government; helping small farmers; separating white and black children in the public schools; exposing the NAACP; and the right of businessmen to operate their business as they see fit. In a television address the night before the Saturday primary, Lake continued on his main theme, attacking the NAACP for promoting integration.

On Saturday, May 28, more than 650,000 voted in the Democratic primary, a new North Carolina record. In the early evening, the candidates waited nervously in Raleigh as polls closed and the results from one hundred counties were counted. Seawell and Larkins headquarters were in the Hotel Sir Walter. Sanford and his supporters moved to the ballroom of the Carolina Hotel, where the returns were posted on a large blackboard. A three-piece band stood by. Lake remained at his home in Wake Forest until 9 P.M., then traveled to see his supporters, who set up in a vacant building in downtown Raleigh. They sipped coffee and soft drinks, yelling each time a return showed Lake in the lead.

The results stunned the state's political establishment. Not unexpectedly, Sanford led the ticket with 41.3 percent of the vote—short of the majority needed to avoid a runoff. Far more surprising was the second-place finisher: Lake won 27.8 percent, finishing well ahead of the other two candidates. Seawell and Larkins split the remainder almost evenly, with Seawell winning 15.5 percent and Larkins 15.4 percent. Seawell, hot-headed until the end, went on television to denounce overactive supporters who moments earlier had invaded Lake headquarters and paraded Seawell placards before the TV cameras. As he trailed Lake, Seawell refused to concede, insisting that some city precincts would revive his chances. They did not.

Lake told a cheering crowd of supporters that he had not made a final decision but that he intended to call for a second primary. He said he had received phone calls and telegrams from supporters of Larkins and Seawell urging him to ask for a runoff. "This, plus the splendid vote I have received today, encourages me tremendously," Lake said. At the Carolina Hotel, Sanford also said he had promises of support from backers of Larkins and Seawell. He had expected a second primary. "I am ready and raring to go," Sanford said. Sanford carried seventy of one hundred counties. He was strong from east to west. He led Lake in his home county of Wake and Seawell in his home county of Robeson. He won every western county except for Madison and Swain, which Larkins won.

Sanford did well among black voters. In Winston-Salem, in ten all-black or mostly black precincts, Sanford won 93 percent of the vote. In Raleigh, in three mostly black precincts, he won 95 percent. In Greensboro, in three mostly black precincts, Sanford won 89 percent. In some other cities results among black voters were more mixed. In Durham, in five mostly black precincts, Seawell won 89 percent and Sanford was second with 7 percent. Sanford later said he intentionally did not seek black votes in Durham because he expected a runoff and did not want to be vulnerable to having received what racial conservatives often called the "bloc vote." "I had seen to it that Seawell got the Durham vote," Sanford said years later. "I just saw to it. I not only didn't lift my finger but I told [a person Sanford believed could deliver votes in black neighborhoods], 'See that Seawell gets that vote.'" In Charlotte, in four all-black or mostly

Former Governor Kerr Scott and Terry Sanford
(Courtesy of the North Carolina Division of Archives and History)

On February 4, 1960, in front of 5,000 people in Fayetteville, Sanford called for a "New Day" in North Carolina.

(Courtesy of *The News and Observer* and the North Carolina Division of Archives and History)

The challengers: John Larkins, Robert Gavin, Malcolm Seawell, and I.
Beverly Lake

(Courtesy of *The News and Observer* and the North Carolina Division of Archives
and History)

His staff said Sanford shook more than 40,000 hands during the campaign.

(Courtesy of *The News and Observer* and the North Carolina
Division of Archives and History)

Sanford, here with lieutenant governor candidate Cloyd Philpott, campaigned relentlessly, visiting each of the 100 counties at least three times.

(Courtesy of the Southern Historical Collection, University of North Carolina, Chapel Hill)

I. Beverly Lake and his campaign manager, future U.S. Senator Robert Morgan

(Courtesy of *The News and Observer* and the North Carolina Division of Archives and History)

Lake, a long-time law professor, was a formal person with little political experience. But after receiving lessons from former student and local pol John Burney, he grew to be a good campaigner.

(Courtesy of *The Charlotte Observer*)

The irrepressible John Burney, holding Lake's arm, came up with the idea of televising Lake's rallies. The rallies, which the Lake campaign believed were the first political rallies televised live in the United States, attracted huge, vocal crowds and became Lake's campaign trademark.

(Courtesy of I. Beverly Lake Jr.)

Among Lake's conservative supporters was future U.S. Senator Jesse Helms (to Lake's left). In this picture, Lake speaks to supporters on the night of the first primary, when he leapt beyond two veteran Democrats and into a run-off against Sanford.

(Courtesy of I. Beverly Lake Jr.)

Many of Lake's most ardent supporters had never been involved before in politics. The Lake campaign assembled an army of supporters who were passionate about preserving segregation.

(Courtesy of I. Beverly Lake Jr.)

Both Lake and Sanford aired television commercials, but most of the campaign was waged face-to-face with voters in settings like this one in rural Anson County.

(Courtesy of *The Charlotte Observer*)

Lake on the night of the second primary when it was clear he had lost to Sanford. Robert Morgan is to Lake's right.

(Courtesy of *The News and Observer* and the North Carolina Division of Archives and History)

Lake congratulates Sanford.

(Courtesy of *The News and Observer* and the North Carolina Division of Archives and History)

Sanford and Governor Luther Hodges

(Courtesy of *The Charlotte Observer*)

"I hope I won't pull you down," Kennedy told Sanford during the Democratic National Convention in July. Sanford was criticized heavily in North Carolina for endorsing the Catholic Kennedy but he never backed away. He adopted the Kennedy campaign as part of his own and carried the state for Kennedy.

(Top and middle: Courtesy of the Rare Book, Manuscript, and Special Collections Library, Duke University Bottom: Courtesy of *The News and Observer* and the North Carolina Division of Archives and History)

President Johnson modeled his War on Poverty on an initiative Sanford started in North Carolina. This picture was taken outside Rocky Mount, North Carolina.

(Courtesy of the North Carolina Division of Archives and History)

Twenty-six years after his triumphant campaign for governor, Sanford attempted a political comeback by running for the U.S. Senate. Sanford won but North Carolina voters turned him out of office six years later.

(Courtesy *The News and Observer* and the North Carolina Division of Archives and History) black precincts, Sanford won 52 percent; the other three candidates split the vote. Lake generally did poorly in the all-black or mostly black precincts in the biggest cities, winning 1 or 2 percent of the vote. In the four Charlotte precincts, however, Lake won 17 percent.

Lake's strength was in eastern North Carolina and along the Virginia border where segregationist views ran strongest. He won twenty-two counties. In the more populous Piedmont, where Sanford built up his big lead, Lake carried Durham and Iredell Counties. Lake ran a strong second or third in many of the counties he did not win. Lake won in New Hanover and Pender in the southeast, where Sanford had said he did not expect to lose.

Sanford and his staff were determined not to repeat Frank Graham's mistakes from ten years earlier, when Graham's campaign lost momentum after the first primary. Sanford's staff worked until dawn Sunday morning analyzing returns but was back at work in room 4-B of the Carolina Hotel by noon Sunday. Sanford sounded a warning. He preferred the race issue not dominate a runoff campaign. "We could do what we have to do a lot better without stirring [it] up," he said. But Sanford said he would not be defensive about his stance. "My position on the race issue is very sound," Sanford said. "I have deliberately refrained from discussing it, although I have laid it out so the public can see it. I have never engaged in personal attacks, mud-slinging or racial or class bitterness. I am going to run a positive campaign but I am not going to be abused."

On that same day, Lake fielded phone calls and met with advisers but did not announce he would call for a runoff. "Dr. Lake has been so overwhelmed with phone calls and telegrams and well wishers that we have been able to confer only a few minutes this afternoon," said Robert Morgan. Lake would announce a decision the following day. There was little doubt, however, about what Lake would do. He had entered the campaign late. He had little money. He had limited political experience. He had a makeshift organization. Yet he had vaulted well beyond two political veterans and into the spotlight of the state's political arena. Now he had four weeks to convince North Carolinians that they should preserve segregation by electing him governor.

Chapter 7

ATTACKS AND LIES

At 4 P.M. Monday at his headquarters, Lake called for a runoff. Democrats would vote in less than four weeks, on Saturday, June 25. It
would not be a fight of personalities, Lake said. He called Sanford "an able
gentleman of pleasing personality and excellent character. . . . He is personally attractive and I like him but I am opposed to his economic policies and program and I am opposed to the mixing of white and Negro
children in our public schools." Lake had received hundreds of phone
calls, telegrams, and visits from people across the state, urging him to call
for a second primary. He believed the people had a right to a clear choice
between Sanford and himself with no distractions from other candidates.

Lake outlined what he saw as their chief differences. He was for a
sound, conservative financial policy for the state; Sanford was for free
spending with heavy taxes. Lake opposed the NAACP and would resist
its program at every step; Sanford did not think the NAACP's program
should be discussed. Lake was supported by rank-and-file workers, union
and nonunion; Sanford had the support of labor leaders. The Raleigh
News and Observer, the *Charlotte Observer*, and their afternoon newspapers opposed Lake and consistently misrepresented his positions; Sanford
had their support.

He said that Sanford's supporters had misrepresented Lake's position
on schools by saying he would close them. The governor did not have the

164

power to close schools and Lake said he had no desire to do so. He would do everything he could to keep schools operating successfully. "For that reason," Lake said, "I shall continue to fight the NAACP and with your help we shall keep your schools open, equal and separate." He urged voters to join him in creating a climate of opinion against integration, as Gov. Ernest Hollings had done in South Carolina. Hollings fought hard against integration, Lake said, yet there had been none of the dire consequences predicted by Lake's foes. There had been no closed schools, no invasion by federal troops, no violence—and no integration. The same was true, Lake said, in Georgia, Florida, Alabama, Mississippi, and Louisiana. (Actually, Florida had token integration and Georgia was under a court order to integrate some of its schools in 1961.) Lake said the troubles in Little Rock, Arkansas, emerged because that city tried moderation and voluntary, token integration. "That is the program which can lead to a similar situation in North Carolina," he said.

He urged North Carolinians to follow the lead of Florida voters. A week earlier, in a primary runoff, Florida Democrats chose hard-line segregationist Farris Bryant over more moderate Doyle Carlton, who had the backing of Gov. Leroy Collins. When they were asked during the campaign if they would carry out an order from the U.S. Supreme Court to integrate schools, Carlton said yes. Bryant said that it was not the function of the governor to see that federal court orders were obeyed and that he would use every lawful means to delay integration. Lake noted that Florida, like North Carolina, had "a moderate administration with its eyes on national political office." Florida Governor Collins had just been chosen chairman of the Democratic National Convention. It was well known in North Carolina political circles that Governor Hodges was interested in serving in the next presidential administration. The Florida runoff had been dominated by issues of race. While there were some parallels, Lake's analogy did not always fit. While Lake would have to come from behind to win, in Florida the stronger segregationist was the front runner. In a ten-candidate field in the first primary, Bryant led Carlton by about seven thousand votes (and then won the runoff with 55 percent of the vote). Lake, on the other hand, trailed Sanford by more than eighty-five thousand votes in the first primary. Nonetheless, Lake could indeed point to another southern state where a strong segregationist recently beat a moderate. Lake said he was confident he could win, but he was out of money. He urged his supporters to contribute to his campaign.

Lake's speech was broadcast live by WRAL-TV and WRAL radio, which were owned by Lake's law partner, A. J. Fletcher. Sanford responded quickly. He already had talked to reporters once that day and told them he would campaign in all one hundred counties in the runoff. But after Lake's speech, he again beckoned reporters to his headquarters at the Carolina Hotel, just a block away from Lake's headquarters. "Let's get this straight right now on the race issue," Sanford said. North Carolina's approach was best and Sanford said he supported it. No other plan would work. As for the NAACP, Sanford said, "I have been and will continue to oppose to the end domination or direction by the NAACP." He said that Lake's approach was riling racial tensions and could lead to more and faster integration. "Professor Lake is bringing on integration when he stirs this up," Sanford said. "I don't believe in playing race against race or group against group. Let's use our common sense and common decency. Let's use our brains instead of our mouths."

The real issue, Sanford said, was about lifting North Carolina's schools from the bottom ten to the top ten. It was about giving North Carolina's children an opportunity to compete on even terms with children from other states. Lake said that the state could not afford Sanford's schools program. "Professor Lake would now join the hold-the-liners," Sanford said. "This, then, is the true issue, the true difference, and I accept the challenge to battle it out on how we can build for the future of our state."

Sanford was asked why he had not discussed the race issue in more detail. He read from a newspaper editorial that said that, unlike other southern states, no governor since 1900 had been elected in North Carolina by campaigning on race-related issues. "I have felt that the best way to deal with this problem was with intelligence, calmness and deliberation," Sanford told reporters. He again issued what seemed to be a warning to Lake to back away from criticizing him on the race question. "I say again, however, that I will not be abused," Sanford said. "I don't think I've ever given any indication that I'm afraid of fighting. If I have, be disabused of that right now." As he had for the entire campaign, Sanford again had attempted to steer the debate away from race and onto improving schools. But he must have sensed that if he were to succeed, he would have to take more drastic measures. On the next day, he had much more to say.

After Lake's call for a runoff was broadcast by WRAL-TV, Sanford requested equal time to rebut what he said were Lake's personal attacks. The station agreed to give Sanford the time on its television and radio stations. If his audiences expected the normally mild-mannered Sanford, the one George Wallace said would "bore yo' ass off," they were shocked. Sanford attacked Lake from the beginning of his address until the end, sometimes personally. On Sunday and Monday, Sanford had spoken cryptically about not being abused and being willing to fight back. Now it became clear what he meant. This was a crucial moment for the state, Sanford said. His voice was clear and forceful, almost belligerent. The runoff, he said, could be the worst and most bitter in state history if it was not conducted with dignity and restraint. The governor's office should not be degraded by a vicious, bitter, or false campaign, he said; the people did not want a campaign of smear or fear.

"I was shocked by the opening tone of Professor Lake's call for a second primary," Sanford said. "From the hundreds of telephone calls we received, I know that other citizens were also shocked. Because he said I was in favor of mixing the races in the schools, and because this is an absolute falsehood, I must take this opportunity to set the record straight. I was shocked to find that instead of running against me, whom he can't beat, Professor Lake tried to set up a straw man to run against. He is injecting a false issue on integration and it is false because I am, and he knows I am, opposed to integration. The difference is that I know how to handle it and he doesn't."

Sanford questioned Lake's motives and his competence to speak on the issue. "Professor Lake yells about mixing of the races, about NAACP domination, and he is appealing to blind prejudice"—for emphasis, Sanford stretched out the *blllind*—"for the pure and simple purpose of getting himself a few votes." He said that North Carolinians wanted to follow the state's current path on school integration and that his rural eastern North Carolina roots would allow him to manage the race issue better than Lake. "I know how the people of North Carolina feel about segregation," Sanford said. "I did not grow up in an ivory tower of a college campus as the professor did. I was raised around the cotton patches and tobacco fields of Scotland County and I know how to handle the situation better than a theoretical college professor." He would no more be directed by the NAACP, he said, then he would blow up the state capitol.

Sanford sought to assure white North Carolinians, especially in the east, that he was one of them. But he also sought to scare them about what a Governor Lake could mean to the state's schools. Lake had used scare tactics throughout the first primary, warning white voters that the token integration that looked benign then could lead to their having mulatto grandchildren. Now it was Sanford's turn. The greatest fear Lake stirred in voters was that his "climate of opposition" would lead to a federal government crackdown involving troops and closed schools. Even for a white segregationist voter, who perhaps did not like the small amount of integration in North Carolina's schools, was Lake worth that risk? Did moderates in North Carolina want a Little Rock–type crackdown in their state? Sanford said that Lake's call for resistance could jeopardize North Carolina's pupil assignment strategy and could be used in court to show the state was not dealing in good faith.

North Carolina's plan was working, Sanford said. Other states were copying it. It gave local school boards and local voters control over their schools. Was it worth the risk of electing Lake and having North Carolina's plan declared unconstitutional? "This would lead to bloodshed and integrated or closed schools," Sanford said. "The people of North Carolina do not want integration and we cannot afford to close our schools, but this is where the professor would lead us. If Professor Lake keeps up his present approach he is inadvertently leading North Carolina down the road to complete integration, to federal troops, to closed schools. We do not want that—we cannot have it." Sanford framed the issues of the second primary this way: Better schools or no schools. Go forward or hold the line. "I take my stand for keeping the schools open and improving them," he said. "And I stand for moving forward with a positive program—not holding the tight line against economic progress in North Carolina." He called on Lake to "debate the true issues of this campaign . . . how we can build a greater future for our state."

It was a new Terry Sanford. "The most striking political development of the week," wrote Jay Jenkins in the *Charlotte Observer*, "was the emergence of Terry Sanford, front-runner in the governor's race, as a different type of campaigner." Different, yes, but not surprisingly so. Those who remembered his role in the 1954 Senate race knew he would not, in his words, "be abused" on the issue of race. In the first primary, as long as it did not detract from his message, Sanford was willing to let Lake, Larkins, and Seawell bloody each other on integration. But now that he and Lake were one on one, Sanford was not going to lay back and let the opposition take the offensive on race, as Frank Graham had allowed Willis Smith to do ten years earlier. At the beginning of the second primary, Sanford immediately returned to Fayetteville to retrieve his notebook on how to combat a racially oriented campaign. "I didn't have to worry too much about that in the first primary because I didn't let them focus on me," Sanford recalled. But in the runoff, Sanford said, "I had to remember the earlier campaigns. You don't let that issue get burning before you stopped it." That meant attacking and neutralizing the race issue, so that he could get his central message out.

That's what he did. In attempting to put Lake on the defensive, Sanford was willing to stretch the truth. In his television rebuttal, Sanford said, "Because he said I was in favor of mixing the races in the schools, and because this is an absolute falsehood, I must take this opportunity to set the record straight." Actually, Lake did not say Sanford was in favor of integration. Lake said he opposed the NAACP, and he said, "Mr. Sanford takes the position that its program for our state should not be discussed." Sanford responded to a charge Lake never made. That is perhaps a fine point; one could conclude that Lake implied Sanford was for integration. Certainly Lake said he opposed integration and he and Sanford were different.

More significant was the second part of Sanford's statement, when Sanford said it was "an absolute falsehood" that he favored school integration. Sanford repeated this point to his television audience. "I am, and he knows I am, opposed to integration," he said. Sanford's future record would show he favored integration. Not long after the 1960 campaign, he would, among other signs that he favored integration, make a statement by sending his children to an integrated public school.

In interviews more than thirty-five years after the campaign, Sanford said he generally was proud of what he had said and thought he had been honest with voters and himself. But he acknowledged he was not completely truthful. "I fudged one time when I said Dr. Lake knows I'm not an integrationist," Sanford said. "I grant you that I knew at that time that I was using that word—I saw it as mildly hypocritical. But I though it was not dishonest because I was not an integrationist as you would define that word in its most extreme manner. I never did think we needed to apologize. . . . I thought I was being very, very careful to not be over-labeled. If I'd said I'm an integrationist, you wouldn't be sitting here talking to me. That word wasn't possible to define in a rational way." To hard-core segregationists, integration meant intermarriage between blacks and whites, Sanford said. He said that it was important to remember what the racial climate was like in 1960, and that strategies and definitions were unsettled. "An integrationist? What the hell did that mean? I wasn't going to let him put that title on me," he said. "You can't let those words be used. You've got to talk about what you stand for. I might be an integrationist in my definition but not in their definition."

Sanford described his challenge this way: "You couldn't get too far ahead of the people and you couldn't say anything that you'd later feel bad about. . . . Under the circumstances, I was cautiously going as far as I could go. . . . This was a campaign about the future of North Carolina. One of the issues in the future of North Carolina was how we handled the race issue. I attempted to give a bright look of the future and not let this be a slamming around on the race issue." There were other ways to talk about opportunities for all people without using words like integration, Sanford said: "A person would have been very foolish to say, 'I'm in favor of integration.' But you could easily say, 'We've got to have equal opportunities in the schools. The Supreme Court has said so. We've got to admit without regard to race in the colleges. . . .' You could have said all of those things, all of which meant integration, but none of them used that explosive, provocative word. So I deliberately wouldn't let them put that title on me."

Sanford's supporters acknowledge his racial sleight of hand but say voters knew he was different than Lake. And he was. Unlike Lake, who believed appropriate opportunities were available to blacks, Sanford believed blacks in 1960 did not have the opportunities that they should. When Sanford was putting together his education platform, he noted that many young blacks neglected or abandoned their education because they saw that their opportunities were blocked. "Every day they saw too many examples within their own race which illustrated to them that education was not likely to lead to jobs commensurate with their abilities and aspirations," Sanford later said. It was a lie, Sanford said then, to encourage blacks to stay in school but not allow them equal opportunities once they left school.

Unlike Lake, who said that whites in North Carolina had no reason to apologize for how they treated blacks, Sanford publicly stated that opportunities for blacks had been limited. When he visited Eastway Junior High in Charlotte during the primary to talk to a ninth-grade civics class of white students, Sanford was asked, "Isn't it true that we have higher I.Q.s and accomplishments than Negro students?" "That is perhaps true," Sanford said, "but they have had only two or three generations of educational opportunity." Unlike Lake, Sanford campaigned before integrated audiences. When he visited Bertie County in northeastern North Carolina during the campaign, he stopped by Monk Harrington's farm-machinery plant in Lewiston. Harrington gathered his 350 or so employees to listen to Sanford. About half were white, half were black. "I never paid attention [to color] when I was hiring people,"

Harrington said. "He just impressed all the people as being a down-to-earth individual."

Sanford's supporters said he was sincere about creating equal opportunities. Clint Newton, the Shelby textile businessman, said he and Sanford talked often in the 1950s about how the South needed to change. "I'm talking about deep down. He just felt that problem was going to have to be settled if indeed we were to grow as a state," Newton said. "Terry and I would discuss these things. He had a deep feeling things needed to be corrected. We'd talk about separate drinking fountains and how that had to change."

Sanford once said that within six months of entering college at Chapel Hill and meeting Frank Graham, he knew racial discrimination was "absolutely wrong and immoral, and ought to be corrected." While Sanford believed change needed to happen, he perhaps wasn't sure what to do. Dickson Phillips, Sanford's law partner and lifelong friend, said that it is difficult to look back after the civil rights movement and remember how confusing the times were. Even white people sympathetic to blacks were unsure of which course to take and how fast. "It's hard to recapture the whole trap the region was in," Phillips said in 1998. Sanford knew changes needed to happen, Phillips said. He had grown up aware of the plight of blacks. His parents were fair-minded and did not tolerate racial slurs. He was disturbed by the inequities he saw.

About Sanford's stated opposition to integration in the runoff, Phillips said, "I think that's politics. It went against his grain. Boy, I tell you, that race thing was hard to deal with. What I think he felt was—what all of us knew was—it cannot last. It [integration] has got to come. But nobody knew how to take the first step." When Sanford said he was opposed to integration, "I'm sure he had his fingers crossed," Phillips said. "I'm sure he meant, 'I don't think that will happen tomorrow.' I'm not sure he could have made it [and won the runoff] without jiggling." Said Sanford supporter Martha McKay, "He treated people equally but he didn't get on the stump for integration, no. He abhorred discrimination and the way many minority people were treated. He did not approve of it. . . . I think he went as far as he thought he could go."

172

* * *

Since the beginning of the campaign, Sanford evaded the race question and sought to assure white voters that he was one of them. Once, campaigning in northeastern North Carolina, he was approached by a man who had been drinking.

"I want you to tell me," the man said, "where you stand on the nigger question."

"Fella, you don't have to ask me where I stand," Sanford said emphatically, locking his eyes on his questioner. "You know where I stand."

"Well, I'm glad," the man said, satisfied with Sanford's answer. "That's just where I thought you stood."

In some northeastern counties, Sanford supporters learned to wink and say, "Don't worry, Old Terry's all right on the Negro question." But now, paired against Lake with no other candidates distracting the public view, Sanford moved aggressively to make sure he would not get beat on race. He was getting plenty of advice on how to handle the issue. Some supporters thought Sanford had not stated clearly enough his opposition to the NAACP and integration. One of the losing campaigns gave Sanford its list of talking points about the other candidates. The Lake items were as follows:

- Has one platform and issue . . . segregation in our public schools.
- No legislative experience or administrative experience.
- No service to the Democratic Party.
- Offers no substitute for the present school plan, which is working well in North Carolina. Would probably lead us to another "Little Rock" re closing of schools.
- Has publicly stated that he would not follow the Supreme Court of the United States which definitely is, whether we like it or not, the law of the land, and without a respect for these laws would lead us to disorder and violence.
- Has led the people to believe that as Governor can alter the present policy re: school integration in North Carolina and yet he stated in Hendersonville at the Kiwanis Club August 20, 1959, "It is for the Legislature, not the Governor, to fix and declare the policy of this State."

Perhaps equally helpful to the Sanford campaign was the list of talking points about Sanford, which included these items:

- Been running for Governor for the past 25 years.
- One term in the State Senate.
- A "B" grade lawyer according to Martindale Hubbell which rates lawyers in America.
- Is denying endorsement of the labor bosses and NAACP. We will know on May 28 for whom they voted.
- Has the endorsement of organized Negro bloc vote—claiming vote that was Kerr Scott's.
- A liberal who has made the most irresponsible promises re integration, roads and farmers ever made by a Gubernatorial candidate in the history of North Carolina. It would take $500,000,000 to do the things Terry Sanford has promised.
- No service to the Democratic Party except one term in the Senate and YDC President for one year.
- No service to the people.
- Attempting to ride a dead man's coattail and yet was never appointed to anything and was not heard of in Scott's Gubernatorial campaign. Was paid $7,500 to manage his Senatorial campaign.
- Is the attorney for the natural gas industry in North Carolina who repeatedly tries to get rates increased, therefore, cost the consumer more money.
- On two occasions, one in Sanford and another on television, Terry Sanford adopted publicly the statement of I. Beverly Lake re segregation, etc.
- Good name—"High Tax Terry."

In early June, Greensboro attorney Clyde Shreve, who had managed John Larkins' campaign, wrote to Bert Bennett, offering advice on Lake and the race issue. Lunch-counter protests led by the NAACP were about to begin in the Wrightsville Beach area, he wrote. "This will play directly into Lake's hands, particularly in eastern North Carolina," Shreve said. "I believe Terry should immediately make a strong statement, clearing himself completely from any NAACP identification. . . . I want to emphasize as strongly as I know how the importance of a well-defined statement relative to NAACP activity and as far in advance as

174

possible of further incidents. I believe it is urgent that such a statement be made now."

Shreve attached a proposed speech for Sanford. In it, he criticized the NAACP, without naming the group, for disrupting the "wholesome" relationship between blacks and whites in North Carolina. "I refer specifically to the lunch counter sit-down strikes in North Carolina and other threatened incidents designed to create tension and turmoil in the state," Shreve wrote in the proposed speech. "This movement merits the condemnation of all responsible citizens." The movement would fail, Shreve wrote, because North Carolinians would use common sense and reason to solve their problems. The NAACP would have destroyed public schools after the Supreme Court's decision in 1954 because it wanted immediate integration. But North Carolina calmly responded with the Pearsall Plan. "This is the North Carolina way," Shreve suggested Sanford say. "I stand solidly behind the North Carolina position. I am dead opposed to integration of our public schools. We will not be prompted to act in anger. We must remain a thinking people. Truly, through the exercise of common sense and reason, there is no problem North Carolina cannot resolve now or in the future."

Sanford did not criticize the sit-in protestors, as Shreve proposed, but he did step up his criticism of the NAACP. He also talked often about the North Carolina way, about how the state could work its way through the problem. "North Carolina has the courage and the wisdom, the strength and the confidence, to shape its own destiny," Sanford told a group from eastern North Carolina in mid June. "North Carolina has never been afraid and we are not afraid now. We are going to continue to go forward to give our children a better chance, to build a better state through better schools." What the state needed, he often said, was not massive resistance, but massive intelligence.

To avoid getting scalded on the race issue, Sanford continued to try to turn the issue back at Lake, even if it meant Sanford was crafty or loose with the facts. Just as the Willis Smith campaign did in 1950, the Lake campaign produced pamphlets attempting to show that its opponent received most of the black vote in the first primary. The Lake pamphlets showed that Sanford received the vast majority of votes in several black or mostly black precincts in Raleigh. Sanford responded by crediting that vote to his energetic campaign managers in Raleigh. Citing the same reason—energetic campaign managers—Sanford said that John Larkins won most of the black vote in Buncombe County and Malcolm Seawell won most in Durham. "And who do you think got the Negro votes—all of them—in Iredell County?" Sanford asked during one speech. "Professor Lake got 'em in Iredell."

Sanford was proud of throwing the "bloc vote" issue back at Lake—even though he later acknowledged that he was not sure what he was saying was true. He said that Larkins won the black vote in Asheville because the sheriff there was for Larkins. "I was reasonably sure he'd gotten it," Sanford recalled. "And I said Dr. Lake got all the black vote in Iredell County. Well, it took him a week to sputter and spew and try to challenge that and deny it. And he got off me for a week. . . . I don't know whether you could identify the black vote [in Iredell] but he had his greatest friend up there and supporter, who had a reputation for buying the black vote in 1960, and I think he probably did. But the point is, that was one of the things of being more aggressive in attacking him, to take the race issue out of the campaign as such." Sanford considered his Iredell offensive one of the best, most effective strategies of his campaign. When he retold the story over the years, he often chuckled at how it flummoxed Lake.

Lake did stay defensive on the issue. Even on the last night before the runoff, when he went on television a final time to talk directly to voters, he was still saying Iredell blacks had not supported him in great numbers. Sanford, he said, was either reckless with the truth or deliberately lying. Lake was right. Blacks made up about 10 percent of the registered voters in Iredell County. There were twenty-three precincts; blacks were not a majority in any of them, making it difficult to determine how they voted. In the precinct with the highest percentage of blacks (Statesville No. 2), about 40 percent of the registered voters were black. In that precinct, Lake won 45 percent of the vote to Sanford's 40 percent.

If Lake had won a lopsided number of black votes in Statesville No. 2, he probably would have dominated that precinct, because he ran strong with white voters throughout Iredell. (Lake lead the ticket in Iredell, winning 45 percent of the vote in the first primary to Sanford's 35 percent.) But Lake did not dominate in Statesville No. 2. Given the scarcity of blacks in Iredell, it was impossible to tell if they had voted strongly for one candidate. There was some evidence that black voters gave most of their votes to Sanford. In the two other precincts with a relatively high percentage of black voters (Turnersburg and Coddle Creek No. 2 were about 20 percent black), Sanford won large majorities. The *Statesville Record and Landmark,* which supported Lake, said that Sanford had the support of "the NAACP-led Negroes." When Sanford said that Lake won "all" of the black vote in Iredell County, he was, at the least, exaggerating wildly.

Sanford did not apologize, though, not during the campaign, not after it. He would do whatever it took to neutralize Lake on the race issue. He wasn't going to be "abused." "Frank Graham wouldn't have done that," Sanford said of his Iredell claim. "That wasn't dishonest. It might have been sneaky. I think it was just aggressive defense of the position. It was, of course, a dishonest issue from the start to finish to talk about a bloc vote. In any event, I learned from Frank Graham not to be that nice on that particular issue."

Sanford stayed on the attack. He continued to say that electing Lake could mean closed schools. "He is the advocate of massive resistance and private schools," Sanford told a group of supporters in mid June. "He tried to defeat the Pearsall Plan—the only hope North Carolina, and especially eastern North Carolina, has to avoid the program of the NAACP. He tried to defeat the Pearsall Plan by preparing a massive resistance plan which was introduced by Robert Morgan, Lake's campaign manager. . . . He advocated private schools as the only hope. . . . By fear he is trying to lead North Carolina down the dangerous path of massive resistance." He said that Lake would hurt economic development because businesses would not relocate to a state where there was strife or danger of schools closing. Sanford later explained his strategy of attacks: "I accused Lake of closing the public schools, he having made statements to that effect. I accused him of running industry away. I accused him of voting Republican in the last three elections. He had to take up a lot of time answering those things."

Sanford also did not want to be seen as soft on the NAACP, which Lake hammered on every day. In the first primary, Sanford mildly criticized the NAACP. In the runoff, Sanford criticized the group more often—even though its leaders supported him. In a paid television show broadcast statewide, Sanford attacked what he said were two extremist groups—the NAACP and the segregationist Patriots—that would destroy the school system. He said that Lake was playing into the hands of the NAACP by giving it free publicity and unintentionally building its membership. Another time, Sanford said, "I don't like the Supreme Court decision. I don't have anything to do with the NAACP. But cussing them is not going to help our problem. It's going to help the NAACP solve one of its problems. That is the sale of new memberships." Lake often asked his supporters to distinguish between the NAACP and blacks. Sanford concurred, saying the NAACP did not control the black people of the state.

Sanford liked to tell a story about his young son, Terry Jr., who asked him what NAACP stood for. Sanford replied, "Nobody Ain't About to Control Papa." That was tame, compared to what Lake was saying. But it put Sanford in the position of criticizing people who were supporting him, such as Kelly Alexander, president of the NAACP in North Carolina. "I had to be very careful about what I said about the NAACP because I was being accused of taking NAACP money, which wasn't true," Sanford remembered. "Kelly was a big supporter of mine but he was very discreet about it. I was right: the NAACP was an extremist group, if you talk about the middle. . . . I wouldn't have any problem with that statement but that's about as brash as I got. But I assure you I wasn't critical of them in a way that offended them."

Lake supporters thought Sanford was not telling the truth about race. They thought he was more liberal on race than he was saying. "He presented himself in a light that was not the true Terry Sanford," Lake supporter Allen Bailey later said. "He made one speech to be elected and one speech to serve. It was a lesson I tried to teach Dr. Lake but never was able to get across to him. And that is, before you can do what you'd like to do, you must first be elected. And that sometimes you must compromise what you believe to be elected. And he was never willing to do that. . . . He [Sanford] did fudge. All you have to do is read his own words. He thought that the end justified the means. That was a widely held perception of Dr. Lake and his staff—that what Terry Sanford was saying was not what he was planning on doing."

Some of Sanford's black supporters essentially agreed. They believed Sanford was saying what he needed to say to get elected. They did not hold it against him. They believed he was doing what he needed to do to win. While Sanford didn't say what they wanted to hear on integration, they thought he was limited by the politics of the era. And they believed he was not trying to set people apart but bring them together. "His dialogue was totally different than that of I. Beverly Lake," said businessman John Winters, a Sanford supporter who would become the first black member of the Raleigh City Council in 1961. "The lines were drawn. While you may not come out and say exactly where you were, your actions spoke louder than your words in many instances. He certainly didn't use the kind of language of George Wallace and [Orval] Faubus and Beverly Lake. . . . Beverly Lake was talking about limiting our access to public accommodations and education." While Sanford always extended his hand and treated him like an equal, Winters said, "I don't think Dr. Lake would have shaken my hand if I'd come into his company."

Sanford tried to offend as few voters as possible by being vague. His aide Graham Jones would later write, "Sanford's position [on race] was short and clear: 'What we need,' he said, 'is massive intelligence, not massive resistance.'" Short and clear? Hardly. It's true Sanford clearly did not support massive resistance. But it was far less clear what he *did* support. Jones acknowledged that Sanford was supported by "strong advocates of civil rights and strong advocates of states rights." Those more conservative on race were assured by Sanford's claims that he was not for integration. Those more liberal on race heard something else—that he accepted the Supreme Court's decisions and believed the state needed to adapt and move forward.

Zechariah Alexander, brother of state NAACP president Kelly Alexander, said that Sanford also worked behind the scenes to win black support. "Those who he had contacted personally and who knew him very well understood his position and knew that he was a friend, even though sometimes he had to say things that looked like he was on the fence," Alexander recalled. If Sanford had pushed faster for racial change, Alexander did not believe Sanford could have won. He did not fault Sanford's strategy. Neither did his late brother, he said. "Sanford was a very astute and smart guy," Zechariah Alexander said. "You could be so outspoken that you'd get yourself killed quickly. And then you'd defeated the whole purpose of your program. I don't think he [his brother] held it against Sanford. I think he had high regard for Sanford. He [Kelly Alexander] understood the politics of the situation. . . . Most of the intelligent black people understood that a politician had to be very astute and careful about what he said in that area if you wanted to make any progress. You can be too outspoken at the wrong time. When the odds are against you, you've got to use your head."

Black newspapers sometimes took a similar, subtle approach. They steadfastly opposed Lake but they did not want to give him ammunition. If they skewered Lake in their editorials, they knew the Lake campaign would make copies and hand them out to whites, many of whom would have been hostile to crusading black newspapers. So they let their readers know what they thought but without arming Lake. Sometimes they described the candidates but didn't name them. "For obvious reasons, we do not need to call names here," the *Carolina Times* wrote in a front-page editorial just before the first primary. "You have the read the newspapers, you have listened to radio. . . . You also know the candidates who have waved a red flag of race hatred and bigotry up and down North Carolina during the present political campaign." Sometimes the black newspapers delayed endorsements as long as possible, to limit the chances their endorsement would be used against them. Many black people accepted these kinds of strategies and Sanford's use of them because they thought it most effective.

Bill Campbell, who became mayor of Atlanta, was seven years old during the Lake-Sanford race but talked later about the contest with his father, Ralph Campbell, who was head of the NAACP chapter in Raleigh and supported Sanford. While Sanford said that he was not for integration, Campbell noted that he did not say he was for segregation. Black people knew Sanford opposed segregation, Campbell said: "Everybody knew where the two stood. . . . There was no misunderstanding the political philosophies of I. Beverly Lake and Terry Sanford. Terry Sanford had 100 percent of the black support in 1960. There was no doubt about where he stood and where his opponent stood."

In their emphasis and tone, Lake and Sanford were different, and the voters knew it. Lake's top priority was preserving segregation; Sanford's was improving schools. Lake opposed the Supreme Court's *Brown* decision and would resist it using all lawful measures; Sanford accepted the Court's decision and would not fight it. "He knew he could not come out and say that he was against segregation," said Sanford supporter Woody Teague. "But he didn't follow the path that Lake went down. The way he handled it was excellent and everybody knew where he stood, that he wasn't going to be in the mold of . . . these other southern governors."

Sanford supporters believe he went as far as he could go on race and still get elected. That is probably true—although it did not justify some of his tactics. His claim that Lake won the black vote in Iredell County was dishonest and unnecessary. He could have pointed out truthfully that other candidates won most of the black votes in other cities and left it at that. Overall, though, Sanford struck an appropriate balance between what he believed and what he said. Was he justified in saying, "I am . . . opposed to integration," when he did not believe in segregation? Perhaps the most telling answer is that the state's black voters forgave him—and overwhelmingly supported him, both in 1960 and after. Black leaders believed Sanford would treat them as his equals. Sanford put himself in a position to win without alienating the black voters he would need to move the state forward. After the election, he would make history promoting civil rights. But he was a smart pol and he knew he could not win the election as a civil rights crusader. He already was fighting one politically risky battle by saying he was willing to raise taxes to make schools better. For him to also fight harder on the civil rights front—and still have a chance of beating Lake—was unrealistic.

Some supporters did want him to fight harder for civil rights. Perhaps they believed white North Carolinians were more receptive to change than Sanford believed. Or perhaps they were more interested in being right than in winning. Sanford protégé Jim Hunt, in an insightful analysis of the campaign, said, "He was smart enough to keep his eye on the ball and figure out how to get there from here. And that's one of the things he ought to be given a lot of credit for. Terry understood about things like human equality and opportunity. He was deeply committed to them. But he also had the smarts to not let what then was a dominant attitude toward segregation in society prevent what he was trying to do from being successful. And that takes a lot of savvy, a lot of discipline. And yet remaining committed to what he believed in and when he was in a position to do it, moving ahead. Obviously, many people would criticize that: 'What you said on integration wasn't strong enough. You should have said more. You left some things unsaid.'" Said Hunt, "Those people would have lost."

Lake was driven to preserve segregation; Sanford was driven to be governor. No doubt part of Sanford's drive to occupy the governor's mansion was to satisfy his own ego and ambition. Yet his gamble on schools and taxes indicated he genuinely wanted to change the state. If he had ambition for himself, he also had ambition for North Carolina. When the race began, Sanford was widely regarded to be the front-runner. With his statement about his willingness to raise taxes he jeopardized that status. Only a politician truly committed to reform would have taken that gamble. Yet his words on integration showed he also was willing to compromise his personal beliefs to get elected. There were more compromises ahead.

On the Sunday after the first primary, Sanford moved to win the support of Governor Hodges. He and Hodges met that day. Shortly after, Bert Bennett also met with Hodges. Bennett knew Hodges would support Sanford. While Hodges and Sanford did not particularly like each other, there was no way Hodges would support Lake. On race, Hodges and Sanford were alike. Lake, on the other hand, had criticized Hodges for years on the issue, often with a harsh and personal tone. Hodges viewed Lake as a dangerous extremist. So Bennett knew the governor would support Sanford. But to what extent? Bennett intended to find out.

When they met, Hodges, supremely confident as always, told Bennett how the Sanford campaign should be run. Then he asked Bennett what he wanted. Bennett said he wanted Hodges to hold some fund-raisers in the governor's mansion for Sanford. "We need it badly," Bennett recalled saying. Hodges didn't like the idea. Bennett persevered: "Governor, we want your support and we need it but we're going to win it. And the state can't afford Lake. It's a question of how much a part you want to play. We really need that money."

Bennett had leverage. Hodges did not want Lake elected. He also had personal ambition: He wanted to be a player in national politics—possibly even vice president. He had organized an effort to seek the vice presidency. Months ago, he had recruited the man scheduled to be John Larkins' campaign manager to run his campaign for vice president at the Democratic National Convention in Los Angeles in July. If Sanford were the Democratic nominee for governor, he likely would have influence with the presidential candidates at the convention. In particular, Sanford, although undecided about whom he would support for president, was forging a relationship with Sen. John F. Kennedy and his brother Robert.

"He [Hodges] had nothing really in common with Sanford, historically, politically or otherwise," Bennett remembered. Sanford was forty-two; Bennett was thirty-nine; Hodges was sixty-two. "He was old to us; he was a generation older," Bennett said. Yet Hodges came around. He never publicly announced for Sanford. That wasn't what Sanford wanted; Hodges was unpopular in the east. But Hodges helped Sanford in other ways. "He stood up like a man and did those things that we requested, and it helped us," Bennett said. "And he knew deep down that Sanford was the answer."

Hodges worked behind the scenes, raising money and calling allies. "He did turn around, obviously, against Lake—he very enthusiastically supported Sanford and was very helpful to Sanford," Luther Hodges Jr. recalled. Sanford was friends with Hodges' nephew and talked with him about getting help from some of Seawell's supporters. One day Sanford called Phil Carlton, a North Carolina State senior who was working nearly full-time for the Sanford campaign, into an office. He asked Carlton to go to Dillon Supply Company in Raleigh and pick up a package from C. A. Dillon, a Hodges supporter who had been Malcolm Seawell's co-campaign manager. Dillon gave Carlton a bag full of cash and a box of postage stamps. "They essentially gave me what was left" of the Seawell campaign, said Carlton, who later would be an associate justice of the North Carolina Supreme Court.

Officially, Hodges was neutral in the runoff. He urged citizens to pay attention and to vote. "There has never been a more vital election," he said in the first week of the runoff. He was concerned about preserving "our precious public schools and the maintenance of peace and order." But officially he was neutral in the first primary, too, and everyone knew he supported Seawell. So reporters pushed him. Near the end of the month, he urged Democrats to vote and said the runoff was "the most important ever held in North Carolina." A reporter asked him if he had met with either Lake or Sanford since the May 28 primary. Hodges curtly replied, "I am not making any further comment."

Lake's warm-up man, John Burney, raised the issue of whom Hodges was supporting. At several rallies, as he worked the crowd into a lather as only he could do, Burney said that Hodges was supporting Sanford. "Hodges is calling industrialists and appointees throughout the state and urging them to support the man whose program he described just three weeks ago as outlandish," Burney told one audience. He said that Hodges was threatening to keep new industry out of some parts of the state if those areas supported Lake. And Burney said that Hodges had let his ally Tom Pearsall, who had led the two committees that developed the state's reaction to the Supreme Court's *Brown* decisions, appear on a paid television program for Sanford.

Burney's accusations prompted Joe Koenenn of United Press International to quiz Sanford at a press conference about whether Hodges was supporting him. Sanford wiggled out of giving an answer but said he had not met with Hodges during the runoff. Sanford, however, had met with Governor Hodges on Sunday, May 29, the day after the first primary. Sanford considered Koenenn a friendly reporter. But when Koenenn asked Sanford about Hodges, Sanford took it as an unfriendly question. "Luther Hodges was not popular," Sanford remembered. "His attorney general and his candidate [Seawell] had gotten something like 15 percent of the vote, which is some indication, and Dr. Lake was attempting to say I was the candidate of the old guard, which was of course obviously far from the truth, but there was no question that Luther Hodges was for me. He couldn't possibly have been for a racist."

Koenenn asked if Sanford had seen Hodges. "I said no, which was a lie in a way but technically it was not, because the second primary was not until Dr. Lake called one," Sanford recalled. "I saw Luther Hodges Sunday morning after Saturday night when the first election took place. I ought to have said something else but I told that little bit of a lie, which was the first lie I told in the campaign, and technically it wasn't, but actually I was misleading him and shouldn't have done it."

Actually, it was more than technically a lie. It was an outright lie, as a transcript of the June 13 press conference shows:

> KOENENN: One of your opponent's leading supporters has said in a
> number of ways and pretty directly that Governor Hodges has not
> maintained his neutrality but that he is supporting you. In fact on Sat-
> urday night he said Hodges was sitting behind closed doors in the
> capitol trying to cut off Dr. Lake's campaign funds. As far as you know,
> has Governor Hodges given you his support in the runoff?
> SANFORD: I would say that the supporter you refer to . . . John Burney
> apparently knows a great deal more about Governor Hodges' activities
> than I do. It is a well-known fact that I was not the candidate of the
> administration and Governor Hodges has expressed his own feelings
> publicly about his position on the campaign. I have nothing to add.
> KOENENN: Have you talked to Governor Hodges since the first primary
> or met Governor Hodges since the first primary?

SANFORD : No, not during the second primary.
KOENENN: That is, since the twenty-eighth?
SANFORD : That's right.

Using his Clinton-esque definition of primary, Sanford had not met with Hodges during the second primary because Lake did not call for a second primary until Monday, May 30. However, Koenenn, apparently recognizing Sanford's hair-splitting definition of second primary, also asked if Sanford had met with Hodges since the twenty-eighth. It was a shrewd question by Koenenn—and a lie by Sanford. He indeed had met with Hodges since the twenty-eighth.

Sanford got away with it. The press reported that Sanford had not met with Hodges since the first primary. No one uncovered the May 29 meeting. But Sanford gave another evasive answer at that same press conference that caused him a week's worth of trouble during a crucial period of the runoff. "That just shows you," Sanford said later, "that one transgression leads to another."

Koenenn asked Sanford if he had seen Kennedy (it's unclear if he said John, Robert, Senator Kennedy, or just "Kennedy") recently in North Carolina. Sanford was perturbed. He already was mad that Koenenn had asked about Hodges. Now he was pressing him on another matter that Sanford did not want to talk about—his recent meeting with Robert Kennedy regarding whom Sanford would support for president. Louis Harris, Sanford's pollster and friend from the University of North Carolina, arranged the meeting and attended. Sanford did not really want to meet with Kennedy representatives but did it as a favor to Harris. Also, Sanford knew if he won the runoff on June 25 he would not have much time to talk with the Kennedy people before the Democratic convention in July. And Kennedy was looking strong. So he decided to meet with Harris and Robert Kennedy, but he wanted the meeting to remain private.

Sanford aides Hugh Cannon and Bert Bennett also attended the meeting, which was at a hotel room in the College Inn in west Raleigh, near the campus of State College. Robert Kennedy, who forgot his belt and kept hiking up his pants, was sick to his stomach and ate only soup.

Kennedy knew all the political players in every state. He had a five-by-eight-inch index card on every North Carolina delegate to the Democratic National Convention. Sanford added information on some of the delegates. Sanford was impressed with Robert Kennedy's organizational skills. He left the meeting convinced Kennedy was going to win the nomination. But Sanford made no commitment.

A few days later, Koenenn asked his question at the press conference. It was Monday, June 13. Sanford's coolness, which became legendary during the campaign, was melting. He was tired. He had been campaigning at a tremendous pace for months. Perhaps more draining was his realization of what was at stake. Lake was no John Larkins or Malcolm Seawell or any other mainstream Democrat. His election would take the state in a direction Sanford dreaded. Sanford told his staff, "I almost wish Seawell or someone else had this burden, this cross to bear. This is the most crucial election of the century, because it's going to determine which way we go."

Sanford was unhappy with Koenenn's line of questioning about Hodges and Kennedy. "Now, both of those questions in the emotion of a second primary, with Lake in there, and my view of the thing was that quite aside from my personal ambitions, I had a banner to carry for the honor of the South and the honor of North Carolina," Sanford recalled. "We were trying to beat a racist campaign and I thought that an enlightened newspaper reporter ought not to ask nasty questions that really weren't on point." Was Hodges supporting Sanford? Was Sanford supporting Kennedy? Maybe those questions didn't seem on point to Sanford, but many North Carolina voters would have found the answers relevant. Koenenn's question was whether Sanford had met with Jack Kennedy, Sanford said. Sanford thought, You little smart aleck.

Sanford said that he had not seen Kennedy. There were no further questions on the subject. He had a plane to catch and bolted to the airport. He believed Koenenn asked him if he had met with John Kennedy. But he suspected Koenenn meant to ask him if he had met with Robert Kennedy. He wished he had said, "No, you mean Bobby Kennedy. I talked to Bobby Kennedy just as I talked to other candidates and I didn't make any commitment to them. They all want to talk with me." But he didn't.

Sanford said later, "I was getting punch drunk. It was day and night in that second primary. That was fatigue. I would never have been smart alecky like that if I'd been rested." Now reporters would find out about the meeting with Robert Kennedy and think Sanford was trying to hide something. "That was the second little shading of the truth that I did and that was a mistake," Sanford said years later. "That was a terrible error and I've never made that mistake again. I've always just told it like it was. But at that time I didn't tell it like it was."

It wasn't long before newspapers carried stories about Sanford's meeting with Robert Kennedy, raising the question of whether he was hiding their meeting. John Kennedy wasn't popular in North Carolina. The Democratic establishment overwhelmingly was for fellow southerner Lyndon Johnson for president. Tom Ellis, one of Lake's key workers, urged campaign manager Robert Morgan to hit Sanford hard on the issue. "Through most of the South, Kennedy was anathema," Ellis recalled. "It would have been very damaging to the Sanford campaign if it were known in the primary that he was going to support Kennedy."

Was Sanford covering up his support for Kennedy? Morgan released a statement questioning Sanford's truthfulness and motives, a statement which was widely carried by newspapers. "Mr. Sanford did see [Robert] Kennedy in Raleigh and had dinner with him at a swank Raleigh motel last Thursday night," Morgan said. "We know that Sen. Kennedy needs just a few more committed delegates to win the presidential nomination next month. Was not Sen. Kennedy's brother here seeking these votes from the North Carolina delegation?"

Morgan also raised the question of whether Robert Kennedy offered to help the Sanford campaign in exchange for Sanford's support. Lake raised similar questions. At a rally, he tied Hodges' support of Sanford to Sanford's meeting with Robert Kennedy: Perhaps Sanford was paying back Hodges by lobbying Kennedy on Hodges' behalf. Lake pointed out that Hodges had once said Sanford's highway program was unrealistic. "Why, then, is Gov. Hodges now supporting Sanford?" Lake asked. "Or has Mr. Sanford agreed in his recent meeting with Kennedy people . . . to help further Hodges' vice presidential aspirations?"

Bert Bennett told reporters it had all been a misunderstanding. When Sanford was asked at the Monday press conference if he had met with Kennedy, Sanford interpreted the question to mean had he met with Jack Kennedy. Bennett said that Sanford, who besides being a candidate for governor also was a delegate to the convention, indeed had met with Robert Kennedy, as he had with representatives of all the other Democratic candidates for president. Bennett said that Sanford had made no commitments. Bennett's statement seemed to satisfy reporters, although their versions of the press conference differed. Sanford said that Koenenn's question was whether he had met with Jack Kennedy and that a tape recording verified that. Some reporters disagreed. Several news reports said that Sanford was asked if he had met with Robert Kennedy.

To help further diffuse the issue, Sanford decided to meet again with Lyndon Johnson's staff. That would show that Sanford indeed was meeting with representatives of each candidate. Sanford had met previously with an old associate from the Kerr Scott campaign who said that he represented Johnson. He had tried to give Sanford a contribution of five thousand to ten thousand dollars if he would support Johnson. Sanford had turned it down. He told the man he wasn't taking campaign contributions if they had strings attached. And he said he wasn't ready to back a candidate for president.

But now, after the Kennedy fiasco, Sanford wanted to meet with Johnson's people. Sanford arranged to meet in a Greensboro hotel room with Bert Bennett, Johnson aide Bobby Baker, and Bill Cochrane, who was Sen. Everett Jordan's administrative assistant. Sanford made a practice of not drinking alcohol during the campaign because he wanted to preserve his energy. He drank Pepsi Colas instead. But that night the men broke out a bottle of whiskey. Sanford was inclined to support Johnson. He liked Kennedy better and thought Kennedy would command more respect across the world. Politically, however, it made no sense for him to support Kennedy. If he supported Kennedy over a southerner like Johnson, he no doubt would pay for it at the polls. And if he endorsed Johnson immediately, it would end the current discussion about his meeting with Robert Kennedy and the speculation that he would support John Kennedy.

Then Baker told Sanford how immoral John Kennedy was, how he participated in orgies, how he was incompetent and would wreck the country. Sanford was turned off by Baker's harsh talk about Kennedy. Still, as the whiskey flowed, Sanford got closer to agreeing to endorse Johnson. If they'd had another half a bottle of whiskey, Sanford later said, he might have gone for Johnson. "I think I might have pledged to Johnson if we'd talked a little bit longer that night," Sanford said, "because I had pretty well made up my mind that this was the easy political course." The whisky ran out and the talk subsided and Sanford had not pledged for Johnson. The next day, Sanford mentioned to reporters that he had met with Johnson's people. The question about whom Sanford would support for president faded—for a while, anyway.

Chapter 8

SHOWDOWN

From the day he announced his candidacy, Lake declared the NAACP the greatest enemy North Carolina faced. In the runoff, he continued his harsh criticism of that group and added a new enemy: the state's major daily newspapers. When he called for the runoff, he made a brief reference to the *Charlotte Observer,* the *News and Observer,* and their afternoon papers, the *Charlotte News* and the *Raleigh Times.* Those papers supported Sanford and school integration and "have consistently misrepresented my program so as to deceive the people of the state," he said.

Two days later in the mountain city of Asheville, he elaborated. Lake said that the state's newspapers had characterized him as an outspoken segregationist to detract from the rest of his program. "The newspapers have pictured me as a man who has talked about nothing but segregation," he said. Not true, he said. He had talked about the financial policies of the state and the right of workers to work without joining a union. He had talked attracting industry, regulating public utilities, repealing the intangibles tax, and improving schools. He did not believe he had received fair coverage on these issues and hoped for better coverage in the runoff.

When a reporter asked him what characterization he would prefer to "outspoken segregationist," Lake said he wished a newspaper would refer to him as an "advocate of sound fiscal policies." He said he had been quoted incompletely and given inaccurate headlines, while Sanford was getting favorable coverage. Lake also said that newspapers were unfairly emphasizing comments that his election could lead to the closing of public schools. This, he said, forced him to bypass newspaper reporters and take his message directly to the people by using paid television time. In his emphasis on television, Lake was ahead of his time. In 1960, television had not yet become the pervasive force that it would become. Most people got their news from newspapers, and newspapers dominated the political debate. But Lake's managers believed television was growing in influence and could be a more effective medium for their man. They did not, however, have much money to pay for TV time.

Lake's criticism of the state's major newspapers became a standard part of his speeches in the runoff, part of his red-meat offering for his conservative audiences. He said he was opposed by a trio of forces—the NAACP, labor bosses, and "the integrationist, left-wing press" of the state. "I welcome the opposition of this partnership for it tends to draw the issues clear and sharp," Lake said. "These people and I do not want the same kind of North Carolina." At a rally in Greensboro, Lake criticized Sanford's education program as being too expensive, then hacked away at the NAACP and the major newspapers. "For if I don't talk about it [the NAACP] in every speech the integrationist press says I have weakened in my opposition to it," Lake said. "Of course, if I do talk about it they say I am nothing but an outspoken segregationist." Lake, however, concurred with that assessment: "Now let me get one thing straight. I am and I have been and I shall continue to be an outspoken segregationist. I know that the policies which North Carolina has followed in the matter of our two great races, in our schools, our eating establishments, our recreation and our social life, are policies which have brought both the white and Negro people of this state to a remarkable and steady advancement." Curiously, Lake managed to both agree with and criticize the newspapers—at the same time—for saying he was an outspoken segregationist.

At another rally, Lake and the irrepressible John Burney took turns hammering the newspapers, especially the *News and Observer*. Lake was going to win, Burney said, despite the lies and inaccuracies of the Raleigh paper. Part of the rally at the Robeson County Courthouse was televised, and Burney coached the crowd of six hundred. When the television cameras started, he would ask them if the people were going to support Lake for governor. "We want the people of North Carolina to know that we aren't sitting up on our backsides and letting the newspapers roll over us," Burney said. Later, Lake supporters passed collection boxes and blank checks from North Carolina banks through the audience. Burney asked the crowd to give. "The people are not going to let *The News and Observer* tell them how to vote!" Burney yelled. "The papers keep talking about unsigned literature. Well, what about these editors who hide behind their pen and do not sign their names? Why don't they come out one time and let the people see who is writing these poison pen letters to the people of North Carolina?" Lake continued the attack. "Wittingly or unwittingly, my opponent's program would permit *The News and Observer, The Charlotte Observer* and their satellites and fellow travelers to bring about a climate of integration," Lake said. The night before in Asheville, Lake said, four hundred people attended his rally. Yet the *News and Observer* reported only two hundred attended. "That is indicative of the half-truths," he said.

Some smaller newspapers supported Lake. The *Statesville Record and Landmark,* in its front-page opinion column, "Down in Iredell," repeatedly criticized Sanford and urged Lake supporters to rally their troops. The paper warned of the growing influence of the NAACP, as shown by the student sit-ins, and said that Sanford had won large majorities of black voters in the first primary. The talk that Lake's election would lead to closed schools was "garbage"; the governor alone could not close schools even if he wanted to, the *Record and Landmark* wrote. At least, the paper said, Lake was confronting the race issue and not trying to dodge it as Sanford was. "What is going to happen when the Negroes begin to insist on mixing not only in the schools but in the parks, playgrounds and swimming pools, in the hotels, lunch counters and restaurants?" the paper wrote. "Could that be the New Day they are all talking about?"

But Lake received little support from editorial writers at the major dailies. The *Asheville Citizen* said that Lake was "a man of unusual ability and considerable personal charm, an able lawyer and former college professor." Much of Lake's program had merit, the paper said, including his calls for fiscal conservatism and agricultural and industrial expansion. However, the paper added, "The fact remains that his position on school segregation is so extreme that his nomination and election could well spell disaster for North Carolina's hard-built, justly prized school system." In another editorial, the paper noted that Lake's campaign was only the second time since the white supremacy campaign of 1900 that a major North Carolina candidate had campaigned on the race issue; the other was the 1950 U.S. Senate race. "Assuredly, Dr. Lake's position, though founded on conviction, is not a wise course, is not in keeping with North Carolina policy, is not calculated to create greater harmony in race relations," it said.

The *Charlotte Observer* said that voters had a choice between a bright future or a dark future, between "a man full of vigor and hope, enthusiasm and confidence and . . . a man wedded to the status quo, obsessed with false fears, who had pandered to the basest and rawest of human emotions in this campaign." Lake had run a negative campaign, the paper said. The *Observer* said that Lake was against the NAACP, which had little influence in the state; against organized labor, which had never been a major factor in a North Carolina election; against Governor Hodges; and against the newspapers, virtually all of which gave Lake more news coverage than the *Observer* said was merited. The paper asked whether the state would continue its forward-looking tradition or "go the way of some other southern states and bind itself with the shackles of bitter racial hatred and gloomy economic pessimism."

The *News and Observer* said that eastern North Carolina was poised for progress—if its people "turned to their best hopes and not backward to their worst fears." Lake was particularly rankled by another *News and Observer* editorial. The paper anonymously received a Lake campaign card. On the back was a swastika and these words: "When we win you'd better leave the state." In the editorial, the paper reported receiving the card. It reproduced the back of the card, showing the swastika and the inscription. The card clearly came from a crackpot, the editorial said. "Such efforts to infuriate the intolerant may not come deliberately from the managers of Dr. Lake's campaign," the paper wrote. But, the editorial continued, the Lake campaign deliberately injected anti-Catholic sentiment into the campaign by harping on Sanford's meeting with Robert Kennedy, who was Catholic. "The clear purpose is to try to add prejudices against Catholics to overwrought racial feelings in this campaign," the paper concluded. "North Carolina will keep the even-tempered, warmhearted tenor of its ways with Terry Sanford, who proffers hope and faith, not hatred and fear."

Lake strongly objected, saying the editorial gave the impression that the swastika and threat represented his views. He said the paper was out of line to base an editorial on an anonymous letter from a disturbed person. No one had ever issued such a card with his consent, he said, and the *News and Observer* knew it. "Here you have the major newspaper in eastern North Carolina writing a smear editorial on no basis whatsoever," Lake said, exasperated, "except an anonymous card it says it received from an unknown 'crackpot.'" He was right to be angry. Writing about the anonymous card and printing the swastika, knowing that it might not have come from the Lake campaign, was a cheap shot.

Lake's criticism went beyond the unsigned editorials opposing him and supporting Sanford. He thought the news reporters and editors, who were supposed to be impartial, were against him. "A lot of people voted against me because they felt I was wrong," Lake said years later. "But a lot of others opposed me because my position hadn't been fairly explained in the newspapers. The headlines were distorted and the cartoons always made me look like a monstrosity. The stories always said Sanford spoke to enthusiastic groups and always said I spoke to a boisterous bunch of rednecks. Newspapers pictured my people as poor white trash and I resented that."

His supporters also said that Lake was not treated fairly. "The five major dailies thought Lake was an extremist and not a good fella," recalled Lake supporter Tom Ellis, referring to the papers in Asheville, Charlotte, Greensboro, Raleigh, and Winston-Salem. "They treated him as some kind of an extremist. What it really comes down to is how the media treats your position. If they're trying to help elect Sam Ervin to the Senate, then he's a great constitutional theorist. If Beverly Lake is trying to be elected governor against Terry Sanford, then he's a racist. It's unfortunate but that's just the way it is." John Burney said years later, "All you had to do was read the way they slanted the articles. They were trying to make a race mongrel out of him and all he was talking about was states rights. They didn't know the difference. They didn't want him to be governor. They were for Terry Sanford." Campaign manager Robert Morgan said that reporters focused on Lake's segregationist views, ignoring the other parts of his platform. "He talked about every issue in the campaign," Morgan recalled. "Basically, the press in the state were more liberal than Dr. Lake."

Sanford's and Lake's relationships with the press were starkly different. During the primaries, Sanford courted reporters and held two press conferences a week. Lake avoided the press. During the first and second primaries, Lake held a total of two question-and-answer sessions with reporters. Sanford tried to make an issue out of Lake's dodging the press. "Why doesn't Dr. Lake hold a press conference?" Sanford asked in mid June at one of his meetings with reporters. "He is unwilling to submit to questions by reporters from newspapers, TV and radio. What is he afraid of? Has it got anything to do with the fact that he doesn't want to say in the Piedmont what he says in the east?" Some reporters believed Lake talked more about race when he campaigned in the east and more about fiscal conservatism when he traveled through the Piedmont. Lake replied that Sanford was more interested in talking to reporters than he was to the people. He said that when given the chance to debate, Sanford chose a thirty-minute format instead of an hour.

During the campaign, Lake cited several examples where he believed reporters were inaccurate. In the last two weeks of the runoff, he said that wire service reporters made three significant errors:

- W. W. Taylor, a Lake supporter and staff member for one of the Pearsall committees, said that the Pupil Assignment Act was the only law that ever had been used to save schools from integration. Lake said that the Associated Press changed "ever" to "never."

196

- The son of the late Harry McMullan, who was Lake's boss when he was attorney general, said that Lake wrote the Pupil Assignment Act. Lake said the Associated Press reported that McMullan had said Lake did not write the law.
- The man who managed Willis Smith's 1950 Senate campaign endorsed Lake. Lake said that United Press International reported that the man endorsed Sanford.

It's possible those mistakes did occur, although highly unlikely any were intentional. For a reporter to intentionally make any of those mistakes would have been grounds for dismissal. At least one of the mistakes appears to have been corrected. Wire services, which dispatch news reports all day, often quickly correct errors. For example, the *Asheville Citizen* published the Associated Press account of W. W. Taylor's comments and they were accurate: the Pupil Assignment Act, Taylor said in the Asheville version, "is the only law that has ever been used in North Carolina for keeping our schools open."

The bigger question is whether Lake got a fair shake in the overall news coverage of the campaign. Many of the reporters did not like Lake or did not want to cover him, or both. While Sanford liked to banter with the press, reporters found Lake rigid and aloof. "Beverly Lake—he was iron minded," said Noel Yancey, who covered the campaign for the Associated Press. "He didn't give on anything. He said everything like it was the Law and Needs of the Persians. He had no sense of humor." Joe Doster, then with the *Charlotte Observer*, said that Lake was not comfortable being interviewed. "He was a more private person than Sanford," Doster recalled. "I thought being out on the campaign trail for him was something he had to do but was something he didn't really enjoy much. He was polite. He didn't kid around any. He never made any little jokes that I could recall. Very serious."

Lake rallies could be uncomfortable for reporters. "Lake would from time to time talk about the press and crowds would get damn hostile," Doster said. "He would name people in the press corps. He'd say, 'Now be nice to these guys.' And they would boo and go on." Roy Parker also remembered the hostile environment of the Lake rallies. "The Lake people didn't like journalists," he said. "That was one of the feelings you got that night from that rally [that Parker covered for the *News and Observer*]. If they find out you're a newspaperman, they're going to beat the hell out of you. . . . Everybody wanted to travel with Terry and no one wanted to travel with Dr. Lake." Parker said that none of the *News and Observer* staff were friends with Lake's key workers: "Dr. Lake didn't have anybody around him that our people cared much of anything about." Jesse Helms, a former reporter and Lake admirer, had been popular with his colleagues years before. Marjorie Hunter, who covered Raleigh for the *Winston-Salem Journal*, remembered Helms then as "a great guy. He was a very fun person to be around. He had some great parties. I enjoyed Jesse then." But by 1960, Helms's relationship with many reporters was strained. Also, Helms said years later that he played no role in the Lake campaign. Neither Helms nor anyone else served as a bridge from the Lake camp to the reporters who covered the campaign.

Did reporters' discomfort with Lake and his supporters affect their news coverage? Some reporters say it did; some say it did not. "I'd like to think we were impartial but personally we were for Sanford," Hunter said. "Professionally, we tried to be honest. I don't think we let it interfere with our writing." Joe Doster said that Lake got a fair shake from reporters. "I tried to report on Lake as objectively as I knew how and I tried to report on Sanford the same way," he said. "If you read all the clips [of stories] you'd come to the conclusion that they came from different directions." The best check on a biased reporter, Doster said, was the competition from other reporters covering the campaign. "You can't play fast and loose with what's out there," he said. "There were a bunch of damn good reporters in the state during that day. If you didn't stay alert, they'd beat your butt."

Roy Parker, however, said that the *News and Observer* favored Sanford. "The *News and Observer* in those days was not the most objective political organ in the world, I won't deny that," Parker said. "We all, everybody on the paper, were rooting for somebody—Larkins or Seawell or Terry—other than Lake. I can't remember anybody [for Lake]. Nobody would speak up for Lake. . . . You could usually tell which side the *News and Observer* was on in the primary, although it wasn't overt."

A contemporary reading of the campaign coverage of Lake finds it generally fair, although there were some articles in which Lake was not treated fairly. For example, a headline in the *News and Observer* said, "Sanford Slaps Back at Racist Campaign of Candidate Lake." Whether Lake's campaign was racist was a matter of opinion. For a newspaper to call it racist on its news pages was inappropriate. The *Charlotte Observer* reported that, on schools and segregation, Lake had "adopted a position of extremism." That, too, was an opinion that should not have been in a news story. But the vast majority of articles were balanced and accurately reported what Lake said. Many of them received prominent display.

Lake's principle complaint was that newspapers focused too much on his segregationist beliefs—a complaint that collapses under scrutiny. Of course newspapers focused on his segregationist beliefs. That's what the Lake campaign was about. That was what Lake himself said it was about. From the beginning, his campaign was built on his belief that schools and society must remain segregated. When he announced his campaign, more than half of his speech was about fighting integration and why candidates needed to debate the issue. In the first primary, he said that the main difference between himself and his three opponents was his approach to fighting integration. He even chided them, one by one, for their positions on integration. Another time, when the four candidates gathered in Charlotte for a forum broadcast on radio, Lake used his ten-minute opening statement to criticize the *Brown* decision and discuss his plan for fighting integration. The next day, on WBTV in Charlotte, Lake said, "If I become governor, the major objective of my administration will be the protection of the present public school system against the NAACP and the progressive improvement of the schools."

When the *Greensboro Daily News* asked each candidate to briefly explain why he was running for governor, Lake said, "Because we must now take a stand on issues going to the foundations of constitutional government and our social order. The governor will affect those decisions." In the runoff, Lake identified fighting integration as one of two main issues in the campaign, the other being Sanford's spending program. He spent most of his speeches talking about fighting integration. When Robert

Morgan sent key Lake supporters a suggested newspaper ad, it said, "Elect Lake . . . The Champion of Balanced Budget . . . Segregation . . . States' Rights . . . And Property Rights." Of those four issues championed by the Lake campaign, three—segregation, states' rights, and property rights— were about saving the South's social order.

Preserving segregation was the dominant issue for Lake and the Lake campaign, and reporters were right in focusing their attention on Lake's segregationist views. Tom Ellis, one of Lake's key workers, said that Lake ran for governor to fight integration. "It was a single-issue campaign, pure and simple," Ellis recalled. "It was about the only thing that was discussed—whether the schools would be integrated or not." Preserving segregation was Lake's dominant issue, and reporters were right in giving it prominence.

Reporters did write about Lake's other proposals. When Lake announced for governor, the *Winston-Salem Journal* listed each of his eleven proposals unrelated to fighting integration. Later the paper ran a transcript of an interview it did with Lake; of the nineteen questions, thirteen were not related to race, including questions about taxes, a statewide liquor referendum, and recruiting industry. When Lake spoke to the Raleigh Civitan Club, almost half the story in the *News and Observer* was devoted to Lake's statements on budget balancing and industry hunting. When the candidates for governor attended a forum on improving public schools, Lake's proposals received as much space as the other candidates' proposals in the *Charlotte Observer*. When Lake said that the state had been unwise in spending a budget surplus, the *Greensboro Daily News* displayed the story at the top of page one.

Given that fighting integration was Lake's dominant issue, one could reasonably argue that reporters did not write *enough* about Lake's proposal for fighting integration. Lake did not propose changing the state laws that allowed local school boards and local voters the power to assign pupils and close schools. But he said he would create a climate of public opinion against integration. How would he do that? Would he travel to local school boards, urging them not to integrate their schools? If they did integrate, would he urge local voters to close them with the power they had under the Pearsall Plan? Lake said he wanted to create a racial climate similar to South Carolina's. Specifically, what was Governor Hollings doing in South Carolina that Lake wanted to emulate in North Carolina? Did it work? Would such resistance—which would defy the Supreme Court's *Brown* decision—jeopardize North Carolina's more moderate approach in Court, as Sanford said it would? Lake said he believed in separate but equal schools. Would he take steps to guarantee that black schools and black colleges received the same level of funding as their white counterparts? What would those steps be? How would he pay for them? Lake said he wanted to drive the NAACP out of North Carolina. Was the group violating the law? If not, how would he drive them out of the state? Lake answered few, if any, of these questions. By not talking with reporters, he made it difficult for them to ask the hard questions— which, no doubt, was his intent all along.

Lake was lucky that reporters did not push him more on budget issues. In early May, Lake predicted the state would need to raise taxes just to maintain current state services. So was he willing to raise taxes? How much? Which ones? If not, was he willing to cut programs? Freeze state salaries? Add Lake's ambitious proposal for reducing class size, hiring clerical workers to relieve teachers from paperwork, and raising teacher salaries, and Lake could have proposed major tax increases or budget cutting or both. Yet he was not held accountable, either in news stories or editorials, for his lack of specificity. Most reporters do not like math and apparently did not push him on the issues of taxes and spending. They could have been more aggressive in covering Lake. Overall, the coverage Lake received was fair and balanced.

Lake had a stronger point when he said that the press treated Sanford favorably. Sanford essentially agreed. He believed reporters and editors were on his side. "The media was very much for me in 1960," Sanford said later. "I suppose I had the endorsement of every major paper and most of the minor ones. I could count on one hand the papers that weren't supporting me. . . . I had a good working relationship with the working press and I felt that most all of them were secretly for me and still trying to be objective." Joe Doster said that Sanford approached the press far differently than Lake. "Sanford knew that the press would give him every break that it could," Doster said. "Sanford saw the press as an ally. Part of it is I think he knew how to engage them better than Lake did. I think Lake didn't quite understand what they were about. He also sort of knew from the editorial policies of the papers [on their opinion pages] that they were not on his side. There was an openness to the Sanford campaign that you didn't see in the Lake campaign and the reporters appreciated that." Sometimes journalists did not try to hide their support of Sanford. Gibson Prather, the managing editor of the *Fayetteville Observer,* was identified in that paper as a member of the Sanford campaign organization.

Reporters did not write many hard-hitting pieces on Sanford. While newspaper articles generally held Lake at a distance, Sanford sometimes was embraced as a friend. In one article about a Sanford rally, Sanford was "an amiable Fayetteville attorney" who despite an exhausting day "was in fine fettle." "If the enthusiasm of the Wake rally is a yardstick," the writer fawned, "Terry Sanford is taking seven-league strides toward becoming this state's governor early in 1961." Lake's rallies were almost fanatically enthusiastic—but articles about Lake's rallies weren't as glowing (nor should they have been). Sanford was often called "Terry" in newspaper headlines. "Two Gunning for Terry," said the *Fayetteville Observer.* "Terry's Campaign a Smooth One," said the *Raleigh Times.* "Terry Held Lead All the Way," the *Charlotte Observer* said the day after the first primary. Headline writers did not call his opponent "Beverly" or "Bev."

Reporters did not push Sanford on his proposals. He said he supported the education proposal of the United Forces for Education, a proposal which would cost about $50 million a year. How would Sanford pay for his education proposals? He said he was willing to raise taxes. Which ones? If state revenues continued to grow at their current pace, how much would taxes have to be raised to pay for Sanford's proposals? How would the tax burden in North Carolina then compare to other states? Could those new taxes put the state at a competitive disadvantage in recruiting new industry? Sanford generally escaped answering those questions.

He also escaped without answering hard questions on race. For example, the *Winston-Salem Journal* conducted question-and-answer sessions with each of the four candidates in the primary. Sanford was asked for his thoughts on the state's approach to school integration. He said he was with the 90 percent of the people of the state who approved of the North Carolina approach. "I haven't seen any better approach suggested," he said, "and I'm with the North Carolina approach." That was it. There was no follow-up question. How did he define the North Carolina approach? Would he suggest changes to the Pupil Assignment Act or the Pearsall Plan? Was the Pearsall Plan too cumbersome, as Lake said? Why had no local system tried to use it? Did he approve of the token integration that had occurred? During the campaign, his hero Frank Graham came to the state to speak at Bennett College in Greensboro. Graham said he was proud that the demonstrations against segregated lunch counters "had their origins in North Carolina." What did Sanford think of those demonstrations? Would a Governor Sanford try to stop them, as Lake said he would? "The press didn't want that stirred up," Sanford recalled. "The press basically was made up of very decent people. They weren't going to try to heckle me on that issue. The press by and large supported me in all my elections."

Sanford's staff did complain about WRAL radio, which was owned by Lake's law partner, A. J. Fletcher. When Lake called for a runoff, Sanford requested equal time to respond to Lake's "personal attack." The station consented—although WRAL news director George Penny did not think it was required by federal regulations. In WRAL's 6 P.M. news program, Penny said that Lake had not attacked Sanford personally. Penny noted that Sanford's response took twice as long as Lake's call for a runoff. He called Sanford "Terry the Tearful" and said that he was crying because Lake had called for a runoff. Bert Bennett asked the Federal Communications Commission to investigate. Bennett pointed out that the station was controlled by Lake's partner and said that WRAL's news programs were being "used to editorialize and propagandize" in favor of Lake. He copied the letter to the state's U.S. senators. WRAL radio was a small player compared to the major dailies but the Sanford campaign was not taking any chances.

It's easy to second-guess newspaper coverage, especially from a modern vantage point. Newspapers in that era gave more emphasis to covering the candidates on the campaign trail and less emphasis to exploring the implications of their platforms. Much of the coverage was excellent. The reporters did well in telling their readers what the candidates said and what they were like as they campaigned. It was an all-star cast of reporters, an unusually talented group. From the *News and Observer*, Gene Roberts became editor of the *Philadelphia Inquirer* and managing editor of the *New York Times* and Roy Parker became editor of the *Fayetteville Times*. From the *Charlotte Observer*, Jay Jenkins was well-regarded by his peers before he went to work for the University of North Carolina system and Joe Doster became publisher of the *Winston-Salem Journal*. Marjorie Hunter of the *Winston-Salem Journal* became a Washington correspondent for the *New York Times*. Noel Yancey spent thirty-nine years with the Associated Press, seventeen as head of the Raleigh bureau. Many others who covered the campaign also had sterling careers. While there were flaws in the news coverage of the campaign, overall the public was given plenty of information to make an informed choice. Lake said that because of incomplete and biased reporting the people didn't know him well enough. Perhaps, some in the press have said, the people knew him too well.

In the first primary, the tone of the Lake-Sanford relationship was cordial and genteel. Sanford publicly praised Lake at the rally in Lee County in February, when he was trying to keep Lake out of the race. After Lake entered the race, there was never much doubt there would be a runoff and Sanford would be in it. Sanford stayed above the fray. Then, when Lake called for a runoff, he maintained a civil tone toward Sanford, twice praising his ability, personality, and character. "This is not a personal fight," Lake said.

That changed when Sanford responded to Lake's runoff call. Sanford accused Lake of "an absolute falsehood," saying Lake had said that Sanford favored school integration (which Lake did not actually say). He said that Lake appealed to "blind prejudice for the pure and simple purpose of getting himself a few votes." He repeated that statement a few minutes later and used barbed, confrontational language. "Every time he opens his mouth," Sanford said, "he is building evidence which is going to be introduced in the Supreme Court." He called Lake "a theoretical college professor" who grew up in an ivory tower and lacked the common sense needed to handle the race problem.

Sanford's hard-edged response ended the polite talk of character and friendship, and exposed the deep differences between the men. They represented different philosophies, appealed to different supporters, and had different dreams for the state each loved. They simply viewed the world differently. When Lake talked about the South, he talked of its glorious past; when Sanford talked of the South, he spoke of its promising future. Lake wanted to preserve the Old South that he loved, with its distinctive traditions and sense of honor; Sanford wanted a modern, inclusive New South more closely tied with the rest of the nation.

Their animosity reflected more than their different visions for the state. Lake was proud to be a teacher and a lawyer; he thought politics was a dirty business. Sanford was proud to be a politician; he thought politics was a noble calling. Lake viewed Sanford as young and unproven professionally, a man who valued the flash of politics over the substance of law. "Dad saw him in that light, as someone who wanted to make a career in politics," Lake's son, I. Beverly Lake Jr., remembered. "He did not like that aspiration in anybody. It was foreign to his nature. He was always a lawyer and a teacher. He did not like that in Sanford, as he did not in anybody he saw it in." Sanford thought Lake was in many ways an honorable man—but with a horrible blind spot that didn't allow him to see the racial injustice of that era. To Sanford, Lake sought to prolong an evil system that held black people down and held the South back. He considered Lake racist and his campaign vicious. "He didn't think he was Bilbo," Sanford said shortly before he died, referring to the race-baiting Mississippi politician. "But he had certainly put himself in a position to make racial strife a terrible problem for us."

With no other candidates around to diffuse the debate, the Lake-Sanford fissures were exposed and broken further. Their dialogue was personal and fierce. Three days after Sanford called him a theoretical college professor, Lake addressed a boisterous crowd of more than twenty-five hundred at the Sudan Temple in New Bern. It was his first rally after calling for a runoff. Lake supporters rang cowbells and arrived in chartered buses. A bus from Wilmington rolled up blaring "Dixie" from a sound system. Before the rally started, supporters chanted, "We want Lake! We want Lake!" Finally, Lake, wearing a dark suit with a white shirt and narrow tie, walked down the center aisle as the crowd cheered. John Burney introduced him. "The masses and not the classes are going to elect Beverly Lake!" Burney bellowed. A supporter from Wayne County held up a sign on a stick that said, "Wayne Says TAKE LAKE for Governor."

If Sanford's attacks on Lake at the beginning of the runoff marked a new Terry Sanford, then the New Bern speech marked a new Beverly Lake. In the first primary, Lake needled his three opponents about their positions on integration but generally did not otherwise discuss them. In the runoff, Lake confronted Sanford head on, with a steely determination that reflected his rising hostility toward his opponent. Sanford's education proposals were too expensive and would cause a dramatic increase in state taxes, Lake told his audience. The entire state budget was $242 million a year. Sanford wanted to spend $50 million a year more on public schools. That's almost what the state brought in each year from personal income taxes. "Do you think you could stand to have your income taxes doubled?" Lake said. If income taxes were not raised to pay for Sanford's program, other taxes could be, Lake said. The state could add a tax of twelve cents per pack on cigarettes. It could add a tax of five cents per bottle on soft drinks. It could remove all sales tax exemptions on food, medicine, feed, seed, and fertilizer—and still not raise $50 million a year.

Sanford's comment about Lake growing up in an ivory tower angered Lake. He deeply loved Wake Forest, the town and the college, and Sanford had insulted him and his family. Lake responded caustically. He said that Sanford did not grow up in a community dedicated to education, as he did, and that Sanford had little teaching experience. Lake pointed out that he taught for eighteen years. Sanford did not know much about schools, Lake said, "but at least my opponent ought to know that you do not necessarily build better educational opportunity for children just by pouring money into the school system." Lake spoke with determination, his voice on the edge of anger. Yes, he grew up in a little college town where his father taught physics for thirty-three years. No, his father never made much money but was able to educate his children and retire comfortably. Sanford said that economic growth would pay for his program. But Lake said that state revenue from corporate income taxes declined in 1959. "If he expects to finance his program from that source he had best get somebody raised in an ivory tower to teach him some elementary arithmetic and economics," Lake said sarcastically. "The only way he could possibly finance his spending program is by laying upon you the people of North Carolina taxes the like of which you have never seen in North Carolina." He waved his finger at the audience: "You will pay if he spends as he said he intends to."

His speech was over—but Lake wasn't through with Sanford. The rally was in two parts. The first portion was taped for television and was to be shown in six cities the following week. In that speech, Lake did not talk about integration. In his second speech, which was seen only by the New Bern audience, Lake discussed race. He was the candidate "most opposed" by the NAACP; Sanford was the candidate "most preferred" by that group. The voting results from black precincts showed that the way Sanford would handle integration "would be acceptable to the NAACP." He referred to a newspaper article that said student sit-down demonstration leaders in Charlotte had handed out lists of recommended candidates to black voters. Sanford was one of the recommended candidates.

As he traveled the state, Lake continued to gig Sanford. He mocked Sanford as "a courageous man," pointing out that Sanford had said he would have the courage to recommend new taxes. "I call upon my courageous adversary to have the courage before the primary to state what new sources of taxation he has in mind," Lake said. In a television address, Lake chided Sanford for dodging the integration issue: "My opponent has said he knows how to handle the integration problem but he has not said how he will handle it."

In another television address, Lake said that black voters overwhelmingly went for Sanford in the first primary, proving that he had the support of the NAACP. That was inconsistent with Lake's previously stated belief that the NAACP was different from the black people of North Carolina. But Lake disregarded his inconsistency and pounded away anyway: "The NAACP also wants to see a new day in North Carolina. The NAACP believes the new day it wants to bring about in your schools, your eating establishments, your barber shops, your beauty parlors, your parks, your beaches, your ballrooms and your children's homes can dawn in North Carolina if Mr. Sanford is your governor."

Sanford gave it back to Lake just as harshly. One Sunday in mid June, he gathered his eastern North Carolina leaders in Raleigh and gave them a pep talk. He said that the same crowd trying to beat them tried to smear Kerr Scott. "We will not be led down the dark trail of fear," Sanford said. In a reference to his opponent's rallies, he said that Lake's "foot-stomping appeal to blind prejudice" wasn't going to work with voters. "They are not going to be fooled by fear, even when it is peddled with foot-stomping, white Cadillac-riding professors," Sanford said. "North Carolina is not going to be fooled by fear even if it dressed up by a combination of Bilbo and Daddy Grace." Bilbo was demagogue Theodore Bilbo, the former governor and senator from Mississippi. Daddy Grace was a black, evangelical minister who founded the United House of Prayer for All People and traveled in a Cadillac, as Lake often did. Lake hated it but it was probably the best line of the campaign.

Sanford sought to turn Lake's aggressiveness on race back at him, believing that North Carolinians did not want a governor who spoke so strongly on the issue. The state's voters, he said, would not reward a gubernatorial campaign that stirred racial fears. He said "old Beverly" would bring "thunderclouds of court orders and lightning bolts of federal troops." Sanford said he didn't like the Supreme Court's *Brown* decision but Lake was making the situation worse. A spectator yelled, "Hit him again, Terry." Sanford did: "It's a naked and immoral appeal to raw race prejudice and the people of North Carolina are not going to put up with it. . . . I did not intend to stand around and be abused by any bigot."

He accused Lake of being a closet Republican. In one-party North Carolina in 1960, to be accused of being a Republican was a slur. When

Lake said that Sanford's program would provoke an era of "tax and tax and spend and spend," Sanford shot back that Lake was taking his phrases straight from the Republican National Handbook. Lake, he said, had no record of service to the Democratic Party and had not always supported Democratic candidates. He said that Lake had put a Republican twist on Franklin D. Roosevelt's saying. Said Sanford, "The only thing he [Lake] has to offer is fear itself."

Other charges and countercharges arose in the final weeks as the candidates fought for position. The stark differences between Lake and Sanford polarized the state. For North Carolinians, there was no middle ground, no compromise. You were either for Sanford or you were for Lake. Friends split in disagreement. Business partners split. Sometimes even families split. "The intensity of the times—I've never seen anything like it," recalled Beverly Lake Jr. "The campaign was extremely intense, very passionate. Unfortunately, I think."

Lake and Sanford started out friends and ended up enemies. Their debate started out civil and ended up personal. There was too much at stake to gloss over their differences, and they were too talented and too articulate to miss an opportunity to slash the other guy. This was not a modern-day campaign dominated by slick commercials and glib spin doctors pimping for candidates who didn't have enough courage or ability to speak without coaching and a TelePrompTer. Sanford and Lake were smart, driven, and competitive, and they didn't need to hire someone to tell them what to say or to say it for them. For a month, they punched and counterpunched, arguing their cases before the people of the state in an attempt to win a majority. They knew each other's strengths and weaknesses, where the other man's arguments rose and fell, and they moved to exploit even the smallest opening. They fought with passion and verve. They weren't just fighting for the governor's office. They were fighting for something much bigger than a four-year term. They were fighting for a way of life, taught to them by their parents when they were children and then retaught by them to their offspring. Each was certain that his way was better. As they fought each other, they became both mortal enemies and yet somehow linked together in the struggle, as fierce competitors often are. No one else could fully understand their deep conflict—except perhaps the other foe. It was a struggle that would bind them together for the rest of their lives.

Three days after the first primary, when Sanford responded aggressively to Lake's call for a runoff, he urged Lake to debate the true issues of the campaign. Lake quickly accepted, saying he was willing to debate Sanford face to face on television. The staffs of the two campaigns negotiated the ground rules and the candidates debated in Charlotte on Monday night, June 13. It had been two weeks since Lake called for a runoff and there were two weeks remaining in the second primary. The candidates debated from the studios of WBTV. Ten television stations carried the event, producing what was believed to be the largest viewing audience ever to see an event originating from a North Carolina television station. It was a thirty-minute debate. Each candidate had seven minutes for an opening statement and six and a half minutes for a rebuttal. The debate was moderated by a television professional.

Sanford won a coin toss and went first. He sold his program to improve schools, saying it was the most important issue the state faced. The state ranked in the bottom ten in the nation in the quality of its schools; Sanford said that his program would bring it into the top ten. He said he would return the Highway Commission to its old form of having members from each highway district and promised to promote industrial and agricultural expansion. He said Lake's characterization of his proposals as a tax-and-spend program was a "direct quote from the Republican National Handbook and they've been using it for years and it hasn't hurt the Democratic Party yet." North Carolina did not reach its present prosperity, Sanford said, by the kind of hold-the-line philosophy that Lake advocated.

Lake, he charged, had said in the past that the only answer to integration was to close the schools. Sanford produced the legislation that Lake wrote in 1956 when Lake and his supporters had opposed the Pearsall Plan in the general assembly. Sanford called Lake's legislation a "massive resistance bill" and also produced what he said was a copy of a charter

Lake had obtained to organize a private school. Sanford said that North Carolina's approach to handling school integration was the best, soundest approach and that he would continue that approach. When Lake asked Sanford what action he would take against the NAACP, Sanford said, "We can handle the NAACP, we can handle it well."

Lake said that the state faced two great dangers: the integration program of the NAACP and Sanford's tax-and-spend proposals. He said that the NAACP was out to integrate the total life of North Carolina and quoted from the 1956 report of the North Carolina Advisory Committee on Education: "If we would preserve our school system, we will have to preserve a segregated system." Lake promised to take "positive action" to lead them "to victory over the NAACP without closing the schools."

On the issue of paying for improved schools, Lake said that North Carolina already spent a higher proportion of its overall income on schools than many richer northern, eastern, and western states. He charged that Sanford had not said specifically where he would turn to for more tax money. He disagreed with Sanford's assessment that the state was prospering financially, saying North Carolina farmers the year before had one of the their worst years of the decade. Lake said he would not recommend any new taxes, except those absolutely necessary to make up for the one-time windfall the state received in the current two-year budget.

Lake also said that Sanford had declined to participate in an hour-long debate for which television stations had offered time. He wished Sanford had not limited the debate to thirty minutes. Sanford replied, "Frankly, I knew nothing about it until I saw their statement [of disappointment about the thirty-minute limit] in the newspapers." He produced telegrams, from television stations in seven cities, that he said showed Lake was mistaken. The Wilmington station offered an hour, Sanford said, but was not suitable for geographic reasons.

It was a cordial, quiet debate. The candidates repeated what they had been saying on the campaign trail but with less rancor. The debate about whether Sanford rejected an hour-long event—a discussion that continued for a week—was more lively than the televised debate. The day after the debate, Lake manager Robert Morgan said that Sanford had misrepresented the facts. Morgan made public a number of telegrams to and from WRAL-TV, showing that the station was willing to host an hour-long debate. Bert Bennett responded by saying WRAL-TV was owned by A. J. Fletcher, Lake's law partner and financial supporter. "Fletcher may be running the Lake's campaign," Bennett said, "but he is not going to run Terry Sanford's."

Morgan did not relent. He was a talented politician with a populist bent, a future U.S. senator who understood the value of staying on the attack. But with his next jab he might have erred. A week before the June 25 vote, Morgan said that union leaders had spent nine thousand dollars on the primary election and that they were supporting Sanford. He referred to federal records that showed labor money was sent to AFL-CIO committees for political education in North Carolina. The state AFL-CIO president said that the nine thousand dollar figure was too high and that none of the money went to the Sanford campaign. Morgan also said that federal records showed that five thousand dollars in union funds was paid to Sanford in 1954, when he managed Kerr Scott's campaign. Those sums were not reported to Scott, Morgan alleged. If the money was intended for Scott, he said that Sanford was required to report the contribution within five days.

Sanford strongly denied that his campaign had received any labor money and said that he would get out of the race if anyone could prove otherwise. He did not directly address the issue about the five thousand dollar contribution from 1954. "This is 1960 and this is my campaign," he said. "I regret that the campaign would ever get to the point when the opposition would attempt in the last hours to smear the name of a great man and a devoted friend like Sen. Kerr Scott." Actually, Morgan was raising questions about what Sanford did with the money—not whether Scott did something inappropriate. The information had been public record for six years, Sanford said, and questioning it now was an act of last-minute desperation. He did not explain, however, how the five thousand dollars was used.

Morgan's attack backfired. It allowed Sanford to rally the Kerr Scott faithful. Scott's family issued a statement, grieving that the Lake campaign would smear the memory of Kerr Scott. "We are confident that those for whom Kerr Scott fought while he was alive will resent with us the tactics now being used by Dr. Lake's forces," the family said. "Kerr is not here to speak for himself but his friends can." Scott supporters took out an ad in the *News and Observer*, decrying Morgan's attack. The ad pictured Scott and his wife. The headline said, "Yes . . . Miss Mary, We will Speak up for KERR SCOTT." The sponsors of the ad—six men from eastern North Carolina—said that they resented the effort to smear Scott's memory. Farmers would rise up to defend Scott's memory at the polls. The ad urged a vote for Sanford and against Lake.

The candidates sought and publicized prominent endorsements. In early June, a wire service caused a stir when it reported that South Carolina governor Ernest Hollings had endorsed Lake. It made sense. Hollings was elected in 1958 over former University of South Carolina president Donald Russell. Hollings was the stronger segregationist. In a runoff primary, Hollings said that Russell offered "a lot of fancy talk" but had failed to take a strong stand on segregation. Hollings assumed office with a promise to "resist the dictation of a power-happy federal government." A few days after the first primary in North Carolina, United Press International reported that Hollings was asked which candidate he preferred. He said he did not know much about either Sanford or Lake. But since Sanford "has been described as a moderate in segregation, I necessarily stand for Dr. Lake, who stands for segregation and our way of life," Hollings said, according to United Press International. Hollings, who would become a longtime U.S. senator, soon said that he was misquoted and that he did not endorse either candidate.

M. A. Huggins, a longtime church leader known in North Carolina as Mr. Baptist, endorsed Sanford—a coup for Sanford because Lake was a devoted Baptist whom Huggins had known since Lake was a child. "I cannot support him for he has sought, wittingly or unwittingly, to intensify those powerful emotions of hate and fear," Huggins said on a television show paid for by the Sanford campaign. Charles Green, who had managed Willis Smith's campaign for the U.S. Senate ten years earlier, endorsed Lake. The Lake and Sanford camps sought endorsements from the losing candidates in the first primary and their prominent supporters. Malcolm Seawell emerged from a month-long silence and endorsed Sanford two days before the runoff. One of his co-managers endorsed Sanford, the other supported Lake. John Larkins remained neutral but his campaign manager endorsed Sanford.

The endorsement that caused the most debate was Tom Pearsall's backing of Sanford on statewide television. Pearsall was a former Speaker of the North Carolina House and one of the state's most respected citizens. He chaired the two committees that developed North Carolina's response to the Supreme Court's *Brown* decision. Pearsall said that Beverly Lake had not, as he claimed, written the Pupil Assignment Act, which gave local school boards power of assignment. For the remainder of the campaign, Lake and his supporters argued back and forth with Pearsall about Lake's role in drafting the legislation. Perhaps more important were the reasons each side gave for why Lake should or should not be elected. Pearsall said that Lake's "massive resistance" program would destroy North Carolina's successful, moderate approach. W. W. Taylor, a former legislator and Lake ally, disputed Pearsall's remarks. He said that the Pupil Assignment Act was passed substantially as written and presented by Lake. He rejected calling Lake's ideas "massive resistance." Of the two candidates, Taylor said that Lake was the one most likely to keep the schools of North Carolina open and segregated.

As Saturday, June 25, drew near, the candidates campaigned feverishly, trying to cover more and more ground. The ever-proper Lake was such a stickler for following the law that he did not believe motorists should drive faster than the speed limit. Lake put a pillow in the back seat. At night, when his drivers heard him snore, they'd drive far faster than the speed limit. "He'd have a fit if he knew how fast we were going," said Roy Green, one of his drivers.

Toward the end of the campaign, Lake apparently stopped worrying about speeding. One day in the last week of the campaign, Lake covered several hundred miles in a frantic swing through the mountains. When they fell behind schedule, the Lake entourage covered the thirty-two miles from Bryson City to Andrews in thirty-two minutes and forty-six seconds, with speeds of up to eighty-five miles an hour on the mountain roads. After shaking hands in the streets of Andrews, Lake traveled to Murphy, where he had lunch and spoke in the blue-marbled Cherokee County Courthouse. He was introduced by a supporter and textile manufacturer from Murphy. "If you want to swap your birthright, then vote for Dr. Sanford," the supporter said. Lake said that his major objective was to preserve the public schools. "I have no program for the advancement of the colored people of North Carolina and I have no program for the advancement of the white people of North Carolina," Lake said. "My program is for all the people of North Carolina."

Sanford also stuck to a vigorous pace. Dave Cooper of the *News and Observer* couldn't keep up. Following Sanford around the state, he wrote, was like trying to compete in the Indianapolis 500 on a bicycle. Three days before Democrats went to the polls, Sanford started early in the morning in Rowan County, northeast of Charlotte in the state's Piedmont, where he was met by a caravan of supporters. The motorcade included a five-piece Dixieland jazz band with a loudspeaker system and about 150 cars, at times snaking for more than a mile. The cars were decorated with pennants, banners, and placards. Drivers repeatedly honked their horns. Sanford rode in an open convertible. In one town Sanford was surrounded by a mob of enthusiastic children. Each wanted Sanford's autograph and got it. During a stop, Sanford tried to help the band by playing saxophone, but he had not practiced in years and could produce only loud honking sounds. That night, Sanford addressed some recent comments from his opponent. Sanford had promised so many gifts, Lake had said, that he rivaled Santa Claus. In trademark fashion, Sanford turned the issue back at his opponent: "If we can hitch up these reindeer and load up this bag with better school opportunities, then I'm all for being called Santa Claus."

On the night before voters would go to the polls, Sanford and Lake each made a final plea over statewide television. In a runoff filled with acrimony, it was fitting that each concluded with a parry at the other. Sanford, speaking from Greensboro, predicted victory. The people wanted to

215

build a better state, he said, and his program would do that. "I am confident that the people of North Carolina are not willing to be led to destruction by a Pied Piper of prejudice," he said. "I am confident that the tons of leaflets prepared in desperation—distributed in the dark of night, oozing with hate and fear—will not fool the people."

Lake spoke from Charlotte. He was hampered by thunderstorms, which interrupted his program over the Durham and Greensboro stations. He defended himself on several fronts. He said he was a loyal Democrat. He said he did not get most of the black vote in Iredell County. He said he would not close schools. He said he was not campaigning on race hatred. Issue after issue, he responded to Sanford. Sanford had knocked Lake off balance, giving him less time to go after Sanford on Lake's issues. Lake did attack, predictably, on his favorite issue—hammering the NAACP. He said Sanford was naive in saying that the NAACP was feeble. "On the contrary, it is a powerful, dangerous enemy which has gained a foothold in North Carolina and which believes that under Mr. Sanford's administration it can grow and flourish," Lake said. He repeated the vote results from the first primary, showing that Sanford had dominated in many black precincts. When Lake finished his television address, the campaign essentially was over. Voters could say much about Sanford and Lake. They could not say that the candidates did not offer a clear choice.

The precinct in secluded Cataloochee Valley in mountainous Haywood County was the first to report its results, twelve minutes and three seconds after the polls opened Saturday morning. The valley, fifteen miles from the nearest store or telephone, once was home to a thriving community before the federal government annexed land for the Great Smokies National Park. Now only the Pilkingtons, Caldwells, and Hannahs remained. All eight registered voters cast their ballots at the abandoned little one-room schoolhouse—all for Terry Sanford. "If he'd been a runnin' back 30 years ago, we'd of give him a thousand," said Lush Caldwell, sporting a Terry Sanford button. Sanford had organized even Cataloochee Valley.

Sanford voted at 4 P.M. in Fayetteville, then drove to Raleigh to listen

216

to the election returns. A reporter asked if he was ready for a vacation. "I'm ready to go again," Sanford said. Lake admitted to being beat. He did not get home from Charlotte until 4:30 A.M. He voted at 11 A.M. and spent the afternoon at home and mingling in downtown Wake Forest before going to Raleigh.

In the early evening, returns slowly arrived at Lake's headquarters in Raleigh. There was a hush in the old garage building. As the returns mounted, Lake was further and further behind. A great cheer arose when it was announced that Lake had carried Wake County, 16,000 votes to 11,000. A few minutes later, there was silence. The tallies had been reported in reverse. Robert Morgan hovered near Lake, whispering in his ear, smiling as best he could. A chalkboard carried the results, which were announced. The gloom thickened. "They know how to handle it in Mississippi," someone said. At 8 P.M., the chalkboard showed Sanford ahead by 50,000 votes. Some people walked outside, where it was cooler. At 8:45 P.M., people murmured that Lake would speak in fifteen minutes. "Listen everybody," said one Lake supporter, "let's all sing 'Dixie.'" Trudy Lake stood with John Burney and they sang the anthem of the Old South, the sound spilling into the streets.

At the Sanford headquarters a block away at the Carolina Hotel, the ballroom squirmed with people. Sanford wore the same striped tie he had worn the last few weeks of the campaign for good luck. It was so crowded, he could move only inches at a time. A woman fainted in the crush. Results from county after county rolled in, giving Sanford an insurmountable lead. In all, he won sixty-six of one hundred counties. Sanford won 56 percent of the vote—352,000 votes to Lake's 276,000. The turnout did not quite match that of a month before, but it was still well beyond the old record set in '52. Sanford won big in the mountains, ran well ahead in most of the Piedmont, and held his own in the east, where Lake was his strongest. He even won four eastern counties that Lake had won in the first primary. Now and then Sanford put his glasses on to read the returns on a blackboard. His mother pressed through the mass of sweaty people and, without a word, kissed him on the cheek. His father gave him a strong pat on the back.

Black voters were an important part of Sanford's success and perhaps won the election for him. Sanford won by 76,000 votes. The *Carolina Times*, the black newspaper in Durham, estimated that there were 150,000 registered black voters in the state and that 70,000 to 90,000 had voted. If 90 percent of black voters went for Sanford, he would have won 63,000 to 81,000 black votes. His margin of victory fell in that range. Sanford and Lake roughly split the white vote. Lake later said with pride that although Sanford won the black vote, he won the white vote. That analysis was too simple. Lake *might* have won a majority of white voters but if he did, it was a narrow majority. The *Carolina Times* credited blacks with providing the winning margin but also said, "It is also encouraging to know that a majority of white voters in North Carolina are no longer duped by a candidate for public office whose major platform plank is the race issue." In the end, the racial breakdown is irrelevant: Sanford won a decisive majority. Lake's pride in winning a majority of white voters assumes that the votes of black citizens somehow are worth less than the votes of white citizens. To him, they were.

At 9:02 P.M., Lake spoke as television cameras watched. "It is apparent to all of us that the Democrats have nominated Mr. Sanford to be our next governor," Lake said. Noting that he had received more than a quarter of a million votes, Lake said he was "thrilled to know so many stand for the principles which are eternal." His supporters interrupted him with a cheer. "I haven't finished saying what I wanted to say," he said. Everybody laughed. Then he and Trudy Lake and some supporters left to walk to the Carolina Hotel and congratulate Sanford. When Lake left his headquarters, John Burney stirred the crowd into stomping and shouting. "This is the last of our camp meetings," Burney said. One elderly woman hugged and kissed Burney.

At the Carolina, Lake pushed his way through the crowd and reached for Sanford's hand.

"Terry, I congratulate you on your fine vote and I wish you a successful administration," Lake said. "Of course, it goes without saying, you have my support in the November election."

"Thank you," Sanford said. "You know the personal regard I have for you. I want to congratulate you on a most vigorous campaign. You certainly had me scared all the way. I do appreciate your coming over here and I am looking forward to working with you and to seeing you and to continuing our friendship, which has lasted so many years."

"Thank you, Terry," Lake said quickly. "Good night to you."

After Trudy and Beverly Lake shook hands with Margaret Rose and Terry Sanford, someone said, "Let's give Dr. Lake a big hand." After the applause, Lake and his party quickly departed.

Sanford moved outside and stood on a park wall to address the crowd. "Get ready for a New Day in North Carolina," Sanford said. The crowd shouted, "We want Terry! We want Terry!" Sanford said, "It's been a hard fight. In any progressive campaign you are going to have a hard fight. But now we need to get on with the job." When he was finished, a photographer hoped to shoot a picture of an exhausted nominee.

"Look beat!" yelled the photographer.

"I'm never beat," Sanford said.

About five hundred miles to the north, the telephone rang, again and again, at the New York City residence of Frank Porter Graham. Telegrams arrived too. The callers told Graham that his defeat in 1950 had contributed to Sanford's victory. Graham was pleased. "If there is any bit of truth in it," Graham wrote Sanford a few days later, "I am deeply glad that such a defeat could be even a small bit of your more enduring and greater victory." Out of the ashes of Graham's defeat, Sanford learned how to control the people's racial fears. The fire did not rage as it did in 1950. It was there, alive, flickering, simmering near the ground, but Sanford built a wall around it so it would not spread. Now that he had controlled the people's fear, perhaps as governor he could turn that fear toward respect and acceptance. First, however, there were some other challenges he needed to meet.

Chapter 9

JFK AND MR. GOP

On Sunday, the day after he had won the Democratic nomination, Sanford sat on his bed at the Carolina Hotel. He might have told the photographer the night before that he wasn't tired, but he was. He had campaigned full-time for six months, traveling to almost every county at least three times. The runoff was particularly demanding. Lake had pushed him hard and, consequently, he had pushed himself hard. As he buttoned his shirt, he said that he would attend a meeting the next day of North Carolina delegates to the Democratic National Convention, which would begin in just two weeks. Then he wanted to take three or four days of vacation at the beach. It would be a quick vacation. There was too much to do. He opened the dresser drawer of his hotel room and pointed to a pile of notes and paper he had accumulated while campaigning. "We've got a lot of thinking and letter writing to do," he said.

On Monday, he talked with reporters. He said his victory showed that a candidate could not win in North Carolina by campaigning on the race issue. "I hope we don't see it again," he said. "An appeal to fear, hate and racial prejudice will not win an election." He added, vaguely, that many citizens were not satisfied with conditions involving race. "I'm not satisfied myself," he said, without elaborating. "But North Carolina has handled it the best way and the election demonstrates that the majority of the people feel that way too." He said he would not be vindictive or hold any grudges against Lake supporters: "I'm ready now to wipe the slate clean."

Sanford also said he had not yet made up his mind about whom he would support for president. He stressed that he would not try to influence any of the other delegates, many of them active workers in his campaign. "I have not had much of a chance until yesterday to talk about the national nominee," he said. "I've been talking with some people since then and will continue to talk about it." He hoped to announce his decision within a week. As he left for vacation two days later, the Associated Press published its survey of North Carolina delegates to the Democratic National Convention. The state had seventy-four delegates to the convention, each with half a vote. Of the thirty-seven votes, Lyndon Johnson had sixteen, Adlai Stevenson two, Stuart Symington two, and John Kennedy one. The rest were undecided.

Governor Hodges would serve as chairman of the delegation and Sanford as vice chairman. Of the seventy-four delegates, Sanford estimated at least two-thirds were friends or supporters of his. He was confident he had the votes to win election as chairman. Hodges, however, sent word to Sanford that he would like to be chairman. Sanford, in the interest of mending the party, agreed. Later Sanford would regret that decision. When the delegation met in Raleigh, Sanford did not commit to a candidate. But he talked with other party leaders—U.S. senators Sam Ervin and Everett Jordan—about making sure that Kennedy won ten to twelve of the delegation's thirty-seven votes. "I think it would help us in the future," Sanford told them. "You know he's going to win." Ervin and Jordan did not acknowledge that Kennedy would win.

Sanford knew Johnson better than he knew Kennedy. When he visited Washington regularly in the mid-1950s to see Kerr Scott, he often talked with Johnson, whom he liked and considered experienced and extremely competent. Sanford had met Kennedy only a couple of times. The first time he spoke with him was in Charlotte in early 1959. Kennedy was considered a possible presidential candidate and the Charlotte Chamber of Commerce invited him to speak. Kennedy asked a Charlotte chamber official to invite delegates who had attended the 1956 Democratic National Convention, where Kennedy made a surprisingly strong showing. Sanford had attended the '56 convention and supported Estes Kefauver. Sanford accepted the invitation to attend the Charlotte event because he wanted the support of the chamber official, who was publisher of the *Charlotte News,* and he wanted to meet Kennedy, whose views Sanford liked.

In Charlotte, Sanford was impressed that Kennedy immediately sought him out and spoke with him, giving him individual attention in the crowded room. Sanford was one of the few delegates from '56 to attend the chamber event and Kennedy knew he was a potential delegate in 1960. Kennedy told Sanford he would be a serious candidate for president. A few days later, Sanford received a letter from Kennedy: "It was a pleasure to be with you in Charlotte last week, and both Jackie and I enjoyed thoroughly our all too short visit to your state." Sanford, in a "Dear Jack" letter, responded: "Many people in North Carolina are very much interested in you and your future, although this is a little early for definite positions." Sanford was impressed, though. He liked the speech Kennedy gave and he liked the one-on-one conversation he had with Kennedy. Sanford admired a well-organized campaign, and he liked the way Kennedy was traveling the country, meeting potential 1960 delegates.

Now Sanford had to choose between Kennedy and Johnson. Sanford leaned toward Kennedy on principle and Johnson on practical politics. Johnson would help him in the fall, while Kennedy could be a burden. In making a decision, he talked individually with a few of his closest friends and advisers. He talked with Henry Hall Wilson, his assistant campaign manager, as Sanford lounged beside a hotel pool in Raleigh. "You don't have any choice," Wilson said. "With what you stand for, you've got to be for Kennedy." Sanford thought that was a good point. Campaign manager Bert Bennett also backed Kennedy. "History knocks seldom and when it does, you'd better open up," Bennett told him. "History is knocking in this opportunity to associate with Kennedy."

Ben Roney, his hard-edged aide and a practical pol, was for Johnson. "You can't be for Kennedy. It will kill you," Roney said. Unless, he said, Sanford had some obligation to Kennedy. Rumors were circulating that the Kennedys had contributed money to Sanford's campaign. Sanford said he did have an obligation. Sanford meant that he had a historical obligation to Kennedy; Roney thought he meant he had a financial obligation to Kennedy. Sanford said years later, "I might have misled him. I didn't really intend to but he didn't ask any more questions. . . . I by that time had made up my mind to be for Kennedy and I simply didn't want to get him too far away from me and too upset and irritated by it."

Sanford went to Myrtle Beach, South Carolina, to vacation for five days at a friend's house. Dickson Phillips, his law partner, came down. Sanford said he thought he was going to be for Kennedy but he wanted to see what Phillips and their other partner and boyhood friend, Don McKoy, thought about it. Phillips agreed with Kennedy. So did McKoy, although he warned Sanford about the political risk.

While he was at Myrtle Beach, Sanford called Robert Kennedy and told him of his decision. "Terrific!" Kennedy said, using his favorite word. After they hung up, Robert Kennedy told his brother of Sanford's support. John Kennedy was delighted—so delighted that he wanted Sanford to second his nomination in Los Angeles. Robert Kennedy called Sanford back and told him. Sanford had reservations about playing such a prominent role. To the home folks, it could look like he was showing off. Also, his decision to back Kennedy instead of Johnson was not going to be popular in North Carolina.

"Don't do me any favors," Sanford said he told Robert Kennedy.

"He really needs you," Kennedy said.

Sanford eventually agreed. He told Robert Kennedy that when he got back to Raleigh, he would hold a press conference and say he was for his brother. But Robert Kennedy wanted Sanford to wait until he got to Los Angeles to make his announcement. A prominent southerner endorsing Kennedy at the opening of the convention would give him a boost, Robert Kennedy said. Sanford said he would think about it. He talked about it with Bert Bennett. "If you're going to help them, you might as well help them their way," Bennett said. They agreed that if Sanford were going to help Kennedy, he would help him as much as he could.

After his trip to Myrtle Beach, Sanford returned to Raleigh and scheduled a meeting with reporters. The *News and Observer,* citing reliable reports, said that Sanford was expected to support Johnson at the press conference. But Sanford did not endorse Johnson for president. He said he would support a ticket of Johnson and Kennedy—but he would not say which for president and which for vice president. He implied that he would not make a decision until he got to California, and said he would announce his decision as the convention was about to open. Years later, Sanford acknowledged that he "was a little bit on the untruthful side" in implying that he had not made a decision.

It was not apparent at the Raleigh press conference, but Sanford was setting the stage to endorse Kennedy. He said neither candidate was from the South. To Sanford, Kennedy was a New Englander and Johnson a westerner. Because of that, he said neither understood the South's challenges with race relations. "Neither fully comprehends as we do more and more that the ultimate solution will be founded in the human heart and not solely in instruments of law," he said. Sanford's assertion that Johnson was not a southerner was news to most people. "Is it official that Texas has seceded from the South?" a reporter asked. Johnson classified himself as a westerner, Sanford said. But both men, he said, were open-minded and would listen to southern leaders on the issue.

Sanford also said the state would gain by going with the winner from the beginning, instead of backing one candidate early on and then switching to the eventual nominee. In the past, southern leaders often supported a southern candidate early on but changed once it was apparent the southern candidate would not win. Going into the convention, Kennedy looked to be the strongest candidate. Sanford added that if Kennedy were the nominee, he could carry North Carolina, despite being Catholic.

In a final hint that he would support Kennedy, Sanford said he wanted North Carolina to move into the national mainstream. Despite Sanford's assertion that Johnson was from the west, most considered him a southerner. That was one of the principal reasons that the vast majority of leaders from across the south—including Governor Hodges and Senators Sam Ervin and Everett Jordan in North Carolina—supported Johnson. "We in the South cannot continue to isolate ourselves from the rest of the nation," Sanford told the reporters. "When we isolate ourselves we invite the rest of the country to use the South as a whipping boy for their political gain. I am tired of this. We do not deserve any whipping and I do not intend to be whipped. I want North Carolina's leadership to be able to walk proudly and confidently into the president's office, which is exactly the place we can start putting a stop to the whipping." He did not say it then, but he thought supporting Johnson was a futile vote—a tip of the hat to the Old South and a wasted opportunity to be a part of an alliance with the Kennedy administration, an alliance that could help North Carolina. Beverly Lake sometimes said he was a North Carolina Democrat, meaning he had no use for the national Democratic Party. Terry Sanford was a national Democrat. He wanted the state to be a part of the national mainstream, and to him that was part of Kennedy's appeal.

Despite Sanford's signals that he was leaning toward Kennedy, they were largely ignored. Few expected him to actually endorse a young senator from Massachusetts over a Senate powerhouse from Texas like Lyndon Johnson. Also, Sanford had enough problems already. While North Carolina had not elected a Republican governor in the century, Sanford had several disadvantages. He had expressed a willingness to raise taxes. Also, he had made enemies during his raw runoff with Beverly Lake. Endorsing Kennedy was simply too risky for a candidate who needed to win the election in November.

Four days later in Los Angeles, Sanford jolted gathering convention goers and shocked the North Carolina political establishment. He endorsed John F. Kennedy for president. At a modest gathering of newspaper reporters Saturday morning, he said that a president should not be decided by sentiment or how he would help the local ticket. A president should be chosen "with a national view toward our own survival and quest for peace." Were arrangements made during his runoff for him to support Kennedy? "Very definitely not," he said. Had Kennedy or any other presidential candidate contributed to his campaign? "The answer is no," he said. Kennedy, it was noted, said that all races should be able to eat at lunch counters. You can support a candidate without agreeing with

him on all matters, Sanford said. Was there friction between Sanford and
Governor Hodges? "I haven't fallen out with Gov. Hodges," Sanford said.
"I respect his right to his opinion and I'm sure he respects my right to
mine." He predicted Kennedy would get about one-third of the North
Carolina delegates' votes and Johnson the other two-thirds. He predicted
Kennedy would carry North Carolina in November.

Sanford's endorsement was a major breakthrough for Kennedy. Although it was mostly a symbolic victory for Kennedy—most North Carolina delegates would still go for Johnson—it broke the solid southern
Johnson bloc and gave Kennedy prestige. "John is deeply grateful," a
Kennedy aide said. "It wasn't the vote or votes. It was the symbol of the
thing—that we could have all sections for us."

The North Carolina delegation buzzed. Their forty-two-year-old nominee for governor, selected all of two weeks ago, had bucked the state's
veteran leadership—Hodges, Ervin, and Jordan. But few delegates followed Sanford. Some were cool to him. Some were bitter. Some were
scared. Some predicted a fight on Monday morning when the delegates
caucused for the first time. "I'm still for Johnson come hell or high water—and they'll probably both come [Monday]," said U.S. representative
Paul Kitchin of Wadesboro.

Sanford was surrounded by criticism. After he announced for
Kennedy, the North Carolina delegation decided that night to host a reception for Johnson. Sanford attended and stood in the middle of the
floor. Johnson immediately went to Sanford and the two shook hands.
"Terry, you and I've got one thing in common," Johnson said. "We out-
married ourselves." Given the circumstances, Sanford thought it was a
good thing to say. Johnson backers continued to work on Sanford. Bill
Cochrane, the Senate staffer who met with Bobby Baker and Sanford
during the runoff, was sent to Los Angeles as an emissary for Johnson. A
Johnson man accompanied him. They tracked down Sanford at night at
a hotel suite. Sanford told Cochrane he wasn't changing his mind.
Cochrane, an old friend and roommate from the University of North
Carolina, said that he knew he wouldn't change his mind but that he
had been asked to talk with him. Once he did, he would fly back to

Washington. When Sanford refused to change his endorsement, the Johnson man cried.

Sanford stood by his decision. "I don't mind taking my knocks," he said the day after he backed Kennedy. "I knew my stand would be unpopular but time will demonstrate that I was right." The almost solid bloc of support for Johnson in the South threatened to further isolate the South from the rest of the nation, he said. "On the question of race," he said, "there really is very little difference among the four major contenders. None of them satisfy us. I think that by being in the corner with the winner—and Kennedy will win—we will be in a better position to soften the attitude of some people toward the South's approach to its problem."

As if Sanford did not have enough problems, he was blind-sided Tuesday by a critical newspaper article. Drew Pearson, a nationally syndicated columnist, implied in a column that Sanford had supported Kennedy in exchange for campaign contributions. Sanford initially was for Johnson and asked for campaign contributions, Pearson said. Then Robert Kennedy visited Sanford in North Carolina and Sanford cooled to Johnson, Pearson said. He also wrote that Sanford promised to call Johnson after the runoff but never did. Sanford was not quoted in the column; he said that Pearson never contacted him to discuss the insinuation. Sanford said he had neither discussed nor received any campaign contributions from Kennedy. There was an element of truth in the column, Sanford said. A man did offer him a campaign contribution if he would support Johnson. Sanford said he turned it down.

Later Sanford would joke that he was honored that Pearson would choose him as his prime target as Democrats from across the nation were getting ready to nominate a president. But it caused him problems both at the convention and for months afterward. When the North Carolina delegation met in Los Angeles, Sanford made a point of denying the allegations. "It's a damn lie," he said. "I did not get one cent from Kennedy or anyone connected with him." The delegation supported Sanford. It considered passing a resolution backing him but then decided just to ignore Pearson's charge. One delegate proposed they accept the description of

Pearson once given by Harry Truman, who called Pearson an SOB. The delegates laughed.

Sanford also told them that he had made no attempt to pressure them to support Kennedy. He pleaded for unity. "I hope there is no lasting division in the delegation and I for one will bear no grudges," he said. He said he would give one of five seconding speeches at Kennedy's nomination. "If you're going to make a fool of yourself, you might as well make a big one," he said. Sanford's words seemed to soothe the delegates. While few delegates joined Sanford in backing Kennedy, none of the acrimony evident before the caucus broke into the open. When the delegation was polled, Johnson had twenty-seven votes; Kennedy had six; Adlai Stevenson had three; and George Smathers had one-half. Sanford did not win the ten votes for Kennedy that he wanted. Hodges, Ervin, and Jordan made sure of that. After Sanford endorsed Kennedy, Hodges predicted Johnson would get at least twenty-five votes from the delegation. That support for Johnson reflected the sentiment back home, Hodges told reporters.

Sanford believed Hodges also had other motives. Hodges still wanted to be vice president. He knew it was unlikely that Johnson would choose a southerner to be his running mate. But Hodges thought that if Johnson were strong enough to deprive Kennedy of the nomination, Democrats might turn to Adlai Stevenson of Illinois—and that Hodges, as a southerner, would be a natural vice president with Stevenson. Hodges had discussed this scenario publicly, saying "if lightning struck" he would accept a nomination for vice president. Sanford said that Hodges, Ervin, and Jordan put tremendous pressure on the delegates to support Johnson. Contrary to what he said publicly, Sanford also did some lobbying for Kennedy. Of the eleven other delegates who supported Kennedy, Sanford would later say, "Half of them came out of there with broken arms and cracked skulls that I had put on them." They would come to be known in North Carolina as the Dirty Dozen.

Sanford resented the opposition of Hodges and Ervin. He wasn't angry at Everett Jordan, whom he considered a gentleman. But he thought Hodges was a mean, vicious, and dirty fighter. Of Hodges, Sanford would later say, "He has got a reputation for being a great reformer and an honest businessman, and he is all of that. But he is a very vicious person in a political situation. I saw him browbeat a little insurance salesman who was half a vote for Harriman in '56 and you would have thought he'd turned on the Christian religion, the way Hodges put the pressure on him and whipped him and ostracized him and did everything he could. He then was governor of course. And he was trying to do that to me [in '60] except I was a little more accustomed to it, and furthermore I had more friends." Instead of coming to his defense after the Pearson article, Sanford said Ervin and Hodges "hopped on that and cut me to pieces." When delegates considered a resolution condemning Pearson, Sanford said that Hodges maneuvered to have it tabled. Sanford and Hodges would later become friends, but Sanford said, "He was just as mean and vicious there and really for his own purposes, I thought."

Sanford went to John Kennedy's hotel and talked to him about Hodges defeating the resolution against Pearson. Kennedy was relaxed and chewing gum.

"You know, if I ever recommend old Hodges for anything, I hope you'll throw me out of your office," Sanford said he told Kennedy.

"He is a bastard, isn't he?" Kennedy replied.

The convention also caused hard feelings between Sanford and Sam Ervin. When the delegates met in Raleigh, Sanford told Ervin and Jordan that he thought Kennedy should win ten to twelve votes. "He keeps telling people that I'm a liar because when I told him that we ought to have a dozen people for Kennedy that I didn't tell him I might be one of them," Sanford said in 1971. "And from that day to this he has been very vicious in his comments about me but I don't care." Sanford considered running against Ervin in 1968 but decided not to.

While in Los Angeles, Sanford received a message from Don McKoy, his law partner in Fayetteville. The reaction back home to his endorsement of Kennedy was not good. Under no circumstances, McKoy said, should Sanford second Kennedy's nomination; Sanford already had enough problems in North Carolina. Sanford tracked down Robert Kennedy on the floor of the convention hall. He told him he did not want to second John Kennedy's nomination. "It might cause me to lose and it's just too big a burden," Sanford said. Robert Kennedy said he would talk with his brother. He came back later and told Sanford that his brother really wanted him to do it, that he needed the regional balance Sanford provided. So Sanford agreed to do it. He tried to telephone McKoy but could not get through. McKoy read in the newspaper about Sanford's seconding of Kennedy.

On Wednesday night, July 13, Kennedy won the Democratic nomination on the first ballot. In seconding the nomination, Sanford said, "John Kennedy is another Franklin D. Roosevelt." Sanford used some of the same language he had used previously in arguing that southerners should not choose a president just because a candidate was from the South. "This election is not to be taken lightly, not to be decided by sentimentality, not to be reached on feelings or emotions," he said. "This election must be made with a national view toward our own survival and quest for peace. Sen. John Kennedy will supply that national leadership."

A short time after Kennedy won the nomination, Hodges approached Sanford. He still wanted to be vice president. Hodges asked him if he would put in a word for him with Kennedy. "No sir," Sanford said with pleasure. "I've already strongly put in a word for Lyndon Johnson." Sanford had told Kennedy that Johnson would help the ticket in North Carolina and the rest of the South.

Years later, Sanford said, "I thought it was so typical of Hodges, that he still was grabbing for this thing, after all he had done to me and after all he had done to Kennedy. At that stage of the game, I wouldn't have lifted a finger to have gotten him out of a sinkhole." Yet only a few months later Sanford visited Kennedy's Georgetown townhouse with Bert Bennett and told Kennedy that he needed to make Hodges his commerce secretary, which he did. Kennedy and Sanford chuckled at the irony. Sanford used to joke that sending Hodges to Washington got him out of North Carolina—and out of his way. Bennett warned Kennedy about Hodges' strong personality. "It was an endorsement but he [Sanford] wanted to be sure Kennedy knew what he was getting, because Hodges was dominant," Bennett remembered. "He didn't like 'No.' I warned the president: If he didn't watch out, it would be 'Move over.' And he [Hodges] would take the seat if he had a chance. You had to let him know who was who."

Sanford pushed Johnson for vice president both before and after Kennedy won the nomination. When he arrived in Los Angeles and endorsed Kennedy, he predicted Johnson would be his running mate. The morning after Kennedy secured the nomination, Sanford was to meet with Kennedy. A top Kennedy aide, either Larry O'Brien or Kenny O'Donnell, urged Sanford to advocate for Johnson at the meeting. Sanford did. But Kennedy did not think Johnson would accept. Sanford told Kennedy he had no doubt that Johnson would accept, for two reasons: Johnson was "a patriot for the party" and he wanted to be president; the vice presidency would put him in line to run for president in eight years. A few hours later, Kennedy asked Johnson to be his running mate. Johnson accepted.

In North Carolina, Sanford's endorsement of Kennedy was unpopular. He expected some resentment—but not the torrent of hostility he received. He later admitted he had underestimated the opposition to Kennedy. "I thought that I could ride out anything by that time, that whatever I wanted North Carolina would go with," Sanford remembered. He found out differently.

Immediately, Sanford was flooded by telegrams in Los Angeles. He received so many that he threw out the first 100 or so. Then, recognizing their historical significance, he began to save them—about 350 more cards, letters, and telegrams. Almost half were favorable, although they often pledged support despite the outcry they said they heard around them. His friend Sonny Boy Joyner wired: "Don't back up. With you all the way. We will be on the firing line always." His friend Lauch Faircloth also wired support: "Think your vote for Kennedy a wise one. Most other people in section feel same way. Kennedy defeated bigger men than Johnson getting to the fight."

The correspondence opposing Kennedy was notable more for its venom than its quantity. Many North Carolinians were emotional and angry. They felt Sanford had betrayed them. They said that they would not have voted for him if they had known he would support Kennedy. A Winston-Salem resident wrote:

> Dear Mr. Carpetbagger,
>
> Drew Pearson in the morning's *Journal* gave us the facts we knew all along. You lied in the beginning about Bob Kennedy so we expected you to lie from then on. Your "sell out," however, is not as honorable as any prostitute that walks the streets of Fayetteville.
>
> I imagine the Negroes and Kennedy money will elect you in November but you can know with surety the people of North Carolina for the next four years will carry nothing but despicability for you in their hearts. I have always voted the Democratic ticket but this is one time when I would vote for a "Block Negro" before I would vote for you.

Three supporters from Lenoir wired: "We wish to express our opinion as supporters of you and Democrats of North Carolina, so don't make it any [harder] for us by helping nominate someone that will shove the Negro situation down our throat. The final election coming up in November, there is still a Republican candidate for governor." A Shelby man wired: "Register my disgust with your support of Kennedy. You have betrayed us. Regret I voted for you." More than one hundred people signed this telegram: "Your friends and workers in Kannapolis and Cabarrus County bitterly disappointed in your failure to support Johnson."

A man who identified himself as the chairman of the Clyde Civic Committee in Haywood County said in a telegram: "Disappointed in your commitment to Kennedy. That has dealt our state worse blow since Civil War. Strongly urge reconsideration for support for Lyndon Johnson." A Winston-Salem woman wired: "The people of North Carolina do not want Kennedy and now we don't want you. Gavin for governor."

Most of the letters and telegrams opposing Kennedy did so on grounds of his Catholicism. A Chapel Hill man telegrammed: "In supporting Kennedy you are betraying North Carolina. You are undeserving of the recent confidence expressed in you by this people. Apparently you are ignorant of the facts of life regarding international Catholicism. The Vatican philosophy is as dangerous as Moscow's despotism. Hope rest of

Carolina delegation uses better judgement and support Johnson." Ten
Concord men signed this telegram: "You may not be our next governor.
Go to Rome with Kennedy." The First Free Will Baptist Church in Rocky
Mount wired: "Because of your decision to support John F. Kennedy we
feel that you have betrayed Jesus Christ and the People of North Car-
olina. Already we regret that you won the gubernatorial nomination in
North Carolina."

A woman from Rocky Point wrote: "You refused to say whom you
stood for as our next president for the fact is you knew many people would
refuse to vote for you. So I say you have betrayed the trust that the people
gave to you. I no longer feel any pride in being a North Carolinian. . . .
He may believe in separation of church and state but will he be able to
put his belief into effect if his superior decides otherwise. No Catholic can
go against his Pope or any other of his superiors. . . . May God have mercy
on your soul." A man who identified himself as a county manager in Sanford's Young Voters program wrote: "I as a Baptist cannot conceive of that
fact that one who is also a Protestant and a Mason can support a man who
owes his allegiance to the Catholic Church, and does not believe in the
separation of Church and State. I do not mind him living under the rule
of the Pope, but do not want to live under the same myself." A man from
Washington, North Carolina, wired: "You are a political Judas to the people of North Carolina. What was the price. Bring fish home."

The Church of God, which was holding its convention in Charlotte,
relayed its opposition in a telegram. A spokesman for the group said it
represented about 270 churches in the state and would oppose a
Catholic candidate from the pulpit, radio programs, and church bul-
letins. The four thousand people attending the convention passed a
unanimous resolution opposing Sanford's support of Kennedy and asking
him to withdraw his support: "We have always been strong advocates of
separation of church and state and . . . it is a widely accepted fact that the
Roman Catholic Church is an advocate of union of church and state.
The papacy exercises dominion over its devout followers in all matters
including politics."

When he returned to North Carolina, Sanford said that his decision to support Kennedy would help the state for years. He knew it would be temporarily unpopular. "But I don't think doing what you believe to be right ever hurt anybody," he said after getting off a plane at the Raleigh-Durham Airport. "And I think this was the right thing to do. It will get us votes and lose us votes." He had gambled that Kennedy would win the nomination—and been right.

He also had gambled that if he backed Kennedy, he could still win his election for governor. It meant he was going to have to work hard in the fall to win. In the past, the Democratic nominee for governor could cruise to victory. There would be no cruising for Sanford. He was going to have to campaign hard. He was determined that he would win and that Kennedy would win North Carolina. Sanford returned home to Fayetteville. "I have given away half of my [winning] margin," Sanford, sitting on his porch, said to aide Tom Lambeth. "I'll win by probably 125,000 votes. But we'll carry the state for Kennedy comfortably. I'll still be governor and we can do everything we wanted to do. And we will have a friend in Washington."

Sanford knew there was risk in endorsing Kennedy—but he thought he could pull it off, Lambeth said. "He also thought Kennedy was a masterful campaigner and the best candidate. He really liked him," Lambeth said. Sanford worked at winning votes for Kennedy in North Carolina. He went all-out for him. He did not apologize. He was not defensive. He embraced him. He made Kennedy's campaign his campaign. When Kennedy came to North Carolina, he traveled with him. When Johnson came through North Carolina on a train—the LBJ Special—Sanford campaigned with him. Johnson helped reassure southerners that Kennedy was acceptable. "Here is the strongest combination of leadership ability ever offered by any political party to the American people," Sanford told Young Democrats in Charlotte. The Constitution protected our right to choose whichever faith we wanted, he said. He reminded his audience of the contributions Catholics had made. The continent was discovered by a Catholic. His hometown of Fayetteville was named for a Catholic. A Catholic had served on the North Carolina Supreme Court.

Pollster Louis Harris showed Nixon ahead of Kennedy in North Carolina by about a two-to-one margin after the convention in July. But Sanford and other Democratic leaders were buoyant after Kennedy toured the state in mid-September and was met by large, vocal crowds. Almost 2,000 people greeted him at 9:30 A.M. at an airstrip in Greenville. In Greensboro, 7,000 attended a rally in his honor. Then 12,500 met him at the Charlotte Coliseum.

Kennedy's Catholicism seemed less important to voters than it once was. When he campaigned in North Carolina, Kennedy said, "We hold the view that every American, regardless of his religion or his race, is entitled to his constitutional rights." The crowd cheered. He had come a long way in North Carolina since July. In mid-October, Harris had Kennedy and Nixon in a dead heat in the state: Kennedy with 45 percent and Nixon with 43 percent and 12 percent undecided. At the end of October, Harris said that Kennedy had gained more ground: He had 51 percent to Nixon's 40 percent.

During the convention in Los Angeles, Kennedy knew Sanford was taking a risk for him. Kennedy did not know if he could win North Carolina. He said to Sanford, "I hope I won't pull you down." As the campaign wore on in North Carolina, Kennedy looked stronger and stronger. Sanford, however, was in the most competitive governor's race of the century.

Shortly after Sanford returned from Los Angeles, he decided to vacation for two weeks in the mountains. He rented a house at Lake Junaluska. He took his family and old friend and press aide Roy Wilder. To his surprise, Sanford found that one of his key mountain supporters had turned on him because he was supporting a Catholic. Sanford worried that the religion issue was getting out of control. He sensed he was in serious trouble and decided he could not sit back for two weeks. So he started holding meetings, shaking hands, and making speeches. By the time Labor Day arrived, he had already covered the west.

As he did in the spring, he would campaign with determination throughout the fall, this time against his Republican opponent, lawyer Robert Gavin. "You know the best approach to a political campaign is to run scared," Sanford said in early September. "Today, I'm running with more confidence than I ever have been. . . . But of course I'm still running scared." In one week, he was scheduled to campaign in twenty-five counties. During the campaign he traveled by car, ferry, horseback, helicopter, airplane, horse cart, mule cart, motorboat, bus, train, and by foot. In October, he campaigned by helicopter; his staff believed this to be a first in North Carolina. It's unclear how they knew for sure, but reporters often said that Sanford campaigned more than any gubernatorial candidate in North Carolina history. His staff estimated that he traveled fifty-four thousand miles in the state and shook more than forty thousand hands during the primaries and fall election.

No Republican had won the governor's office since 1896, but Gavin campaigned far more aggressively than his GOP predecessors. Gavin and Sanford knew each other from Chapel Hill. Gavin, forty-four, had attended the University of North Carolina as an undergraduate and a law student at about the same time as Sanford. Each graduated from law school in 1946. Gavin was a large (six feet, one inch tall, 185 pounds), amiable man and possessed a good political pedigree. He was a North Carolina native who had grown up in the town of Sanford. His father, E. L. Gavin, was elected to the state senate in 1918 and served one term in an era when Republicans were rare in the legislature. Calvin Coolidge later appointed E. L. Gavin federal attorney for the state's middle district, headquartered in Greensboro. Robert Gavin later held the same post. He was appointed assistant U.S. attorney in the middle district by Dwight Eisenhower in 1954 and became U.S. attorney three years later. He resigned in 1958 to return to his law practice. Like his father, Gavin long had been active in Republican politics, serving as a delegate to the national convention in 1948 and 1960. Because of his dedication to the party, including his run for governor in 1960, Gavin would become known in North Carolina as "Mr. Republican."

Gavin campaigned like he could win—the first time in the century the Republican nominee had done so. Previously, Republican nominees did not start campaigning until summer or even the fall. Gavin started

campaigning in the spring, frequently getting equal billing at forums with
the four Democrats. Democratic presidential candidates were fading with
each election in North Carolina. Franklin Roosevelt won 74 percent in
1940 and 67 percent four years later. Harry Truman won 58 percent in
1948. Adlai Stevenson won 54 percent in 1952. Stevenson won less than
51 percent in 1956, edging Dwight Eisenhower by less than sixteen thousand votes. If the trend continued, Republican presidential candidate
Richard Nixon would carry North Carolina in 1960.

Gavin, who seconded Nixon's nomination at the Republican convention, wisely hitched himself to the Nixon ticket. GOP candidates for governor in North Carolina had not won votes as their national ticket had.
Since 1936, the most a Republican candidate for governor received in
North Carolina was 33 percent. But in Sanford's endorsement of
Kennedy, Gavin saw an opening. The chief issue in the governor's race,
he said, was Sanford's endorsement of Kennedy and his platform. "I be-
lieve those ideas are more radical than we want in North Carolina,"
Gavin said. He told Democrats that Sanford had betrayed them. He said
that Sanford deserted his party to join the "radical-socialist wing of the
Kennedys" and that Kennedy people were running the Sanford campaign.
Sanford, Gavin said, didn't speak unless he'd been "briefed by the Sen.
John Kennedy machine."

Sanford's endorsement of Kennedy—announced not in North Carolina but three thousand miles away in Los Angeles—seemed sneaky to
some. Gavin questioned whether Sanford could be trusted. Previous Democratic candidates for governor were high-minded, Gavin said, but he
questioned whether Sanford's motives were as lofty. He said that Sanford
was supported by labor unions. He asked what would happen if the
tremendous power of the governor's office fell "into the hands of a man
who is committed to the Northern radical liberal policies so expounded
by the Democratic national platform?" Gavin said he would not raise the
race issue. But he attacked the Democratic Party's national platform on
civil rights and said that would be part of his central message in eastern
North Carolina. In one speech in Rocky Mount in eastern North Carolina, he said that black U.S. representative Adam Clayton Powell of

Harlem "wanted to integrate every school and home in North Carolina" if Democrats were elected.

Although Gavin was an amiable person, when gigged he retaliated. Defeated Democrat Malcolm Seawell, who once lived down the street from Gavin, campaigned for Sanford and said that Gavin was not qualified to be governor. Gavin retorted, "They brought in a 'B' grade lawyer to introduce a 'B' grade lawyer to say an 'A' grade lawyer isn't qualified to be governor." He said, "[Sanford] hasn't had an original thought on education in North Carolina." When Sanford joked that he couldn't remember his opponent's name, Gavin said, "A man who can't even remember his opponent's name in a gubernatorial competition is in poor shape to be governor of North Carolina."

Gavin said that the state would be better off with two strong parties. He said that Democrats had led the state "to last or nearly last in every significant statistic in the country except one—we are on top in major crimes." Now that the state was competitive for presidential candidates, Gavin said that it attracted the candidates' attention. Kennedy and Nixon had visited. So had Kennedy's mother and brother and Nixon's wife. Lyndon Johnson and his wife had traveled through the state, as had Nixon running-mate Henry Cabot Lodge, former president Harry Truman, and Agriculture secretary Ezra Taft Benson. Likewise, Gavin said that state government in North Carolina would be better off if its gubernatorial races were more competitive. Sanford knew this was a different, more competitive governor's race than what the state was used to. "He was playing the issues," Sanford recalled, "and giving me the devil for selling out to everybody, including . . . the NAACP and the Kennedys and all that crowd of subversives."

Gavin hit on state issues, too. He said that Sanford lacked fiscal integrity and had endorsed the program of every education group in the state. "His programs cannot be computed as to total cost," Gavin said. "Indeed, if they could today, they would change tomorrow, because my opponent will grab the next pamphlet he sees and endorse that as well, and hang the cost to the taxpayers." Gavin scored on fiscal issues. When Louis Harris asked voters in mid October which candidate would better handle various issues, respondents ranked Sanford ahead on every issue but one—keeping state taxes down. (Overall, Harris had Sanford leading 53 percent to 35 percent, with 12 percent undecided.) Gavin also called for consolidating city and county school systems to reduce administration and save money. He urged that local school board elections be nonpartisan. He called for better training of teachers. "We have education majors in this state who cannot spell," Gavin said at Western Carolina College in Cullowhee. Unfortunately for Gavin, he and his staff did not do a good job of proofreading his speech and press release on the subject; they had misspelled "pertinent," "about," "Cullowhee," and "capital."

Perhaps Gavin's strongest state issue was in calling for civil service reform. Democrats had distributed letters through state government department heads and state employees' associations asking for political contributions. One department set up a scale that showed how much each employee should give, based on his or her salary. State employees were afraid to support him, Gavin said. He said that they traveled sixty miles at night to attend a rally, instead of attending one in Raleigh, for fear of being spotted and punished. "I am running against an opponent called fear," Gavin said at one rally. "The race against the man who opposes me is not a difficult race but I have been confronted in recent days with fear."

Republicans raised questions about whether Sanford had received inappropriate help from the Kennedys. Gavin's campaign manager said that John Kennedy had sent three of his staff members to run Sanford's campaign. The chairman of a national Nixon group reportedly said Gavin would win "over resentment of Robert Kennedy going down and paying Terry Sanford's campaign expenses"; the man said he had been misquoted.

Nonetheless, Drew Pearson's allegations followed Sanford throughout the fall campaign, even though Pearson himself said he did not believe them. About a month after the convention, Pearson wrote another piece on Sanford and Kennedy. "I have now talked at some length with Terry Sanford and am convinced that he was telling the truth," Pearson wrote.

Sanford gave details of his meeting with Robert Kennedy in Raleigh and his reasons for supporting Kennedy, and he explained his campaign finances. "I came to the conclusion that . . . North Carolina will be in the hands of an able and scrupulously honest man as governor," Pearson wrote.

Rumors of financial assistance from Kennedy persisted. When John Kennedy campaigned in Charlotte in September, reporter Roy Parker asked him if he had given money to Sanford in exchange for his support. Even with his deep tan, Kennedy's face flushed. His eyes narrowed. He grabbed Parker's arm hard and shot back: "The answer to that is a categorically flat denial." A dozen other reporters and Kennedy staffers saw his anger. Later, as he waited to drive to the Charlotte Coliseum, Kennedy questioned reporters about the allegation. He appeared never to have heard it before. "That is the most below-the-belt thing I ever heard," Kennedy said.

Sanford was pleased with Kennedy's response—but it did not kill the rumor. Four decades after the campaign, Lake supporters still believed Sanford received an infusion of Kennedy money during the runoff. Sanford was dismayed that the allegation lived on and on. Actually, he said years later, his campaign contributed money to the Kennedy campaign. After the Democratic convention, he and Bert Bennett signed a fifty thousand dollar note to contribute to Kennedy, Sanford said; they put up the money until they could raise it for the party. "So it was the other way around," Sanford said.

Kennedy's religion also followed Sanford during the fall campaign. Even Sanford's minister at his Methodist church in Fayetteville was upset that he endorsed Kennedy. Sanford was scheduled to make the Laymen's Day speech in October but his minister thought it best if Sanford didn't. Sanford resented it. He thought his minister should have said that it didn't make any difference that he had endorsed Kennedy. "I wouldn't have made the speech anyhow in the middle of a hot political campaign because I never do that, but it irritated me," Sanford recalled. Another time, he said, "The Methodist Church virtually excommunicated me. . . . We were carrying a terrible burden by carrying Kennedy in this state."

Margaret Rose Sanford said, "People would hardly speak to us on the street. They thought Terry had sold out the state."

Anti-Catholic pamphlets and mailings circulated across the state. In tone, many of them were hysterical. More than a generation later, it is difficult to imagine that the anti-Catholic literature was widespread and effective in 1960, but it was. One pamphlet said that a Catholic president would control military bases across the world; if the president worked with Catholic diplomats in each country, "the world-wide massacre of non-Catholics could be accomplished simultaneously." Another pamphlet said that the Roman Catholic Church did not recognize the concept of innocent until proven guilty and worked against freedom of speech. Presidents Abraham Lincoln, James Garfield, and William McKinley all were assassinated by Catholics, according to the anti-Catholic literature. It also said that Theodore Roosevelt was wounded by a Catholic because, when visiting Rome, he insulted the Pope by choosing to visit a YMCA instead of the Vatican.

The state Republican Party said that it had nothing to do with circulating anti-Catholic literature. But local GOP officials were involved. The chairman of the Craven County Republican Party placed an anti-Catholic newspaper ad. The chairman of the state GOP asked him to resign. Local Republicans openly raised the issue on other occasions. At a GOP rally in Forsyth County, one of the speakers said, "We want 'In God We Trust' on our coins, not 'In the Pope We Hope.'"

Bert Bennett urged local leaders to address Kennedy's Catholicism head on. After the second primary, Bennett became chairman of the North Carolina Democratic Party. He directed a united effort to elect Democrats. At the top were Kennedy, Sanford, and Everett Jordan for Senate. Bennett mailed county chairmen a suggested newspaper advertisement that struck back at "Democrats for Nixon." With tongue in cheek, the ad announced a revolutionary political organization—Democrats for the Democratic Ticket. Not eligible were

- People who have such blind prejudice against a candidate of another faith that they can even concoct reasons for voting for Nixon.

- People who are using the so-called religious issue as a screen to hide their opposition to the aims and purposes of the Democratic Party.
- People who are out-and-out Republicans, but who are so fearful of the stigma attached to that word that they have slunk for years under the cover of phony slogans such as "Democrats for Dewey," "Democrats for Ike," "Democrats for Dick," and "Democrats for Gavin."

Just to be sure, the Sanford campaign ran newspapers ads reminding voters that Sanford was a good Protestant. "Whatever makes men good Christians makes them good citizens," the ad said. Among other things, it said that Sanford was chairman of the board of Methodist College and a lay leader in his church. "His background in home, church and government qualifies him for Governor," the ad said. Sanford sometimes spoke at Protestant churches on Sundays. In a note to an aide, Sanford said that he should not be scheduled for political events on Sundays and that he personally would accept or decline invitations from churches to speak.

Late in the campaign, Sanford said that the issue of Kennedy's Catholicism had faded. "If the people don't pay any more attention to their preachers on this issue than on other matters, we're going to be OK," he quipped. Nonetheless, Robert Kennedy said on NBC's *Meet the Press* that Governor Hodges had told him that Kennedy's Catholicism would cost Kennedy two hundred thousand votes—but that he still would carry the state.

Gavin, a Baptist, did not directly discuss Kennedy's religion. He did, however, want to debate on television the issues of the campaign. Sanford did not want to. He did not want to give Gavin free air time or equal billing. WRAL-TV in Raleigh offered one hour in prime time for a debate between Gavin and Sanford. The offer was made through the station's new vice president for news, Jesse Helms. Gavin immediately accepted. Bert Bennett said he would prefer a debate including all state candidates running for statewide office—that would have meant more than twenty people on camera. Bennett did not trust Helms and station owner, A. J. Fletcher. "They'd kill us if they could," he said years later. Helms said there would be no shenanigans. "Our sole interest lies in informing the people of the important issues at hand," he said.

Helms eventually withdrew WRAL-TV's offer. In a telegram to Sanford in late October, Helms said, "[I am] surprised that I have not had the courtesy of a response from you or your associates regarding our wire of Oct. 19, offering one hour free prime television time for a debate between you and candidate Gavin." Sanford and Helms would be adversaries for years. "Jesse's biggest problem is he's not educated," Sanford would say years later, referring to Helms's lack of a college degree. "He's a good writer. But I never thought Jesse was broadly educated." Sanford thought Helms had exploited racial issues to maintain his seat in the U.S. Senate. "Was that a backlash to what we did in the '60s? Maybe. Or maybe he was just lucky," Sanford said. In 1990, when Sanford was a U.S. senator, he campaigned for Harvey Gantt, the black former Charlotte mayor who was trying to win Helms's Senate seat.

Sanford did not debate Gavin but he did engage him on the issues. He questioned Gavin's competence and knowledge of state government. Gavin originally called for raising teacher salaries by 50 percent but backed away once he realized that it would require a major tax increase. Lamely, he said he did not have contacts in the state budget office to educate him on the state's fiscal condition. Sanford pointed out that budget information was published and readily available. "He doesn't know his position, I don't know it and no one knows it," Sanford said.

Later, Gavin said he supported the North Carolina Education Association's program for improving schools but not the program of the United Forces for Education. The programs, however, were identical. Sanford gave reporters a copy of the questionnaire Gavin had filled out for the United Forces for Education; in the questionnaire he had endorsed its program. Sanford said, "[Gavin] has been totally reckless in the advocating and endorsing of programs which he does not understand." In the spring, when he sat on a panel with the four Democratic candidates, Gavin supported new taxes on tobacco, soft drinks, and certain luxury foods. The money was needed to help make schools better, he said. In the fall, Gavin denied that he ever had supported those taxes. Sanford's wit flourished: He said he would debate Gavin when Gavin was finished debating himself.

Sanford also sought to raise bad memories of the Republicans, often referring to the Depression days of Herbert Hoover. The Republican approach on schools and farms was "negative, backward and confused," Sanford said. "The spirit of the Democratic Party is to point with pride at past progress and to look with confidence to the future. We are not going back to Hoover days." During the Hoover days, Sanford said, "The only way to get meat on the table was by setting rabbit boxes." National Democrats had brought the country social security, rural electrification, and improved farm programs. State Democrats had run North Carolina well for sixty years, he said. "People who believe in a forward-moving program for the state of North Carolina have no other place to go but join the Democrats," Sanford said.

As part of his attacks on Republicans, Sanford, like many Democrats, enjoyed mocking Richard Nixon. After Nixon's first debate with Kennedy, Nixon said he appeared tired because of improper makeup and lighting. Sanford told more than one thousand cheering, foot-stomping Democrats at one rally that Nixon was the first man in American history "to have as an alibi that he didn't have his lipstick on straight." Another Nixon-Kennedy debate was to be held that night. Sanford said that Nixon was a cry baby and an opportunist. "The people of the United States won't be taken in by Nixon and his make-up men," Sanford said. "We've known all along he was a synthetic, that there was a false front there."

Sanford said it was a time for being bold, not timid. Some said his plan to make schools better was too expensive. "North Carolina has never taken a step forward in its history which some of its citizens said it could not afford," he said. In a speech to the North Carolina League of Municipalities in Charlotte in mid October, Sanford bypassed the politics of the moment and instead evoked the promise of a new era. At certain periods in the state's history, he said, events led great men to step forward and take the state to new heights in government, business, and education. At the turn of the century, Charles Brantley Aycock, then in his early forties, was elected governor and dramatically improved schools in the state. Another crucial period was in the late 1920s, Sanford said. Almost within a year, Spencer Love became president of Burlington Industries, which became the largest textile company in the world; North Carolinian Thomas Wolfe wrote *Look Homeward Angel*; and Frank Graham became president of the University of North Carolina, which some called "the capital of the Southern mind."

The new decade was another one of those special times, Sanford said, when a new generation would take over, with fresh energy and ideas, and usher in a golden period for the state and nation. Sanford said that there were vital men in the arts and sciences, business, industry, agriculture, and politics who would raise the state to new heights, just as other great men had done earlier in the century. He did not say it, but it was understood: John Kennedy and Terry Sanford could best lead the country and state toward this New Day.

North Carolina voters agreed. On November 8, they gave Sanford 54.5 percent of the vote and Kennedy 52 percent. Sanford's percentage of the vote was the smallest of the century, to that point, for a Democratic candidate for governor. Yet it was almost exactly what he had predicted. He was an uncanny pol. When he returned from Los Angeles after the Democratic convention, he said that his endorsement of Kennedy would cut his winning margin from 250,000 votes to 125,000; he beat Gavin by 121,000 votes. In October, Sanford said that Kennedy would win in North Carolina by at least 50,000 votes; Kennedy won by about 58,000 votes.

He had to work harder than any Democratic gubernatorial nominee in the century, but Sanford had gambled and pulled it off: He won, and Kennedy won North Carolina and the nation. Now Sanford could pick up a phone and immediately get to Robert Kennedy whenever he needed. In one of the closest presidential races in history, Sanford delivered North Carolina's fourteen electoral votes to Kennedy—and the Kennedys were not going to forget it. "North Carolina was the most pleasant state to win for me," said Robert Kennedy, who would attend Sanford's inauguration. "We started off even or behind. We had the party organization with us—

Terry Sanford, Bert Bennett, Gov. Hodges—and we sent in some help [John Kennedy, Lyndon Johnson, Harry Truman, Adlai Stevenson, and Sam Rayburn]. We won. It was a pleasant thing to see."

On election night, Sanford, who didn't usually smoke, puffed on a victory cigar. He felt good physically. "I could start a fourth primary tomorrow," he said. Just before 11 P.M., when it was clear he would win, Sanford and Margaret Rose left the ballroom of the Sir Walter Hotel and took the elevator upstairs. Margaret Rose was on her way to the tenth floor, where a crowd of friends was watching television. Sanford got off at the ninth floor for a few minutes of quiet in their room. "I'll be up in a few minutes," he said to her. In their room, Sanford pulled off his shoes and reclined on the bed. He was satisfied but not giddy. "I don't feel the elation I felt in the second primary," he said. Of course, it was good to beat the Republicans. But it wasn't as good as beating Beverly Lake.

Chapter 10

EPILOGUE

In the fall campaign, Beverly Lake was like a ghost. The grim vestige of his candidacy hovered near Sanford, dark and menacing, threatening to drag him down to defeat. The primary runoff left scars and ill will. Many Lake supporters were hostile toward Sanford *before* he endorsed Kennedy. After the endorsement, they disliked him even more. To Lake's strongest supporters, Sanford represented a liberalism and racial accommodation they could not tolerate. Lake did nothing to soothe their bad feelings toward Sanford.

The day after Sanford defeated Lake in the second primary, Sanford met outside Fayetteville with Robert Morgan. They were friends before the campaign and Sanford wanted their friendship to resume. "I knew Robert underneath was redeemable," Sanford said years later. Morgan agreed to do all he could to help Sanford win the November election. Sanford aide Tom Lambeth attended the meeting. "They had always been friends and the friendship came right back together as soon as the primary was over," Lambeth said. Their friendship endured until Sanford's death. In 1972, when Sanford ran for president, Morgan traveled to New Jersey to pay his filing fee.

Margaret Rose Sanford was dismayed that her husband reconciled with Morgan so quickly. "What in the world are you doing with Robert Morgan?" she asked him. Sanford's staff was incredulous. "It absolutely confounded a lot of our people who were mad at Bob, who was the chief architect of that [Lake] campaign," recalled Dickson Phillips. "But that was old Terry. He was skeptical of ideological feelings so strong that they made you lose your sense of proportion. He knew he and Bob had been friends and could be again. He would never get his emotions caught up. There was an element of shrewdness but I think it went deeper than that. He was a person who was innately tolerant."

Morgan worked hard for Sanford, traveling the state, introducing him, sometimes speaking for Sanford when he could not attend, always urging Lake's supporters to back the man they recently fought. Sanford later credited Morgan's enthusiastic support for his November victory. "He carried the Lake forces back around to me, or I would have lost, especially [with my] carrying Kennedy," Sanford said.

For Sanford, it was good that he had Morgan's support—because he did not have Lake's. Lake was sullen, hurt, and unforgiving. He thought Sanford was unfair when he said that Lake appealed to "blind prejudice" and made similar remarks casting Lake as a hate monger. "That's why Lake never would come out for Sanford. Lake was very sensitive to that," Morgan recalled. "I sort of carried the [Lake] wing of the party for Sanford. I bet I introduced him 50 times. But Dr. Lake wouldn't do it because of words like 'blind prejudice.' It hurt him."

In particular, Lake would not forgive Sanford for saying Lake was "a combination of Bilbo and Daddy Grace." Lake told Sanford that it bothered him. It was unclear whether Lake objected to being compared to a white demagogue, a flamboyant black minister, or both. Sanford had intended to get under Lake's skin and had succeeded. Years later, Sanford relished the memory with a chuckle: "That stuck in Lake's craw." At the time, though, with all the problems he was having after the Democratic convention, Sanford wanted Lake's endorsement. While he didn't outwardly oppose Sanford, Lake did not specifically endorse him, either. He had neither forgotten nor forgiven.

The best Morgan could do was to get Lake to appear at a few Democratic rallies with Sanford. Lake agreed to support the Democratic ticket, but his ambivalence was apparent. At a speech in Williamston in eastern

North Carolina in early October, Lake urged one thousand Democrats to reject the national platform when it differed from that of the North Carolina Democratic Party. The party had problems, Lake said. He did not share the opinion that a Catholic should not be elected president because of his religion. But he said he respected the sincerity of those who did believe that. Democratic leaders should not drive those people from the party "by abusing them as hate mongers and bigots or by planning reprisals against them in years to come."

Kennedy's church affiliation was not the party's main problem, he continued. The main problem was the platform of the national party, which included a call for integration decrees and repeal of the literacy test for voters. He said that the leaders of the national Democratic Party believed in different principles than those cherished by North Carolina Democrats. When he urged the crowd to repudiate parts of the national platform, he was met by dead silence. In his fifteen-minute speech, Lake did not mention the names of any of the Democrats on the state or national ticket. He repeatedly referred to himself as a "North Carolina Democrat."

Sanford followed Lake and set a different tone. "I am proud tonight to be a Democrat running as a Democrat on the record of the Democratic Party!" Sanford yelled. He said the Kennedy-Johnson ticket was "the finest ticket ever offered the nation by any party." He continued to reach out to Lake, despite their bitter runoff and apparent differences. He noted Lake's presence, saying it showed Lake was "a good man and a good Democrat." Sanford was in Lake territory; Lake had carried that county in both primaries. He wanted to say something else good about Lake, so he fell back on his old, reliable words about the loyalty Lake inspired in his former law students. He had used similar words in February, the night when it seemed Lake was pulling out of the race. Much had transpired between the two of them in the eight months since then—a lot of bitterness and anger and name-calling. They did not have much in common before the campaign, and the second primary had emphasized their differences. They might have liked each other at one point, but not now. But winning is a lot better than losing, and Sanford no doubt felt better about the primary than did Lake. Also, Sanford had an election to win. "I know of no other college professor in North Carolina who has the love and admiration of his former students any more than he does," Sanford told the Democrats in Williamston. "That is the mark of a splendid gentleman and Dr. Lake is a splendid gentleman." As Sanford praised him, Lake sat off to the side and behind him, his face blank, not showing even the hint of a smile.

Kind words from Sanford were not going to sway Beverly Lake. He was too wounded. Three weeks later in Statesville, at another Democratic rally in a county he had won twice, Lake gave a similar speech and received a similarly cool reception. He again criticized parts of the national platform. The people of North Carolina want separate, equal schools for white and black children, he said. Yet the Democratic platform adopted in Los Angeles called for the integration of schools, restaurants, and housing built with the aid of federal money. North Carolinians were "properly disturbed" by that platform. He criticized Republican vice presidential candidate Henry Cabot Lodge. He said, "[Lodge,] in an appeal for votes unexcelled for sheer demagoguery in the history of our country, promised that a cabinet post will be given to a Negro on the basis of race, not ability." During his speech, Lake received polite applause several times. Otherwise, when he spoke there was almost complete silence.

Lake also warned the row of Democratic leaders sitting behind him, including Sanford. Lake referred to himself as merely a private in a great army of North Carolina Democrats. But, he reminded the party leaders, there were more privates than generals in the army. He urged them "to sound the clear call for those principles of the party of Thomas Jefferson." Lake referred to Jefferson six times in his speech, prompting Sanford to say slyly years later, "Lake never endorsed me. He endorsed Jefferson two or three times."

In late October, Lake's supporters gathered in Raleigh to pay tribute to him. The event, which was designed to be like one of Lake's campaign rallies, was held in the same building where Lake and his supporters had gathered on the warm night of the second primary in late June. Television cameras whirred. John Burney warmed up the crowd. An overflow crowd of more than four hundred people saluted Lake and gave him a new Buick. Robert Morgan said he'd never seen so many people come so far to honor a candidate who had lost, and he was probably right. Lake had not let down the true believers of segregation. He had not moderated his position. He did not let his supporters down during the primary or the aftermath, and he wasn't going to let them down that day at their last camp meeting. He had lost a battle but the war was not over.

Dr. Lake thanked the audience for the car and for its support. He urged them not to support a write-in movement that had been started on his behalf. But, he said, the fight was not over. In the strongest signal that he considered Sanford's nomination unsatisfactory, Lake said that his forces would rally again four years later around another candidate. "The last time I spoke in this room I acknowledged we had been defeated in that battle but I did not surrender," Lake said. "I say now to you and through you to the people of North Carolina we shall never surrender! For we are fighting, as we fought last May and June, for the state we love and the principles which are the foundation stones of the liberty we inherited and are determined to pass on to our children and grandchildren."

He did not mention Sanford by name, but his criticism of his former opponent was apparent. To Lake, Sanford was not a patriot but a common politician, a man lacking in substance, who would make promises he could not keep in order to get elected. "We did not seek for or proclaim catch phrases and slogans in order to get an office," Lake told his supporters. "We sought an office in order to serve and defend North Carolina. We did not win that office but we are still going to serve and defend North Carolina, and four years from now our candidate is going to win that office. Not a single one of the 276,000 North Carolinians who stood with us had been promised appointment to any office or job. Not a one of them was promised a road or a bridge. They stood with us then and they stand with us now because they believe as we believe that the program of the NAACP and its friends, in or out of office, will destroy that which we love in North Carolina; because they believe as we believe that the malignant cancer of integration will destroy the effectiveness of our public schools."

Lake would stand and fight, as his grandfather had for Kentucky in the Civil War. As long as he had a voice, Lake said, he would use it at the courthouse, the lunch table, and the speaker's rostrum against the NAACP, spendthrift policies, and an overbearing federal government. He would not waver. He was still committed to the cause. In four years, he said, he would support the leader who would arise and carry them to victory.

If Sanford thought he could exorcize the ghost of Lake by winning the November election, he was wrong. Lake periodically surfaced to criticize the Sanford administration and its allies. When Bert Bennett and the state Democratic Party announced that New York mayor Robert Wagner would be the speaker at the party's Jefferson-Jackson Day Dinner in 1962, Lake objected. He said that Wagner was "an extremist liberal representative of . . . big-city machine politicians." He wanted the party to invite a southern Democrat from the U.S. Senate, such as Harry Byrd of Virginia, Richard Russell of Georgia, or John Stennis of Mississippi. All were strong segregationists. Lake warned that the Republicans could take over in North Carolina in 1964 if North Carolina Democrats did not return to "sound, conservative Democratic thinking." Lake later criticized Bennett's tenure as party chairman, saying the party had lost strength.

In 1963, Bennett was considering a run for governor—and so was Lake. By state law, Sanford could not run for reelection. Lake traveled the state, often criticizing Sanford. Lake, who did not like to fly, criticized Sanford's use of a state-owned airplane to travel, saying it was extravagant. He said that the state was suffering from poor management and that teachers had been pressured to give campaign funds to the Democratic Party or risk losing their jobs. "This is not quality education," he said, mocking Sanford's education slogan. At Sen. Strom Thurmond's invitation, Lake testified before the U.S. Senate's Commerce Committee and said that President Kennedy's public accommodations bill "would fan racial differences to the white heat of hatred."

In the closing hours of the 1963 legislative session, legislators passed what came to be known as the Speaker Ban Bill. It barred from speaking at any public college or university anyone who was a "known member" of the Communist Party or who was "known" to advocate the overthrow of the Constitution of North Carolina or the United States. Sanford opposed it, although some thought tepidly, and sought its reversal. Lake was an ardent supporter of the ban and said that those who wanted to reverse the ban wanted "a socialist dictatorship in America."

That was harsh criticism—too harsh, a kind of North Carolina McCarthyism that went beyond the bounds of fair debate. Allowing a communist to speak on a college campus made one a socialist? Lake was, in effect, questioning the patriotism of those who wanted the Speaker Ban Bill repealed. But Sanford wasn't going to engage Lake on this or most other issues. He often ignored Lake or responded mildly. In one speech, Sanford said that critics of government were distorting the facts. He did not name Lake, but he said that critics had "called up the ghosts of early patriots like Thomas Jefferson as an indictment against our present government." Sanford said that North Carolina ranked near the bottom in the costs of state and local government per person, that it had a low number of government employees, and that Wall Street had given the state the highest credit rating in the country. It was a measured reply to Lake's criticism. Sanford was not going to give Lake more attention and raise his profile.

After he lost in 1960, Lake said that a conservative would arise and lead his followers to victory four years later. In late 1963, Lake unveiled that candidate—and it was I. Beverly Lake. When he announced his candidacy at the Sir Walter Hotel in Raleigh, Lake, without criticizing Sanford by name, said that he would take office with no commitments other than those he would make publicly. He also indicated that race would not be the chief issue in the campaign. "I certainly hope it will not be. It ought not to be," Lake said.

Lake's views on race had not changed. Earlier in the year, he had quit teaching Sunday school at Wake Forest Baptist Church after two black seminary students from Africa were accepted as members. He began teaching a private Bible class in a vacant store building in downtown Wake Forest. Though his views had not changed, North Carolinians saw a different Lake campaign in 1964. His manager, attorney Allen Bailey of Charlotte, steered Lake away from race. "I thought that in 1964 I could present him in a different light than he had been perceived to be as a person in 1960," Bailey remembered. "The perception that the public had from 1960 in no way represented the man. So my goal in 1964 was to try to help the public see some of the fine qualities that I knew existed." The public perception of Lake from the campaign against Sanford was that he was racist, Bailey said.

Lake generally stayed away from racial issues. Sometimes he even sounded more moderate on the issue: He assured voters he would never use force to block any student from entering a school or college. Still, it was clear Lake strongly disliked the civil rights protests that were spreading across the country. Civil rights, he said during the campaign, should be gained through "the friendly spirit of helpfulness." He said that professors convicted of violating laws in connection with racial protests should not be allowed to teach in state universities.

He also criticized Sanford for how he handled a threatened protest. In early 1964, the Congress of Racial Equality promised to make Chapel Hill the focal point of the civil rights protest movement in the state if its demands were not met. Sanford rebuked the group, but Lake said that he was three years too late. He believed Sanford's accommodation of civil rights groups had emboldened them. The state should not tolerate any ultimatum, Lake said, and the governor needed to move quickly when one was issued. "The governor of North Carolina," Lake said, "must not stand by and permit such an outrage to go unanswered."

Bert Bennett did not run for governor in 1964 but he and Sanford recruited Richardson Preyer of Greensboro, who had been appointed a federal judge by John Kennedy, to represent the liberal wing of the party. Sanford did not publicly endorse Preyer until just before the spring primary, but it was clear all along that he backed Preyer. (Jesse Jackson, then a student at North Carolina A&T, who sometimes worked with Sanford, wrote him in fall 1963: "If we handle ourselves properly, we can swing a helluva lot of votes out of this county for Preyer, also.") Preyer and Lake were joined in the Democratic primary by former superior court judge

Dan Moore of Canton. Moore was seen by voters as more moderate than Preyer and Lake. In the first primary, Preyer led with 37 percent and Moore finished second with 34 percent, eliminating Lake, who won 29 percent.

In the runoff, Lake supported Moore, and both men criticized the Sanford administration repeatedly. Preyer had pledged to continue Sanford's emphasis on education but Moore refused to do so. In a television address, Lake asked viewers to note the men who would advise Preyer. He mentioned Bert Bennett, Terry Sanford, Kelly Alexander of the NAACP, and "all of those block voters who are captive pawns in the hands of Bobby Kennedy and Martin Luther King." Lake said that a vote for Preyer was a vote for Sanford, civil rights, and left-wing liberals. Lake and Jesse Helms, the editorialist at WRAL-TV, were the state's two leading segregationists of the era. Both publicized the high level of black support Preyer received in the first primary and questioned the depth of his commitment to segregation. One Moore supporter framed the runoff like this: "It's a race between the white people and the colored people."

Moore, in a stunningly strong reversal, defeated Preyer, 62 percent to 38 percent. Lake supporters switched overwhelmingly to Moore. "It's pretty obvious," Lake crowed, "that the people who supported me supported Judge Moore." About a year later, Governor Moore appointed Lake to the North Carolina Supreme Court. It took four years, but Lake had won his revenge over Sanford, denying Sanford the successor he badly wanted. In doing so, Lake achieved his dream of a seat on the state supreme court—making his retribution against Sanford doubly sweet.

During Lake's 1960 primary runoff, one of the black newspapers, the *Carolinian*, said in an editorial that it was praying for him. Candidate Lake might accumulate many hatreds, prejudices, and narrow-minded beliefs, but some day, the paper predicted, Lake would realize he was mistaken. "He will realize that the time has come to clean out the rubbish, get rid of the outmoded ideas and shopworn theories," it said. "Then he will want to rebuild his life and a complete overhauling will be necessary to deliver him from dilapidation." The *Carolinian* was wrong. Lake's views on race never changed.

He served on the supreme court until his retirement in 1978 at age seventy-two. He was respected by his peers for his scholarship and intellect. He enjoyed his colleagues and the exclusive, clubby atmosphere of the state's most elite, tradition-bound court. He loved the supreme court—its traditions, its precedents, its role in the state's history.

Only occasionally did his views on race make their way into court decisions. One case involved bonds that were approved to build segregated schools. Lake noted that it was, in 1966, legally and practically impossible to operate segregated schools. He said, however, that segregated schools were "tested and proved to be wise and beneficial by over 65 years of experience in this state." He continued to rail against the U.S. Supreme Court, saying just because a majority of that Court issued a certain opinion, it did not mean that opinion was in keeping with the U.S. Constitution. He warned against "the smothering of freedom beneath the robes of judicial despotism."

North Carolina Supreme Court justices generally work out of the public view. From time to time, though, Lake emerged in the news. He declined to give his papers to East Carolina University in 1969 because of a disagreement with the school over the display of the Confederate flag and the singing of "Dixie." Lake wrote to the school: "I do not care to have anything belonging to me in the custody of an institution that finds it necessary to apologize for displaying the Confederate flag and singing Dixie."

A year later, in an address to students, parents, and staff of Wake Christian Academy, Lake praised them for starting the school, which was founded by a group opposed to the integration of public schools. These were perilous times, especially in social matters, Lake said. Such private schools, he said, offered the state its best chance for safe passage through the perils. In his speech, he recycled a racist phrase he had used in his first campaign for governor a decade earlier. "In city after city," he said, "the blackboard jungle has replaced the institution of learning and the undisciplined products of those jungles are now at large upon college and university campuses, disrupting and destroying that which they do not have the knowledge or the intellectual maturity to understand and evaluate."

To Lake's delight, in 1980 his son ran for governor. Beverly Lake Jr. was elected to the state senate in 1976 as a Democrat from Wake County and served two terms. With the backing of Tom Ellis's and Jesse Helms's Congressional Club, Lake Jr. switched his registration to Republican and ran for governor—against Sanford protégé Jim Hunt. It was, in many ways, a rematch of the 1960 campaign: Son of Lake versus (Political) Son of Sanford. Hunt and Lake Jr. each had been baptized politically in the 1960 campaign. Each relied heavily on supporters of their political fathers. Ellis was the key man behind Lake Jr.; Bert Bennett was a key Hunt backer. Lake also sought to rally his old supporters for his son. Lake's 1960 campaign had not been forgotten. Hunt's campaign distributed information on Dr. Lake's racial beliefs. "I hope you won't portray Beverly's campaign as a mere continuation of mine because it is not," Lake told a reporter. "Segregation is not an issue in this campaign."

Beverly Lake Jr. accused Hunt of making a race issue. But he refused to repudiate his father's views on segregation. "I would never repudiate my father," Lake Jr. said. "He is the finest Christian gentleman I have ever known. . . . I am proud to have him up front in the campaign and I'm proud of his public record." A group of Republicans, including Robert Gavin, formed a Republicans for Hunt group. The chairman of that group, John A. Walker, said that Lake Jr.'s campaign was causing turmoil by endorsing "outdated and discredited political views." Asked how Lake Jr. was creating turmoil, Walker said, "He embraces the philosophy of his father." Hunt beat Lake Jr. easily.

Twenty years later, Lake Jr., then a member of the North Carolina Supreme Court, decided to run in 2000 for chief justice against incumbent Henry Frye, the first black person elected to the North Carolina legislature in the twentieth century and the first black chief justice in state history. The irony—Beverly Lake's progeny and namesake running against a black man—was inescapable, but Lake Jr. said that his father's views on race were not relevant to his 2000 campaign. He did, however, offer a spirited defense of his father's campaign. "My father's views on race have been totally misunderstood. He was not a racist. I am not a racist," Lake Jr. said. "He was a strong friend of the black citizens of North Carolina and wanted to do everything he could to preserve that friendship that existed at the time, he thought, generally, between the two races. . . He believed in segregation, which was the law of the land at the time, and he was very fearful that forced integration would damage the public school system and maybe even cause it to go out of existence. He said time and again that his purpose was to preserve the public schools of North Carolina and the equal education of all of our children, regardless of race. That was his position. No, I don't repudiate that. . . . The times were different. You have to judge him in light of the times. He was trying to preserve our society. He was trying to preserve the school system."

As he got older, Dr. Lake lost the bitterness he once felt about his 1960 run for governor. Reporters, who were never his natural allies, visited him periodically over the years and found him warm and engaging, with no trace of anger about his two campaigns for governor. "I have no regrets about running," Lake said in 1970. "I think our campaigns contributed a great deal to North Carolina and made this a better state. It would have been a great honor to have been governor, and no one likes to lose, but it was never a life or death thing with me."

In a 1986 interview, when he was eighty, Lake said, "I thoroughly enjoyed my two campaigns for governor. You're not going to be involved with political campaigns long before you get involved in 'pleasant' controversies." He added, "I've had a remarkably happy life." In that same interview, Lake said that the Supreme Court's *Brown* decision was "constitutionally indefensible" because the Court departed from what he called "the 'plain teachings of the Constitution' to do what they thought was sociologically desirable."

Two weeks after he was elected governor, Terry Sanford returned to his alma mater to give a speech to educators at the University of North Carolina's Memorial Auditorium, just a short walk along leafy Cameron Avenue from Frank Graham's old office. Sanford gave one of the longest speeches of his career, outlining his plan for improving North Carolina's public schools. "Good Lord!" said an elderly professor sitting on the back row in the cavernous auditorium. "He meant what he said during the campaign."

He was inaugurated in January 1961. Two months later, Sanford asked legislators to remove exemptions from the state's 3 percent sales tax, including those on food and prescription medicine. For ninety days, it was a tough fight. No legislature, including this one, which was dominated by conservative, rural Democrats, wants to approve new taxes. Critics picked up on John Larkins' campaign nickname for Sanford, calling him "Food Tax Terry." Sanford worked to win legislators, one by one. In contrast to Governor Hodges, who was aloof to legislators, Sanford courted their favor. He lobbied legislators over breakfast at the governor's mansion and with late-night cigars there, too. He visited them on their turf, at the lobby of the Sir Walter Hotel, where legislators were flattered to have the governor in their presence. Sanford was at his best—friendly, reasonable, persuasive. One columnist called it "the most astute salesmanship campaign ever conducted by the chief executive of North Carolina."

During the fight, Sanford again took to the campaign trail, this time seeking not his election but a victory for his most important program. He attended education rallies across the state, giving as many as twelve speeches a day. He cited a long list of statistics showing that North Carolina lagged behind the rest of the nation. The state ranked forty-fifth in spending per student, forty-first in pupil-teacher ratio, and fiftieth in raising teachers salaries in the last decade. No wonder, Sanford said, that North Carolina also ranked forty-first in the percentage of adults with college degrees, forty-first in the percentage of adult illiterates, and forty-fifth in per capita income. "We have cultivated our children's minds less well than we have cultivated our tobacco and cotton and peanut acres," he told a crowd in the middle of tobacco country.

At first, Sanford spoke with school administrators, school boards, and PTAs. Then in Brunswick County, in the southeastern corner of the state, a school official asked Sanford to stop by a school and speak to students. Sanford received such an enthusiastic response from the students that he said it was "almost magic." Sanford stopped visiting courthouses and in-stead spent his time in schools talking to children and invited adults. Three decades later, Sanford remembered his school visits—"one of the best things we did"—when he was governor: "I constantly run into peo-ple who remember the visit." Most of the schools were segregated. San-ford made it a point to visit both white and black schools. Sanford's schools program was not designed to specifically assist black students or to promote school desegregation. But the program helped all schools and all children—a point Sanford often made. His schools program was a way to improve opportunities for all children without embarking on a politically difficult civil rights crusade. John Batchelor, a local superintendent in North Carolina who studied the state's desegregation efforts, concluded, "By linking the educational fate of all races together, Sanford made sig-nificant steps toward establishing the basis for a single, racially integrated school system providing quality education to all the state's students, re-gardless of race."

In the end, legislators voted overwhelmingly for Sanford's $100 mil-lion Quality Education Program (worth more than $500 million in to-day's dollars). Sanford's program added twenty-eight hundred teachers, raised average teacher pay by 22 percent, added home economics and vo-cational teachers, provided more training for teachers, doubled library money to $1 per student, and increased money for instructional supplies by 33 percent. Educators and politicians across the nation took note. San-ford's "imaginative leadership . . . made possible the changes which were not only significant for his state but in many instances useful as models in other states as well," said James Conant, retired president of Harvard University. Sanford received invitations from all over the nation to speak about his education programs, and he traveled to thirty states (including giving speeches at Harvard and Yale) to talk about making public schools better.

While Sanford was in demand outside his state, he was troubled in it. In November, in the first major public vote since legislators approved his sales-tax proposal, state voters slammed ten bond proposals to spend $61.5 million for university buildings, state ports, state government buildings, community colleges, juvenile training schools, prisons, and mental health hospitals. It was the first time since 1924 that North Carolina voters rejected a statewide bond issue. Most of the votes weren't even close. For example, only twenty-seven of the state's one hundred counties approved the education bonds. Sanford and other state leaders were shocked. Were voters rebelling against the new sales tax on food? Were they saying state government was too big? Did they just want the state to slow down? A Louis Harris poll taken after the vote showed three out of five North Carolina voters were dissatisfied with Sanford's job performance.

Sanford remained upbeat, but his job was getting tougher. The civil rights movement was growing, putting more pressure on him from both sides. In his inauguration speech, Sanford said, "We are not going to forget, as we move into the challenging and demanding years ahead, that no group of our citizens can be denied the right to participate in the opportunities of first-class citizenship. Let us extend North Carolina's well-known spirit of moderation and good will, of mutual respect and understanding, in order that our energies and our resources, our abilities and our wills, may be directed toward building a better and more fruitful life for all the people of our state." Then civil rights moved off his agenda—if it was ever really on it—as he worked on the sales tax, schools, and other issues.

But in January 1963, Sanford revived the issue. He could not have done it for political reasons. Just two months earlier, Republicans won two U.S. House seats in the state for the first time in thirty years. They also increased their strength in the state house of representatives from fifteen to twenty-one seats, with some predicting that Republicans would win the governor's election in 1964. Some white voters were unhappy with what they considered the liberalism of the Kennedy and Sanford administrations. Yet even with the losses at the polls, Sanford mulled giving a speech on civil rights, a speech that would alienate those white voters even more. The issue kept coming up. He didn't know whether to tackle it or leave it alone. Sanford was troubled from his visits to public schools two years earlier. He gave the same speech then to white and blacks chil-

261

dren about the promise of America—but he knew the speech did not truly apply to black children. He would have to change his speech or change the state. He decided he'd try to change the state.

In early January, Sanford invited a group of twenty-five for breakfast at the governor's mansion. Six were black. Included in the group were leading figures from state government and politics. The night before the breakfast, Sanford gave a handwritten statement on a large, yellow pad to his aide John Ehle. In the morning, the group would decide how good the statement was and whether it should be released. In his book *The Free Men*, Ehle wrote, "I remember thinking that this would be the first time in history that a Southerner while governor of a state had taken a stand openly, avowedly in favor of Negro rights."

At breakfast, Sanford told the group he was thinking about publicly giving his thoughts on the race problem. "No doubt," wrote Ehle, who attended the breakfast, "some of his visitors could not have been more surprised if he had said he was going to open the doors of the sixty state prisons at noon." Sanford read the draft of his speech. John Wheeler, a black banker from Durham, had the most trouble with it. Wheeler thought the statement was too moderate. It relied on good will and persuasion. Wheeler thought it should call for new laws to ensure blacks' rights. Sanford disagreed. There was a lengthy discussion. Wheeler, by attacking the draft as too moderate, had shifted the debate away from whether it should be released and on to the question of whether it was aggressive enough. Sanford seemed content with Wheeler's premise that the speech should be given.

A few weeks later, Sanford gave the speech to the North Carolina Press Association at its meeting in Chapel Hill. At the beginning of his speech, Sanford noted that it had been one hundred years since Abraham Lincoln had issued the Emancipation Proclamation. "The time has come for American citizens to give up their reluctance, to quit unfair discrimination and to give the Negro a full chance to earn a decent living for his family and to contribute to higher standards for himself and all men," Sanford said. "North Carolina and its people have come to the point of recognizing the urgent need for opening new economic opportunities for

Negro citizens. We also recognize that in doing so we shall be adding new economic growth for everybody. We can do this. We should do this. We will do it because we are concerned with the problems and the welfare of our neighbors. We will do it because it is honest and fair for us to give all men and women their best chance in life."

Sanford said he was creating an integrated Good Neighbor Council to establish voluntary nondiscriminatory hiring practices and to urge youth to become better trained for jobs. The council also would work with local committees to be established by local leaders. The head of each state agency would create nondiscriminatory policies. And Sanford asked churches and civic organizations to support the objectives of the Good Neighbor Council. Sanford had noted previously that if the wages of blacks in the state were raised to the level of whites' wages in the state, North Carolina's per capita rank would rise ten spots in national rankings. In giving his speech, Sanford became the first southern governor to call for employment without regard to race. John Ehle said a few years later that the speech "might prove to be one of the greatest political errors, yet one of the finest achievements, of Terry Sanford's life."

Among Sanford's enemies, and there seemed to be more and more of them, the backlash was immediate. Two weeks after his Chapel Hill speech, a group of four hundred angry whites gathered in the courthouse in Caswell County, along the Virginia border in a swath of the state where Lake had run strong. Lake had won that county twice, in the runoff whipping Sanford by more than a two-to-one margin. The local chapter of the North Carolina Defenders of States Rights gathered to support segregation and build enthusiasm for private schools. "Unless we take a firm stand and use the word 'never,' and that's what they're using in Alabama and Mississippi, we're not going to lick this thing," said Allison James, a pharmacist from Winston-Salem. He said, "[Sanford] is a carpet bagger in the same sense and definition as they used after the Civil War. He is against the white people. . . . We are fighting for the preservation of the white race!" A motion was made that the group support Beverly Lake for governor in 1964. It passed unanimously. That summer, President

Kennedy sent to Congress the most far-reaching civil rights bill ever proposed. Among its principal features was a ban on discrimination in places of public accommodation. The proposal hurt Kennedy—and Sanford—with many whites. Sanford acknowledged that if Kennedy were running for reelection in North Carolina in November 1963, he would not win.

Sanford expected resentment from conservative whites. What disappointed him was the anger some blacks held toward him. He thought it clear, through his words and deeds, that he was on their side. He routinely met with black leaders. He sent his children to an integrated school. He called for an end to discrimination in hiring. He and Hargrove Bowles, his director of Conservation and Development (and father of future White House chief of staff Erskine Bowles), integrated all state parks. He appointed blacks to thirty state boards. He personally called white business owners and asked them to integrate. While other southern governors were standing in doorways, blocking integration, Sanford steadily was pushing for it. When President Kennedy sent federal marshals to the University of Mississippi in 1962 to ensure the enrollment of James Meredith, every southern governor responded with outrage—except Sanford, who said he'd never been prouder of Kennedy. "There wasn't any chance of my being elected chairman of the Southern Governors Conference," Sanford once said wryly.

Yet the pressures on him to move faster on integration increased. Members of the Congress of Racial Equality (CORE) traveled the highways of North Carolina with its Freedom Highways campaign, seeking access to public accommodations and picketing hotels and restaurants that did not provide it. In 1963, rallies and protests, mostly by young blacks, gained strength in cities across the state. In Greensboro in May and early June, fourteen hundred black students went to jail as they tried to integrate cafeterias and theaters—perhaps the largest jail-in of the civil rights movement. They were led in part by charismatic North Carolina A&T quarterback and student leader Jesse Jackson. Sanford, always creative, had them released from jail and taken back to campus; one civil rights leader called this "the first and only jail lock-out in the movement."

On a Friday in May, in a speech at Pembroke State College, Sanford called for "civilized and mature acts" to handle racial disorder. In the two prior days, more than 150 black demonstrators had been arrested in Raleigh during attempts to integrate theaters and restaurants. Sanford believed the participants had a right to protest. But he was determined to avoid violence. "I don't know . . . the full answer to the tension of Negro youths who feel, apparently with justification, that they are left out of the full advantages of American citizenship," Sanford said in his speech. He urged blacks and whites to talk about their problems.

Back in Raleigh that night, a crowd of about five hundred, most of them black college students, marched to the governor's mansion and demanded to see the governor. Sanford was hosting a party for the North Carolina Symphony. In those days, there was no fence around the mansion grounds, which occupy a full city block on all four sides, and the students proceeded to the south edge of the mansion. The students sang hymns and chanted, "We want the governor," for nearly twenty minutes.

Finally, Sanford, wearing a tuxedo, emerged and spoke with the students. "I have enjoyed the singing," he said. The students booed. Sanford had several testy exchanges with students. "I'll be glad to talk to you about any of your problems, any of your grievances, any of your hopes," he said. "This is not the time or the place." John Winters, a black businessman and confidante of Sanford's, was part of the crowd. Winters initially feared the tense encounter would turn violent. Eventually, Sanford diffused the situation and the students left the grounds peacefully. They weren't satisfied but they respected Sanford for speaking to them. "It was a sign of hope," Winters said later. "That in itself was a memorable thing. A southern governor—who had troopers on the premises that he could call and say, 'Get rid of these students because they are trespassing'—took a different tack. He talked with them."

Given the stands he had taken, Sanford sometimes resented the public pressure put on him by black protestors. Perhaps it was inevitable that even a fair-minded white man like Sanford could never fully understand the frustration of blacks who had waited centuries to be treated as first-class citizens. Historian William Chafe, in his 1980 book on the Greensboro civil rights movement, *Civilities and Civil Rights,* was among those

265

who questioned whether Sanford pushed hard enough. Chafe said that Sanford's leadership was more enlightened and more imaginative than that of any other southern governor, and that he made an important contribution to the civil rights movement by recognizing its legitimacy. But Chafe said that Sanford's reliance on local, voluntary efforts meant integration would occur only where people were committed to bringing racial change. "Even as Sanford sanctioned black demands and raised black hopes, he proved unable to alter the underlying structure and substance of race relations," he wrote.

Chafe's point hinges on the belief that Sanford could have accomplished more by proposing new laws. Sanford could have proposed new laws—but he almost surely would not have won passage. By North Carolina law, he had a single, four-year term as governor and no veto, giving him few formal powers compared to governors in other states. He'd been elected by the narrowest margin of the century. He had spent considerable political capital in getting the sales tax placed on food. He was not a popular governor. The legislature was dominated by rural, conservative Democrats. The strong segregationists, with Beverly Lake warming up for another run for governor, were ready to pounce. It's unfathomable that Sanford could have won majorities in both chambers for a civil rights bill. When Sanford decided to take the voluntary approach on race issues, he said privately that he could not have won legislative approval of a civil rights measure—and no one was a better, shrewder vote counter than Sanford. If he had risked the issue in the legislature and lost, Sanford very well could have been left a crippled and ineffective governor. Sanford went for what he thought he could get, and in doing so he moved the state forward.

While many black leaders wanted more, they also thought Sanford was a man with whom they could work. They respected him; some admired him deeply. James Farmer, the founder of CORE and one of the "Big Four" civil rights leaders (along with Martin Luther King Jr., Roy Wilkins, and Whitney Young), called Sanford "a fine and liberal gentleman, and highly competent." The NAACP's Wilkins, in his March on Washington speech in 1963, called on lawmakers "to be as brave as our sit-ins and marchers" and "as forthright as the governor of North Car-olina." John Winters, the first black member of the Raleigh City Council, said, "Terry Sanford was just a genuinely good person. I loved him as a hu-man being."

There can be no doubt that Sanford's willingness to talk with black leaders, and his desire to seek more opportunities for all people, hurt him with many whites. Still, Sanford did not let it get to him. He didn't dwell on his losses or his lack of popularity. He kept his cool, as he had on the campaign trail. His aide John Ehle wrote, "I often wondered how he could exist in a world in which he was forever being petitioned or advised or pestered or telephoned or questioned or challenged or charged with something, and still remain as casual as if he had just come in off the golf links. Nor was he ever hurried or distressed." Margaret Rose Sanford said that her husband never seemed discouraged: "He never let things bother him. I think that helped him through a lot of difficult times." Even with the pressures of the job, Sanford loved being governor. He surrounded himself with young, talented aides and asked for their best ideas. He kept busy with new programs and initiatives and maintained a good relation-ship with legislators, who funded most of his key programs. At one point he counted eighty-eight programs and projects he was working on. His single four-year term was one of the most productive governorships in the history of the United States.

Yet, when the 1964 governor's race in North Carolina became a refer-endum on his policies, his candidate lost badly. After four years of helter-skelter government activity, voters wanted to slow down. Dan Moore campaigned as the anti-Sanford and won big. Still, Sanford left office gung ho. "I'd do it again, yes sir. And I may," he said. He didn't run for governor again, but he didn't leave politics either. He became president of Duke University in 1970 and guided the university to new prominence during his fifteen years there. He was drafted by students to run for presi-dent in 1972 and entered the race, hoping to win the primary in North Carolina and go to the national convention as a compromise choice if the convention were deadlocked. Instead, he was humiliated in his home state by an old rabid segregationist, Alabama Gov. George Wallace, who beat Sanford 50 percent to 37 percent. Sanford ran for president again in 1976 but withdrew before the North Carolina primary. Ten years later, at age sixty-nine, having not won an election in twenty-six years, he attempted a political comeback by running for the U.S. Senate—and won. After one term, voters rejected him, choosing instead his estranged friend Lauch Faircloth, an ally from the gubernatorial campaign who switched parties and ran as a Republican. In his long career, Sanford ran statewide four times. Twice he won; twice he lost. When Sanford died of cancer in 1998, his former aide Tom Lambeth said that if at times North Carolina was not with Terry Sanford, he was always with North Carolina.

Sanford never stopped working on issues of race. In the mid-1990s, he asked retired Duke University historian John Hope Franklin, who is black, to lunch. They began meeting monthly. They agreed that the nation needed a national dialogue on race. Sanford contacted Erskine Bowles, the White House chief of staff and son of one of Sanford's closest political allies from the 1960s. That led to President Clinton's creation of a high-profile advisory panel on race, chaired by Franklin, who said, "It all began, in a sense, with Terry Sanford."

His 1960 triumph was never far from Sanford's mind. He was proud of beating a man he considered a racist, proud of vindicating Frank Graham's loss from ten years earlier, proud of his place in southern political history. Although for years he and Lake lived near each other—Sanford's Durham home was about twenty-five miles from Lake's in Wake Forest—the two did not see each other often. In September 1986, Dan Moore, the man who succeeded Sanford as governor, died. Sanford attended his funeral at Edenton Street United Methodist Church in downtown Raleigh, just a few blocks from the capitol. So did Lake. After the service, as Moore's casket was carried to nearby Oakwood Cemetery, Sanford and Lake engaged in a long, warm conversation in front of the old church. Each had meant to attend the graveside service but instead the two old foes, who had not seen each other in a long time, were engrossed with each other. The next day, Sanford, who was campaigning for a seat in the U.S. Senate, handwrote a letter to Lake.

Dear Beverly,

Seeing you at Governor Moore's funeral was a touch of delight in an otherwise somber occasion, and it reminded me that I have thought of you often as I have criss-crossed the state in recent months, and have been wanting to visit with you. After the election, I'll call, if I may.

Time passes too rapidly. I do not want any more to pass without reaffirming to you that I did, as I think you know, greatly admire you before our campaign, and I do today admire you for your high qualities of manhood—intelligence, steadfastness, dedication to principles, courage.

Somehow as I have campaigned I have felt a sort of oneness with you, a companionship that comes from the same ordeal, even as adversaries. I have just been wanting to say this to you, and the warmth I felt in seeing you on Tuesday prompted me to do so. We are moving down the road, and I do not want to leave lingering doubts of my regard and appreciation for you and your life.

Sincerely,

Terry

Lake responded the following week with a typed, single-spaced letter:

Dear Governor Sanford:

Your gracious letter of September 10 is much appreciated. The knowledge that I fall far short of meriting the nice things you said in it causes me to be even more grateful for your kindness in writing as you did.

It is said that politics makes strange bedfellows. It also produces unexpected adversaries. When you were in the State Senate and I was in the Attorney General's Office we were often in agreement, especially in public utility matters. Later, in the upheavals resulting from the so-called Civil Rights Movement, it became apparent to both of us that we have widely differing political philosophies. . . .

My deeply felt beliefs concerning the fundamental purposes of our State and Federal Governments, and the appropriate means for achieving them, simply differ from those you feel and believe. That, not personal ill will, brought us to the leadership of the opposing forces in the 1960 campaigns, just as former classmates at West Point fought so fiercely against each other a century earlier. I still believe the losing side was right in each instance.

Now, you are leading one side in another campaign, while I have become an aged-out noncombatant spectator on the sidelines. Neither of us has changed his fundamental beliefs about the purpose of government in America or the most effective means for attaining it. Consequently, I cannot wish you success in your present campaign, but, as in the days gone by, I wish for you and Mrs. Sanford happiness and well-being. . . .

Kathleen and I would always welcome you and Mrs. Sanford as guests in our home.

Sincerely,

Beverly

They saw each other for the last time seven years later. Each attended a ceremony in Raleigh, in the courtroom of the state supreme court, during which a portrait was presented to honor a former chief justice. Sanford and Lake were old men. Lake, who had retired years before, was eighty-six; Sanford, who was practicing law and teaching at Duke after being turned out of the Senate, was seventy-five. Neither had changed his fundamental beliefs. As they were parting, Lake told Sanford that the greatest tragedy in American history was that the South lost the Civil War.

Sanford once said that after the 1960 runoff, he quickly put his hard feelings toward Lake behind him. "I got over being upset with him a whole lot quicker than he got over being upset with me," Sanford said. "I got over it in about a half hour." Maybe so. But on the April day in 1996 when Lake died, it was clear Sanford still had mixed feelings toward his old adversary. Sanford was finishing his meal at a restaurant at about 10 P.M. when he received a phone call from a reporter informing him of Beverly Lake's death and seeking comment. Sanford dodged the interview. Thirty-six years after his showdown with Lake, he said he did not have anything nice to say. Sanford turned to two dinner companions and said, "What am I supposed to say—he died 40 years too late?" When Sanford died two years later, he was working on a sweeping historical novel of the twentieth century. Among the characters was a darkly tragic figure, trapped in the past. That character was based on I. Beverly Lake.

* * *

It is tempting to look at the Lake-Sanford second primary and say it brought out the worst in each man. Lake, a cheerful political innocent until he was burned by Sanford's aggressive rhetoric, became cynical and defensive. Sanford, locked in a death match he was determined not to lose, shaded the truth, occasionally lying outright.

Focusing on their shortcomings, however, takes too narrow a view and ignores the positive leadership each man displayed. The Lake-Sanford showdown inspired great passion among North Carolinians because Lake and Sanford represented their viewpoints so well. Each was the best his side had to offer. Often in politics, voters believe they are settling for a candidate less than best. That was not the case in 1960. Lake was the conservative's conservative; Sanford was the liberal's liberal. The most passionate partisans on each side had deep faith in their man and for good reason. Lake and Sanford were strong leaders with a vision for the state. They were men of character and ability.

Clearly, each had flaws. Lake's were more glaring because, as a matter of public policy, they were more harmful to more people. He was wrong to seek to preserve segregation and wrong in his belief that blacks were inferior. Unlike many strong segregationist politicians across the South, he was not hostile toward blacks and repeatedly and publicly preached friendship between the races. If segregationists were to have a candidate—and in the South in 1960 that was inevitable—then Beverly Lake was the best, most able, most ethical person to run on that platform.

As governor, Sanford proved to be a public figure of unusual vision. He led the state through a period of innovation and racial adjustment that led to North Carolina's prosperity of the 1970s, '80s, and '90s. The first glimpse of his greatness was apparent in his campaign for governor. Sanford's waffling, dodging, and shading of the truth in 1960 should not obscure the important consensus he built during the campaign. He knew where he wanted to take the state—to better schools and more opportunity for all people. He was determined to build support for improving public schools. He started building that support when he said he was willing to raise taxes to improve schools. Then he campaigned not just for his election but for making public schools better, at whatever cost.

Sanford also helped build another consensus—toward a thoughtful, constructive approach to race relations, based on good will. Some of Sanford's younger admirers are disappointed to learn that he did not campaign in 1960 as a supporter of integration. Their disappointment should be not with Terry Sanford but with the white voters of 1960. In general, Sanford did what was necessary to win enough support from whites to beat Lake.

Sanford's message was a gamble. For him to campaign in the South, six years after the *Brown* decision, on a platform of expanding opportunities for all people was truly a risk. That message had not often, if ever, succeeded in the South. Yet Sanford proclaimed it loudly. Sanford believed in the North Carolina described a decade earlier by the political historian V. O. Key Jr. In his seminal book, *Southern Politics*, Key detected a mood in North Carolina different from the rest of the South. The state's residents were energetic and ambitious, determined and confident. In the areas of industrial development, education, and race relations, the state was more like the rest of the nation than any other southern state. North Carolinians knew there was hard work ahead, Key wrote, and they were ready to tackle that hard work with good will and patience.

Yet a political candidate could not be sure of that. Only a year after Key's book was published, North Carolina voters had rejected Sanford's hero, Frank Graham, after a campaign of racist tactics that taunted Key's optimism. Sanford could not be sure if North Carolinians were ready for his message. But he was brave enough to try to show them the way. David Gergen, a North Carolina native who has advised four presidents, said Sanford believed that racism not only divided blacks from whites but also divided the South from the rest of the nation. If freed from the scourge of racism, everyone would have a better chance to grow. Sanford believed he could lead North Carolinians away from the paralysis of prejudice and into the national mainstream. Gergen described Sanford's philosophy like this: "A leader's role is to raise people's aspirations for what they can become and to release their energies so they will try to get there." To raise their aspirations, Sanford had to rely not on the political climate of the moment but on his own sense of right and wrong learned from his parents back in Laurinburg. Sanford, Gergen said, showed how a single, fearless leader can release the best in his people.

Sanford opened doors not only for blacks and whites in his state but for others like him across the South. His election as governor, and his accomplishments in the next four years, showed other southern politicians that they could succeed with a similar message. In some southern states, it happened almost immediately; in others, it took years. But eventually, every southern state had a governor—often they were Democrats, sometimes they were Republicans—who sounded much like Terry Sanford in the early 1960s. Some, like Gov. William Winter of Mississippi, intentionally modeled themselves after Sanford. Others, probably unsure of the origin, knew only that they were following a formula that was working across the region. And it has worked. In the forty years since Sanford's election as governor, the South has been transformed. It has changed from an Old South of racism, ignorance, and poverty to a New South of opportunity, optimism, and economic vitality. Terry Sanford is as responsible for that transformation as any other single person.

Like all of us, Sanford was flawed. This book points out how he stretched the truth several times during his 1960 campaign. Occasionally, in seeking to firm up support among white voters, Sanford went too far and made statements he should not have made. It's also true, however, that Sanford could have been far more conservative on race than he was. He did not have to publicly remind white schoolchildren in Charlotte that whites had been given opportunities that blacks had not. He did not have to campaign before integrated audiences. He did not have to have blacks within his campaign organization. Blacks and white liberals were going to vote for Sanford; they were not going to vote for Lake. White conservatives were going to vote for Lake. Sanford and Lake were fighting for the white voters in the middle.

Sanford could have tried to win those white voters in the middle by scaring them about the impending black threat. He would have won more votes if he had. But he did not use that tactic. That's because he ran not just to win but to build a foundation for governing, one that included expanding opportunities for all citizens. Instead of scaring voters, he gave an optimistic view of the future and said that together, we could work it out. In doing so, he helped create an implicit agreement among most North Carolinians that change was coming and they could handle it. That consensus on race allowed the state to work through a transition period without becoming paralyzed by fear. In helping to build that racial consensus among people of good will, Sanford showed a rare kind of political and moral leadership. He led North Carolinians well. He led them to a new day.

NOTES

I. Beverly Lake's speeches are courtesy of I. Beverly Lake Jr. They are not in a university collection. The Terry Sanford Papers are from the Southern Historical Collection at the University of North Carolina, Chapel Hill, unless otherwise noted. The Southern Oral History Program at the University of North Carolina, Chapel Hill, is abbreviated SOHP. The University of North Carolina is abbreviated UNC.

INTRODUCTION

Page xv, paragraph 2. Governor Sanford's accomplishments: Foon Rhee, "Terry Sanford dies at 80," *Charlotte Observer*, Apr. 19, 1998; Associated Press, Apr. 18, 1998.

Page xvi, paragraph 1. One of twelve best governors: Sabato, *Goodbye to Good-Time Charlie*.

Page xvi, paragraph 2. Glendening on Sanford: "Next Governor Will Lead Maryland in New Direction," Washington Post, Oct. 31, 1994; author interview with Glendening.

Page xvii, paragraph 1. Riley on Sanford: *Charlotte Observer*, Apr. 23, 1998.

Page xvii, paragraph 1. Clinton on Sanford: Associated Press, Apr. 18, 1998.

Pages xvii–xviii. Winter and Hunt on Sanford: Author interviews with Winter and Hunt.

Notes

Page xix, paragraph 2. The "fighting words" in Sanford's inaugural address: Jonathan Yardley, "Trailblazer in N.C. Education," *Washington Post,* July 4, 1985.

Page xix, paragraph 2. Employment without regard to race or creed: Sanford, *But What About the People?*

Page xix, paragraph 2. Sanford on dealing with race as governor: Rob Christensen, "Terry Sanford dead at 80," *News and Observer,* Apr. 19, 1998.

Page xx, paragraph 2. Record turnout: Associated Press reports from June 26, 1960, and figures supplied by the North Carolina Board of Elections.

Page xx, paragraph 2. Robert Morgan and Lake and Sanford: Morgan interview with Jack Bass and Walter DeVries, SOHP.

Page xx, paragraph 3. Moderates and segregationists in the South from 1957 to 1973: Earl Black, "Southern Governors and Civil Rights" and "North Carolina Governors and Racial Segregation," in *Politics and Policy in North Carolina,* MSS Information Corporation, 1975.

Page xx, paragraph 4. William Campbell's first day at Murphey: Mary Burch, "'I felt so small,'" Raleigh Times, May 17, 1979; Katie Mosher, "School becomes historic site," *News and Observer,* May 20, 1989.

Page xxi, paragraph 2. Sanfords attend Murphey School: Author interview with Margaret Rose Sanford; Chafe, *Civilities and Civil Rights.*

Page xxi, paragraph 3. Bill Campbell on Sanford: Author interview with Campbell.

CHAPTER 1: SANFORD

Page 3, paragraph 2. Sanford and Graham at UNC: Sanford interview with Brent Glass, May 14, 1976, SOHP.

Page 4, paragraph 3. The White People ad and other dirty tricks from the Smith-Graham campaign: Pleasants and Burns, *Frank Porter Graham and the 1950 Senate Race in North Carolina.*

Page 5, paragraph 2. Turning around Cumberland Mills: In an interview with the author, Sanford noted that another precinct that switched from Smith to Graham was in Madison County, which had a history of election-day shenanigans. In Madison County, Sanford said wryly, "They turned that election around very differently than how I turned Cumberland Mills around."

Page 5, paragraph 2. Mob mood: Attributed to political scientist Samuel Lubell in Chafe's *Civilities and Civil Rights*.

Page 5, paragraph 3. Sanford's visit with Graham: Ehle, *Dr. Frank*.

Page 5, paragraph 4. The notebook: Sanford interview with author, as well as Glass interview and Sanford's interview with Jack Bass and Walter DeVries, SOHP. The contents of the notebook are based on these Sanford interviews. Sanford was organized and meticulous, and kept many notes and documents related to his political life. But he told the author he did not save the notebook.

Page 6, paragraph 2. Spankings: "'Miss Betsy' Talks about Son Who Is Running for Presidency," *Pilot of Southern Pines*, June 18, 1975.

Page 7, paragraph 3. Sanford's youth: Much of this information comes from Sanford interview with Brent Glass, SOHP; and Sanford interview with Robin Minietta of UNC-TV in the summer of 1997.

Page 7, paragraph 3. Camping out in the swamp: Joan Brock, "Mother Recalls Governor as Mischievous Boy," *News and Observer*, Jan. 7, 1961. The anecdote about Sanford traveling in the trunk also is from this article.

Page 8, paragraph 1. Prodigal son: Barbara McAden, "Pride and Pain Mark Son's Governorship," *Charlotte Observer*, Dec. 8, 1964. This story also includes the anecdote about Mrs. Sanford making coconut cake for her son.

Page 8, paragraph 1. As a teenager: Julian Scheer, "Friends Knew Terry as Leader, Loner," *Charlotte News*, Dec. 27, 1960. Several paragraphs have been lifted almost word for word.

Page 8, paragraph 2. Average at sports, and the Latin teacher: Joan Brock, *News and Observer*, Jan. 7, 1961.

Page 8, paragraph 2. Blushing about his dimples: "Terry Sanford . . . Oh, You Mean 'Miss Betsey's' Son," *News and Observer*, June 16, 1975.

Page 8, paragraph 3. Not one of the boys: From author interview with Dickson Phillips.

Page 9, paragraph 2. A nice fellow: Charles Dunn, "Terry's New Day Will Face Lots of 'Old Hat,'" *Durham Morning Herald*, Jan. 8, 1961.

Page 9, paragraph 3. Margaret Rose, first steady girlfriend: Joan Brock, *News and Observer*, Jan. 7, 1961.

Page 10, paragraph 1. St. Louis FBI days: From Oct. 4, 1960, letter from Thomas F. McDevitt, in Sanford papers.

Notes

Page 10, paragraph 2. Paratroopers and steak: Jack Riley, "Tar Heel of the Week," *News and Observer*, Sept. 10, 1950.

Page 10, paragraph 3. Stick with Terry: Wilder, *You All Spoken Here*; and author interview with Wilder.

Page 10, paragraph 3. Sanford and the 517th: Sanford interview with Robin Minietta of UNC-TV in the summer of 1997.

Page 11, paragraph 1. A hillside in Belgium: David Rice, "Sanford, Leader in Politics, Dies at 80," *Winston-Salem Journal*, Apr. 19, 1998.

Page 11, paragraph 2. His friend Bill Friday: Link, *William Friday*.

Page 15, paragraph 4. Scott appointment of black man to Education Board: Don C. Shoemaker, "Tar Heels Hope for Segregation Compromise," *Asheville Citizen*, Sept. 22, 1953.

Page 16, paragraph 1. Lennon says Scott opposes segregation: "Sen. Lennon Injects Race Issue into N.C. Campaign," Associated Press, *Durham Morning Herald*, May 19, 1954.

Page 17, paragraph 2. The fake flyers: Sanford gave consistent, detailed accounts of his response to the ad in interviews with the author and with Glass, Bass, and DeVries. Also, the *News and Observer* covered the flyers story extensively on May 28, 1954, and the following day. In an interview with the author, Woodrow Price provided further detail.

Page 20, paragraph 2. Scott and Sanford at the beach: Reese Hart, "Short Vacation Planned by Tired, Happy Sanford," Associated Press, June 27, 1960.

Page 20, paragraph 3. Sanford on Hodges: Sanford interview with Brent Glass, SOHP.

Page 21, paragraph 3. One dollar to the Sanford campaign: Associated Press report, May 19, 1960.

Page 21, paragraph 3. Kerr Scott on Sanford for governor: "Sanford Attends Chitlin Supper," *News and Observer*, Jan. 5, 1960.

Page 22, paragraph 1. Meeting at Roy Wilder's house: Author interview with Wilder.

Page 22, paragraph 2. Sanford critical of Jordan appointment: Bob Brooks, "Terry Sanford Blasts Appointment of Jordan," *News and Observer*, Apr. 21, 1958.

Page 22, paragraph 3. Liver lips: Author interview with Wilder.

Page 23, paragraph 2. Letters from Bob Scott and Mrs. Kerr Scott: Letters dated Jan. 27, 1960, and Aug. 24, 1959, respectively, in Sanford Papers.

Page 23, paragraph 2. Helms says Mrs. Scott mistaken about his TV appearance: Letter from Sen. Jesse Helms to the author, Dec. 23, 1998.

Page 24, paragraph 2. Sanford speech at Kerr Scott portrait unveiling: Howard White, "Portrait of W. Kerr Scott Officially Given to State," *Burlington Times-News*.

Page 24, paragraph 3. A move for governor every day: Foon Rhee, "Terry Sanford Dies at 80," *Charlotte Observer*, Apr. 19, 1998.

Page 26, paragraph 1. The gas station owner and Christmas cards: Ragan, *The New Day*.

Page 26, paragraph 2. Sanford letter to Sonny Boy Joyner: Letter dated Dec. 9, 1957, in Sanford Papers.

Page 26, paragraph 2. Sanford and Faircloth sleep in same bed: Jim Morrill, "Does Faircloth Snore? Rival Says He Knows," *Charlotte Observer*, Apr. 6, 1992; Jim Morrill, "Longtime Political Buddies Fight It out for the U.S. Senate," *Charlotte Observer*, July 6, 1992. Joyner said he heard Sanford and Faircloth laughing when they got in bed. "I asked them the next morning what they were laughing about," Joyner said. "They kidded with me, said it got cold as hell."

Page 28, paragraph 2. "Bore yo' ass off": Ken Eudy, "Sanford Seen as Folksy, Quick Witted," *Charlotte Observer*, Oct. 7, 1986. The Brandt Ayers quote also is from this article.

Page 29, paragraph 3. Sanford speech lesson: Memo from Roy Wilder in Sanford Papers. Also, author interview with Wilder.

CHAPTER 2: LAKE

Page 32, paragraph 2. The Willis Smith motorcade and Lake's comments to his son: From author's interviews with I. Beverly Lake Jr. and Tom Ellis.

Page 33, paragraph 1. Lake's radio address: Allen Langston Papers, Duke University, Durham, N.C.

Page 33, paragraph 3. Lake's letter to Graham: Frank Graham Papers, UNC Chapel Hill.

Page 34, paragraph 3. Lake's early life: Most of the information and quotations from Lake come from two interviews he gave that are part of the SOHP.

Page 36, paragraph 1. Sneaking away to watch practices: Lake campaign speech, Jan. 23, 1964, Edenton.

Page 36, paragraph 2. "Ikey": From author's interview with I. Beverly Lake Jr.

Notes

Page 38, paragraph 1. Norman Wiggins: From his eulogy to I. Beverly Lake, published in the *Campbell Lawyer*, spring/summer 1996, and from his speech given at the presentation of Lake's portrait at the North Carolina Supreme Court, June 15, 1994.

Page 38, paragraph 1. Pulling his hair out: Myra Knight, "Politicians pack birthday fete for I. Beverly Lake," *News and Observer*, Sept. 15, 1986.

Page 38, paragraph 2. Trudy Lake's favorite meals: Jean Powell, "Mrs. I. Beverly Lake Looks to the Future while Studying Past," *News and Observer*, Jan. 26, 1964.

Page 40, paragraph 1. The clear garment bag: Matt Schudel, "I. Beverly Lake: A Portrait at 80," News and Observer, Sept. 12, 1986. Also, several other details about Lake's childhood are from this article.

Page 40, paragraph 3. Scholars reaction to *Brown*: Richard E. Morgan, "Coming Clean about Brown," *City Journal*, summer 1996.

Page 41, paragraph 1. School funding figures: Bagwell, *School Desegregation in the Carolinas*; and *Southern School News*, Sept. 3, 1954.

Page 44, paragraph 1. The Pearsall committee and Lake: Batchelor, "Rule of Law, Accommodation of Faith."

Page 44, paragraph 3. Lake before the Supreme Court: Jay Jenkins, "Attorney Lake Says Supreme Court Decree Would Place Schools in 'Gravest Danger of Abolition,'" *News and Observer*, Apr. 14, 1955.

Page 44, paragraph 4. Frankfurter's questioning of Thurgood Marshall: Williams, *Thurgood Marshall: American Revolutionary*.

Page 45, paragraph 1. Lake, Frankfurter exchanges: From transcript of Lake's appearance before the court. I. Beverly Lake Jr. attended oral arguments and provided the detail about Lake pointing his finger at Justice Frankfurter. Lake Jr. also is the source for Frankfurter teaching his father at Harvard. Author interview with Lake Jr.

Page 45, paragraph 4. Helms' praise of Lake: Batchelor, "Rule of Law, Accommodation of Faith."

Page 46, paragraph 1. Justice Warren's memo: Schwartz, *The Unpublished Opinions of the Warren Court*.

Page 47, paragraph 3. Hodges gets word of NAACP request: Hodges, *Businessman in the Statehouse*.

Page 48, paragraph 1. Lake and Hodges: Batchelor, "Rule of Law, Accommodation of Faith."

Page 48, paragraph 1. "Life won't be the same:" From author interview with I. Beverly Lake Jr. He also said that Lake had received support to run for governor in 1956.

Page 49, paragraph 1. Lake disappointed he was not named attorney general: In *The Making of a Governor*, James R. Spence wrote, "When a vacancy arose in the position of attorney general, Lake expected to move up but Hodges bypassed him." Beverly Lake Jr. believes his father would have liked to have been appointed attorney general but did not expect to be appointed for the reasons given in the text.

Page 50, paragraph 1. Lawyer on the Pearsall Plan: Ed Rankin, an aide to Luther Hodges, attributed that quotation to Paul A. Johnston, Governor Hodges' lawyer. Interview with Ed Rankin, SOHP.

Page 51, paragraph 1. Sanford and Pearsall Plan: Jay Jenkins, "Scott's, Hodges' Forces in Accord," *Charlotte Observer*, Aug. 2, 1956. Also, Terry Sanford, "Pearsall Plan: The Spirit of Moderation," *Greensboro Daily News*, Sept. 2, 1956.

Page 52, paragraph 3. Lake denounces three school boards: Bagwell, *School Desegregation in the Carolinas*.

Page 52, paragraph 4. Lake WRAL-TV address: "Gradual Integration in North Carolina," from Lake's speeches, courtesy of I. Beverly Lake Jr.

Page 53, paragraph 2. Hodges and blacks: Batchelor, "Rule of Law, Accommodation of Faith."

Page 54, paragraph 1. Dr. Wesley Critz George and the Patriots of North Carolina: Steven Niven, "Wesley Critz George: Scientist and Segregationist," *North Carolina Literary Review*, no. 7, 1998. Also, Roslyn Holdzkom's description of the George Papers at the Southern Historical Collection, UNC Chapel Hill.

Page 54, paragraph 1. Protoplasmic mixing of the races: Wesley Critz George, "Human Progress and the Race Problem," an address given at Dartmouth College, in the George Papers, UNC Chapel Hill.

Page 54, paragraph 2. George introduces Lake in Mecklenburg: George Papers, UNC Chapel Hill.

Page 54, paragraph 3. George correspondence: George papers, UNC Chapel Hill.

Page 56, paragraph 3. Morgan on Lake: Author interview and Morgan interview with Jack Bass and Walter DeVries, Dec. 13, 1973, SOHP. Also, Morgan interview with author.

Page 57, paragraph 1. Support for Graham: J. A. C. Dunn, "Lake: No Burning Ambition to Be Governor," *Chapel Hill Weekly*, Aug. 12, 1962.

CHAPTER 3: KICKOFF

Page 59, paragraph 1. Louis Harris polling information: Sanford Papers.

Page 63, paragraph 1. Larkins announces for governor: Jay Jenkins, *Charlotte Observer*, Jan. 21, 1960.

Page 63, paragraph 2. Larkins' experience: Guy Munger, "Larkins Linked Closely to Party," *Greensboro Daily News*, May 17, 1960.

Page 64, paragraph 2. Larkins and Barden, and Larkins on Sanford: Larkins, *Politics, Bar and Bench*.

Page 66, paragraph 1. Politics in the east: Sanford interview with Brent Glass, SOHP.

Page 66, paragraph 4. Sanford's kickoff speech in Fayetteville: Marjorie Hunter's story in the *Winston-Salem Journal*, Feb. 5, 1960. Also, the author viewed film of Sanford's speech. The footage is part of Sanford's Papers at UNC Chapel Hill.

Page 67, paragraph 4. Visit to Charles Cannon: Author interview with Tom Lambeth; and Sanford interview with Brent Glass, SOHP.

Page 69, paragraph 2. The Texas funny line: Sanford interview with Robin Minietta of UNC-TV in the summer of 1997. Also, Sanford said in this interview that most political consultants would advise against talking about raising taxes.

Page 70, paragraph 1. "I'm not tired": Bob Wilson, "At Big Day's End, Still Full of Run," *Fayetteville Observer*, Feb. 5, 1960.

Page 70, paragraph 2. Jefferson-Jackson Day: Simmons Fentress, "The Old Pros Like Sanford, Jordan," *Charlotte Observer*, Feb. 8, 1960; and Julian Scheer, "If Election Were Today, Sanford Could Win," *Charlotte News*, Feb. 7, 1960.

Page 71, paragraph 2. Description of the Greensboro sit-ins: Chafe, *Civilities and Civil Rights*; Associated Press, Dec. 31, 1989; and Constance Simpson, "Anniversary of Defiance," *Charlotte Observer*, Jan. 28, 1990.

Page 71, paragraph 3. Durham, Charlotte, and Raleigh sit-ins: From Associated Press accounts.

Page 72, paragraph 1. Franklin McCain: Ricki Morell, "Anniversary of Rights Legislation Bittersweet to Some in the Struggle," *Charlotte Observer*, July 2, 1989.

Page 73, paragraph 2. King at Durham: Branch, *Parting the Waters*.

Page 75, paragraph 2. Lake wanted the bench, not governor's office: Lake said this in SOHP interviews. Also, his son said the same in an interview with the author. Beverly Lake Jr. noted the irony: His father thought getting involved in politics would hurt his chances of a supreme court appointment. But he was appointed to the bench by Gov. Dan Moore after Lake finished third in the 1964 Democratic primary and threw his support to Moore. Running for governor led directly to his appointment.

Page 75, paragraph 2. Lake friendly with Sanford: Spence, *The Making of a Governor.* Spence wrote that Lake encountered the Sanford friend in the spring of 1963, but it's clear from the context of the anecdote that it was the spring of 1959.

Page 75, paragraph 3. Lake comments at Lee County: "A Look Ahead for North Carolina," Lake speeches.

Page 78, paragraph 1. Audience reaction at Lee County and Lake comments afterward: Gene Roberts, "Lake Says He Won't Enter Campaign for Governor," *News and Observer,* Feb. 11, 1960.

Page 78, paragraph 3. Sanford on his comments to Lake: Sanford interview with author.

Page 79, paragraph 2. Seawell reaction to Lee County rally: Jay Jenkins' articles in the *Charlotte Observer* on Feb. 12 and Feb. 14; and Associated Press reports.

Page 80, paragraph 1. Seawell told Sanford he would not run: Spence, *The Making of a Governor.*

Page 80, paragraph 2. Seawell and Sanford at the Green Lantern: Author interview with Dickson Phillips. Phillips could not confirm that Seawell already had told Sanford he would not run, as James R. Spence reported. But Phillips believed there was a good chance that was true, because Sanford was deeply surprised to learn Seawell was considering getting into the race.

Page 80, paragraph 3. Luther Hodges on Sanford and Larkins: Luther Hodges Jr. interview with Ben Bulla, SOHP.

Page 81, paragraph 2. Chub Seawell: Julian Pleasants, "Call Your Next Case," *North Carolina Historical Review,* January 1999.

Page 81, paragraph 3. Seawell announces: Jay Jenkins, "Attorney General Lists 19 Objectives," *Charlotte Observer,* Feb. 19, 1960; and the Associated Press report.

Page 81, paragraph 4. Unsigned letter: United Press International report, Oct. 4, 1958.

Page 82, paragraph 2. Seawell and the Klan: "Malcolm Seawell Is Klan Nemesis," *Charlotte Observer,* Apr. 6, 1958.

Page 83, paragraph 3. Seawell and the Patriots: "Patriots Tell Seawell to Resign," *Charlotte Observer,* Jan. 17, 1959.

Notes

Page 84, paragraph 1. Hodges and the cartoon: "Seawell Gets Hodges' OK," *Charlotte Observer*, Nov. 4, 1958.

Page 85, paragraph 1. Sanford's frustration: Author interview with Sanford.

Chapter 4: Wild-Card Lake

Page 86, paragraph 1. Larkins talks with Lake: Larkins, *Politics, Bar and Bench*.

Page 86, paragraph 2. Letter from Paul Hastings to Lake: Wesley George Critz Papers, UNC Chapel Hill.

Page 88, paragraph 1. Lake's pivotal meeting in Rocky Mount with Clarence Bailey: Author interview with Jack Bailey and John Lewis.

Page 88, paragraph 3. Lake's letter: Ferrel Guillory, "Justice Morgan Withdraws Backing of Morgan in Race," *News and Observer*, Oct. 13, 1974; Ned Cline, "Lake's Rocky Road Takes New Direction," *Charlotte Observer*, July 14, 1978; and Nadine Cohodas, "Retired Justice Retains His Controversial Views," *News and Observer*, Sept. 3, 1978.

Page 89, paragraph 1. Morgan never opened Lake letter: Morgan interview with Howard Covington, Feb. 8, 1995, SOHP.

Page 89, paragraph 2. Morgan interview: Author interview with Morgan.

Page 89, paragraph 3. Not a campaign of racial hatred: Associated Press report, Feb. 27, 1960, based on an interview Morgan gave Henry Belk, editor of the *Goldsboro News-Argus*.

Page 89, paragraph 3. Morgan speech: *Greensboro Daily News*, May 15, 1960.

Page 89, paragraph 4. Morgan in memo to Ben Roney: Memo dated June 1959 in Sanford Papers.

Page 89, paragraph 4. Sanford and Morgan: From Henry Hall Wilson letter to Terry Sanford, October 1959, Sanford Papers. Sanford and Morgan comments from author interviews with each.

Page 90, paragraph 2. Morgan raising money: "Fund Drive Began by Lake Followers," *News and Observer*, Feb. 13, 1960; Associated Press report, Feb. 15, 1960; "Morgan Says Lake May Get Back in Race," *Raleigh Times*, Feb. 25, 1960; Associated Press report, Feb. 26, 1960.

Page 91, paragraph 1. Morgan opponents: In interviews with the author, Tom Lambeth and Bert Bennett praised Morgan's running of the Lake campaign.

Page 91, paragraph 2. Lake and the Supreme Court offer: *Charlotte Observer*, July 14, 1978.

Page 91, paragraph 4. Larkins on Lake and Seawell: Larkins, *Politics, Bar and Bench*.

Page 92, paragraph 3. Lake announces his candidacy: Marjorie Hunter, "Lake Enters Race for N.C. Governor," *Winston-Salem Journal*, Mar. 2, 1960; Jay Jenkins, "Lake Grabs N.C. Spotlight," *Charlotte Observer*, Mar. 6, 1960.

Page 93, paragraph 4. Description of Lake's speaking style: This is Marjorie Hunter's description, almost word for word, in "Lake Enters Race for N.C. Governor," *Winston-Salem Journal*, Mar. 2, 1960

Page 93, paragraph 4. Lake on the *Today* show: Associated Press, Mar. 2, 1960.

Page 94, paragraph 2. NAACP opposition: Associated Press, Mar. 3, 1960.

Page 96, paragraph 1. Kendall column: *Greensboro Daily News*, Nov. 15, 1959.

Page 96, paragraph 1. No mention of Lake: Guy Munger, "Gill Ponders Governor's Contest," *Greensboro Daily News*, Dec. 18, 1959.

Page 96, paragraph 2. Larkins, Sanford in runoff: Simmons Fentress, "The Old Pros Like Sanford, Jordan," *Charlotte Observer*, Feb. 8, 1960.

Page 96, paragraph 3. Lake fourth: Burke Davis, "Tar Heel Notebook," *Greensboro Daily News*, May 1, 1960.

Page 97, paragraph 1. Lunch-counter protests put Lake in runoff: *Rockingham Post-Dispatch*, Mar. 24, 1960.

Page 97, paragraph 2. Black newspapers think Lake could win: "The Qualifications of That Candidate," *Carolinian*, Mar. 12, 1960; "A Challenge to Progressive Citizens," *Carolina Times*, Mar. 5, 1960.

Page 97, paragraph 3. The April Louis Harris poll: Sanford Papers, Duke University Archives. Harris didn't charge Sanford for this second poll. Sanford wrote Harris a check for $6,000. Harris returned it with a note that said, "Here is your check. Give 'em hell from here on in and we'll all be praying on election night. Good luck."

Page 98, paragraph 1. Larkins' campaign crumbling: Larkins, *Politics, Bar and Bench*.

Page 98, paragraph 2. Sanford feared Lake: Author interview with Terry Sanford.

Page 100, paragraph 1. Burney and Lake: Author interview with John Burney.

Page 100, paragraph 2. Ellis on Lake: Author interview with Tom Ellis.

Page 100, paragraph 2. Lake's size: Estimate from Beverly Lake Jr.

Page 100, paragraph 3. Campaigning in Wake County: Gene Roberts Jr., "Lake Caravan Tours Wake County Towns," *News and Observer*, May 27, 1960.

Page 101, paragraph 3. Shoestring campaign: J. A. C. Dunn, "Lake: No Burning Ambition to Be Governor," *Chapel Hill Weekly*, Aug. 12, 1962.

Page 102, paragraph 2. Helms's comments on Lake and his involvement in the campaign: Letter from Sen. Jesse Helms to the author, Dec. 23, 1998.

Page 102, paragraph 3. Lake and the 1972 Helms campaign: Author interview with Beverly Lake Jr.; and Covington, *Terry Sanford: Politics, Progress, and Outrageous Ambitions*.

Page 102, paragraph 3. More of Helms' comments on Lake: Helms' letter to Hy Jackson, Nov. 7, 1988.

Page 103, paragraph 2. Helms and Lake campaign: Author interviews with Jack Bailey and Beverly Lake Jr.

Page 103, paragraph 3. Ellis and Burney on WRAL: Author interviews with Ellis and Burney.

Page 104, paragraph 3. The Lake bus: Author interview with Beverly Lake Jr., who has photographs of the tour, including the Sanford donkey.

Page 106, paragraph 1. Sanford's shot at Burney: *News and Observer*, June 21, 1960.

Page 106, paragraph 2. Description of the Lake rallies: I relied heavily on two *News and Observer* articles by Gene Roberts on June 12 and June 24, 1960. Also, I reviewed videotape of two Lake rallies.

Page 107, paragraph 2. The Rocky Mount rally: From videotape owned by I. Beverly Lake Jr.

Page 108, paragraph 3. Morgan on Lake's speaking style: Author interview with Robert Morgan.

CHAPTER 5: SHOOTING AT SANFORD

Page 113, paragraph 2. Sanford's Greensboro speech: Sanford Papers

Page 115, paragraph 4. Harris on taxes: April 1960 poll, Louis Harris and Associates, Sanford Papers, Duke University Archives.

Page 116, paragraph 2. Taxes a great issue: Sanford interview with Robin Minietta of UNC-TV in the summer of 1997.

Page 116, paragraph 3. Sanford was a risk taker: Author interview with Robert Morgan.

Page 116, paragraph 3. Sanford on taking political risks: Interview with Joe Frantz, SOHP.

Notes

Page 117, paragraph 2. Sanford attacks Hodges: Spence, *The Making of a Governor.*

Page 117, paragraph 3. Bert Bennett's notes: Sanford Papers.

Page 119, paragraph 2. Role of women in Sanford campaign: Sanford, *But What About the People?* Also, author interview with Martha McKay.

Page 119, paragraph 2. Strong Mecklenburg organization: Kays Gary, "Terry Sanford Leads Pack in Mecklenburg," *Charlotte Observer,* Apr. 24, 1960.

Page 119, paragraph 3. Larkins astounded: Larkins, *Politics, Bar and Bench.*

Page 120, paragraph 1. United Forces program: Associated Press report, May 3, 1960.

Page 120, paragraph 2. Seawell on Sanford's school proposal: Jay Jenkins, "Candidates Express Segregation Views," *Charlotte Observer,* Apr. 13, 1960; and "Candidates Enliven Campaign," *Greensboro Daily News,* May 3, 1960.

Page 120, paragraph 2. Seawell and Sanford on taxes: "Leaf Tax Comments Given," *Greensboro Daily News,* May 7, 1960.

Page 120, paragraph 3. Lake on schools and taxes: Kays Gary, "Candidates for Governor Call for Improved Schools," *Charlotte Observer,* March 30, 1960; and "Here's What They're Saying," *Charlotte Observer,* Apr. 17, 1960.

Page 121, paragraph 2. Hodges' revenue projections: Guy Munger, "N.C. Revenue Shows 13.4 Per Cent Gain," *Greensboro Daily News,* May 5, 1960; and United Press International reports.

Page 121, paragraph 4. Sanford attacked at campaign event: Charles Clay, "Sanford Front-Runner in Gubernatorial Race," *News and Observer,* May 18, 1960.

Page 122, paragraph 2. Larkins on Sanford's promises: Associated Press report, Apr. 24, 1960.

Page 122, paragraph 2. Moon shots and a brass stopper: Guy Munger, "Candidates Issued, Reviewed as Democratic Primary Looms," *Greensboro Daily News,* May 1, 1960.

Page 122, paragraph 2. Poster on a boy and a man: *Charlotte News,* July 14, 1960.

Page 122, paragraph 2. Batch of cure-all programs: Guy Munger, "Experience Pointed out by Larkins," *Greensboro Daily News,* May 11, 1960.

Page 123, paragraph 1. Questioning Sanford's Kerr Scott credentials: "Seawell, Larkins Lambast Sanford," *Charlotte Observer,* May 12, 1960.

Page 123, paragraph 2. D. K. Stewart comments: These apparently are from a speech given by Stewart. Sanford Papers.

Page 123, paragraph 3. Sanford never said who he supported in 1948 for governor: Marjorie Hunter, "Sanford: Next Young Governor?" *Winston-Salem Journal,* June 27, 1960.

Notes

Page 123, paragraph 3. Mayne Albright in 1948: Interview with Brent Glass, SOHP.

Page 124, paragraph 1. So many asked to do so much: "Candidates Campaign up to Finish Line," *Greensboro Daily News*, May 28, 1960.

Page 124, paragraph 2. Pie in the sky: *News and Observer*, Apr. 13, 1960; and "Two Gunning for Terry," *Fayetteville Observer*, May 11, 1960.

Page 124, paragraph 2. They are all mixed up: Guy Munger, "Political Campaigns Head for Finish Line," *Greensboro Daily News*, May 15, 1960.

Page 125, paragraph 1. Keep the sons of bitches out: Author interview with Bert Bennett.

Page 125, paragraph 2. Visits law office once and home a dozen times: Reese Hart, "Short Vacation Planned by Tired, Happy Sanford," Associated Press, June 27, 1960.

Page 125, paragraph 2. Blister in January: Roy Thompson, "Terry Sanford's Long, Long Trail Comes to an End," *Winston-Salem Journal*, Nov. 10, 1960.

Page 125, paragraph 2. Shaking forty thousand hands: From an undated campaign press release in the Sanford Papers. It could have included the fall campaign.

Page 125, paragraph 3. Long day campaigning in Wake County: Gene Roberts, "Sanford Caravan Tours Wake," *News and Observer*, May 5, 1960.

Page 126, paragraph 3. Sanford on toughness: Sanford interview with Charlie Rose, Aug. 20, 1997, USA Network.

Page 129, paragraph 2. Sanford on relaxing: J. A. C. Dunn, "A Talk with Terry Sanford," *Chapel Hill Weekly*, Dec. 8, 1960.

Page 129, paragraph 2. Bennett on Sanford campaigning: Author interview with Bert Bennett. Also, Bennett's 1973 interview with Jack Bass and Walter De-Vries, SOHP.

Page 129, paragraph 4. Roney and Bennett: The characterization of their relationship comes from Phil Carlton, who worked actively in the campaign as a senior at North Carolina State. In the interest of full disclosure, Carlton is the author's father-in-law. Roy Wilder and Roy Parker also talked about how different Roney and Bennett were. The Bennett memo comes from the Sanford Papers.

Page 131, paragraph 2. Sanford on sit-ins: Author interview with Terry Sanford

Page 131, paragraph 4. Response to Seawell on race: Sanford Papers.

Page 133, paragraph 2. Chapel Hill speech: Sanford Papers; and Bill Kezziah, "Sanford Is Mum on Racial Issues," *Chapel Hill Weekly*, Mar. 17, 1960.

Page 133, paragraph 3. Sanford TV commercial: Sanford Papers.

Page 134, paragraph 2. Bennett letter to Reidsville supporter: Sanford Papers.

Page 134, paragraph 4. Leaflets: Associated Press reports; Jay Jenkins, "Controversial Leaflet 'Doesn't Violate Law,'" *Charlotte Observer*, May 24, 1960; "SBI to Continue Investigation of Leaflet Attacking Candidate," *News and Observer*, May 24, 1960; "Sanford Hits at Leaflets," *Charlotte Observer*, May 26, 1960.

Page 135, paragraph 1. Morgan on Sanford's claim: Campaign letter from Wesley George Papers, UNC Chapel Hill.

Page 136, paragraph 1. Dropped the ball: Motte V. Griffith Jr., "Terry's Campaign a Smooth One," *Raleigh Times*, May 25, 1960.

CHAPTER 6: LAKE, APART AND AFIRE

Page 137, paragraph 1. Lake's assessment of three opponents: Marjorie Hunter, "NAACP Blasted by Beverly Lake," *Winston-Salem Journal*, Apr. 5, 1960.

Page 138, paragraph 1. Lake and the National Guard: "Lake Outlines Position on Segregation," *Winston-Salem Journal*, May 9, 1960.

Page 138, paragraph 2. Lake talks with reporters in Wilmington: United Press International report, Apr. 20, 1960.

Page 138, paragraph 3. Wilmington rally: Author interview with John Burney.

Page 139, paragraph 1. Lake's comments in Wilmington: Lake speeches.

Page 141, paragraph 1. Eastern North Carolina more like the Deep South: Chafe, *Civilities and Civil Rights*. I've used V. O. Key's regional divisions in defining eastern North Carolina. Smith-Graham returns are from Pleasants and Burns, *Frank Porter Graham and the 1950 Senate Race in North Carolina*. Population figures are from the U.S. Department of Commerce, Bureau of the Census, *Census of Population: 1960* (Washington, D.C., 1961). Voter registration figures are from the North Carolina Advisory Committee to the U.S. Commission on Civil Rights, June 4, 1961, as quoted in Lefler and Newsome, *North Carolina: The History of a Southern State*.

Page 142, paragraph 3. Larkins and Sanford on NAACP: Jay Jenkins, "Candidates Express Segregation Views," *Charlotte Observer*, Apr. 13, 1960; and United Press International report, Apr. 23, 1960.

Page 142, paragraph 3. Greensboro editorial on the NAACP: "Campaign Will-O'-the-Wisp," *Greensboro Daily News*, May 7, 1960.

Notes

Page 143, paragraph 1. Blacks have no candidate: Kays Gary, "Terry Sanford Leads Pack in Mecklenburg," *Charlotte Observer*, Apr. 24, 1960.

Page 143, paragraph 2. Lake's sharp speech in Greenville: Associated Press report, May 5, 1960; and text of Lake address, Lake speeches.

Page 143, paragraph 3. Negotiate with the NAACP about the sit-ins: Lake referred to each of his three opponents. The first reference was to Larkins and the third reference was to Seawell. In another speech, given later in the campaign, Lake makes it clear that his second reference was to Sanford.

Page 144, paragraph 3. Criticism of King and Hughes appearances at UNC: Lake speech on WBT radio, May 17, 1960, courtesy of Beverly Lake Jr.

Page 145, paragraph 1. "I shall not be a moderate": "Lake Sees Threat to Public Schools," *News and Observer*, Mar. 9, 1960.

Page 145, paragraph 1. Black child an invader: *Charlotte Observer*, May 4, 1960.

Page 146, paragraph 1. Blackboard jungle: From Lake's address on WBT radio forum, May 3, 1960, Lake speeches.

Page 146, paragraph 2. Lake warns whites about being surrounded by blacks: Text of Lake TV commercial on the dangers of the NAACP; also, text of Lake TV commercial on a business owners' freedom to run his business as he desires, from Lake speeches.

Page 146, paragraph 3. School integration figures: *Statistical Summary of School Desegregation in the Southern and Border States*, Southern Education Reporting Service, 1961.

Page 147, paragraph 1. Seawell on Lake: Associated Press report, May 5, 1960; and Jay Jenkins, "Lake's School Plan Is Hit by Seawell," *Charlotte Observer*, Apr. 29, 1960.

Page 147, paragraph 3. Hodges defends North Carolina's approach: Associated Press report, May 13, 1960.

Page 148, paragraph 2. Legal advice from X: "Personal memo to Terry," Sanford Papers.

Page 149, paragraph 1. Sanford and community dialogues: *Winston-Salem Journal*, May 11, 1960.

Page 151, paragraph 2. Lake on the radio call-in show: *Charlotte Observer*, May 4, 1960.

Page 151, paragraph 3. Lake's speech at Grove Presbyterian Church: Lake's speeches, courtesy of Beverly Lake Jr.

Page 153, paragraph 2. Governor for the black people too: "Lake attacks NAACP; Gets Rebel Yells," *Greensboro Daily News*, May 18, 1960.

Page 153, paragraph 2. Lake calls for new medical school: Lake for Governor campaign information on health care, Sanford Papers.

Page 154, paragraph 1. Appeal to blacks to fight NAACP: "Integration of the Schools," speech by I. Beverly Lake, WNCT-TV, May 5, 1960, Lake speeches.

Page 154, paragraph 2. Lake wholeheartedly preserves black-white friendship: Lake 15-minute TV commercial on the dangers of the NAACP, Lake speeches.

Page 154, paragraph 2. George Wallace approach ridiculous: Ned Cline, "Lake's Rocky Road Takes New Direction," *Charlotte Observer*, July 14, 1978. Two other nearby quotes also are from this article: Lake's saying that he got more black votes than reported, and Lake's saying that tests showed the average black does not have the intelligence level of the average white.

Page 154, paragraph 3. Lake said that he was not a racist: Matt Schudel, "I. Beverly Lake: A portrait at 80," *News and Observer*, Sept. 12, 1986.

Page 154, paragraph 3. Did not speak against blacks: J. A. C. Dunn, "Lake: No Burning Ambition to Be Governor," *Chapel Hill Weekly*, Aug. 12, 1962.

Page 155, paragraph 1. Ten generations for black students to catch up: Luther Shaw, "Lake Hits at Newspaper Coverage," *Asheville Citizen*, June 2, 1960.

Page 155, paragraph 2. George speech: George Papers, UNC Chapel Hill.

Page 156, paragraph 2. Lake letter to George: George Papers, UNC Chapel Hill.

Page 156, paragraph 3. Lake's 1992 interview: Lake's interview with Edward L. Harrelson, SOHP.

Page 158, paragraph 2. No apologies for how black people are treated: "Conservation and Development," speech by I. Beverly Lake, Siler City Lions Club, March 28, 1960, Lake speeches.

Page 158, paragraph 2. Separate and equal has worked: "Integration of the Schools," speech by I. Beverly Lake, WNCT-TV, May 5, 1960, Lake speeches.

Page 159, paragraph 1. Description of Democratic Convention: Guy Munger, "Happy Bedlam Opens Meeting of Democrats," *Greensboro Daily News*, May 20, 1960; and Pat Reese, "Party Meet Like Carnival," *Fayetteville Observer*, May 20, 1960.

Page 160, paragraph 2. Kendall at the convention: H. W. Kendall, "Buttons and Beaux," *Greensboro Daily News*, May 22, 1960.

Notes

Page 160, paragraph 3. Reporter surveys of voters: Kays Gary, "Terry Sanford Leads in Mecklenburg," *Charlotte Observer*, Apr. 24, 1960; and Jay Jenkins, "Terry Nabs Shaky Lead in Piedmont," *Charlotte Observer*, Apr. 17, 1960.

Page 161, paragraph 2. "We dare you!": The ad ran in the *Greensboro Daily News* on May 27, 1960.

Page 162, paragraph 2. Primary night: Jay Jenkins, "Their Faces Told a Story," *Charlotte Observer*, May 29, 1960; Guy Munger, "Top Candidate Ready, Raring for Runoff," *Greensboro Daily News*, May 29, 1960; and "County Backs Terry," *Fayetteville Observer*, May 29, 1960.

Page 162, paragraph 3. Black precinct totals: Associated Press report, May 29, 1960.

Page 162, paragraph 3. Sanford did not seek black vote in Durham: Sanford interview with Brent Glass, SOHP. Sanford made similar comments in his interview with Robin Minietta of UNC-TV in the summer of 1997.

Page 163, paragraph 2. Sanford's staff at work by noon Sunday: See Graham Jones' introduction in Sanford's *Addresses and Papers of Governor Terry Sanford*.

Page 163, paragraph 2. Sanford's warning: United Press International report, May 30, 1960.

Page 163, paragraph 3. Lake's day of phone calls: Guy Munger, "Lake May Give His Decision on Runoff," *Greensboro Daily News*, May 30, 1960.

CHAPTER 7: ATTACKS AND LIES

Page 164, paragraph 1. Lake's press conference calling for a runoff: Statement courtesy of I. Beverly Lake Jr.; Guy Munger, "School Integration, Spending Labeled Campaign Issues," *Greensboro Daily News*, May 31, 1960; and *Charlotte Observer*, May 31, 1960.

Page 165, paragraph 2. Florida governor's race: Bruce Jolly, "N.C., Florida Campaigns Differ," *Greensboro Daily News*, May 31, 1960. Figures from Florida Division of Elections. In the first primary, Bryant won 193,507 votes (20.65 percent) to Carlton's 186,228 (19.9 percent). After he won the runoff, Bryant was elected governor later in 1960.

Page 166, paragraph 1. Sanford's initial reaction to Lake's call for a runoff: Charles Craven, "Lake Calls Runoff," *News and Observer*, May 31, 1960; and "Sanford Joins Runoff Battle," *Greensboro Daily News*, May 31, 1960.

Page 167, paragraph 2. Sanford attacks Lake and his policies: "Here's Sanford's Statement," *Charlotte Observer*, June 1, 1960; and Woodrow Price, "Sanford

Slaps Back at Racist Campaign of Candidate Lake," *News and Observer*, June 1, 1960.

Page 169, paragraph 1. Sanford returns to Fayetteville to get notebook: Sanford interview with Jack Bass and Walter DeVries, SOHP.

Page 170, paragraph 2. Sanford explains his statement saying he opposed integration: Author interviews with Sanford.

Page 171, paragraph 2. Sanford believes blacks have limited opportunities: Sanford, *But What About the People?*

Page 171, paragraph 3. Sanford speaks to ninth graders: Kays Gary, "Sanford Gets an 'A,'" *Charlotte Observer*, Apr. 8, 1960.

Page 172, paragraph 2. Sanford knows discrimination wrong: Sanford letter to Richard Donahue, Apr. 22, 1991, John F. Kennedy Library Foundation, Boston, Mass.

Page 173, paragraph 1. You know where I stand: Ken Eudy, "Sanford Seen as Folksy, Quick-Witted," *Charlotte Observer*, Oct. 5, 1986. Bert Bennett and Lauch Faircloth told the author similar versions of this anecdote. In Eudy's version, the confrontation occurred in Ahoskie. Faircloth said that it happened one county over, in Woodland in Northampton County. Bennett said that it happened at a courthouse; Ahoskie is the county seat of Hertford County but Woodland is not the county seat of Northampton County.

Page 173, paragraph 5. Terry's all right on the Negro question: Spence, *The Making of a Governor*.

Page 173, paragraph 5. Talking points from opponent: Sanford Papers. The talking points probably were from Larkins. He liked to call Sanford "High Tax Terry."

Page 174, paragraph 2. Clyde Shreve letter: Letter dated June 1960, in Sanford Papers.

Page 175, paragraph 2. North Carolina has the courage and the wisdom: From statement to supporters, June 12, 1960, Sanford Papers.

Page 176, paragraph 3. Black voters in Iredell: 1964 precinct registration figures from the Iredell County Board of Elections. Registration by race for 1960 was not available but it is unlikely there was a dramatic change from 1960 to 1964.

Page 177, paragraph 2. Frank Graham would not have done what Sanford did on black votes in Iredell: Sanford interview with Brent Glass, SOHP.

Page 177, paragraph 3. Lake for massive resistance: Sanford speech to supporters, June 12, 1960. Sanford Papers.

Notes

Page 178, paragraph 1. Sanford's criticism of the NAACP: "'Mr. Baptist, Judge Endorse Sanford," *Charlotte Observer*, June 16, 1960; Jay Jenkins, "Terry Urges Support of 'Positive Program,'" *Charlotte Observer*, June 23, 1960; and *Charlotte News*, June 21, 1960.

Page 179, paragraph 3. Graham Jones on Sanford's "short and clear" position on race: See Jones's introduction in Sanford's *Addresses and Papers of Governor Terry Sanford*.

Page 182, paragraph 3. Bennett's meeting with Hodges: Author interview with Bert Bennett.

Page 183, paragraph 3. Hodges for vice president: Larkins, *Politics, Bar and Bench*.

Page 184, paragraph 1. Sanford and Hodges' nephew: Sanford interview with Brent Glass, SOHP.

Page 184, paragraph 1. Seawell camp gives cash, stamps to Sanford: Author interview with Phil Carlton.

Page 184, paragraph 2. Hodges' officially neutral: *Charlotte Observer*, June 5, 1960; and "Under the Dome," *News and Observer*, June 24, 1960.

Page 185, paragraph 4. Transcript of questions to Sanford about Hodges: Sanford Papers.

Page 186, paragraph 4. Sanford's meeting with Robert Kennedy and his view of the questions at the press conference: Sanford interviews with Joe B. Frantz and Brent Glass, SOHP; and Sanford interview with Ann M. Campbell for the John F. Kennedy Library, Boston, Mass.

Page 187, paragraph 1. After meeting with RFK, Sanford confident Kennedy would win: Drew Pearson syndicated column, Aug. 20, 1960.

Page 187, paragraph 2. Sanford understands significance of the race: Author interview with Sanford.

Page 188, paragraph 1. Sanford tired: Author interview with Sanford; and Sanford interview with Brent Glass, SOHP.

Page 188, paragraph 4. Lake raises questions about Hodges, Sanford, and Kennedy: Gene Roberts, "Lake, Burney Flail N&O at Lumberton," *News and Observer*, June 22, 1960.

Page 189, paragraph 3. Sanford's meeting with Bobby Baker: Sanford interview with Joe B. Frantz, SOHP.

CHAPTER 8: SHOWDOWN

Page 191, paragraph 1. Lake criticizes newspaper coverage: Luther Shaw, "Lake Hits at Newspaper Coverage," *Asheville Citizen*, June 2, 1960.

Page 192, paragraph 3. Lumberton rally: Gene Roberts, "Lake, Burney Flail N&O at Lumberton," *News and Observer*, June 22, 1960.

Page 193, paragraph 2. *Statesville Record and Landmark*: June 4, 10, 17, 22, 24 and 27, 1960.

Page 194, paragraph 1. *Asheville Citizen* editorials: June 5 and 7, 1960.

Page 194, paragraph 2. *Charlotte Observer* editorial: June 24, 1960.

Page 194, paragraph 3. *News and Observer* editorials: June 23 and 24, 1960.

Page 195, paragraph 3. Lake says his position not fairly explained: Ned Cline, "Lake's Rocky Road Takes New Direction," *Charlotte Observer*, July 14, 1978.

Page 196, paragraph 2. Lake's lack of press conferences: Jay Jenkins, "Sanford: Lake Fears the Press," *Charlotte Observer*, June 11, 1960. The *News and Observer* also reported on June 25, 1960, that Lake held two press conferences.

Page 196, paragraph 2. Lake's message in the east: Jay Jenkins reported this in his June 11, 1960, article for the *Charlotte Observer*: "Lake has been bearing down on the race issue in the East while stressing his fiscal conservatism in the Piedmont." When the author interviewed former *Observer* reporter Joe Doster, he also believed Lake's message was different in different parts of the state.

Page 197, paragraph 1. W. W. Taylor's comments: From an Associated Press report published in the *Asheville Citizen*, June 18, 1960.

Page 198, paragraph 1. Helms was popular: Author interview with Marjorie Hunter. Roy Parker said that Helms was not popular with reporters in 1960, which was logical; Helms supported Willis Smith in 1950 and many reporters disliked the tactics of Smith supporters.

Page 199, paragraph 2. Lake at the candidates' forum: Julian Scheer, "Local 'Experts' Fire Questions at Candidates," *Charlotte News*, May 17, 1960; and text of Lake speech on WBTV, Lake speeches.

Page 201, paragraph 3. "The media was for me in 1960": Sanford interview with Brent Glass, SOHP.

Page 203, paragraph 1. "The press didn't want that stirred up": Author interview with Sanford.

Notes

Page 203, paragraph 2. Sanford's dispute with WRAL: Transcript of May 31, 1960, "News of Raleigh" program; and Bert Bennett's letter to the FCC, June 10, 1960, Sanford Papers.

Page 206, paragraph 1. Lake's New Bern rally: Text of Lake's first speech, Sanford Papers; video of speech, courtesy Beverly Lake Jr.; and Roy Covington, "Sanford Program Lashed by Lake," *Charlotte Observer*, June 4, 1960.

Page 207, paragraph 3. Lake says Sanford courageous: Speech at Greensboro rally, June 9, 1960. Lake speeches.

Page 207, paragraph 3. Lake says Sanford silent on how to handle integration: "Integration of the Schools," 15-minute television address on WNCT-TV, June 1960, Lake speeches.

Page 208, paragraph 1. Lake on the bloc vote: "Block Voting by the NAACP," 15-minute television address on WRAL-TV, June 1960, Lake speeches.

Page 208, paragraph 2. Bilbo and Daddy Grace: Press release of Sanford statement, June 12, 1960, Sanford Papers; and "Charges Lake Playing into Hands of NAACP," *News and Observer*, June 13, 1960.

Page 208, paragraph 2. Sanford criticizes Lake on the campaign trail: "Sanford Draws Good Crowds in East, West and Piedmont" and "Candidate Terry Sanford Tours Wake after Western Trip," *News and Observer*, June 19, 1960; Jay Jenkins, "Sanford Steps up Runoff Campaign," *Charlotte Observer*, June 19, 1960; *Charlotte News*, June 21, 1960; Jay Jenkins, "Terry Urges Support of 'Positive Program,'" *Charlotte Observer*, June 23, 1960; and *News and Observer*, June 23, 1960.

Page 208, paragraph 4. Sanford says Lake is a closet Republican: David Cooper, "Lake Brought 'Republican Twist' into Campaign, Sanford Charges," *News and Observer*, June 24, 1960.

Page 209, paragraph 2. Friends, business partners, families split: H. W. Kendall, "Buttons and Beaux," *Greensboro Daily News*, May 22, 1960.

Page 210, paragraph 1. The televised debate: Roy Covington, "Sanford, Lake Clash Politely in TV Debate," *Charlotte Observer*, June 14, 1960; and United Press International Report, June 14, 1960.

Page 211, paragraph 4. Lake criticizes Sanford on thirty-minute debate: Associated Press report, June 15, 1960; Gene Roberts, "Lake Makes Fast Tour in Mountains," *News and Observer*, June 21, 1960; and Philip Clark, "'I'll Close NAACP,' Lake Declares Here," *Asheville Citizen*, June 21, 1960. Also, June 2, 1960, telegram from A. J. Fletcher to Bert Bennett, Sanford Papers.

Page 212, paragraph 3. Sanford and labor money: Associated Press report, June 19, 1960; Sanford statement, June 22, 1960, Sanford Papers; Associated Press report on Scott family reaction, June 22, 1960; and newspaper ad in the *News and Observer*, June 24, 1960.

Page 213, paragraph 2. South Carolina governor Ernest Hollings: United Press International report, June 1, 1960; and Associated Press report, June 3, 1960.

Page 213, paragraph 3. Huggins endorsement a coup for Sanford: David Cooper, "Sanford Draws Good Crowds in East, West and Piedmont," *News and Observer*, June 19, 1960.

Page 214, paragraph 2. Pearsall says Lake did not write Pupil Assignment Act: Julian Scheer, "Sanford, Lake Head for the Hills," *Charlotte News*, June 16, 1960.

Page 214, paragraph 2. Taylor defends Lake: Associated Press report, June 18, 1960.

Page 214, paragraph 3. Lake did not like speeding: Author interviews with Roy Green and Allen Bailey. According to Bailey, one night during the 1964 campaign Bailey drove Lake back from an eastern North Carolina town near the Virginia border. When Lake fell asleep, Bailey hit the gas. He was pulled over by a highway patrolman, who saw the "Lake" bumper sticker on the car. "If you weren't supporting my man, I'd give you a ticket," the trooper said. "Your man," Bailey responded, "is in the other side, asleep." Even with the stop, Bailey made it in record time to Raleigh. When Lake woke up and looked at his watch, he said, "They must have shortened the distance" between the two cities.

Page 215, paragraph 1. Lake campaigning at the end: John Parris, "Swain, Cherokee, Macon See, Hear Touring Lake," *Asheville Citizen*, June 21, 1960.

Page 215, paragraph 2. Sanford campaigning at the end: Article by David Cooper in the *News and Observer*, June 23, 1960.

Page 216, paragraph 3. Cataloochee reports first: John Parris, "Cataloochee in Early—8 for Sanford and Taylor," *Asheville Citizen*, June 26, 1960.

Page 217, paragraph 2. Runoff night: Anne Sawyer and Julian Scheer, "Terry's Sun Reached Zenith as Darkness Fell on Lake," *Charlotte News*, June 27, 1960; Jay Jenkins, "Lake: 'I Congratulate You,'" *Charlotte Observer*, June 26, 1960; David Cooper, "Lake's Camp Sang 'Dixie' in Defeat," *News and Observer*, June 26, 1960; Associated Press report, June 26, 1960; and Bette Elliott, "A Personal Glimpse of Margaret," *News and Observer*, June 27, 1960.

Page 218, paragraph 1. Estimates of black turnout: "Negro Vote Sanford's Win Margin," and "The Defeat of Dr. Lake for Governor," *Carolina Times*, July 2, 1960.

Page 219, paragraph 6. Frank Graham's phone calls on election night: Graham letter to Margaret Rose and Terry Sanford, June 28, 1960, Sanford Papers.

CHAPTER 9: JFK AND MR. GOP

Page 220, paragraph 1. Sanford in his hotel room: Associated Press report by Reese Hart, June 27, 1960.

Page 220, paragraph 2. Sanford's Monday press conference: Jay Jenkins, "He Hopes Question Is Politically Dead," *Charlotte Observer*, June 28, 1960; Charles Craven, "Sanford Hopes Race Question Laid to Rest," *News and Observer*, June 28, 1960; and Jay Jenkins, "Sanford's Favorite Unknown," *Charlotte Observer*, June 30, 1960.

Page 221, paragraph 3. Kennedy, Sanford talk in Charlotte: Sanford letter to Donavon Luhning, Oct. 29, 1990, Sanford Papers, Duke University. Also, Sanford interview with Ann M. Campbell for the John F. Kennedy Library.

Page 222, paragraph 2. Sanford's decision to support Kennedy: Based principally on Sanford's interview with Joe Frantz, SOHP; and Sanford interview with Ann M. Campbell for the John F. Kennedy Library. Also, Sanford's interviews with Brent Glass, SOHP; with Robin Minietta of UNC-TV in the summer of 1997; and with Charlie Rose, Aug. 20, 1997. Much of the information about Sanford at the Democratic convention comes from these interviews.

Page 224, paragraph 1. *News and Observer* reports Sanford to back Johnson: "Sanford Support Seen Going to Sen. Johnson," *News and Observer*, July 5, 1960.

Page 224, paragraph 1. Sanford "a little bit on the untruthful side": Sanford interview with Ann M. Campbell for the John F. Kennedy Library.

Page 225, paragraph 1. Johnson a futile vote: Sanford interview with Joe Frantz, SOHP.

Page 225, paragraph 3. Sanford backs Kennedy: Jay Jenkins, "Johnson's 'Solid' Dixie Bloc Cracks," *Charlotte Observer*, July 10, 1960; and Jack K. Russell, "Sanford for Kennedy; Tar Heel Split Looms," *News and Observer*, July 10, 1960.

Page 226, paragraph 2. Kennedy deeply grateful: Julian Scheer, "Sanford's Choice Not Sitting Well," *Charlotte News*, July 11, 1960.

Page 227, paragraph 1. Sanford stands by decision: Jack K. Russell, "Terry Sanford Defends His Support of Kennedy," *News and Observer*, July 11, 1960.

Page 228, paragraph 1. Truman called Pearson an SOB: Marjorie Hunter, "Sanford Denies Kennedy's Help," *Winston-Salem Journal*, July 14, 1960.

Page 228, paragraph 2. Hodges discusses vice presidency: United Press International report, Apr. 28, 1960.

Page 230, paragraph 3. Sanford pushes LBJ for vice president: Roy Parker, "Terry Sanford Involved in LBJ-JFK Sidelight," *News and Observer*, July 21, 1965.

Page 231, paragraph 1. Larry O'Brien or Kenny O'Donnell: In Roy Parker's 1965 article, Sanford said that it was Kenny O'Donnell who urged him to push Johnson, "Terry Sanford Involved in LBJ-JFK Sidelight," *News and Observer*, July 21, 1965. In his 1971 interview with Joe Frantz (SOHP), Sanford said that he thought it was Larry O'Brien.

Page 231, paragraph 3. Telegrams and letters on JFK endorsement: Sanford Papers.

Page 233, paragraph 3. Church opposition to JFK: "Churchmen Tell Sanford Not to Back Kennedy," *Charlotte Observer*, July 11, 1960.

Page 234, paragraph 1. Sanford back in North Carolina: "Sanford Defends His Endorsement of John Kennedy," *News and Observer*, July 18, 1960.

Page 234, paragraph 3. Sanford on religion: Jack Claiborne, "Sanford: Faith Isn't an Issue," *Charlotte Observer*, Aug. 8, 1960.

Page 235, paragraph 1. Nixon up two-to-one in North Carolina: Sanford interview with Robin Minietta of UNC-TV in the summer of 1997.

Page 235, paragraph 1. Kennedy's September visit: Julian Scheer, "'Horses Are Ready to Run,'" *Charlotte News*, Sept. 19, 1960.

Page 235, paragraph 2. Louis Harris' October polling figures: Sanford Papers.

Page 235, paragraph 3. "I hope I won't pull you down": Charles Craven, "Sanford Sure All Along," *News and Observer*, Nov. 9, 1960.

Page 235, paragraph 4. Starts campaigning during mountain vacation: Sanford interview with Joe Frantz, SOHP.

Page 236, paragraph 1. Running scared: United Press International report, Sept. 4, 1960.

Page 236, paragraph 1. Campaigning by ferry, horseback, etc.: Roy Thompson, "Terry Sanford's Long, Long Trail Comes to an End," *Winston-Salem Journal*, Nov. 10, 1960.

Page 236, paragraph 1. Shaking forty thousand hands: Sanford press release, Sanford Papers.

Page 236, paragraph 2. Biographical background on Gavin: James Ross, "GOP Nominee to Tour State," *Greensboro Daily News*, 1964; and resume that Gavin supplied to the *News and Observer*.

Notes

Page 237, paragraph 1. Gavin campaigns in spring: Marjorie Hunter, "Gavin Is Getting Equal Billing," *Winston-Salem Journal*, Apr. 20, 1960.

Page 237, paragraph 2. Gavin says biggest issue is Kennedy: *Winston-Salem Journal*, Oct. 5, 1960.

Page 237, paragraph 3. Gavin on race: Roy Parker, "Gavin Looks to the East," *News and Observer*, Sept. 24, 1960.

Page 238, paragraph 1. Gavin's retorts to Seawell: Roy Thompson, "Gavin Blasts Seawell," *Winston-Salem Journal*, Oct. 26, 1960.

Page 238, paragraph 2. Gavin says one-party system bad: Associated Press and United Press International reports, Oct. 7, 19, and 23, 1960.

Page 238, paragraph 3. Gavin says Sanford free spender: United Press International report, Oct. 15, 1960.

Page 239, paragraph 2. Gavin for civil service changes: United Press International reports of Oct. 22 and 30, 1960; and "Gavin's Most Effective Issue," *Winston-Salem Journal*, Nov. 1, 1960.

Page 239, paragraph 1. Gavin says education majors can't spell: United Press International report, Oct. 5, 1960; and "Spelling the Issue Out," *Winston-Salem Journal*, Oct. 7, 1960.

Page 240, paragraph 2. Kennedy angrily denies he gave Sanford money: Roy Parker, "Kennedy Denies He Gave Funds to T. Sanford," *News and Observer*, Sept. 18, 1960.

Page 240, paragraph 3. Sanford signs note for Kennedy: Sanford interview with Brent Glass, SOHP.

Page 240, paragraph 3. Sanford on his minister's reaction to his endorsing of Kennedy: Sanford interviews with Joe Frantz and Brent Glass, SOHP.

Page 241, paragraph 1. Anti-Catholic literature: Jesse Poindexter, "Anti-Catholic Literature Criticized," *Winston-Salem Journal*, Oct. 28, 1960.

Page 241, paragraph 2. GOP county chairman asked to resign: Associated Press report, Nov. 7, 1960.

Page 241, paragraph 3. Bert Bennett on religion: Memo from Bert Bennett to county chairmen, Langston Papers, Duke University.

Page 242, paragraph 2. Sanford ad on good Christians: *Winston-Salem Journal*, Oct. 30, 1960.

Page 242, paragraph 2. No political events for Sanford on Sundays: Sanford's handwritten note, Langston Papers, Duke University.

Page 242, paragraph 3. Sanford on people not paying attention to their ministers: Associated Press report, Nov. 5, 1960.

Page 242, paragraph 3. JFK's Catholicism cost him 200,000 votes in North Carolina: Associated Press report, Nov. 7, 1960.

Page 243, paragraph 1. Helms and no debate: Associated Press and United Press International stories, Oct. 21, 22, 24, and 27, 1960.

Page 243, paragraph 1. Sanford on Helms: Author interviews with Sanford.

Page 243, paragraph 2. Sanford hits Gavin on budget issues: United Press International report, Sept. 4, 1960.

Page 243, paragraph 3. Sanford hits Gavin on education issues: Associated Press report, Oct. 1, 1960.

Page 244, paragraph 1. Not going back to Hoover: Jesse Poindexter, "Democratic Leaders Rap GOP at Rally," *Winston-Salem Journal*, Oct. 5, 1960.

Page 244, paragraph 1. Social security and more: "Sanford Cites Good Record of Democrats," *Winston-Salem Journal*, Oct. 18, 1960.

Page 244, paragraph 1. Sixty years of good Democratic leadership: Jeanette Reid, "Sanford Applauded at Dobson," *Winston-Salem Journal*, Oct. 4, 1960.

Page 244, paragraph 2. Sanford on Nixon's makeup: Marjorie Hunter, "Sanford Hits a 'Made-Up' Nixon, GOP," *Winston-Salem Journal*, Oct. 8, 1960.

Page 244, paragraph 3. Sanford says state poised for new era: Marjorie Hunter, "N.C. Ready to Move Ahead, Sanford Says," *Winston-Salem Journal*, Oct. 12, 1960.

Page 245, paragraph 4. Robert Kennedy happy with North Carolina: Julian Scheer, "N.C.'s Future Looks Bright," *Charlotte News*, Nov. 9, 1960.

Page 246, paragraph 1. Sanford smokes a victory cigar: Roy Thompson, "Terry Sanford's Long, Long Trail Comes to an End," *Winston-Salem Journal*, Nov. 10, 1960.

Page 246, paragraph 1. Sanford in his hotel room: Charles Craven, "Sanford Sure All Along," *News and Observer*, Nov. 9, 1960.

CHAPTER 10: EPILOGUE

Page 247, paragraph 2. Morgan redeemable: Sanford interview with author.

Page 248, paragraph 2. Morgan's support key to victory: Sanford interview with Jack Bass and Walter DeVries, SOHP.

Page 249, paragraph 1. Lake criticizes national Democratic platform: Lake speeches. Also, Woodrow Price, "Beverly Lake Critical of National Platform,"

News and Observer, Oct. 7, 1960; and video of the Williamston rally, Sanford Papers.

Page 250, paragraph 2. Lake's Statesville speech: Lake speeches. Also, Marjorie Hunter, "Lake Pledges Support," *Winston-Salem Journal*, Oct. 27, 1960.

Page 250, paragraph 3. Lake endorsed Jefferson: Sanford interview with author.

Page 250, paragraph 4. Tribute to Lake: Lake speeches. Also, Gene Roberts, "Lake Says His Backers Will Try Again in '64," *News and Observer*, Oct. 22, 1960.

Page 252, paragraph 2. Lake's criticism of Robert Wagner: Associated Press report, Feb. 2, 1962.

Page 252, paragraph 3. Sanford's use of state airplane: Associated Press report, May 11, 1963.

Page 252, paragraph 3. Lake testifies at Thurmond's invitation: Jack Claiborne, "Lake Says Rights Bill Would Intensify Hate, Imperil Lives," *Charlotte Observer*, July 30, 1963.

Page 253, paragraph 1. Lake supports Speaker Ban: "Lake Defends Speakers Ban," *News and Observer*, July 5, 1963.

Page 253, paragraph 3. Lake announces for governor: Tom Inman, "Beverly Lake in Governor's Race," News and Observer, Dec. 1, 1963.

Page 253, paragraph 4. Lake quits Sunday school post: Bill Connelly, "Lake Quits Teaching at Church," *Winston-Salem Journal*, Apr. 24, 1963.

Page 254, paragraph 1. Bailey reshapes Lake's image: Author interview with Allen Bailey.

Page 254, paragraph 2. Lake on race in 1964 campaign: Associated Press report by Rob Wood on Lake's appointment to supreme court, Aug. 26, 1965.

Page 254, paragraph 4. Jesse Jackson letter: Sanford Papers, Duke University Archives.

Page 255, paragraph 2. Helms and Lake on Preyer: Luebke, *Tar Heel Politics*.

Page 255, paragraph 4. *Carolinian* prays for Lake: "A Second Look at Beverly Lake," *Carolinian*, May 14, 1960.

Page 256, paragraph 2. Lake's school bond opinion: "Under the Dome" column, *News and Observer*, June 19, 1968.

Page 256, paragraph 3. Lake denies Eastern Carolina University his papers: Russell Clay, "Justice Lake Denies His Papers to ECU," *News and Observer*, Apr. 10, 1969.

Page 256, paragraph 4. Lake speaks to Wake Christian Academy: "Lake: Public Schools Hamstrung," *News and Observer*, May 23, 1970.

Page 257, paragraph 2. Lake Jr. defends his father: Paul T. O'Connor, "Conservative Unmoved by Past Defeats," *Raleigh Times*, Sept. 15, 1980.

Page 257, paragraph 2. Republicans for Hunt: A. L. May, "Former Hunt Opponent Supporting Governor," *News and Observer*, Sept. 30, 1980.

Page 258, paragraph 2. Lake not angry about his campaigns: John Kilgo, "Beverly Lake Looks Back without Anger," *Chapel Hill Weekly*, Dec. 16, 1970; and Matt Schudel, "I. Beverly Lake: A Portrait at 80," *News and Observer*, Sept. 12, 1986.

Page 258, paragraph 4. Sanford's University of North Carolina speech: Sanford, *Addresses and Papers of Governor Terry Sanford*.

Page 259, paragraph 1. Sanford's "astute salesmanship": Covington and Ellis, *Terry Sanford: Politics, Progress, and Outrageous Ambitions*.

Page 260, paragraph 1. Governor Sanford's visits to schools "one of the best things": Sanford letter to Tom Lambeth, Oct. 25, 1989, Sanford Papers, Duke University.

Page 261, paragraph 1. Bonds issues defeated in 1961: Lefler and Newsome, *North Carolina: History of a Southern State*.

Page 261, paragraph 1. Harris poll after bonds: Covington and Ellis, *Terry Sanford: Politics, Progress, and Outrageous Ambitions*.

Page 262, paragraph 1. Sanford's decision to give a civil rights speech: Ehle, *The Free Men*.

Page 263, paragraph 3. Caswell Defenders' rally: Joseph Knox, "Caswell Rally Held to Fight Racial Mixing," *Greensboro Daily News*, Feb. 4, 1963.

Page 264, paragraph 2. Greensboro rallies: Chafe, *Civilities and Civil Rights*; and Farmer, *Lay Bare the Heart*.

Page 265, paragraph 1. Sanford's Pembroke speech: Jane Hall, "Governor Urges Tension Calmness," *News and Observer*, May 11, 1963.

Page 265, paragraph 2. Protest at the mansion: Bob Lynch and Roy Parker Jr., "Negroes Boo Gov. at Mansion," *News and Observer*, May 11, 1963.

Page 266, paragraph 3. Farmer on Sanford: Farmer, *Lay Bare the Heart*.

Page 266, paragraph 3. Wilkins on Sanford: Covington and Ellis, *Terry Sanford: Politics, Progress, and Outrageous Ambitions*.

Notes

Page 268, paragraph 2. Clinton's race commission: Author interview with Erskine Bowles; and "Sanford's Work on Race Issue Recalled," *News and Observer*, Apr. 26, 1998.

Page 269, paragraph 1. Sanford's and Lake's 1986 letters to each other: Sanford Papers, Duke University.

Page 270, paragraph 2. The last Lake-Sanford meeting: Author interviews with Terry Sanford and Willis Whichard.

Page 270, paragraph 3. Sanford on Lake's death: Sanford commented while walking out of the restaurant of the Washington Duke Inn in Durham with his former aide Ed Wilson Jr. and the author.

Page 272, paragraph 3. Gergen on Sanford: David Gergen, "'A Conscience with Bite,'" *U.S. News and World Report*, May 4, 1998.

BIBLIOGRAPHY

BOOKS

Bagwell, William. *School Desegregation in the Carolinas*. University of South Carolina Press, 1972.

Bass, Jack. *Unlikely Heroes*. Simon and Schuster, 1981.

Batchelor, John. "Rule of Law, Accommodation of Faith: North Carolina School Desegregation from *Brown* to *Swann*, 1954 to 1975." Personal manuscript.

Beyle, Thad L., and Merle Black. *Politics and Policy in North Carolina*. MSS Information Corp., 1975.

Black, Earl. *Southern Governors and Civil Rights*. Harvard University Press, 1976.

Branch, Taylor. *Parting the Waters*. Simon and Schuster, 1988.

Chafe, William H. *Civilities and Civil Rights*. Oxford University Press, 1980.

Covington, Howard E., and Marion A. Ellis. *Terry Sanford: Politics, Progress, and Outrageous Ambitions*. Duke University Press, 1999.

Ehle, John. *Dr. Frank*. Franklin Street Books, 1993.

———. *The Free Men*. Harper & Row, 1965.

Farmer, James. *Lay Bare the Heart*. Arbor House, 1985.

Hodges, Luther H. *Businessman in the Statehouse*. University of North Carolina Press, 1962.

Jones, H. G. *North Carolina Illustrated, 1524–1984*. University of North Carolina Press, 1983.

Bibliography

Key, V. O., Jr. *Southern Politics in State and Nation*. Knopf, 1949.

Larkins, John Davis, Jr.. *Politics, Bar and Bench*. Historical Society of Eastern North Carolina, 1980.

Lefler, Hugh Talmage, and Albert Ray Newsome. *North Carolina: History of a Southern State*. 3rd ed. University of North Carolina Press, 1973.

Link, William A. *William Friday: Power, Purpose, and American Higher Education*. University of North Carolina Press, 1995.

Luebke, Paul. *Tar Heel Politics: Myths and Realities*. University of North Carolina Press, 1990.

Pleasants, Julian, and Augustus M. Burns III. *Frank Porter Graham and the 1950 Senate Race in North Carolina*. University of North Carolina Press, 1990.

Ragan, Sam. *The New Day*. Record Publishing Co., 1964.

Sabato, Larry. *Goodbye to Good-Time Charlie: The American Governorship Transformed*. D. C. Heath and Co., 1978.

Sanford, Terry. *Addresses and Papers of Governor Terry Sanford*. Edited by Memory Mitchell. North Carolina State Department of Archives and History, 1966.

————. *But What About the People?* Harper & Row, 1966.

Schlesinger, Arthur, Jr. *A Thousand Days*. Fawcett Premier, 1965.

————. *Robert Kennedy and His Times*. Ballantine Books, 1979.

Schwartz, Bernard. *The Unpublished Opinions of the Warren Court*. Oxford University Press, 1985.

Sorensen, Theodore C. *Kennedy*. Harper & Row, 1965.

Spence, James R. *The Making of a Governor: The Moore-Preyer-Lake Primaries of 1964*. John F. Blair, Publisher, 1968.

Statistical Summary of School Segregation-Desegregation in the Southern and Border States. Southern Education Reporting Service, 1961.

Williams, Juan. *Thurgood Marshall: American Revolutionary*. Times Books, 1998.

Wilder, Roy, Jr. *You All Spoken Here*. Viking Penguin, 1984.

Transcripts of Interviews

Bennett, Bert. Southern Oral History Project, University of North Carolina, Chapel Hill (hereafter cited as SOHP).

Graham, Frank Porter.. SOHP.

Helms, Jesse. SOHP.

Hodges, Luther, Jr. SOHP.

Lake, Beverly. SOHP.

Morgan, Robert. SOHP.

Rankin, Ed. SOHP.

Sanford, Terry. John F. Kennedy Library, National Archives of the United States.

Sanford, Terry. SOHP.

Scott, Bob. SOHP.

ORAL INTERVIEWS CONDUCTED BY THE AUTHOR

Adams, Hoover. June 1998.

Alexander, Zechariah. Dec. 14, 1998.

Bailey, Allen. May 20, 1998.

Bailey, Jack. July 28, 1998.

Bennett, Bert. Feb. 10, 1998; Dec. 21, 1998.

Bowles, Erskine. Aug. 16, 1999.

Burney, John. June 1, 1998; June 8, 1998; Nov. 23, 1998.

Campbell, Bill. Sept. 16, 1998.

Carlton, Phil. Sept. 4, 1998.

Cromartie, Doris. Apr. 28, 1998.

Doster, Joe. June 30, 1998.

Ellis, Tom. August 1998.

Evans, Eli. July 2, 1998.

Faircloth, Lauch. Sept. 29, 1998.

Glendening, Parris. Dec. 23, 1999.

Goodman, Raymond. June 1998.

Green, Roy. May 15, 1998.

Hair, Liz. Nov. 4, 1998.

Harrington, Monk. June 23, 1998.

Hunt, Jim. July 20, 1998.

Hunter, Marjorie. Sept. 30, 1998.

Jackson, Angus. Aug. 9, 1998.

Jackson, Hy, Aug. 9, 1998.

Bibliography

Joyner, Sonny Boy. Dec. 27, 1998.

Lake, Beverly, Jr. Apr. 23, 1998; June 12, 1998; Aug. 9, 1998; Oct. 19, 1998; Dec. 28, 1999.

Lambeth, Tom. Feb. 11, 1998.

Lewis, John. July 28, 1998.

McKay, Martha. Nov. 5, 1998.

Mitchell, John. Sept. 12, 1998.

Morgan, Robert. Apr. 6, 1998.

Newton, Clint. July 9, 1998.

Parker, Roy. Sept. 11, 1998.

Phillips, Dickson. Nov. 14, 1998.

Price, Woodrow. June 18, 1998.

Sanford, Margaret Rose. Dec. 1, 1999.

Sanford, Terry. July 19, 1996; Jan. 20, 1997; Feb. 3, 1998.

Scott, Bob. June 15, 1999.

Scott, Jessie Rae. June 15, 1999.

Staton, Bill. June 19, 1998; June 30, 1998; Nov. 30, 1998.

Teague, Woody. June 29, 1998.

Yancey, Noel. June 1998.

Whichard, Willis. Aug. 23, 1999.

Wilder, Roy, Jr. Aug. 7, 1998; Nov. 5, 1998.

Wiggins, Norman. June 26, 1998.

Winter, William. July 28, 1999.

Winters, John. Nov. 6, 1998.

CORRESPONDENCE WITH AUTHOR (LETTERS)

Helms, Jesse. Dec. 23, 1998.

Wiggins, Norman. June 22, 1998.

NORTH CAROLINA NEWSPAPERS

Asheville Citizen

Asheville Times

Charlotte News

Charlotte Observer

Durham Carolina Times

Fayetteville Observer

Fayetteville Times

Greensboro Daily News

Raleigh Carolinian

Raleigh News and Observer

Raleigh Times

Statesville Record and Landmark

Winston-Salem Journal

VIDEOCASSETTES

Lake, Beverly I. Beverly Lake campaign speeches. Courtesy of I. Beverly Lake Jr.

Sanford, Terry. *Biographical Conversations with Terry Sanford.* UNC-TV, aired May 25–27, 1998.

Sanford, Terry. *Charlie Rose interview with Terry Sanford.* USA Network, aired Aug. 20, 1997.

Sanford, Terry. Terry Sanford campaign commercials and speeches. Sanford Papers, University of North Carolina, Chapel Hill.

INDEX

Adams, Hoover, 128, 141

Adler, Richard, 9

Albright, Mayne, 123

Alexander, Kelly, 94, 178, 255

Alexander, Zechariah, 180

Archie, William, 56

Aycock, Charles Brantley, 244

Ayers, Brandt, 28

Bailey, Allen, 37, 108, 142, 149, 178, 254

Bailey, Clarence, 87–88

Bailey, Jack, 88, 102–03, 106–07, 112

Baker, Bobby, 189–90, 226

Barden, Hap, 64

Barnett, Ross, 99

Bass, Spencer, 55

Bennett, Bert: black voters, 134; Burney's skills, 106; considers run for governor, 252, 254; criticized by Lake, 255; debates, 212; Democratic party chairman, 252; early days as campaign manager, 30; Hodges'

strong personality, 230–31; Hunt supporter, 257; Kennedy's visit and Sanford's endorsement, 186, 189, 222–23, 240–42, 246; money from Texas, not taxes, 69, 116; Roney's opposite, 130; Sanford's gut desire, 26, 125, 129; Scott supporters, 117–18; skeptical of Supreme Court offer to Lake, 91

Benson, Ezra Taft, 238

Best, Robert, 57

Bilbo, Theodore, 208, 248

Black newspapers, 180–81, 218, 255–56

Blair, Ezell, Jr., 71

Bowles, Erskine, 264, 268

Bowles, Hargrove, 264

Branch Head Boys, 15, 21, 117–18

Broughton, Mel, 59

Brown decision, 40–46, 56, 112, 133, 137, 147–48, 199, 208, 272

Bryant, Farris, 99, 165

Burney, John, 100, 103, 105, 108, 138, 184–85, 192–93, 218, 250

Byrd, Harry, 252

Caldwell, John, 34

Caldwell, Lush, 216

Campbell, William, xx–xxi, 181

Cannon, Charles, 67

Cannon, Hugh, 186

Carlton, Doyle, 165

Carlton, Phil, 184

Carter, Betty, 22

Carter, Jimmy, xvii

Chafe, William, 265

Clinton, Bill, xvii

Coates, Albert, 29

Cochrane, Bill, 189, 226

Collins, Leroy, 165

Conant, James, 260

Cooper, Dave, 215

CORE, 254, 264, 266

Cromartie, Doris, 127

Davis, Jimmie, 99

Dillon, C. A., 184

Doster, Joe, 14, 151, 197, 201–02

Drake, Ormand, 29

Duke University, 267

Ehle, John, 262–63, 267

Eisenhower, Dwight, 27, 60, 237

Ellis, Tom, 49, 100–01, 103, 188, 195, 200, 257

Ervin, Sam, 196, 221, 228–29

Evans, Eli, 27

Faircloth, Lauch, 26, 231

Farmer, James, 266

Faubus, Orval, 99, 179

FBI, 10

Fletcher, A. J., 49, 166, 203, 212, 242

Frady, Marshall, 31

Frankfurter, Felix, 36, 44–46

Franklin, John Hope, 268

Friday, Bill, 11

Frye, Henry, 257

Gantt, Harvey, 243

Gardner, O. Max, 7

Gardner, O. Max, Jr., 11, 12

Garfield, James, 241

Gary, Kays, 119, 160

Gavin, Robert, 235–39, 257

George, Wesley Critz, 54, 155–56

Gill, Edwin, 59

Gleaves, J. H. R., 16–17

Golden, Harry, 72

Good Neighbor Council, xix, 263

Goodman, Raymond, 27, 128

Grace, Daddy, 208, 248

Graham, Frank, 3–5, 9, 13, 15, 17–18, 28, 31–32, 56–57, 61–62, 70, 141, 163, 172, 177, 203, 219, 245, 268, 272

Green, Charles, 213

Green, Roy, 150–51, 214

Greensboro sit-ins, 71–75, 131, 203

Harlan, John Marshall, 44

Harrington, Monk, 27, 171

Harris, Louis, 9, 59–63, 97–98, 115–16, 131, 134, 235, 238

Hastings, Paul, 86–87

Helms, Fred, 45

Helms, Jesse, 23, 51, 55, 101–03, 242–43, 257

Hewlett, Addison, 59, 96

Hodges, Luther: appointment of Sen. Everett Jordan, 22; decision not to run for Senate, 59; disagreements with John Larkins, 64–65; meets with Sanford, Bennett, 182–83; Pearsall committees, 43, 49; presidential nominee, 226, 228, 242, 246; revenue projections, 121; Sanford's criticism as governor and lieutenant governor, 20–22; sit–ins, 74; strained relationship with Lake, 47–51, 53–54, 76, 147; support of Malcolm Seawell, 79–81, 84; support of Pearsall Plan, 50, 147–48; support of Sanford in runoff, 184–86; vice presidential aspirations, 165, 183, 188, 228, 230

Hodges, Luther, Jr., 184

Hoey, Clyde, 7, 59

Hollings, Ernest, 99, 165, 213

Hoover, Herbert, 244

Hoover, J. Edgar, 10

Huggins, M. A., 213

Hughes, Langston, 144

Hunt, Jim, xvii–xviii, 27, 127, 182

Hunter, Marjorie, 66, 198, 204

Jackson, Angus, 35

Jackson, Jesse, 254, 264

James, Allison, 263

Jefferson, Thomas, 250, 253

Jenkins, Jay, 160, 169, 204

Johnson, Charlie, 123

Johnson, Lyndon, xv, 189–90, 221–28, 238, 246

Jones, Charles, 72

Jones, Graham, 179

Jones, Woodrow, 65

Jordan, Everett, 22, 221, 228, 241

Joyner, Sonny Boy, 26–27, 128, 231

Joyner, William, 37

Joyner, W. T., 159

Kefauver, Estes, 222

Kendall, H. W., 96, 160

Kennedy, John, 25, 28, 188–90, 221–35, 238, 240, 263–64

Kennedy, Robert, 186–90, 223, 230, 245–46, 255

Kerr, John, Jr., 55

Key, V. O., Jr., 272

King, Martin Luther, Jr., 73, 144, 266

Kirkman, Arthur, 59, 75

Kitchin, Paul, 226

Koenenn, Joe, 185–86

Ku Klux Klan, 82–83, 99

Kurfees, Marshall, 17–18

Lake, I. Beverly: Asheboro Lion's Club speech, 46–47, 56; attorney general's staffer, 39; "blackboard jungle," 146; *Brown* decision, 40–46, 56, 137–38, 144; campaigning style, 100–01; childhood, 34–36; concession to Sanford, 218–19; correspondence with Wesley Critz George, 55; criticism of Luther Hodges, 53–54, 76, 93, 110, 143; criticism of NAACP, 46, 110–11, 139–40, 216; eastern North Carolina, 141; education proposals, 110, 120–21, 139, 201, 211; enters race for governor, 92–94; fall campaign, 247–52; fear that blacks and whites would marry, 52–53, 144, 153, 156; Graham campaign, 32–34, 56–58; hints he will run for governor, 54–55, 70; law teacher, 37–38;

Lake, I. Beverly (*cont.*)
Morgan's involvement in campaign, 88–91; newspaper coverage, 191–201; opposition to Pearsall Plan, 50, 144; Pearsall committee, 43–44; polling from Louis Harris, 62, 97–98; private schools, 145–46; religious beliefs, 151–53; Rocky Mount speech, 107–12; runoff announcement, 164–66; second gubernatorial campaign, 253–55; segregationist views, 137–41, 143–46, 149–59; sitins, 77; Supreme Court justice, 255–56; talking points from opponent's campaign, 173; withdrawal from race and reconsideration, 75–79, 86–88, 91–92

Lake, I. Beverly, Jr., 32, 205, 209, 257–58

Lake, Trudy, 38, 218

Lake, Virginia Prudence Caldwell, 34–35

Lambeth, Tom, 27, 68–69, 126, 128–29, 234, 268

Larkins, John, 31, 60, 63–65, 84, 86, 91, 96, 98, 119–20, 122, 135, 142, 148, 162, 214

Lassiter, Thomas, 30

Lennon, Alton, 15, 16, 19, 64, 122

Lewis, John, 88, 102, 106, 150

Lincoln, Abraham, 241

Little Rock, Ark., 30

Lodge, Henry Cabot, 238, 250

Love, Spencer, 245

Marshall, John, 95

Marshall, Thurgood, 44, 46

Maupin, Armistead, 84

McCain, Franklin, 72, 76

McClelland, Royce, 138

McCoy, Donald, 12, 229–30

McDonald, Ralph, 7

McKay, Martha, 119, 126, 131, 172

McKinley, William, 241

McMullen, Harry, 39–40, 43, 45, 48, 49

Meredith, James, 264

Mitchell, John, 6–7

Moore, Dan, 255, 267–68

Morgan, Robert: alleges labor money to Sanford campaign, 212–13; fall campaign, 247–48; involvement in getting Lake to run, 55, 78, 88–91; Kennedys' role in campaign, 188; Lake's segregationist views, 56, 108, 150; law student of Lake's, 37; loyalty inspired by Lake and Sanford, xx, 127, 251; newspaper coverage, 196; Pearsall Plan, 50, 177; running Lake's campaign, 103, 135, 163, 217

Murphey Elementary School, xx–xxi

NAACP: *Brown* decision, 44; calls for Lake's resignation, 47; criticism from candidates, 142–43, 174–75, 178, 207–08, 211, 216; Hodges' treatment of, 47–48, 53; Lake's criticism of, 46, 139–40, 146, 252; Morgan's 1974 meeting, 88; opposes Lake, 94

Newton, Clint, 12, 25, 128, 172

Nixon, Richard, 237, 244

O'Brien, Larry, 231

O'Donnell, Kenny, 231

Parker, Roy, 25, 103, 197, 204

Patriots of North Carolina, 54–55, 83, 86

Patterson, John, 98
Peacock, Bruce, 102
Pearsall Plan, 49–52, 144, 168, 177
Pearsall, Tom, 30, 43, 184
Pearson, Drew, 227–29, 239–40
Penny, George, 203
Phillips, Dickson, 8, 12, 21, 27, 91, 150, 172
Powell, Adam Clayton, 237
Prather, Gibson, 202
Preyer, Richardson, 254
Price, Woodrow, 14, 17, 19

Rabenhorst, Harry, 36
Rayburn, Sam, 246
Riley, Dick, xvii
Roberts, Gene, 97, 100, 204
Rodman, William, 47–48
Roney, Ben, 17, 22–23, 29, 89, 129–30, 222–23
Roosevelt, Franklin, 7, 28, 209, 230, 237
Rose, Charlie, Jr., 12
Russell, Donald, 213
Russell, Richard, 252

Sanford, Betsy, xxi, 125
Sanford, Cecil, 6–8, 217
Sanford, Elizabeth, 6–8, 217
Sanford, Margaret Rose, xxi, 9–10, 11, 28, 66, 125, 241, 246, 247, 267
Sanford, Terry: announces candidacy, 66–68; attacks Lake at beginning of runoff, 167–69; attitudes toward women, blacks, and young people, 118–19; on blacks and black voters, including issue of integration, xix, 30, 62, 130–34, 142, 148–49, 162–63, 166–75, 208, 210, 220, 271–74; "bloc vote" in Iredell, 176–77; campaigning style, 125–29, 235–36; childhood, 6–8; civic activities in Fayetteville, 12; civil rights as governor, 261–68; criticism of Hodges, 20–22, 117; Drew Pearson column, 227–29, 239–40; friendship with Robert Morgan, 90, 247–48; Hodges' support in runoff, 182–86; Kennedy endorsement, 186–90, 221–35, 240–42; legislative term, 13–14; NAACP, 174–75, 178, 207, 211; newspaper coverage, 201–04; notebook of strategies, 3, 5, 16, 19; polling from Louis Harris, 59–63, 97–98, 115–16, 131, 235, 238; public schools and taxes, 30, 60, 68–69, 113–17, 120–21, 206, 210, 259–60; relationship with Lake after primary runoff, 247–50, 268–70; Scott campaign, 15–20, 28, 123, 189; sense of humor, 118, 124, 243–44; sit-ins, 74–75, 131; support of Pearsall Plan, 51–52, 168, 177, 210; talking points from opponent's campaign, 174; unsigned leaflets, 134–36; World War II, 10–11
Sanford, Terry, Jr., xxi, 125, 178
Satterfield, Byrd, 50
School integration figures, 146–47
Scott, Bob, 22–24, 28, 67, 129
Scott, Jessie Rae, 20, 28
Scott, Kerr, 13, 15–16, 21, 23, 28, 59, 70, 90, 116, 123, 189, 212–13
Scott, Mary, 23–24, 67
Scott, Ralph, 21–22
Seawell, Chub, 81

Seawell, Malcolm, 74–75, 79–85, 96, 120, 124, 135, 144, 147–48, 162, 214, 238
Shreve, Clyde, 174–75
Smathers, George, 228
Smith, Willis, 3–5, 15, 23, 32, 37, 103, 141, 175, 213
Speaker Ban Bill, 252–53
Staton, Bill, 12, 25, 55–56, 150
Stennis, John, 252
Stevenson, Adlai, 221, 228, 237, 246
Stewart, D. K., 123
Symington, Stuart, 221

Taylor, Archie, 89
Taylor, W. W., Jr., 49, 196
Teague, Woody, 24–25, 27, 56, 126, 181
Thompson, Paul, 11, 25
Thurmond, Strom, 12, 252
Truman, Harry, 12, 237–38, 246

Umstead, William, 14, 20, 43
University of North Carolina, 9, 11
Upchurch, Abie, 18, 122–23

Vandiver, Ernest, 99
Voter registration of blacks and whites, 141

Walker, John, 257
Wallace, George, 28, 98–99, 154, 179, 267
Ward, Hiram, 38
Warren, Peggy, 22
Weaver, L. Stacy, 12
Wheeler, John, 262
Whitley, Charles, 38
Wiggins, Norman, 38
Wilder, Roy, 22, 29–30, 106, 235
Wilkins, Roy, 48, 266
Wilson, Henry Hall, 25, 89, 222
Winter, William, xvii, 273
Winters, John, 179, 265, 267
Wolfe, Thomas, 245
Women for Sanford, 118–19

Yancey, Noel, 197, 204
Yardley, Jonathan, xix
Young, Whitney, 266